INSIGHT GUIDES

Created and Directed by Hans Höfer

BELGIUM

Edited and Produced by Martha Ellen Zenfell
Photography by Carl and Ann Purcell

Editorial Director: Brian Bell

Houghton Mifflin

APA PUBLICATIONS

Except perhaps for the realm of sport, where the cyclist Eddy Merckx is about the only international star the country has ever produced, Belgium seems to excel by almost any criterion against which one wishes to measure it. It was a therefore a natural title for Apa Publications to add to its award-winning Insight Guides series, which covers nearly 190 destinations all over the world. The Insight Guide series is complemented by Pocket Guides and Compact Guides to the capital, Brussels.

Müller

Project editor **Kristiane Müller** focused the skills of Insight Guides writers and photographers on this small country with so much to offer. Grand' Place in Brussels, for example, is considered by many to be the world's most beautiful market square. And beyond are no fewer than 30 cities whose architectural and artistic treasures are lasting memorials to the golden age of Brabant and Flanders, when the city of Ghent was the most important north of the Alps after Paris; when Antwerp's port was the key to enormous prosperity.

Throughout the centuries, these towns and cities have nurtured the talents of artists and writers such as Jan van Eyck and Peter Paul Rubens, Georges Simenon, René Magritte and Hergé. The art of oil-painting was perfected in Belgium, and Inspector Maigret and Tintin were invented there.

But it isn't only cultural achievements which entice visitors. For those who like the fresh air, there are more than 40 miles (60 km) of inviting coastline, as well as vast expanses of unspoilt moor and heathland. When Lord Byron claimed "a molehill would make the inhabitants think that the Alps had come here on a visit," he must have forgotten about the Ardennes.

Although the country is divided into two linguistic and cultural spheres, between the Walloons and the Flemings, certain common denominators have always prevailed, notably good hospitality and good food. The cuisine includes such old favourites as the internationally acclaimed Celerie Belge. And there are 550 beers to choose from.

It was the country's cuisine that clinched Kristiane Müller's acceptance of the editorship of *Insight Guide: Belgium*. She likes to sample local specialities wherever she can, and has already done so for her Insight Guides to The Rhine, Düsseldorf and Brussels. For this book, she travelled the length and breadth of the country with **Eberhard Urban**, who has written about Belgium's artistic treasures. He has a Frankfurt-based business which produces calendars.

E. Urban

His daughter, **Susanne Urban**, a historian, provided a number of the background articles, including the piece on the Belgian Congo and "Belgium and the World Wars".

S. Urban

Kirsten Kehret is also from Frankfurt. In this book she discusses the "Age of the Burgundians" and the "Kingdom of Belgium". **Gisela Decker**, a language specialist, teaches English and literature. Here, she offers an insight into the problems of the continuing language dispute between the Flemings and the Walloons.

Born of Russian parents, **Nina Köster** works as a freelance journalist in Hamburg. A regular contributor to Apa guides, she edited *Insight Guide: Cologne*. To these pages, she has contributed some historical articles as well as the essay on music and literature and the chapter on the port and city of Antwerp.

Köster

Dierks

Schmerfeld

Wendt

Hartmut Dierks works as a journalist and radio producer in northern Germany. For this book, he travelled through the provinces of Limburg, Namur, Hainaut, Brabant and Luxembourg, and to Liège and Brussels.

The author and journalist **Rosine de Dijn** has lived for 20 years in Cologne. Here, she writes about the task of tracing the fate of Jewish children during the war.

Joseph Lehnen, a Brussels journalist, describes the development of the country after World War II and also looks at Brussels' fascinating Marolles district. **Erika Dreyer-Eimbcke** has travelled throughout Europe for many years, and is particularly interested in following the courses of old trading routes. She describes the importance of the Hanseatic League for the development of trade in Belgium. As an editor of the monthly magazine *Europa*, **Michael Brückner** was ideally placed to write about diplomacy and spas.

Wolfgang Schmerfeld, who has also contributed to several Apa guides, most notably *Insight Guide: Düsseldorf*, looks at the way of life in Brussels' Upper City and examines what's on offer at some of the city's markets.

Few people know the Royal Greenhouses at Laeken better than local man **Edgar Goedleven**, director of the "society for the preservation of monuments and the landscape". The historian and author **Dr Barbara Beuys** takes us to the battlefield of Waterloo to relive the events of Wellington's finest hour and Napoleon's final defeat.

The travel writer and photographer **Christoph Wendt** lives just on the German side of the Belgian border. Here, he takes us on a journey through West and East Flanders. **Michael Bengel**, from Cologne, is a literary critic and writes cultural features for a Cologne newspaper. Here, he recounts the deeds of the rogue Tyl Ulenspiegel from Damme.

It was in Belgium that journalist **Heidrun Noblé** learned all about the "Catholic way of life". Today she lives in Cologne, which is also brimming with good beer and joie de vivre, especially during the carnival. But in Belgium, festivities seem to go on all year.

Helmut Müller-Kleinsorge, who refers to himself as an "all-weather journalist", examines how remarkably sporty a nation Belgium is. Having lived in the country for five years, he also looked at the problems of communication caused by three official languages.

Journalist **Hans-Hermann Frobenius** has explored every corner of Belgium. Together with Kristiane Müller, he samples both the Flemish and Wallonian cuisine. He also penned the article on Georges Simenon.

Noblé

Bondzio

Fritz

The photographs come from many specialists, including the portraits of Cologne-based **Bodo Bondzio** and the work of Apa old hand **Wolfgang Fritz** who travelled extensively to assemble his contribution. Further shots were supplied by **Henning Christoph**, **Thomas Mayer** and **Jörn Sackermann**, who have a photo agency in Essen. Last but not least is **Ingeborg Knigge**, who has lived in Brussels for some years.

The original German text, supervised by managing editor **Wieland Giebel**, was translated under the direction of **Tony Halliday**, and the English edition was produced in Apa's editorial office in London by **Dorothy Stannard**. This edition has been updated by **Jane Hutchings**.

CONTENTS

Maps

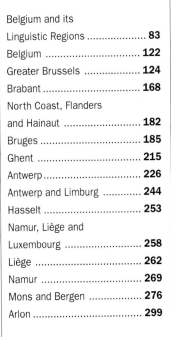

THE LAND AT THE HEART OF EUROPE

Belgium was always at the centre of the action when it came to European power struggles. Altercations started more than 2,000 years ago with the Celtic tribe of the *Belgae* spearheading the brave fight against the northward march of the Roman legions. But the latter won through and made themselves at home here for nearly 500 years. After the Romans, Belgium was ruled by Frankish overlords, and then came the French, the Spanish, the Austrians and, from 1815, the Dutch.

There had been popular revolts all down the ages, of course. But the ultimate rallying cry for independence, for the revolt against the Dutch government, didn't come until the evening of 25 August 1830, during a performance of Auber's opera *Masianello* ("The Dumb Girl of Portici") in Brussels' opera house, the Théâtre de la Monnaie. The audience became restless during the aria *Sacred Love of our Fatherland*. "Far better to die than to live a wretched life in slavery and shame! Away with the yoke before which we tremble; away with the foreigner who laughs at our torment!" The Belgians had finally succeeded where the *Belgae* had failed.

In 1831 Leopold of Saxe-Coburg became king and took up residence in the palace in Brussels. He was followed by Leopold II, Leopold III, Albert I and King Baudouin I. Today, the head of state is King Albert II.

When one considers how much this country was once fought over, it is somewhat surprising that it has never appealed quite so much to the travellers of today. All the more so when one thinks of its compact size, which makes it an ideal place for planning a trip. Belgium has a population of some 10 million and consists of nine separate provinces spread out over a total area of almost 12,000 sq. miles (46,000 sq. km). There are three official languages: the Flemings in the north speak Flemish, which is very similar to Dutch, the Walloons in the south speak French and a small minority of the population in the east speak German. Located right in the middle of the country, the province of Brabant maintains a special status and speaks both Flemish and Walloon.

The capital Brussels is also the capital of Brabant. With such a multi-cultural metropolis at their centre – a city which is set to become the capital of Europe – it is easy to see why the Belgians are so obliging and hospitable towards outsiders. The Belgians are both generous and tolerant, they love good food, and they celebrate their festivals all the year round.

Preceding pages: a view of medieval Bruges – the jewel of Flanders; wrought-iron artistry in Mons; Tournai, a view from the bell tower; requisites for the garden in Limburg; the Carnival in Binche. **Left**, not all the masks are the same.

The history of Belgium begins several decades before the birth of Christ. Julius Caesar recorded that the *Belgae*, a conglomeration of Celtic tribes in the northern part of Gaul, fought with great valour against his forces in 58 BC. They lost, however, and the Romans remained in the region for almost 500 years, establishing an urban infrastructure, building roads and bridges and developing trade.

Following the collapse of the Western Roman Empire, the power vacuum was filled by the Franks. Tournai was the centre of their empire. They helped spread Christianity throughout western Europe.

Belgium became the focal point of world events during the reign of Charlemagne, who was born in Liège in 742. Before his reign as King of the Franks, invasions from the Barbarian north and Muslim south were eroding Frankish power in Europe. He quickly set about rectifying the situation, subduing the Saxons in the northeast and the Lombards in northern Italy. He established a "Spanish March" south of the Pyrenees to keep the infidel at bay and the Eastern March in the middle of the Danube basin as a buttress against the Hvars and later the Magyrs. Under Charlemagne the Frankish Empire extended from the Elbe to the Atlantic and from the North Sea to the Mediterranean. For services to Christianity and, in particular, for restoring papal lands in Italy, he was crowned Emperor of the West ("Holy Roman Emperor") on Christmas Day 800.

Charlemagne's successors, however, could not retain control over such an enormous territory. Two generations later the Frankish Empire was divided into three parts by the Treaty of Verdun. Charles the Bald was granted sovereignty over the region west of the Scheldt, an area which evolved into the West Frankish Empire and later became France. The region east of the Scheldt was granted to Lorraine. Later on Lorraine was divided between France and the German Empire and, in the year 925, it came under the sovereignty of the Germans. The Scheldt

was, from then on, the boundary between the German and French spheres of influence.

The Belgians did not concern themselves with any of these affairs. They took advantage of the fall of the Frankish Empire and developed extensive independent feudal dynasties. In Flanders, Baldwin the Iron Arm profited from the weakness of the French throne. In his efforts to make himself Count of Flanders, he stopped at nothing, kidnapping the daughter of the French king and making her his wife. He responded to the

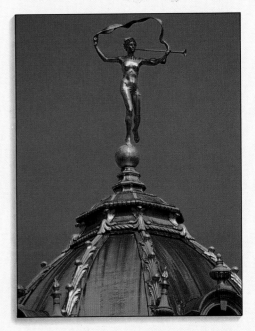

anger of his father-in-law by threatening to enter into an allegiance with the Normans. Wishing to avoid this, the French king had no choice but to go along with Baldwin's wishes.

Baldwin's successors soon extended the sovereignty of Flanders to the south as far as the Somme. In the 11th century, the region controlled by Baldwin V reached eastward beyond the Scheldt. By extending their reign beyond this river, the Flemish counts, from 1056 onward, became vassals of the French king as well as of the German emperor. This strengthened even further their already powerful position. The importance of Flanders in 11th-century Europe is demonstrated by the

Preceding pages: the Grand' Place in Tournai. **Left,** the city of Ghent around 1800. **Right,** the dome of the Bakers' Hall in Brussels.

fact that in 1060 Baldwin V was made regent for the French king, who was not yet old enough to rule. He held this position until 1065. In 1070, Robert the Frisian ascended to the Flemish throne. This was the first time that a non-descendent of Baldwin the Iron Arm occupied that position. This did not lessen Flemish influence, however.

At the same time, the feudal dynasties of Lorraine were becoming increasingly powerful. For a long time, the development of the principalities of Hainaut, Brabant, Limburg, Namur and Liège, in the German fiefdoms east of the Scheldt, progressed at a slow pace. In the middle of the 11th century, all the powers of the empire were tied up in the

it was not only trade which led to these cities' increasing wealth and prestige: the growing textile industry was also a vital factor.

The influence of the Flemish cities became clear after the murder of Charles the Good in the 12th century. Charles, who had fostered good relations with the cities, left no heir. In this event, it was the duty of Louis VI of France to appoint a successor. He chose William of Normandy, but the cities wanted Dietrich of Alsace and, in the end, the king was forced to yield to their demand.

The reign of the Alsatians began with great promise. Dietrich, and later his son Philip, relied on the support of the cities, as well as a series of arranged marriages, to

Investiture Dispute, giving the princes of Lorraine the opportunity to gain greater independence. Brabant, where the Dukes of Leuven ruled, profited most from the weakness of the empire.

Prosperous trading cities: From the 12th century, the cities developed into important centres of power. This was especially the case in Flanders, but later also in Lorraine. The blossoming trade between the Continent and England resulted in the rapid growth of the cities. Bruges became the trading centre for goods from Italy, France, Germany and England, and merchants from far and wide offered their wares for sale in Flanders. But

increase Flanders' sphere of influence. Philip of Alsace even served for a time as adviser to Philip-August (Philip II), grandson of Louis VI, a position which enabled him to control the strings of French politics.

In the year 1181, however, a dispute arose between France and Flanders. In the ensuing conflict, Philip of Alsace unfortunately overestimated his strength. He died during the siege of St Jean d'Acre. Basing his claims on previously made agreements, Philip II, the first great Capetian king of France, was able to gain control over southern Flanders. Shortly thereafter, however, the pendulum of fortune once again swung over to the side of Flanders, and Baldwin VI, through his alliance with England, was able to reconquer some of the lost territories. In the end, however, France was the victor: in 1214, Philip securely established his throne by defeating the Flemish, the English and the emperor Otto IV at the Battle of Bouvines.

In the 13th century, France succeeded in consolidating its position not only in Flanders but also in the German fiefs of Lorraine. It was only owing to the tremendous power of the cities that the territory of today's Belgium did not come under French rule for once and for all.

Rebellion of the cities: At the start of the 14th century it looked as if France, under

Philip IV (Philip the Fair), would succeed in completing the annexation of Flanders, a task which had been started by Philip II. Guy of Flanders entered into an alliance with England in order to oppose French sovereignty, but still he was unsuccessful. A French governor was sent into Flanders to rule. His power, however, was shortlived.

Emotions were at a high pitch within the cities. The craftsmen, under the leadership of the weaver Peter de Coninck, rebelled against

Left, the main entrance to Bruges town hall. **Above**, a participant in the Procession of Our Dear Lady.

the patricians and the French who supported them. The rebellion was suppressed several times, but during the night of 18 May 1302, the rebels overcame the French guards in Bruges. The result was a bloodbath. Anyone who couldn't correctly pronounce the Flemish cry "*schild ende vriendt*" was killed.

Encouraged by the success in Bruges, the common folk all over Flanders reached for their weapons. Armed only with spears, the Flemish craftsmen and peasants faced the French cavalry on the battlefield of Courtrai on 11 July 1302. The French, although confident of an easy victory, were decisively defeated. Not one French soldier survived and, when the fighting had come to an end, the rebels collected 700 golden spurs.

Finally, Philip the Fair yielded to the demands of the rebels and granted Flanders its independence, but stipulated that large compensation sums had to be paid. The peace treaty did not herald the onset of peaceful times in Flanders. It was only after years of fighting that, in 1329, the aristocracy was able to crush the rebellious peasants in maritime Flanders. The citizens of Bruges and Ypres had allied themselves with these peasants. Ghent, a city which had in the main stayed loyal to the rulers, was the spearhead of new popular rebellions at the end of 1337.

At the beginning of the Hundred Years' War, Flanders sided with France, causing England to boycott delivery of wool to the region. Trade in Flanders came to a complete halt. The people of Ghent – including merchants and craftsmen, rich and poor – were all in agreement about what should be done. In order to get the economy back on its feet, they must rebel against the politics of their rulers. The wool merchant Jacob of Artevelde was the rebels' leader. It was under his influence that Edward III of England, who viewed himself as the rightful heir to the French throne, was proclaimed king of France at the Ghent market in January of 1340.

The alliance with England meant that trade blossomed once again, but it also meant a revival of the old conflicts of interest between merchants and craftsmen. In July of 1345, the weavers murdered Jacob van Artevelde and usurped power in the cities. Their action attracted the hatred of the other craftsmen and a civil war ensued in which they lost all the power they had gained. A half century of constant unrest was thus brought to an end.

THE AGE OF THE BURGUNDIANS

The Burgundian Empire, which included the area comprising modern Belgium, came into existence during the period of the Hundred Years' War, a war waged spasmodically between France and England from 1337 to 1453. The major point of dispute was the succession to the French throne. The claimant Edward III of England was pitted against the Valois line which had ascended the French throne when the Capetian dynasty died out. The war was fought solely on the Continent – mainly in France.

Because of their vacillating position, the Burgundians were again and again drawn into the war. Burgundy basically consisted of two regions, separated from one another geographically. The southern region, in today's eastern France, comprised an area stretching from Dijon to Basle. The other sector, the one which was actually the more important in terms of the war, consisted of today's Belgium, plus the French territory near the border, and a large portion of today's Netherlands. The Burgundians sided with England, though not because they wanted to see France ruled by Edward III. In fact, they saw themselves as the potential rulers of France, and their goal was the elimination of French supremacy in Europe. Whoever controlled the Belgian sector of Burgundy was guaranteed access to the sea, proximity to England and therefore the best trade connections.

Four great dukes: The Burgundians increased their power and their sphere of influence by means of diplomacy, military endeavours and cleverly arranged marriages. The fortunes of this powerful, though short-lived empire was moulded by the four "great dukes". These four rulers were in power for barely more than 100 years between them (1364–1477); and yet this was time enough to earn Burgundy an important place in the annals of history.

The French dynasty of the Capetians, from whose line the French king had descended since the year 987, expired in 1328, when

Charles IV died leaving no heirs; the stuggle for power in France was now on. Who would be the first to occupy the throne and remain in the saddle of power?

King John II was crowned in 1350. In order to ensure that his son, Philip the Bold, had a position in life he granted him the title of Duke of Burgundy in 1363. The next year, Philip's elder brother Charles ascended the French throne. In 1369, Charles decided that Philip, born in 1342, should marry Margaret of Flanders. She was the daughter and heir-

ess of the Count of Flanders, and by marrying her Philip gained more than merely a wife and family. In 1384–85, after the death of the Count of Flanders, Belgian Flanders, Artois and other territories were incorporated into the Burgundian duchy. This meant that Burgundy now controlled the area which makes up today's Netherlands and Belgium. But the acquisition of this new territory was not painless.

Insurrections against the nobility: The rulers of the Belgian territory continually underestimated the dissatisfaction of the craftsmen and peasants of Burgundy. The working classes had played no role in the battles for

Left and above right, Philip III (the Good), Duke of Burgundy and his third wife Isabella of Portugal. (Flemish master, 1450.)

EMPEROR CHARLES V

Charles V, Holy Roman Emperor and King of Spain lived in the saddle of a fast horse or on the creaking deck of a sailing ship. His territories and responsibilities were vast. Despite his sickly constitution, the last emperor of the Middle Ages made nine journeys to Germany, seven to Italy, six to Spain, four to France, two to England and two to Africa.

Flanders and Brabant were the nearest thing to home that Charles ever knew. He was born on 20 February 1500 in Ghent, the son of Philip the Handsome, King of Castile, and Joanna the Mad. His childhood was spent in Mechelen, but it was in

Emperor's crown. In 1522 Charles returned to strengthen his hold on Spain, which was torn apart by rebellion.

He had no chance to settle down. The Spanish and Habsburg empire he had inherited extended across Europe from Spain and the Netherlands to Austria and the Kingdom of Naples, stretching across the Atlantic Ocean to Spanish America. Time and again he was forced to take up arms – to put down his archrival, François I of France or to quash the infidels (Turks and Protestants) within and without his realm.

In the final analysis, he failed on both these counts. By the end of his life he had managed to prevent neither the schism within the Christian church nor the fragmentation of his empire. Charles's fortunes waxed and waned as King

Brussels that he was declared of age, being nominated Duke of Brabant and King of Spain (as Charles I) in 1516. He returned again and again to his native land; and at heart he remained a Netherlander all his life. He shared with his compatriots a love of good food, riotous feasting and fine art. As an old man he referred to the Netherlands in a letter to his son Philip as "Our Father Burgundy".

And yet he never had the chance to settle there. His life of travelling began when he was only 17. After the death of his grandfather, Ferdinand of Aragon, he sailed to Spain in order to take up the reins of government there. But three years later, in the summer of 1520, before he had a chance to win over the proud southerners to his cause, he had to hurry to Germany to receive the Holy Roman

Henry VIII of England and the popes in Rome transferred their allegiance between his cause and that of François I and back again.

In 1553, old, sick and disillusioned after a lifetime of almost continuous war, he returned to the Netherlands. It was here that he made his last public appearance in October 1555. In a moving speech before the assembled estates of the 17 provinces in the Great Hall of his castle in Brussels, Charles V renounced the throne of the Netherlands in favour of his son Philip.

At the beginning of 1556 he also relinquished the Spanish crown; and shortly after that he abdicated as Holy Roman Emperor in favour of his brother Ferdinand. Divested of power, he left the Netherlands for ever, retiring to San Geronimo de Yuste in Spain, where he died in 1558.

European supremacy, but they had suffered greatly under increasing exploitation of the ruling aristocracy, especially within the flourishing cities. Insurrections had already taken place in several cities long before the death of the Count of Flanders. The centres of the first revolts (1338–45) were in the cities of Ghent, Bruges and Ypres. The rebels were led by Jacob van Artevelde, elected by the population as Captain of Ghent in 1338. He made a commercial treaty with Edward III of England in 1340, but was killed during an insurrection by the Ghent weavers in 1345 after supporting the cause of Edward the Black Prince to become Count of Flanders.

Artevelde's son Philip took over where he

to stabilise and consolidate his empire. In 1385 he signed the Treaty of Tournai, a peace treaty with the county of Flanders and the city of Ghent.

When Philip's brother, King Charles V, died in 1380, his son, Charles VI (Charles the Well-beloved), became king of France. Charles, however, suffered increasingly from periods of insanity – resulting in his new nickname of Mad King Charles – and three of his uncles ruled as regents in his name, beginning in 1392. One of these uncles was Philip the Bold.

The ongoing war between France and England, however, had driven a wedge between these three uncles. England took ad-

had left off. Starting in 1382, Philip led the new outbreak of insurgency, directed against the count and the Burgundian plan of annexation, a plan which the rebelling craftsmen feared would lead to more exploitation.

Artevelde, together with his followers, managed to capture Bruges but were subsequently defeated. Ultimately, the revolts, which lasted almost 35 years, were brutally crushed. Philip Artevelde met his death in 1382, during the Battle of Roosebeke in Flanders. Philip the Bold was thereafter able

Left, Charles V abdicates the throne in 1555 and hands over power to his son Philip (**above**).

vantage of the conflict between Orléans and Burgundy, a conflict which was to last for the next decade. Whereas Charles VI's brother Louis of Orléans was interested in continuing the battles against England, his uncle Philip was eager to enter into a truce. In fact, he was able to bargain for peace on his own in 1392. Philip died in 1404 in the Belgian province of Brabant and was succeeded by his son, John the Fearless.

This second Duke of Burgundy remained a foe of Louis of Orléans. John the Fearless made himself not only protector of the peace with England, but also of the bourgeoisie and the peasants. His aspirations were aimed directly against his uncle Louis and the incalculable king. John had Louis of Orléans assassinated, defending his action as the necessary removal of a tyrant. Soon thereafter, a French civil war broke out, dividing the nation into two camps – those supporting Burgundy and those supporting Orléans. The Belgians did not take sides, preferring to steer their own course and retain as much freedom as possible for themselves.

Mad King Charles took no clear stand in the dispute between Burgundy and Orléans. Thus, it was not difficult, in the year 1411, for John of Burgundy to convince the people of France to side with him and to rebel against Orléans and the French king. The

actually worthy of the name fearless, saw no other alternative but to sign the Treaty of Arras in 1414.

John cooperates with England: Before his defeat, John had approached the English king, hoping for good neighbourly relations and the support of England. A trade agreement between Burgundian Flanders and England had already been signed in 1406. In an attempt to increase British influence on the Continent, English troops had landed repeatedly in Normandy from 1385 onwards. In 1415 they defeated the French army near Agincourt, not far from Arras. It was after this victory that John, Duke of Burgundy, entered into a secret alliance with King Henry

leader of the revolt was Simon Caboche, a Parisian butcher. However, the actions of Caboche and his followers, the "Cabochians" as they were called, got so out of hand and their blows against the aristocracy became so atrocious that John the Fearless lost complete control over them. He decided to flee Paris and allow the troops of Orléans to conquer the city. Louis of Orléans and his soldiers entered Paris, granting no mercy to the population.

In 1414, John was defeated by his enemies. His allies rescinded their loyalty to him and surrendered to Orléans. John, perhaps for the first time in his life no longer

V of England. He supported Henry's claim to the French throne and in return received military support against Orléans.

John let the British do his fighting for him and used this short period of time, during which his troops were not engaged in any fighting, to gain advantages for himself. He kidnapped the French queen Isabeau in Champagne, carrying her away to Troyes, and formed a new government. Then he found himself faced with a new problem: his English allies were continuing their attempts to capture Paris.

John could not decide whether he should maintain his alliance with England and open the city gates to the English troops, or whether he should make peace with his French opponents and fight with them against the British. Both the English and the French noticed his indecision. John delayed too long and in July of 1419, during a conference with representatives of the Count of Orléans, he was assassinated.

The Burgundian title which he passed on to his son, Philip the Good, was at best questionable. Philip's wife, Michelle of Valois, had become a dangerous partner. It was her brother who had murdered Philip's father. In 1420, the Treaty of Troyes was ratified by France, England and Burgundy. The English king retained the right of suc-

cession to the French throne and was granted the daughter of the French king as his wife. The crown prince, Charles VII, was denied his rightful title to the throne. Charles had no choice but to join with Orléans in fighting against Burgundy, England and France. In 1429, Philip bought the estate of Namur, inheriting Brabant and Limburg in 1430. Four hundred years later, these territories became part of the Kingdom of Belgium.

In 1422, the French king died, and the new king followed him to the grave soon after.

Left, Leo Belgicus, a powerful symbol for the nation. **Above**, historical Bruges.

With the despised English successor dead, the disinherited crown prince was free to ascend the French throne. The reign of Charles VII was accompanied by further battles in and around France. The French pushed the English out of France, thanks to a large extent to the efforts of Joan of Arc. The Duke of Burgundy, however, turned her over to the British who burned her at the stake in 1431 in Rouen. Belgian Hainaut was added to Burgundian territory in 1433, and a treaty was signed in Arras in 1434 between France and Burgundy, which had by then dissolved its alliance with England. Philip the Good and Charles VII made peace with one another, or at least attempted to.

Philip the Good died in 1467. His successor was Charles the Bold. In 1477, the last "great duke" was killed in a battle just outside the city gates of Nancy. Shortly before his death he had added Liège to his duchy, a city which was granted to Belgium in 1831.

Belgium falls to the Habsburgs: Mary of Burgundy, the daughter and heir of Charles, was forced to fight the French king for control of her territory. Her saving strength was her marriage to the Habsburg Maximilian I, an alliance set up by her father. Tragically Mary died young. Maximilian entered into the Treaty of Arras which granted him sovereignty over the Netherlands as well as Belgium. After many years of fighting between France and Burgundy (now a part of the Habsburg Empire), Maximilian was victorious and was granted control over the entire territory.

The daughter of Maximilian, Margaret of Austria, ruled the Burgundian Empire from 1506 onwards. As guardian of Maximilian's grandson, the future Charles V, she prepared him for his royal duties. He became the German king in 1516 and the German emperor in 1530. Under Charles V, the disputes with the neighbouring French over the right to rule Flanders and other Habsburg territories continued.

When the Habsburg Empire was divided between the Spanish line and the Austrian line in 1556, Philip II, the son of Charles V, was granted sovereignty over Belgium as well as other regions. Brutal suppression of the Reformation in Belgium continued under his rule, but the fierce resistance which the Belgians had exercised throughout the centuries could not be broken.

The Hanseatic League was founded as a commercial association of German merchant cities located along the North and the Baltic seas. Its goal was to promote trade between the cities, and exclude other competition. The power and the glory of the Hanseatic cities blossomed in the 12th century and lasted until the 17th century. The League was at its most powerful in the 15th century, but even by the mid-13th century, it practically monopolised trade in northern Europe and had established a transport route from

During this period, Cologne occupied a superior position both economically and culturally among the cities along the Rhine. It enjoyed the unique position of being located on the two largest trade routes of northern Europe: the Rhine route running between Italy and England, and the Hanseatic route between Novgorod and Bruges.

The trading centres: The routes from Cologne to Brabant and Flanders were especially busy. The trading centres along the roads were important to the Hanseatic League

Novgoro via Tallinn, Lübeck, Hamburg and Bruges to London.

The history of the Hanseatic League in the 14th and 15th centuries reveals the unique significance of Flanders. Hanseatic League merchants purchased cloth and fine fabrics from the people of Flanders (textiles being their most important industry) and sold them furs, grain, wood, wax, iron, hemp, amber and wine in return. Additionally, the steady stream of traders from further afield – including the Italians, Iberians, French and English – visiting the cities of Bruges and Antwerp offered the Hanseatic League unlimited scope for further trading activities.

cities as well as for the Netherlands region. One of the most important centres was Deventer, where many of the goods destined for Flanders were loaded on to ships. Other commodities were transported overland, along the "Flemish Road" between Bremen and Haselüne to Kampen and Deventer. A road also led from Deventer through Hertogenbosch and Antwerp to the city of Bruges.

The merchants controlling trade along the River Meuse transported wine from the Rhine and metal products, gems and luxurious textiles from Regensburg, or even Constantinople, across southern Belgium to the coastal towns. From there they were shipped to

England. Every August the Meuse merchants from Liège, Huy and Dinant travelled to the trade fair in Cologne, taking with them samples of their metal products.

One of the most important overland routes was the road leading from Cologne through Roermond to Mol and Antwerp; this route became increasingly important as the centre of trade shifted from Bruges to Antwerp. It wasn't just the merchants who benefited from the movement of goods: wealthy landowners saw it as an opportunity to impose tolls on the merchants. The Duke of Jülich, for example, collected a customs toll at Kaster Toll House near the hamlet of Kaster. Robbers were another hazard of the roads. Several merchants and a merchant's servant were robbed near Wasserberg in 1484. Eight years later, a number of barrels of herring were confiscated here from drivers returning from Antwerp. The records of Wasserberg's customs office show that the carriers had refused to pay customs duties.

Roermond, at the point where the river Meuse became navigable, was another big trading centre. A road from this town led directly westward to Antwerp. In 1490, 10 Cologne merchants travelling home from Antwerp were abducted by highway robbers between Roermond and Horn.

Pilgrim routes: The route between Cologne, Antwerp and Bruges crossed the Meuse at Maastricht; along with Jülich and Valkenburg, Maastricht was named a custom station in 1249. The itineraries of two Cologne emissaries cite the cities of Bergheim, Jülich, Herzogenaurath, Valkenburg and Maastricht as resting places. Around 1250, Maastricht was mentioned as a stopping-off point for pilgrims on their way from Münster to Rome.

From Maastricht, the route ran through the towns of Hasselt, Riest and Lier to Antwerp. Attacks, abductions and murders along this

route were common. A Cologne merchant on his way to Antwerp was murdered at the marketplace in Lier in 1446.

A number of other routes are worthy of mention: firstly, the one which led from Maastricht through Mechelen to Bruges. The distinctive cloth used to make the garments of the Teutonic Knights came from Mechelen. In 1490, eight relay horsemen galloped along a route between Innsbruck and Mechelen. They were carrying a letter which was addressed to Emperor Maximilian I. The deliv-

ery of the letter took five days and the ride is said to have marked the birth of the German postal system.

Other routes of note included the one from Dinant to Brussels and Antwerp and the one from Namur through Nivelles to Brussels, which was called the "Steenway".

The German painter Albrecht Dürer travelled from Antwerp through Mechelen to Brussels in the year 1520. The diary of his travels throughout the Netherlands is a rich source of information on the subject of trading routes: he recorded which routes he travelled, where he rested and exactly how much money he spent.

Left, excursions by boat in the old Hanseatic city of Antwerp. **Above**, three-masted schooners (*Kogge*) used by Hanseatic League merchants.

The Spanish king, Charles II died unmarried and without heirs on 1 November 1700. With him died the Spanish line of the Habsburg dynasty.

Spain, at this time, was a world power with numerous colonies and possessions. Among these were the Spanish Netherlands, to which today's Belgium and Luxembourg belonged. Charles had designated as his successor Philip V of Anjou, a Frenchman and grandson of the reigning king of France, but because the accession of Philip would have meant France and Spain being ruled by the same dynasty, Emperor Leopold II of Austria protested vehemently. Such a concentration of power was just not in the best interests of the Austrian Habsburgs. His protests, however, went unheeded and Leopold deemed it necessary to send the Austrian army into battle in 1701 in order to enforce his will. This war, known as the Spanish War of Succession, lasted from 1701 to 1714.

Austrian realm of power: The peace treaties signed at the end of the war granted sovereignty over the Spanish Netherlands, as well as other regions, to Austria. Belgium thus came under Austrian rule. A short time later, however, a new battle of succession was brewing. Emperor Charles VI, who occupied the Austrian throne from 1711 to 1740, had no male heirs. Without an heir, the whole Habsburg empire could fall apart. In order to prevent another war, he issued a "pragmatic sanction" allowing the crown if necessary to pass to a female. This meant that his daughter Maria Theresa could ascend the throne on his death.

This was an audacious move. It was completely without precedent. In order to ensure future peace, he appealed to other European powers to sanction his plan. He bought their approval by, among other things, agreeing to liquidate the Belgian Ostend Trading Company. This trading company had been founded in 1722 and was already making huge profits in overseas trade. Although the maritime powers tolerated the

Left, fine stained glass in the town hall of Bruges. **Right**, Beguine convents are a common feature of Belgian towns.

company, it was not without a good deal of ill feeling, and they were greatly relieved by its dissolution.

After the death of Charles VI in 1740, however, the European powers wasted very little time in forgetting their agreement to recognise Maria Theresa as the legitimate heir to the Austrian throne. Maria Theresa wrote of her succession: "I found myself without money, without credit, without an army, without experience and knowledge..." In order to defend her right to the throne and

the sovereignty over her inherited lands, she was forced into a war which lasted eight years. In the end, she was victorious and Belgium remained under Austrian rule.

Boom time: Under Maria Theresa, Belgium experienced enormous economic prosperity. Trade and the import business as well as industry were subsidised. Roads were built linking the important cities; the "royal road" linked Brussels to Vienna. Although the Austrian government, the Belgian industrialists and the merchants were all turning huge profits during this period, the common folk of Belgium came out empty-handed. Low wages, unemployment and social destitution were the lot of a large portion of the Belgian population. The main interest of the rulers and the wealthy class lay in the development of fine arts and crafts. Tournai was a manufacturing centre for porcelain and faïence. Maria Theresa granted the city a monopoly, giving it exclusive rights to produce these wares for the whole of the Austrian Low Countries. The gold and blue decorations of Belgian porcelain were recognised in the very finest drawing-rooms of Europe.

The fashion for lace reached its peak during this period and the lace-making industry entered one of its most productive periods. Brussels lace was worn by anyone in a position of power and wealth, both at home and

however, his introduction of freedom of religion (his mother had been a devout Roman Catholic) as well as his relatively liberal innovations in education and health were viewed as reforms "dictated from above" and were thus considered despotic.

Joseph's reforms were felt as far away as Belgium. He established a strong central bureaucracy in the hope of eliminating regional patriotism. He attempted to bring the Church under the control of the state except in purely spiritual matters, a measure which paved the way for secularised education and civil marriages. His decree of 1784 made German the official language of all countries within the empire. His widespread reforms

abroad. Architecture, too, flourished during the reign of Maria Theresa. Brussels became known for its magnificent buildings and splendid squares.

The distrusted revolutionary: The opening of the Theresienne Academy in the year 1772 and the establishment of a public library are among the most important accomplishments attributed to the Austrian empress, a ruler who considered herself a follower of enlightened absolutism. Maria Theresa died in the year 1780 and her son, Joseph II, her coregent since 1765, succeeded. A student of radical French philosophy, he wished to revolutionise his whole empire. Unfortunately,

met with ever-increasing resistance within the countries under his rule.

In Belgium, resistance to Joseph II was divided into two very different camps. The followers of the *ancien régime*, who believed in the absolutist form of government, formed the mute opposition. Their leader was the lawyer Henri van der Noot, a radical opponent of enlightenment. The other camp, led by the lawyer Jean Vonck, was opposed to reforms imposed by a single monarch. They demanded a liberal and modern state, and embraced the ideas coming out of prerevolutionary France.

Starting in 1788, insurrections broke out

in Belgium and a national volunteer army was formed. Van der Noot's conservatives eventually became the dominant revolutionary force. On 11 January 1790, one month before the death of Joseph II, the "United States of Belgium" was proclaimed. Every province retained sovereignty over its own territory, but the Supreme Congress exercised control over the areas of foreign affairs, defence and currency. Van der Noot was elected by the *Congrès Souverain* as prime minister, and Prussia, England and Holland recognised Belgium as an independent country at last.

This new state of affairs was not to last for very long. The new Austrian emperor, Leo-

pold II, sent troops into Belgium to pull the country back into the empire. Being a weak and small country, Belgium was quickly defeated and after just one short year of freedom the country once again, in 1791, came under Austrian rule.

In 1792 the Austrian and Prussian war against revolutionary France broke out and Belgium was drawn into the battle. On 6 November 1792, the French, with the aid of a Belgian legion, defeated the Austrian army

Left, Belgium became prosperous through the weaving industry. Above, the art of lacemaking is slowly dying out.

near Jemappes. It seemed that Belgium was at last free of the Habsburg Empire.

In June 1794, however, France occupied Belgium and the Netherlands. The two countries were united and renamed the Batavian Republic. They remained under French dominion for the next 20 years. The French administration proved to be reformist and succeeded in dismantling, piece by piece, the old absolutist system.

The first order of business was to divide Belgium into nine departments, according to the French pattern of government. The possessions of the Church were transferred to the state and Church and state were officially separated. Inherited titles, as well as the outmoded guild system, were abolished and a reformed judiciary was pledged to ensure equality for all. The "Code Napoleon", which served as the law of the land, became the basis of the new legal system. Duties levied on peasants also became a thing of the past as did the unjust system of taxation.

Industrial state: The fact that the economy was subsidised by the government helped Belgium develop into the most progressive industrialised state on the Continent. The amount of coal mined increased steadily and the metal and textile industries flourished. France became the largest consumer of the goods produced in the country's metal and textile factories.

But French domination had its drawbacks. Starting in 1797, young Belgians were conscripted to serve in the campaigns of Napoleon. A Belgian opposition developed and in 1798 rebellions broke out. Liberal Belgians, as well as those who supported France, distanced themselves from these revolts.

The so-called Holy Alliance defeated Napoleon once and for all near the Belgian village of Waterloo in 1815. The Batavian Republic was dissolved; but a large number of Belgians were to regret the departure of the French, in view of what was decided at the peace conference. The object of the Congress of Vienna in 1815 was to establish a new order in Europe. A resolution was passed perpetuating the unification of Belgium and the Low Countries in one state, but ruled over by the Dutch House of Orange.

Just 15 years later, the patience of the Belgians was at an end. The revolution of 1830 was to result in a free and independent Belgium at last.

THE KINGDOM OF BELGIUM

After the battle of Waterloo in 1815, the country which would later be known as Belgium once more found its fate in the hands of foreign powers. The members of the "Holy Alliance" – Austria, Britain, Russia, Prussia, France and the papacy – linked Belgium with the Netherlands to form the "United Netherlands". This union imposed from above took no account of the historical, political and economic differences between the two halves of this uneasy partnership.

Dissatisfaction with this arrangement quickly took root, with the Belgians seeing themselves as victims of discrimination. Catholics, liberals, supporters of the French connection and conservatives all united with the common aim of ridding their land of the rule of the Dutch House of Orange. When a number of petitions sent to the foreign rulers brought about no improvement in the situation, social and national tensions increased to bursting point.

National independence: France became a role model for Belgium. In France itself, the July Revolution of 1830 aimed to revive the ideals of the 1789 French Revolution. For the Belgians this was to prove the signal to rise up against the House of Orange. In August 1830 the War of Independence began in Brussels, actively supported by the French government.

The events of 4 October were to go down in the annals of Belgian history. On that day, Belgium officially declared itself to be an independent country. The provisional government demanded instant recognition of the new state by other European governments. A few months later, on 26 January 1831, during the London Conference, the great powers of Europe confirmed Belgium's independence and guaranteed its neutrality.

This acceptance of the new nation's autonomy marked the first step along the road towards true independence. As the next step, the newly created parliamentary monarchy needed a suitable king. In their search for an appropriate sovereign, the political leaders of the country agreed upon Leopold of Saxe-

Coburg. By virtue of his blood ties with the English monarchy (he was the uncle of Queen Victoria), his education, his skill in diplomacy and his interest in military matters, Leopold united all the qualities considered to be desirable prerequisites of a representative royal sovereign.

In 1831, the National Congress voted Leopold of Saxe-Coburg King of Belgium, and 21 July was proclaimed a day of national rejoicing. In 1832, Leopold I married Louise, a daughter of King Louis Philippe of France

– an act which strengthened the friendly links between the two countries.

Under Leopold I, relations between Belgium and the Netherlands improved considerably and the foundations were laid for industrial expansion. Despite such measures an undercurrent of restlessness could be detected beneath the apparently calm surface and, from 1840, workers began to rebel against their appalling living conditions. Leopold I was unable to live up to his task as mediator and unifier of the Flemings and the Walloons and against the background of the language dispute, initially regarded as a secondary problem, violence repeatedly broke

Left, Leopold II in formal dress. **Right**, informal escapades with his mistress, the dancer Cleo.

out. Flemish nationalists in the north became increasingly vociferous in their call for independence from the south. On his death, in 1865, Leopold bequeathed a range of social problems to his successor, Leopold II.

Private colony: The new king had various aims, principally characterised by his own personal interests rather than those of the nation as a whole. First, he attempted to boost the national economy by bringing his influence to bear on Belgian financial policy, and then, having achieved this goal, he set about realising his long-cherished dream of colonial power.

The king's intermediary in the African Congo was an Englishman, Sir Henry Morton

private colony was growing, and in 1908 Leopold found himself obliged to subordinate his sovereignty over the Congo to the Belgian parliament.

Leopold, a man who had repeatedly managed to assert his personal will against the liberal powers of parliament, died one year later. The next king, Albert I, was his nephew. In 1914 German troops marched into Belgium at the beginning of World War I and Albert I declared war. Belgium was defeated later that same year but at the Treaty of Versailles at the end of the war Belgium gained the German-speaking territories of Eupen and Malmedy.

Albert I died near Namur during a moun-

Stanley. Through the offices of Stanley and by pursuing a policy of murder, deception and colonialism of the worst type, Leopold II gained control of the entire Congo basin. The region, half the size of Western Europe, in effect became his private property.

Leopold II's coup in the Congo was sanctioned in 1885 by 14 nations at the Berlin Congo Conference, under the chairmanship of Bismarck. In return, Leopold agreed to allow unrestricted trade and freedom of navigation within the Congo basin. Belgium's economic upswing profited still further from this exploitation of the colony. Meanwhile, in England and Belgium, opposition to this

tain walking trip in 1934. His son was crowned Leopold III at the height of the Great Depression. He had married Princess Astrid of Sweden in 1926 and the royal couple had three children: a daughter, Josephine Charlotte (the current Archduchess of Luxembourg), and two sons, Baudouin and Albert, who made their political debuts after World War II.

The German invasion: In the face of the increasing threat from Germany, the king was able to have Belgium reinstated as a neutral country in 1936. Only a few months after the beginning of World War II, German troops invaded Belgium. Leopold III capitulated in the name of his country on 10 May 1940. Although the government fled to London, the king remained at home. Until 1944 he was interned by the forces of occupation in Laeken Castle; then, as the Allied army advanced, he was moved to Germany. He remained there while Belgium was liberated, his brother, Prince Charles, becoming temporary regent.

When Leopold III returned it was not possible to quash all rumours of his collaboration with the Germans, but a referendum as to whether he should continue to reign voted in his favour. In 1950, however, he abdicated and handed over the throne to his son, Baudouin, then aged 20. The new king was

gian troops were firing on a population which – despite international protests – had been thrust into independence without any preparation. The royal couple were married in December 1960.

Future hope: The rights and duties of the King of Belgium were laid down by the country's constitution of 1831. A number of modifications have been made to the clauses of that first constitution, but those referring to the sovereign have remained unchanged. According to Article 65, the king is responsible for nominating and dismissing his prime ministers. In practice, of course, the choice lies in the hands of the politicians and the king has no real power of his own. As Article

crowned on 17 July 1951. One of Baudouin's most pressing official duties was to supervise the decolonisation of the Belgian Congo. Before that came about, however, there were private matters to attend to: in September 1960 he became engaged to a Spanish noblewoman and trained nurse, Doña Fabiola de Mora y Aragon.

Whilst the engagement celebrations were taking place in Brussels, in the Congo Bel-

Left, the merchants became wealthy at the weavers' expense. **Above**, the Grand-Place in Brussels has hardly changed since this photograph was taken in 1890.

64 of the constitution says, all documents signed by the king also require the signature of a minister to make them valid.

The marriage of Baudouin and Fabiola was childless, so when the king died suddenly in 1993, his brother succeeded to the throne as Albert II, with his Italian-born wife Paola as queen. In the longer term it seems certain that Baudouin's eldest nephew Prince Philippe will ascend the throne. Philippe is being prepared for his role in the traditional manner: he is already a colonel in the Belgian army and has studied political sciences. Much depends on Albert's performance of his duties, following the popular Baudouin.

For many years Belgium kept out of the race to acquire colonies. Leopold I, who became the first King of Belgium in 1831, refused to be involved in an official state colonial policy. After his death in 1865, however, his son, Leopold II, made up for lost time.

The groundwork was laid by Sir Henry Morton Stanley (1841–1904), the British explorer and journalist, who led an expedition to Central Africa in 1874. He had already travelled extensively in Africa, America and the Far East.

Stanley's first expedition to the River Congo concluded that the river's wide channel made it an ideal trading route. In 1878, Leopold II commissioned the explorer to undertake a second trip to the Congo. Following the instructions issued by the Belgian monarch, Stanley came to "agreements" with several of the native tribes.

The basis of these contracts was that the Africans would receive fabric and similar items in return for granting the white intruders property rights to their land. The wording was such that the terms could be interpreted as a purchase. In this way, by 1884 Leopold II had gained possession of almost the entire area. He named it the "Congo Free State".

The 19th-century colonial powers soon began to demand a formal agreement on the Congo State. The "Congo Conference" was held in Berlin between November 1884 and February 1885. Belgian authority over the Congo was recognised – with the proviso that henceforth in perpetuity there should be freedom of trade within the country.

At the instigation of Leopold II, the Berlin Conference also passed a resolution repudiating the slave trade. In reality, things were very different. Within Africa, slavery was at its peak. Natives were unscrupulously sold as cheap labour and porters, or press-ganged as soldiers. Whippings and murder were daily occurrences. Between 1889 and 1890 the "Anti-Slavery Conference" was held in Brussels; once more, lip service was paid to the noble aims of colonialism.

From 1890 the Socialists and progressive

Left, the slave trade and brutal exploitation of the colonies made Leopold II, and Belgium, wealthy.

Liberals protested with increasing frequency against the king's colonial policy. In the meantime, the Congolese themselves took up the fight for their own freedom. Between 1895 and 1897 a series of riots in the Congo were brutally quashed.

In 1908 the criticism openly voiced in Europe concerning the king's authoritarian system of exploitation forced the Belgian government to transfer the monarch's power over the new Belgian Congo to the state.

When Leopold II died in 1909 his nephew, Albert I, became king of Belgium and the Belgian Congo. Between 1912 and 1918, the determined resistance of the oppressed Congolese led to further unrest. Following the arrest of ringleader Simon Kimbanga, the leader of the African National Church and a Congo resident (he was imprisoned until his death in 1959), there was a general strike. The ruling powers replied with a machine-gun salvo from the "Force Publique" and the internment of freedom fighters in so-called "improvement camps".

After World War I the Congo experienced an economic boom, and the outbreak of World War II overshadowed the problem of independence. After 1945, the unrest flared up anew and the citizens of the Congo demanded their independence with increasing vehemence. But King Baudouin and the majority of Belgians were disinclined to relinquish the colony, whose minerals, rubber, palm oil and ivory contributed to the national prosperity.

Unrest, however, could not be contained. The revolt which erupted after the First African Peoples' Conference in 1958 finally led to the Belgian government's precipitate agreement to independence on 30 June 1960. Inter-tribal conflict subsequently broke out in the newly independent state and the breakaway of the rich mining province of Katanga (now Shaba) led to fresh conflict.

The superior attitude of the Belgians who had remained incited the Congolese to stage a desperate rebellion. Once more, Belgian soldiers fired their guns at the native population. The unrest led to the first Congo Crisis. In 1971 the state, still tottering, assumed a new name: the Republic of Zaire.

Belgium's independence was recognised by the superpowers of Europe at the London Conference of 1831 – a very shortly after the Belgian nation was founded. In order to ensure the European balance of power, the countries participating at the conference demanded a permanent guarantee of the new state's neutrality. Many Belgians had become tired of their country being used as a pawn in the power games of their European neighbours and were more than willing to accept this forced neutrality.

Indeed, this neutrality became the cornerstone of Belgian foreign policy. On the positive side, it meant, among other things, that no foreign troops could cross through Belgian territory and it guaranteed that sovereignty over territorial waters would be respected (any country which did not comply would have to reckon with military resistance). On the negative side, a neutral state was forbidden from supporting foreign troops either with weapons or with soldiers.

The neutrality of Belgium, however, was latently threatened from the start, particularly by the German Empire, established in 1871. The Germans resented Belgian colonisation of the Congo and disliked the fact that the Belgians refused to enter into an alliance with the Empire. On 3 August 1914, the Germans demanded that the Belgian government allow their army passage through Belgian territory. They claimed France was making plans to invade Belgium; in fact, the Germans planned to invade France using Belgium as a base.

The Belgian government denied the request, but the Germans ignored it and marched into Belgium anyway on 4 August. Great Britain, France and Russia called for an immediate retreat of the German forces, but the war could no longer be stopped. Despite intense resistance by the Belgian army, almost all of the country was in the hands of the Germans by the end of 1914.

Left, the destruction of war. A woodcut by Frans Masereel from his *From Black to White* series. **Right**, a "V1" rocket homes in on Antwerp after the liberation of Belgium by the Allied forces in September 1944.

The fiercest battles were fought in Tirlemont, Liège, Antwerp and Brussels. The massacres carried out by both sides are still remembered in the towns today. The battles in Flanders began in October 1914. Continuous fighting in Ypres, where poison gas was used, led to countless deaths.

Langemark, a village near Ypres, was considered by the Germans to be impregnable, but on 22–23 October 1914 the German army's supreme commanders, quartered securely away from the battlefields, ordered

several regiments to attack the village. The regiments were composed mainly of teenage volunteers. These young men, with an enthusiastic commitment to their cause, stormed blindly onto the "Field of Honour". Today, a cemetery with 45,000 graves of soldiers of different nationalities serves as a memorial to the victims of that action.

Resistance: Even after the Germans were securely entrenched in Belgium, the fighting continued. The Belgian civilian population countered the occupation with a variety of attacks designed to weaken the German position, including destroying train tracks and telephone and telegraph lines in order to hinder the supply of reinforcement troops and the transmission of military reports. The German reaction to such attacks was to seize and kill random hostages. Another means employed to break the population's resistance was to send Belgian women, teenagers and elderly men to Germany to work as forced labourers. The German administration also attempted to stir up animosity between the Flemings and the Walloons.

As the war drew to a close, the fiercest battles were fought on French soil and in the Ardennes, resulting in horrendous loss of human life and widespread destruction of property. By the time a ceasefire was declared on 11 November 1918, millions lay

and Belgium agreed to recognise the existing borders. England and Italy were to serve as guarantors of the borders. Belgium returned to its policy of neutrality in 1936, a move designed to guarantee the country's security and to prevent its involvement in any further war.

Society was also very different after the war. Belgium introduced universal male suffrage (women were not given the vote until 1948) and the right to strike. The economy, badly damaged by the war, was slow to recover. During the Great Depression, unemployment rose rapidly and, as in other cities across the Continent, fascist groups profited from the general unrest.

dead and Flemish soil had been turned into a massive graveyard. Mines, grenades, weapons and skeletons are regularly uncovered to this day.

King Albert I acquired a glorious reputation during World War I. He had become regent in 1909, and personally led the Belgian army as well as encouraging the country's citizens to resist the foreign invaders.

After the war, Belgium was granted sovereignty over the German-speaking region of Eupen-Malmedy. The Belgian government abandoned its position of neutrality and moved politically closer to France. In the 1925 Treaty of Locarno, Germany, France

World War II: German troops invaded Poland on 1 September 1939, signalling the start of World War II. After the Third Reich's victory over Poland, Norway and Denmark, it attacked France, the Netherlands, Luxembourg and Belgium on 10 May 1940. The Belgian government fled the country and set itself up in exile in London. King Leopold III, however, elected to remain in Belgium where he was held prisoner by the Germans until the end of the war. He was later unable to dispel suspicions that he had collaborated with the occupying forces.

The number of collaborators in Belgium is reckoned to have been considerable. They came mainly from the ranks of the fascist-monarchist movement, a movement which still exists today. The monarchists, under the leadership of Degrelle, supported the activities of the Nazi occupying forces from 1940 onwards. Later, the weapon-bearing SS even boasted two Belgian units, composed mainly of Flemings and French-speaking monarchists. These units were sent into action on the eastern front in 1945 where they were almost totally annihilated.

Belgium and northern France were under a common military administration during the war. Eupen-Malmedy was "reabsorbed" into the German Empire and Flanders was granted special status. Many residents of

Flanders belonged to the Flemish movement and enthusiastically supported the German annexation of their land.

Germany thus considered Flanders an "area capable of being resettled". This meant that, after the elimination or deportation of all opposition elements and Jews, Flanders could be recognised a German region.

Many Belgian Jews, as well as the many German and Austrian Jews who had fled to

Belgium in order to escape persecution at home, were murdered after the invasion of the Nazis. But some – calculations suggest about half – were hidden by Belgium's non-Jewish population and thereby saved from deportation and certain death. The Nazis' first step in controlling Belgium's Jews was to introduce registration. A large "J" was stamped in every Jewish passport. From 1941, Jews were prohibited from leaving their houses, and one year later they were forced to wear a yellow star. The Germans issued an order in July of 1942 that all Jews must appear at the Dossin military base near Mechelen, a base which had been turned into a camp. From there they would be transported to the east to be used as forced labourers. This led the Belgian resistance to distribute leaflets warning the Jews that they would meet certain death if they allowed themselves to be transported to the east. The result was that many Jews fled underground.

Nevertheless, the trains from Mechelen to Auschwitz began rolling on 4 August 1942. Most of the deportees did not go voluntarily, but had been randomly arrested or dragged out of hiding. The last train departed on 31 July 1944. Among the deportees was Felix Nussbaum, a German artist who had fled to Belgium from Osnabruck. By the end of the war, a total of 25,000 Jews living in Belgium had been murdered.

Many Belgians showed great courage in their commitment to aid the persecuted and become active in the resistance movement. These men and women, of all ages, destroyed train tracks, bridges, roads and telephone lines in order to hinder the occupying forces. It was to their credit that they were willing to suffer torture and death at the hands of the Nazis rather than reveal the names of their fellows. Socialists, communists, liberals and Christians fought side by side as Belgians and anti-fascists.

Liberation: The allied forces landed in Normandy on 6 June 1944 and on 25 August Paris was liberated. By 3 September Belgium was rid of the Nazis and the Belgian army joined forces with the Allied troops.

When Germany surrendered on 8 May 1945, Belgium, like many other countries, lay in ruins. But the Belgian people had another priority apart from reconstruction – identifying those who had collaborated with the Germans.

Left, the famous "Moules et Frites" were served in the "Friture Léon" as long ago as 1936. **Above**, German soldiers of occupation thinking of their sweethearts.

WHAT HAPPENED TO BELGIUM'S JEWS?

There are few people who do not know the poignant story of Anne Frank (1929–45), the daughter of a Jewish businessman from Frankfurt, who along with her family fled to Amsterdam early in the Hitler regime. In 1942 she and her family went into hiding. With the help of Dutch friends, they managed to survive for over two years in a secret annex in a warehouse. Then, in 1944, they were betrayed to the Gestapo by Dutch informers and transported to concentration camps in Germany. Anne's father alone survived; her mother died in Auschwitz in 1944, and she and her sister in Bergen-Belsen in 1945.

Returning to Holland after the war, Anne's father found the diary she had kept during her years in hiding. The *Diary of a Young Girl*, recording the events of her life during World War II, was published in 1947 and quickly became a classic of its kind. It serves as a memorial to the millions of Jews exterminated in the Nazi Holocaust.

In Belgium, a total of 2,700 Jewish children survived the persecution of the Nazi era. Their escape was thanks to the relentless efforts of a unique underground organisation that hid the children under false names in convents, boarding schools and private families.

But inevitably rescue came at a price to the children. The children had to live under the enormous strain of an assumed identity, a burden later replaced by feelings of guilt associated with being one of the "lucky" ones who escaped.

Now the generation of those who helped them is dwindling one by one. Many members of the underground rescue operation lost their lives at the time, or have died in the intervening years. Most of those who remain are now about 80 years old. Some of them have written accounts of the period of history through which they lived; none of them can free themselves from its shadow.

After the war and its aftermath, the generation of children they saved withdrew into a sort of emotional no man's land. Even today, so many years on, few of them are willing to talk about their years in hiding. This is an account of what happened in Belgium.

From 1 June 1942, Belgian Jews were required to wear the yellow Star of David. When they were called upon to volunteer for the labour camps in the early summer of 1942, many of them actually did so, believing this was their safest course of action. This led to thousands going unwittingly to their death. In the 100 days between 4 August 1942 and 31 October 1942, more than 17,000 Belgian Jews were deported from the Flemish town of Mechelen alone. In the two-year period between October 1942 and September 1944 (Brussels was liberated by the Allies on 4 September) the Germans captured 8,000 Jews, less than half the number in that 100-day period in Mechelen. The reason for this was that, from October 1942, those remaining realised the outcome of surrendering. By then, they knew that their only hope of survival lay in flight or in going underground, and they began to organise themselves accordingly.

Their principal aim was to save their children. Adults were in a position to arrange a life on the run, but the question of what they could do with their children was difficult. In this time of desperate need, an organisation of Jews and non-Jews – Belgian resistance fighters, social workers and idealists – joined forces to do whatever they could.

Organisation and co-ordination were vital to their success, but so was absolute secrecy. Maurice and Estera Heiber, a Jewish couple whose child also had to be hidden, set up an illegal coordination centre. Yvonne Rospa, a Jewish social worker and dedicated anti-racist, set out with a group of Belgian supporters to find accommodation and hideouts for the children who were at risk. Under the fictitious name of Madame Pascal, Estera Heiber could be found each morning in the flat of a Belgian opera singer. Here she could be consulted, could receive and pass on information, provide money for accommodation and distribute food ration cards.

The helpers were faced with a gargantuan task, not least how best to persuade loving parents that it was better for all concerned if they agreed to separate from their children. Parents had to accept the fact that they would receive no details of the name and address of the prospective foster parents. The separation of family members in such dangerous circumstances was heart-rending, but knowledge and information represented an additional risk of discovery.

Yvonne Jospa says that not all Belgians were prepared to help, but she refuses to judge those who failed to do so. Some were too afraid; others were unconcerned. She says that assistance came from isolated individuals from every social class. Those who agreed to take a Jewish child into their families were well aware of the risks involved and prepared to face them. The child had to remain as inconspicuous as possible, adopting the customs of the host family, attending the local state or

dren unscarred. Those children who survived refer only occasionally to their years spent in hiding. The parents on the other hand, especially those who were actively involved, find it easier to convey their experiences. They were able to join the resistance movement, whereas their children were helpless in the face of their fate.

Andrée Geulen, a former Belgian partisan married to a Jew, has six grandchildren. She lives in Brussels. She knows from the annual meetings with "her children" (those she helped rescue) just how sensitive these Jews are today. Now aged between 45 and 55, they have made their homes all over the world.

"It is amazing," she says, "to discover that only now, more than 45 years later, are some of my

confessional school with the other children in the family and going to church. They had to pray and eat exactly as the family did.

False passports were issued with the help of Belgian officials. Names were changed to disguise Jewish origins – Apfelbaum, for example, became Appelmans – so that a ration card could be claimed. Without one, survival in wartime Belgium was impossible.

The tragedy of being separated from their parents, of having to live with the permanent anxiety of an assumed identity and with the ever-present fear of being discovered, did not leave these chil-

Left, Jewish children deported and murdered by the Nazis. **Above**, many Jewish girls were hidden by Catholic schools; they survived the Holocaust.

protégés willing to permit others to see just how deep these unhealed wounds go. Only now have they begun to speak hesitatingly about their repressed, deep-seated fears. How can we possibly comprehend the feelings of a six-year-old girl snatched away from the bosom of her family and burdened with the inhuman knowledge that she must never reveal that her real name is Rachel, must never betray the fact that she is Jewish, for to do so would mean death?

"I knew personally the little girl called Rachel. Throughout the war she was known as Monique. Today she is almost 50 and admits she never answered when called by her assumed name. People tended to think she was retarded, but – as she recently told me in tears – 'I just didn't really know who I was'."

In September 1944 the Allies liberated Belgium from the German occupation. The Belgian government, reconstituted on 3 September, returned from its exile in London and assumed its administrative functions.

This government, although recognised by the Allies, was not fully accepted by the Belgian population. Both chambers of the legislature (with the exception of those members who had collaborated with the enemy) were to convene, but the question was raised as to whether the members of the government were representative of the Belgian people. The monarch, King Leopold III, had been deported by the Germans to Germany in June of 1944 and was not in Belgium at the time of the liberation. The chambers voted on 20 September to make Prince Charles, the brother of the king, prince regent.

Reconstruction: Compared to neighbouring countries, Belgium's economic recovery after the war was quite rapid. The harbour of Antwerp had been spared major damage during the conflict, and the country's energy reserves were adequate to supply all the necessary power.

Reorganisation on the political level, on the other hand, was very slow in coming. The country returned to the same structures and institutions which had been in place before the war. Parties that had collaborated with the Germans were banned, but changes in the other political parties were slight. The Christian Socialist party, founded in 1945, distanced itself from its forerunner, the Catholic party; it termed itself non-confessional and unitarian, and based itself on individual support as opposed to being church affiliated. Within the party, a Flemish and a Walloon wing were established. In the first parliamentary election after the war, in February 1946, this party was the victor.

The Socialist party, too, turned away from its practice of recruiting members collectively through the trade unions, cooperatives and sick-funds and began instead to enlist

support on a direct basis among individual voters. The Liberal party and the Communist party based their appeal on their existing platforms and programmes. The Communists temporarily replaced the Liberals as the third strongest faction in parliament, but by 1949 the three traditional parties were once again in the forefront of Belgian politics.

The purges which took place within the population immediately after the war belong to a depressing chapter in the history of Belgium. Some 53,000 Belgians were con-

demned for collaborating with the enemy.

The king returns: In May 1945, King Leopold III returned to Belgium from his exile in Germany and the crisis between the king and his ministers turned into an open conflict. Every one of the parties took a stand on the issue: the Christian Socialists supported the return of the king, the Socialists and Communists demanded that he abdicate, and the Liberals were in favour of abolishing the monarchy altogether. The Christian Socialists resigned from the government in protest, leaving only opponents of the monarch and of monarchy still represented.

A short time after, the Communists also

Left, symbols of economic progress; with the introduction of nuclear power, lamps were erected along the motorways. **Right**, the Atomium in Brussels, built for the 1958 World Exhibition.

resigned from the coalition, leaving the government unable to function. The Christian Socialists were thus forced to return. The government, now a coalition of Socialists and Christian Socialists, implemented a series of economic reforms. A central economic council, as well as councils for the professions and for management, was established. The parliamentary elections of 1949 were the first in which women could vote.

The Christian Socialists gained an absolute majority in the Senate and the Liberals became the third strongest party in Belgium. A popular referendum was held on 12 March 1950 to determine what constitutional rights the monarch should be granted. Fifty-eight percent of the voters were in favour of allowing the king to return to the throne.

But the results of the election demonstrated a polarisation of feelings on the issue. In Flanders, 72 percent of the population favoured the return of the king to office. In Brussels, on the other hand, it was only 48 percent, and only 42 percent of the Walloons voted in favour of the king.

In June 1950, new parliamentary elections were held. The Christian Socialists gained the absolute majority in both chambers of the legislature. The parliament voted to reinstate the king, and, on 22 July 1950, Leopold III returned to Laeken Palace. This resulted in a mighty wave of protest in the Walloon industrial areas. The king announced that he would be willing to abdicate in favour of his son within one year and, on 17 July 1951, Baudouin I was duly crowned.

The Christian Socialists retained an absolute majority in the legislature from 1950 to 1954. In the following legislative period, however, a coalition of Socialists and Liberals took the reins of power.

Regionalism: It was during this time that the education reform debates between the Catholics and non-confessionals (Socialists, Liberals and Communists) were raised. The Catholics demanded a more autonomous form of education while the anti-clerics supported a standard public education. The same fronts that had formed during the referendum on Leopold III reappeared. On the one side were the Catholics and on the other side the Socialists, Liberals and Communists. It soon became clear that a schism between north and south was a likely possibility and that the only thing which had prevented this from

happening so far was the existence of the large national-based parties.

Since the war, there had been differences in the way the Flemish north and Wallonian south had developed and the first regionalist demands were heard. For the time being, however, the federalists and supporters of cultural autonomy were in a minority. The politics of economic and social solidarity practised by successive governments were enough to keep the north and south from drifting too far apart. However, on 3 December 1953 both the Walloon and the Flemish federalists called for a reform of the centralised state.

Even though the Socialist party was actu-

ally in opposition, the three unity parties signed a "schooling pact" on 20 November 1958. This agreement introduced new regulations for the educational system from kindergarten all the way up through high school. It was more democratic, the federal budget included more funds for education, new schools were built and the free religiously affiliated educational institutions were subsidised. A commission was set up to oversee the implementation of the agreement.

While it would be wrong to place the full blame for the ensuing linguistic disputes on this agreement, it is true to say that it stirred up differences within the parties. All the parties were now divided on the language question. It was during these years that new economic structures had been established. Although these had worked to the advantage of the Walloons up to this time, the reverse was now starting to be the case. The Walloon mines were closing down, the related heavy industry was suffering setbacks, regional development organisations were being established and American industry was getting a foothold on the Continent. In Flanders, these developments were greeted enthusiastically and the port of Antwerp boomed.

At this point, a tribute should be paid to King Baudouin and his queen, Fabiola de Mora y Aragon. The king and his prime

tic disputes and regional economic questions came to the forefront of Belgian domestic politics. The social climate was marked by strikes during the winter of 1960–61. Demonstrations were held to protest against the so-called "law of uniformity" regulating economic development, social progress and the reorganisation of state finances. The strikers demanded federalism and structural reforms. Tensions developed not only between the language groups and different religions, but also within the parties and trades unions. One result was an increase in pluralism. Parties and pressure groups sprouted up all over the place. Their main concern was to ensure that they retained their position and

ministers, from the Socialist Van Acker to the more recent Christian Socialist Martens, were able to defuse the worst of the country's problems: linguistic disputes, governmental reforms, independence for the Belgian Congo (1960) and economic crises. A common spirit reigned over party politics, extreme solutions were rejected and the strict neutrality of the king, required by the constitution, gave him an important role in attempts to solve these conflicts.

Even so, as the new decade began, linguis-

Left and above, some consumer products of a prosperous society.

their voice in a future regionalised Belgium.

This was all taking place in a climate of economic prosperity. The "golden '60s" lasted 15 years in Belgium, until the economic crisis of 1974. Consumer spending and construction boomed. Household appliances, televisions and cars headed the list of consumer goods; department stores and supermarkets proliferated. Belgium was paved with super highways. But the prosperity of some highlighted the poverty of others. Some 900,000 people, a tenth of the entire population, were either living on the edge of poverty or could not support themselves at all. Gradually, reforms began to take place.

The Flemings wanted cultural, linguistic and territorial autonomy. The Walloons wanted to remain in control of their own affairs and sought to pull themselves out of the economic slump brought on by the decline of their traditional industries. They demanded new and more efficient industry, a new division of the territory and the right to administer their own natural resources.

State reform: The constitutional revisions of 1970 ("the centralised state has been superseded by the facts," according to Prime Minister Gaston Eyskens) and of 1980, and the accompanying legislation, were all designed to preserve the language, culture, lifestyle and spiritual beliefs of the different groups

The latest reforms provided for a redistribution of authority and finances among the various administrative levels. Currently the state is responsible for about 60 percent of the national budget; local and regional governments must divide the remaining 40 percent between them.

The development of the Brussels region is the latest outcome of the constitutional reform. There are many facilities around Brussels which serve both the Flemish and Walloon communities. The institutional reform has brought a temporary halt to the historic development toward a federal state.

In total there are six governments, 60 ministers, nine provincial governors and 550

within the country. Since 1970, three communities and three regions have existed within Belgium: the Flemish, the French and the German-speaking communities; the Flemish, the Walloon and the Brussels regions.

In 1980 measures were taken to expand the authority of the regions, which were granted their own rights and institutions. In order to regulate the balance of power between the central organs of the state, the different communities and the regions, a committee of accordance and a disputes court was established. Today Belgium has a complex system of municipalities, provinces and regions as well as a centralised state.

communes. Many Belgians feel that this policy, known as the *Compromis à la Belge*, attempting to devolve power to every conceivable minority, has got out of hand.

The influence of the European Union over different sectors of communal life is increasing, especially in regional relations. In Belgium, the zones of development recommended by the EU have been imposed on the autonomous Flemish-Walloon regions. European resolutions concerning production capacities for the steel industry have led to additional friction.

The central state has authority in national defence, foreign affairs, social issues, agriculture, justice and financial and monetary issues. Policy-making in areas such as the economy, education, transport and the environment have all been passed to the regions.

There is growing pressure from Flanders to devolve social security; the Flemish feel they are bearing the brunt by financing the large welfare payments being dished out to the growing numbers of sick, aged and unemployed in Wallonia. Friction between the language groups is exacerbated by an influx of foreigners, particularly the well-heeled Eurocrats who are forcing up house prices and making it difficult for young couples to find affordable housing.

The rivalry between the language groups

is best illustrated by the row which forced the election in November 1991 (the 10th election in 12 years). When the Flemish refused to grant export licences to two Wallonian arms manufacturers poised to sign a contract with Saudi Arabia on the grounds that Belgium should not be supplying arms to the Middle East, the Walloons retaliated by refusing to sign contracts to provide telephone exchanges to the Middle East, as the lion's share of the contracts were to be handled by Flemish companies.

Left, a comfortable life in the country. **Above**, strife on the streets.

In spite of such incidents, it does not mean that there are no forces at work to prevent Belgium from being torn apart. Indeed, the opposite is true. Admittedly, Belgium has historically always been a divided country, but paradoxically, it has also managed to remain unified.

But where is the counterweight to this over-structured and unwieldy state system? The Belgians themselves, who are individualists and protective of their privileges. And Belgium is an integral part of a European movement within a Europe which, with the new opening up of the eastern European countries, is itself being fundamentally restructured.

Belgian society has been completely transformed since the end of World War II. For the past several years, there has been a growing feeling among some Belgian intellectuals that the economic, social and political significance of these developments should be seen in terms of a geographical entity which is a product of constantly changing social processes. The geography of Belgium becomes a comparative study of the socio-economic forces at play within this entity. The Belgian landscape is torn and divided in all directions. Of course there is the geographic boundary between the Walloons and the Flemings, but there is also a division between the wealthy and the poor .

Strong constitution: The competition between regions, cities, ports and industrial zones is increasing. Conflicts between social groups with different, often opposite, ways of looking at things, are developing. The young intellectuals of a group called Mort-Subite describe today's Belgium as "an entity resulting from the relationships between the economic, social, political and cultural dimensions of the region".

Anyone who travels through Belgium and views the country in this light will surely notice the underlying differences and yet, at the same time, understand its unity. "What actually unites you the most?" is a question often asked by perplexed onlookers.

One answer often given by Belgians is: "Our constitution." This constitution, constantly evolving, is the epitome of a commitment to liberty. Recognised as one of the world's most modern constitutions, it often serves as a model for newly-established governments in the developing world.

A VISITOR'S FIRST IMPRESSIONS

Heidrun Noble left her home in Cologne to go to work in Antwerp. Here she describes her first impressions of her new environment and its inhabitants.

"Where are you going?" asked my neighbours as they helped me to carry all my worldly goods to the removal van. "I'm leaving for Antwerp," I replied.

It wasn't a distant move. Antwerp lies less than two hours from Cologne, but it was a different country with a different culture and I felt a mixture of apprehension and excitement. As I crossed the border into Belgium I felt I was entering a new chapter in my life.

Despite the doom-laden warnings about Belgian drivers being among the worst in the world, I managed to arrive safely at my destination. The rules of the road in Belgium seem to be quite easy to follow; the most important thing is to watch the car in front like a hawk. In Belgium manoeuvres are rarely signalled in advance. Only when a driver has successfully completed a manoeuvre will he set his indicator flashing – presumably, I reasoned, in pleasure at a mission accomplished.

Tongue-tied: One of the first things I did after unpacking my belongings was to watch the news on television. The city of Antwerp lies in the Flemish half of Belgium. A visitor who speaks both English and German will quickly be able to comprehend the gist of a news report, and he will soon be able to follow a conversation; speaking and being properly understood, however, is a much more difficult matter – unless you are prepared to sacrifice your larynx in the interest of international relations.

I had been warned about the language conflict before arriving in Antwerp and I fully expected to find Flemish and Walloon activists throwing bombs at each other. In fact, though feelings on the subject are still running high, the extent of the violence seems to be limited to the odd stink bomb – usually announced so far in advance that the opposi-

tion has plenty of time to duck for cover. History testifies to the fact that the Flemings and Walloons are about as capable of patching up their quarrel as the cartoon characters Tom and Jerry. Yet, in spite of their differences, they have repeatedly managed to unify in the face of an external enemy. Together they have managed to evict all forces of occupation from their country – irrespective of whether they spoke Spanish, French, Dutch or German.

Apart from Flemish and French, there is a

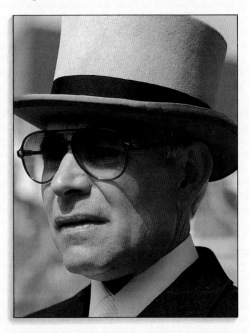

third official language in Belgium: German. Despite the devastating experiences of two world wars there are no discernable anti-German feelings here. The fact that King Albert II is descended from a family of German princes and the presence of some 60,000 German-speaking citizens living between Eupen and Malmedy, a region ceded to Belgium after World War I, has helped to repair relations.

The problems of trilinguality are most keenly felt during Christmas speeches and at state receptions, when feelings can be at their most sensitive; even the names of places and people give rise to complications. Still, the

Preceding pages: at a gathering of transvestites in Echternach. **Left**, a smile from the Ardennes. **Right**, a coachman in Mechelen.

third official language can be useful at times. Flemish is best for striking up friendships, but German is useful for dealing with red tape. Along with French – spoken by virtually everyone – German is spoken in restaurants and hotels.

When communicating in Flemish it can be unwise to try to draw any inferences as to the meaning of a word or phrase on the basis of its similarity to German. To do so is to invite misunderstanding. When, for example, an advertisement for a job seeks *bekwame* applicants, the post is for diligent workers, not easy-going (*bequem*) ones, as German-speakers might think. The lack of capital letters and seemingly arbitrary syllabifica-

especially for the Dutch. The brew, invented by a Trappist monk, is lovingly produced in Belgian monasteries to this day. It comes served in shallow glasses and should be drunk with due devotion.

The punk and his granny: There must be some reason why there are so few punks, skinheads and hell's angels on the streets of Antwerp, and it probably lies in the fact that there is nothing to rebel against. Young and old alike are easy-going and tolerant of one another. Community ties are based on kin and the closely-knit extended family is common. Should a bored teenager decide to dye his hair red and purple, squeeze himself into skin-tight leathers and march into the nearest

tion do not make comprehension any easier for the outsider.

Belgium's French and Dutch neighbours – who are as fond of telling jokes about the Belgians as the English are about the Irish – frequently cross the border if they want to eat well or paint the town red. One of the biggest attractions for these visitors are Belgian chips (though the standard of more exalted culinary achievements is also high). The secret of their distinctive flavour lies in the method of their cooking. Belgian chips are removed from the frying pan just before the end of the normal cooking time and tossed in a different fat. Belgian beer also proves a popular draw,

pub with the intention of scaring the living daylights out of the regulars, he is most likely to meet his granny, cheerfully dealing out the cards and volunteering to buy him a beer. And in the next hostelry he will probably meet his mother, surrounded by shopping bags, enjoying a little refreshment on her way home.

Without doubt, the Flemings' greatest love is their home. The region's architects and builders seem to have only one model available, however – a timber shoe-box packed with ornate wall units and armchairs so solid that they leave the German rustic oak three-piece in the shade. Here, antimacassars and tassels have never really gone out of fashion.

Although interiors tend to be conservative, Belgian imagination is given free rein when it comes to the letter-box; in many cases it reaches Breughelian proportions – adornments ranging from carved birds of prey, baroque mausoleums, classical temples and marble pedestals are not uncommon.

No Belgian home is complete without a garden. Whether for flowers or vegetables, a Belgian's patch of earth is a symbol of success. Apart from the ubiquitous easy-care conifers, the monkey puzzle tree is particularly popular in Belgium its tentacle-like branches looming nightmarishly over the unadorned cube of the house.

"Belgian weather is quite straightforward," explained one long-term resident. "Most of the time it rains; apart from that, there are the March and November storms, which we also call 'spring' and 'autumn' storms, because the March storms sometimes last until July and the November ones often start in September. In good years, August is relatively calm – at least, for a few hours here and there." The Belgians take advantage of these lulls to carry out repairs to their homes, working at the speed of light before the next shower sets in.

It is advisable to keep the following table of wind speeds in mind during your visit to Belgium: dead calm – the washing flaps

Mark Twain maintained that New England had the widest range of possible weather conditions; he obviously never visited Belgium. Those who imagine Belgium to be a small, flat land engulfed in perpetual drizzle are completely wrong; the weather, unlike the equable nature of the Belgian people, is tempestuous. If you did the splits and stretched out your arms you would have your left leg in a cloudburst, the right one in a hurricane, and one arm in sunshine and the other in a thunderstorm.

Left, "Your final bid!": the Belgians love bargains. **Above**, market scene.

vigorously on the line; gentle breeze – button your coat and hang on to your hat; moderate wind – watch out for loose roof tiles; windy – progress possible only on all fours; strong wind – buy stocks of food for several days, board up windows and wait for it to pass; storm – run for your life.

Well, I expect I shall survive here for a while. After all, if nothing else, I am now living in one of the two most prominent places on the face of the earth. Astronauts in orbit can discern just two man-made details on the globe – the Great Wall of China by day and the gleaming ribbons of Belgian motorways by night.

Eddy Merckx, the legendary racing cyclist of the 1960s and '70s, is probably the only Belgian sportsman whose name is familiar to non-Belgians. At various stages in his career, Merckx won every major international cycling race, gaining the coveted Tour de France trophy no fewer than five times.

All in all, however, Brussels does not play an important role on the international sporting scene and Merckx is the only world-calibre athlete that the country can boast. Even so the majority of Belgians enjoy participating in one or more sporting activities and support their national teams with enthusiasm.

Brussels' sports fans are particularly well catered for, with a choice of six stadiums, three horse-racing tracks and several ice rinks. There are top-ranking football teams such as R.S.C. Anderlecht, and an internationally famous light athletics meeting (Ivo van Damme Memorial).

Since 1985 Brussels has been haunted by the curse of Heysel Stadium. This tragedy occurred when hooligan supporters of the British national champions, Liverpool, staged a brutal riot during the European Cup Final against Juventus Turin. The tragic episode cost the lives of 39 Juvenutus fans and resulted in British clubs being banned from European tournaments. The event had a profound effect on the city, though it had very little to do with the everyday reality of sport in Belgium – active or passive – for the average citizen of Brussels.

A nation on its bike: Cycling is without doubt the favourite national sport. It holds a place in the national soul comparable to that of baseball in America, cricket in England, bullfighting in Spain, or ice hockey in the Soviet Union and Canada. Cynics maintain that its popularity represents an escape from the boredom of a Belgian Sunday. Indeed, hardly a day goes by on which there is no cycling race somewhere or other, and they are always supported by thousands of enthusiastic spectators; a classic cycling race from

Liège to Bastogne and back, for instance, will be lined by throngs of spectators all along the route.

But it isn't just the cycling that people come to see. A rally is also a social event. Friends meet, drink a beer together, become carried away by the speed at which the cyclists race past, and enjoy listening to the results on the radio later on. In addition, cycling events are invariably attended by fairs and other attractions appealing to younger family members.

Speculation as to why this enthusiasm for cycling should have grown up in Belgium usually cites the topography of the land. One ideal precondition is without doubt the flatness of the countryside. Except in the hilly eastern provinces, Belgium – like the Netherlands – makes the bicycle the most convenient and inexpensive mode of transport. Children organise impromptu races on the way to school, and farmers' wives use their ancient bone-shakers to reach the nearest village. When national heroes such as grocer's son Eddy Merckx make headline news in the international press, their success fires the enthusiasm of the aspiring youth. The popu-

Left, crags on the Mass, a paradise for climbers. **Above right**, a cycling race gets underway at the Zandpoortvest in Mechelen.

larity of the sport has little to do with the prospect of monetary gain; apart from the trophies, the prizes are not usually very significant. In a small country like Belgium, the few top sportsmen become role models to a far greater extent than elsewhere.

The Belgians are a convivial people; they love their families and enjoy celebrating with friends. A Belgian who participates actively in some form of sport will naturally tend to belong to a club. For Flemings and Walloons alike the latter performs the role of a second family, a second home.

An example of this sociability can be found in the cycling club at Plombières, in the three-country triangle between Aachen, thousands flock to the race from Spa to Francorchamps, hoping to witness as many hazardous thrills as possible. Celebrations know no bounds when a compatriot wins, and heavy disappointment descends if a Belgian entry is eliminated early on in the race. However, competing is considered the most important thing.

Bar billiards: Brussels citizens with more limited sporting ability tend to retire to the city's bars to indulge in a game of billiards, a favourite evening pastime. The professional standards reached by some of these players are documented by the string of world championship titles won by the nation's experts.

Maastricht and Liège. Although the lively club has had no active cycling members for years, it still continues to organise a "Grand Prix de Plombières" each autumn. The winner is invariably from the Netherlands. A crate of beer is the prize for the fastest circuit, and the winner is rewarded with a trophy and a certificate.

Sport in Belgium has a great deal to do with spectacle. The louder and more colourful the event, the better. Motor races are frequent events; many take place through the streets of towns, with all speed limits temporarily lifted (be warned: barriers to protect the spectators are seldom erected). Tens of

Apart from cycling, football and billiards, the other sports enjoying popularity in Belgium include tennis and golf – both as fashionable here as elsewhere on the Continent. Cross-country skiing is practised in the winter in the hills of the Ardennes; and during the summer months, sailing and surfing are both very popular pastimes on the English Channel coast between Knokke and De Panne. Rugby is played mainly in the French-speaking provinces, where it is a favourite spectator sport.

Top sportsmen have a difficult time in a small country. Belgium has produced few world-class athletes, although it has established a winning tradition in a number of disciplines. Gold medals or unexpected success produce a spirit of national euphoria. In the 1986 World Football Championship in Mexico, the Belgian team reached the semifinals. Nobody slept during the victory night; celebrations lasted until well into the small hours. Apart from that, however, things are quiet on the higher sporting plane.

Rat catching: The combination of sport and spectacle has a long tradition in the country. Every August in the village of Zaffelare, near Ghent, an archery contest is held – a sporting event, but with the spirit of a funfair. The chief aspect of the contest is somewhat gruesome. The targets are not the normal

Twice a week between 15 October and 1 May (on Tuesdays and Saturdays), a hunt takes place in the Vielsalm region. It is a full-blooded mounted chase in which a stag is pursued by hounds and horsemen to the bitter end. The hunt can last as long as 10 hours. The host of the event is Baron Eric Jansen, whose guests for the occasion are drawn from the aristocracy and the highest echelons of industry. After the killing, the hunting party recovers at an exclusive champagne reception.

Public outcry at blood sports of this nature is vociferous in Belgium. Organised protest is also directed against a substantial number of birdcatchers, who prefer to describe

ones used in archery, but cages full of rats which are suspended at a height of 27 metres (86 ft). The event marks a plague of rats that descended on the village over a century ago. The archers attempt to shoot down the containers; if they succeed in their aim, the cages shatter in mid-air; the rats fall to the ground and lie stunned until their throats are slit. The local newspaper, *Het Nieuwsblad*, which sponsors the event, maintains that this grisly slaughter is more humane than poisoning.

Left, Belgium is mostly flat, so ideal cycling territory. **Above**, billiards is one of the most popular pastimes.

theselves as animal lovers and sportsmen. Each year in the late autumn and early winter, almost 1 million migratory birds are caught; they end up in cages on balconies, in the bird market in Brussels, and even in cooking pots.

This love of birds extends to pigeon racing, another popular sport throughout the country. The sport is covered by radio, with regular bulletins on the times when different groups of birds have been despatched and weather reports detailing flight conditions. In summer the railway stations are full of people carrying wicker baskets full of gently cooing birds.

It is almost impossible to travel through Belgium without coming across a celebration of some kind. The government recognises only 10 official annual public holidays – New Year's Day, Easter Monday, May Day, Ascension Day, Whit Monday, 21 July, 15 August, 1 and 11 November, and Boxing Day – but these occasions, adding up to a total of 2.74 percent of the entire year, represent only a fraction of the country's countless celebrations.

A favourite saying maintains that it only takes three Belgians to make a party; in fact, the entire nation loves to celebrate at the drop of a hat. The Belgians' nonchalant approach to life can easily stand comparison with the famous savoir-vivre of the neighbouring French. In Belgium you will find a unique combination of French, Dutch, and German attitudes and philosophies.

Public holidays: Each nationality also contributes its own traditional festivals. With the consequences of this in mind, the government has deliberately restricted the number of official public holidays. In practice, however, Belgians take little notice of government kill-joys and frequently take time off for unofficial holidays too. In many districts, for example, the people cheerfully ignore the fact that the pre-Lenten festival is not a public holiday.

For the visitor this hidden agenda of unofficial holidays can present problems. The uninitiated may arrive in a town or village only to find themselves confronted on all sides by locked doors and hardly a soul in sight. However, their disappointment is usually dispelled when the scene of revelry occupying the entire community has been tracked down and they are invited to join in the fun.

It isn't just festivals which are cause for celebration. The Belgians are a spontaneous people and are apt to rejoice over almost anything – from a sporting success to a sunny day. A visitor to the provinces may find that ordering a simple beer or coffee in an inn

leads to his inclusion in a full-scale party. As evening approaches the place will become busier and busier, and the local accordion player will be invited to strike up a tune. A minute later, the gathering will have become a party with singing and dancing. And yet, nobody was actually invited – neither the guests nor the musician.

Beer is tops: In spite of being neighbours of the French, Belgians are not great advocates of wine. The Belgians' favourite drink is undoubtedly beer. It is usually served in

small glasses, as in the Netherlands, and bottom-fermented. Local pilsner is relatively mild in flavour. The Belgians' favourite chaser is *jenever* (juniper-flavoured gin). But be warned: *jenever* causes a thundering hangover when consumed in quantity, especially in the novice.

Festival time: As a rule, the Walloon provinces tend to celebrate carnival with rather less gusto than the Flemish ones, paying more attention to the religious aspects of the event. Dancing, however, forms an important part of carnival almost everywhere. In some towns a carnival ball is held virtually every day of the festivites; and many people

Left, the Belgians love a chance to dress up. **Right**, giants at Brussels' maypole celebrations – for some reason held in August.

wouldn't miss a single one of them. Usually they are accompanied by traditional Belgian folk music. Strongly influenced by French and Dutch traditions, this is based on wind and percussion instruments augmented by the accordion.

The annual round of carnival celebrations kicks off in the town of Ronse in East Flanders on 6 January. Its pre-Lenten carnival, known as *bommelfeesten*, is marked by an endless round of celebrations. One of the most spectacular carnival celebrations takes place in Binche (Hainaut), where festivities start a good four weeks before Mardi Gras proper. Festivities reach a climax on Shrove Tuesday with the antics of the so-called

notably in the towns of Fosses-la-Ville and Stavelot (Liège).

Summer celebrations: As summertime approaches, the calendar of festivals fills up rapidly. The first important celebrations after Easter are the May parades. On 30 May, festivals are held in Hasselt and Genk (Limburg). Genk goes one step better than the usual maypole dancing and feasting and holds a grand procession led by the specially elected May Queen.

On the second Sunday in May, Ypres (West Flanders) celebrates its Cats' Festival, in which floats and costumes sport a feline theme. The origins of this festival lie in the time when Ypres was an important wool-

Gilles. Some 1,500 people, colourfully dressed in special costumes, stage a 24-hour display of dancing on the market square, showering the spectators with oranges as they perform.

Malmedy (Liège) is another town which celebrates carnival in a big way. The fun continues well into Lent, long after Ash Wednesday is past and the religiously inclined have started fasting. Carnival parades on the Sunday following Ash Wednesday are held in the towns of Fosses (Namur), Hasselt (Limburg) and Tilff (Liège). The fourth Wednesday before Easter is also an important date for carnival parades, most

weaving town. In the winter cats were encouraged to live in the Weavers' Hall on the Grote Markt, where the wool was stored, in order to keep the mice down. When summer arrived, however, the cats were deemed dispensable and thrown out of the window to meet with certain death at the hands of the crowd. The last of the original, blood-thirsty Cats' Festivals was held in 1817; it was revived in 1938, when cloth cats replaced the real thing.

The third weekend in May sees the Windmill Festival in Lembeke (East Flanders) and the exciting Witches' Procession in Nieuwpoort (West Flanders).

Visitors who like processions will find plenty to amuse them during the month of June. On the first Sunday of the month they can witness the Hundred Days Parade in Ligny (Namur). During the same weekend the town of Tournai (Hainaut) celebrates its Day of the Four Processions.

The Peasants' Festival during the second weekend in June in Turnhout (Antwerp) is considered great cause for merrymaking. A fine array of folkloric costumes can be seen on the third Sunday in July in Verviers (Liège). The international costumed parade attracts thousands of visitors.

Visitors keen to explore the many facets of Belgian beer will find the ideal opportunity mally held on the second Sunday in July.

There seems no historical justification for the fact that in Baardegem the harvest festival is celebrated as early as the last weekend in July, when the crops are still ripening in the fields and a long way off being gathered in. Some think it indicates that the festival was originally a fertility cult rather than a festival of thanks. Cynics put it down to just another case of the Belgians seeking any pretext to celebrate.

Also on the last weekend in July, there's another Witches' Procession, this time in Breslare in West Flanders (the other takes place in Nieuwpoort in May).

The Ommegang festival is celebrated in

in Oudenaarde (East Flanders) on the 30 June. Then virtually the entire population of Oudenaarde – translated, the name means "Old Earth" – celebrates the "Adriaen-Brouwer-Feest", dedicated to the glory of the national drink. Needless to say, the local beer flows in impressive quantities during the festival – mainly down the throats of thirsty visitors.

Those whose interests are more culturally inclined shouldn't miss the International Folk Dance Festival in Schoten (Antwerp) nor-

Brussels on the first Thursday in July. This famous parade commemorates the arrival of a miraculous statue of the Virgin Mary in the 14th century. It's a spectacular affair and one of the biggest festivals in the whole country; more than 2,000 participants, all dressed in historical costumes and bearing banners, assemble on the Grand' Place; actors dressed in royal attire represent the family of the Emperor Charles V.

August activities: The capital's other big festival celebrates the erection of the *meyboom* (maypole) on 9 August (no explanations are available as to the reason for a maypole in August). The Giants' Parade

Left, the traditional Ros Beiaardommegang in Dendermonde. **Above**, at the fair in St Druiden.

begins on the third Sunday in August in Heusden (East Flanders), as does the Heathens Festival in Nassogne. Bruges holds a triennial Canal Festival (August 1992, 1995, 1998) and, every five years the Golden Tree Parade (catch it in 1995).

August also sees a number of festivals in honour of the harvests. Anyone who imagines that the Belgians do not produce wine, or even that they do not appreciate it, should visit the wine festivals in Beaumont (Hainaut) and Overijse (Brabant), where many a local connoisseur can be observed sampling Belgian vintages.

Alternatively, you might like to visit the medieval fair at Franchimont Castle, which

takes place at the same time. The castle is situated at Theux (Liège).

Even when the evenings start to draw in with the onset of autumn, there is no let-up in the calendar of events. On the first Sunday in September, a magnificent flower show is held in Ghent as a farewell to the flower-filled summer months. On 3 and 4 September Antwerp celebrates its Feast of Liberation and the Festival of the Guilds. Antwerp's citizens celebrate with great gusto, even though the liberation in question occurred many years ago. On the second Sunday in September in nearby Mechelen the festival of Op Signoorke is held. Op

Signoorke is a giant doll which traditionally symbolised male irresponsibility (it also went by the name *vuilen bras* (unfaithful drunkard) and *vuilen bruidegom* (disloyal bridegroom); every year the doll was paraded through the streets and tossed in a sheet. In 1775, however, the doll acquired a new significance when a young man from the rival city of Antwerp tried to steal it. The robber failed in his attempt and was badly beaten, but the outraged citzens of Mechelen decided to rename their doll "Op Signoorke", a derisive nickname for the people of Antwerp which came from the word "signor", a reference to Antwerp's favoured status under the Spanish.

The beer festival in Diksmuide (West Flanders) is popular enough to rival the Oktoberfest in Munich. In fact, it has even borrowed the name of the famous Munich original. Another popular Oktoberfest is held in the little town of Wieze (East Flanders). The atmosphere in the marquee, large enough to hold 10,000 people, is enlivened by the thigh-slapping music of Bavarian bands. Beer from the local brewery is served until the small hours.

It is impossible to list all the beer festivals which take place during the autumn. At no other time do the Belgians devote so much attention to their national drink. Even small towns and villagers are likely to be holding a festival. Visitors are always welcome to join in. Since many Belgians are multilingual you will encounter few problems. A beer festival can be the best place to get to know the Belgians. The relaxed atmosphere of the village festivals are often more conducive to friendship than the more elaborate events staged in the towns.

Finally, before closing this calendar of festivals, mention should be made of the Feast of St Martin on 11 November. The festival is celebrated with great enthusiasm throughout the country. Children receive presents, and many Belgians still observe the tradition of the St Martin's Day bonfire. The town of Eupon celebrates the day with particular panache, with a candle-lit procession.

Christmas celebrations in Belgium are very like those in France. After New Year the whole calendar begins again.

Left, where drinkers are spoilt for choice. **Right**, a sunny day in a beer garden in Liège.

A BELGIAN STEW OF TASTES

If you are feeling hungry in Belgium you have two choices: you can select an inn or a restaurant at random and sit down at one of the tables or you can purchase a satisfying snack from one of the numerous street vendors. Few European countries have such a range of portable food. Wherever hunger strikes, you can be sure of finding, close at hand, a chip stand (French: *frites*; Flemish *frieten*) or a waffle stall and – if you are lucky – a vendor selling snails, a hot, satisfying snack, served wrapped in paper. Many people would say you haven't tasted chips, waffles or snails until you've tried the Belgian varieties.

Belgium embraces two regions, each of which has its own language, customs and culinary traditions. The northern provinces speak Flemish, a language strongly akin to that of their Netherlandish neighbours; the southern part of the country speaks French. Brabant, together with its capital Brussels, is bilingual, lying as it does at the heart of the country and possessing no external borders. In addition to the culinary traits of these neighbouring countries, the discerning diner may also be able to detect influences from Spain and Austria, originating from the time when Belgium was part of the Spanish Netherlands and the Habsburg Empire.

Although Belgium's neighbours, France and the Netherlands, have undeniably left their mark on Belgian cuisine, it would be an oversimplification to claim that the Flemings favour the good, plain cooking of the Netherlands while the Walloons prefer the refined and subtle flavours of French cuisine. In the Netherlands, a *hutspot* is a stew of puréed vegetables with large chunks of meat. The Flemish *hochepot*, by contrast, consists of pieces of meat and vegetables in a clear stock flavoured with herbs. The Walloon cuisine tends to be somewhat more substantial, more spicy and have more calories than modern French cusine.

The different provincial cuisines of Belgium, however, are no longer as distinct as

they used to be. The country's top chefs have borrowed and combined elements from all regions and the average cook has followed suit. Belgian cuisine is at times light and delicate, and at other times flavoursome and rich. One thing is certain, though: whatever you choose to eat, it will be delicious.

The still-lifes of numerous Flemish artists, from Pieter Breughel and Pieter Aertsen to Adriaen Brouwer and Frans Snyders, feature the hearty food of their native Flanders. Their pictures express the Belgian delight in good food of all kinds.

Specialities: Fish and crustaceans occupy a prominent place in the Flemish cuisine. Mussels are ubiquitous, especially served with chips. The herring is also popular and is cooked in a wide varietiy of ways; as steamed herring, herring Nieuwpoort-style (marinated herring), fresh herring *bonne femme* (herring in red wine), green herring with spring vegetables, smoked herring in onion sauce or kippers *en papillote*. Lobster, shrimps and oysters round out the Belgian seafood platter. Oysters are usually swallowed raw, but you may also like to try them *au gratin* – covered with a crust of breadcrumbs, cheese and fine spices.

All Belgians are fond of a good, hearty soup. It is invariably brought to the table in a huge tureen, from which guests are invited to help themselves to as many helpings as they like. The variety of soups in Belgium is endless, but just some of the local specialities include carrot soup, cauliflower soup, red cabbage soup, endive soup, cress soup and – more a meal than a soup – a hearty green pea soup with cured pork, potatoes, plenty of vegetables and a slice or two of spicy sausage.

Many regions have their own particular soup – for example, Flemish soup, Ardennes soup, Liège soup and Brabant soup. Regions are also proud of their own traditional dishes. Mechelen, for example, is famous for its excellent asparagus and chicken; Liège boasts fine white sausages, Antwerp has its meat loaves, the province of Luxembourg is renowned for its venison chops and its stuffed goose *à la forestière*. And good food is not always synonymous with haute cuisine. The

Excellent seafood in a restaurant in Brussels' "Ilot Sacré", an area packed with good eating establishments.

district surrounding Verviers on the edge of the Ardennes, for example, is known for its fried eggs and bacon. Even the local chips, often lovingly prepared, are good enough to win the acclaim of gourmets.

Brussels, the national and provincial capital, the self-styled "Capital of Europe", is also the uncontested culinary capital of the country. Its restaurants rival the top establishments in Paris. One speciality which always features prominently on the menus of all classes of restaurants are *choesels* (sweetbreads) considered a great delicacy.

Three restaurants in the Brussels area have been awarded the ultimate accolade – the coveted three Michelin stars – and many

by Reny Goscinny attributes its invention to an incident during the time of the Roman invasion. According to the story, when the Belgians unexpectedly turned up in the Roman camp, the soldier in charge of what the Belgians took to be a giant chip pan (in fact, a cauldron of boiling oil to douse the enemy) collapsed like a sack of potatoes. "Potatoes," thought the Belgian to himself, and decided to give further thought to the subject of fried potatoes when he was at home with his wife again. His ruminations on the matter were interrupted by another battle, during which a Gaul named Obelix appeared on the battlefield with a piece of planking from a ship, covered with gleaming black mussels. This

others restaurants are in the *haute cuisine* bracket (*see Travel Tips section*); but, as in any other major European city, good but inexpensive establishments are plentiful. For those on a budget, the best place to head to is the Ilot Sacré, otherwise known as the "Stomach of Brussels".

One of Brussels' favourite specialities is *moules et frites* – mussels and chips – though you will find them on menus all over Belgium. *Chez Léon* in Brussels is rated as one of the best places to eat them, but even the street stall version is excellent.

How this unusual culinary combination came about is uncertain but one unlikely tale

set the mind of the budding Anton Mossiman working. "Mussels? mussels?" he thought to himself, "I wonder if they taste good with chips?" The Belgians enjoyed the mussels and chips so much that they have been cooking them regularly ever since. (For more details, read *Asterix and the Belgians*).

Other keen cooks might like to try their hand at reproducing some of Belgium's specialities at home. Recipes for some of the most popular dishes are given below.

In South Belgium, in the area adjoining the French border, the culinary influence of France is very evident. On the Belgian side of the border, however, everything is somewhat spicier and a little richer. Two favourite dishes are ragoût of lamb with chicory and rabbit with prunes and bacon.

Ragoût of lamb: To prepare the ragoût of lamb, heat some oil in a frying pan and gently fry onions and garlic. When cooked, add the lamb and brown. Add sufficient lamb stock to cover and braise until tender. Fifteen minutes before the meat is cooked, add some chicory and continue to braise until lamb and vegetables are tender. Season with plenty of fresh thyme, salt, pepper, a bay leaf, cloves and parsley. Thicken the sauce slightly with potato flour before serving.

Rabbit with prunes and bacon: Soak 15 dried prunes in brandy. Cut the rabbit into 6–8

pieces, brown in oil, add some finely chopped onion and soup vegetables and cook in light beer or white wine. Season with salt, pepper, thyme, mustard and a generous pinch of sugar. Add the soaked prunes when tender. Before serving fry 150gm of lean bacon until crisp and add to the rabbit stew.

Two delicacies which no connoisseur should fail to try during his stay are *anguilles au vert* ("green eel") and *waterzooi*.

Anguilles au vert: In order to prepare green eel in the Belgian manner, select approxi-

Left, pickled allsorts in Antwerp. **Above**, cheese galore in the market.

mately 1 kg of young, lean eels. Skin and clean them and cut them into pieces approx. 6 cm long. Heat 2 tablespoonfuls of butter in a large frying pan and add 3 coffee cups of chopped fresh herbs, choosing a combination of some or all of the following: parsley, sage, thyme, sorrel, spinach, tarragon, dill, chervil, coriander, lemon balm and cress. Toss the herbs in the butter for a few minutes, then add one cup of dry white wine and bring to the boil. Arrange the eel on the bed of herbs, cover and braise for 10 minutes. Remove the eel and keep warm.

Purée the herbs, thicken the sauce with two egg yolks and season with pepper, salt, a few drops of Tabasco and lemon juice. Stir 3 tablespoonfuls of butter into the sauce, return the eel to the pan and warm through again, taking care not to allow the sauce to come to the boil again to prevent curdling. Allow the eel to cool in the green sauce or serve hot at once. The Flemish name for this dish is *paling in't groen*.

Waterzooi: This traditional Flemish speciality, which translates rather oddly as "hot water", is prepared from poultry – usually chicken – or fish (if possible turbot or eel). You will need 1½ litres of fish or chicken stock. Flavour the stock with freshly prepared soup vegetables, peppercorns and slices of onion. Add either 1 kg fish (turbot, eel, perch etc), cleaned and cut into cubes approx. 4 x 4 cm, or a whole chicken (approx. 1.2 kg). Simmer until cooked. Remove the fish or poultry (take the chicken meat off the bones, removing and discarding the skin); and cut into pieces.

Pour the soup through a sieve or place in a blender, puréeing the vegetables. In the case of fish, allow the soup to simmer for at least 30 minutes, then season to taste, and pour over the warm fish. Serve immediately. For the chicken soup, thicken with four egg yolks and 120 ml of *crème fraîche*. Add the chicken pieces and reheat, but do not allow to boil. The addition of the egg yolks will thicken the soup slightly; the stock can also be enriched and flavoured by the addition of a glass of white wine.

This "hot water" is a delicious Flemish speciality; if you sample it in different regions – on the coast and inland in Brabant – you will discover that *waterzooi* never tastes the same twice running, since each family has its own particular recipe.

THE LANGUAGE PROBLEM

Most citizens of Belgium speak either Walloon – a form of French – or Flemish, a Netherlands dialect. However available information on the percentage of the population belonging to each linguistic group is vague. The most recent figures date from the Language Census of 1947.

Since then, the Flemish, finding themselves to be losing ground to the French speakers, have sought to prevent any formal tally in case it should highlight their plight. Even areas traditionally Flemish-speaking – for example, the technological zone of Brussels – have seen an influx of French-speaking residents and workers.

The term "Flemish" is used imprecisely to describe a language spoken for the past 1,000 years north of a linguistic boundary running from Aachen to north of Lille. lacks precision. Flemish is actually a mixture of Flemish dialects and standard Dutch. Walloon, on the other hand, is nothing more than French with a number of Walloon idiosyncrasies.

Flemish never developed an independent written language of its own. Instead, it uses standard Dutch, enriched by a number of Belgian characteristics. This form is used in a spoken form by the media, the Church and in schools, although both teachers and pupils revert to the dialect form after hours.

The quarrel between the two linguistic groups has ancient roots. Originally, German peasants came from the north, whilst settlers from the Romance countries bordering the Moselle and the Mediterranean made their homes primarily in the remote regions of the Ardennes, which long remained undeveloped. No formal boundary was ever drawn between the two groups; their different lifestyles were adjuncts to their specifically Belgian political culture and mentality.

Historical evidence: When the first modern nation arose within the boundaries of the present-day Benelux States under the Dukes of Burgundy, French – the language of the court – became the symbol of power and social success. Simultaneously, however, the

flourishing cloth trade with England enabled the Flemish provinces of Flanders and Brabant to win high economic status.

When, during the 16th century, the Netherlands (including present-day Belgium) revolted against the Spanish Habsburgs, a clear north-south division within the Dutch-speaking area was already evident. The predominantly urban north, devoutly Calvinist in the wake of the Reformation, contrasted starkly with the more rural, overwhelmingly Catholic south. Not all Flemings became citizens

of the hard-won "Republic of the United Netherlands". The frontier remained some 50 km (30 miles) north of Antwerp; south of this border, what would later become Belgium started to develop.

Belgium was still far from independent, however, as it formed part of the Habsburg empire. The language which enjoyed the higher prestige – especially during the Age of Enlightenment – was still French. When, in 1794, post-revolutionary French troops began to conquer Belgium for France and a rigid centralised government as well as a compulsorily introduced "Religion of Reason" took over, the most impassioned resist-

Left, celebratory drum roll for the Walloons. **Right**, confrontation with the police: a Flemish farmer's determined wife.

ance fighters were the peasants from Flanders. The Flemish legacy stood them in good stead against France on the battlefield.

At the Congress of Vienna in 1815, Belgium was annexed as part of the newly-created Kingdom of the Netherlands under William I, who introduced Dutch as the official written language. It transpired, however, that even the Flemings found the language forced upon them boorish (*boerentaal*) and regarded their new masters as heretics. The border established 50 km before Antwerp divided a population which had diverged linguistically and culturally. Catholic Flemings and French-speaking Liberals united in revolt against the rulers of the United Neth-

the language used in public administration, and continued to be regarded as the language of the refined classes. Flemish was considered the language of the man in the street.

This was the situation when *The Lion of Flanders*, a novel by Hendrik Conscience (1812–83), was published in 1838. The book, still counted amongst the works of world literature, fired the imagination of the Flemings. From then on, the Flemings began to demand the *taalvrijheid*, the right not to be forced to use French in their dealings with official bodies.

In 1898 both languages were declared of equal official status. No boundaries were laid down to define the areas in which each

erlands. In October 1830 a temporary government proclaimed the newly formed state of Belgium. From this point onwards, controlling the linguistic power struggle in the country was a balancing act.

The Belgian Constitution of 1831, created in the prevailing spirit of liberalism, called for a strict principle of neutrality regarding the linguistic education of the nation's children. This clause tended to work to the disadvantage of the Flemings. Their children were mostly instructed in the less well-equipped confessional schools while the more prosperous private schools introduced French as the teaching language. French also became

should be considered predominant.

The divide widens: The language dispute became even more acute during the 20th century. On two occasions, German troops invaded Belgian territory. The subsequent occupation exacerbated the internal conflict between Flemings and Walloons. Most Belgians remained anti-German, but one Flemish group, the "Activists", campaigned for an independent state as a German protectorate; during World War I, the group collaborated with the forces of occupation.

In 1917, two separate linguistic regions were determined within Belgium. Each had its own ministries in Brussels and Namur.

Only a mass demonstration in Brussels on 11 February 1918 prevented total separation. After World War I, everything Flemish was anathema and was despised as being anti-Belgian. In its external policies, Belgium moved closer to France.

During the 1920s the language dispute was most heated in the universities, particularly in Ghent. Justified claims for a separate Flemish institute of higher education, realised during World War I, were shelved after the war. There was frequent unrest among the Flemish speakers.

During the 1930s, the nationalist spectrum became polarised in accordance with the spirit of the times. Laws governing the use of collaborators not only amongst the Flemings (in fact, this time most Flemish associations resisted the German temptation). Walloon monarchists under the leadership of Leon Degrelle dreamed of Belgium belonging to a fascist corporate state. When the war was over, each language group ostracised the other in attempts to find a better concept than peaceful coexistence.

Violent protest: Since July 1966 the governing principle has been one of strict monolinguality in predetermined regions (Brussels, which is bilingual, and a small number of linguistic enclaves enjoy special status). The Flemings were forthright in asserting their claims and they were not afraid to use

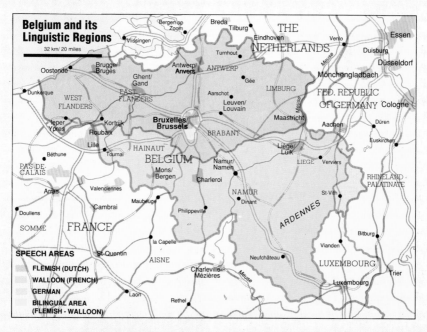

language in administrative circles, and the insistence on the use of the local language as the official language in courts and classrooms, made Belgium a state with two linguistically homogeneous regions with equal rights. A strongly centralist principle continued to dominate; most leading officials in Brussels were either Walloons or non Flemish-speaking citizens. The validity of the French speakers' claims of "cultural superiority" was too obvious to be ignored.

World War II completely destroyed the status quo once more. This time there were

Left, Flemish nationalists at a demonstration.

violence: their repeated interruption of French church services and funerals during the 1960s resulted in a series of television reports that shocked the world.

But some of the statistics are less controversial. For example, many schools in the Flemish-speaking regions offer French teaching of such a high standard that parents whose homes lie south of the language border send their children to them.

It is fair to say that the Flemings tend to speak better French than the Walloons speak Flemish. It is also clear that English is making rapid progress as a language of wider communication.

One Country – But A Babel Of Tongues

The Flemish-speaking region of Belgium lies in the north of the country; the French-speaking region lies to the south. In Brussels both languages are spoken. This basic rule of thumb may seem to be an over-simplification; it nevertheless summarises the linguistic situation prevailing in the country today. Provided travellers always bear in mind that place names are written on road signs in the language of the region in question (Luik/Liège or Brugge/Bruges), they are likely to encounter few insurmountable problems on their journey through the country.

The French dialect spoken by the Walloons of Belgium is a frequent source of amusement to the French. A native of France can seldom suppress a smile when conversing with a French speaker from across the border. The French refer to their linguistic partners somewhat disparagingly as *moules-frites* (mussels with chips is of course the national dish of Belgium).

To the unaccustomed ears the Walloon language has an unattractively hard, provincial ring to it. The Flemish-speaking Belgians, in their turn, experience a similar reaction from their Dutch neighbours. The Flemish language differs from standard Dutch in hundreds of dialect expressions.

But this is not the whole story; there are also the German-speaking inhabitants. Within the national borders there are a number of linguistic grey areas. They lie on the geographical periphery of the country, on the border with Germany and Luxembourg. In the eastern cantons one will often hear a person saying, almost apologetically: "I am Belgian, but I speak German." Whereas in other regions the inhabitants claim to belong first and foremost to either the Flemish or the Walloon groups, here – in the district between Eupen in the north and St Vith in the south – you will encounter people who classify themselves simply as Belgians.

The Germans in Belgium: The strip of Belgium running along the German frontier covers some 854 sq. km (330 sq. miles) and is inhabited by less than one percent of the Belgian population. This German-speaking population's loyalty to Belgium is all the

more surprising when one looks back at history. Since 1794 these citizens have had their nationality changed no fewer than seven times. They were successively Austrian, French, Prussian, Belgian, German and – from 1944 – Belgian once again.

In spite of being the victims of past injustices, they are reconciled with their Belgian identity. The young people in particular, who converse in German at home and French at school, have led the campaign against any resurgence of nationalism, a force which dominated the area in the 1920s and 1930s. They go to the discotheques in Eupen or Verviers, in Maastricht or Aachen. The significance of the actual national frontiers has

drawn between soldiers who had been compulsorily conscripted by the Germans and Nazis by conviction.

But it wasn't all bad for the German-speaking population. On the plus side, they were increasingly able to profit from the growing conflict dividing the Walloons and the Flemings; the minority, originally seen as an unwelcome addition in the Belgium state, came to be regarded as a stabilising influence.

In 1963 German was recognised as the country's third official language. Since 1973 the Council of the German Cultural Community has been responsible for decision-making; the Council's 25 members have taken

been greatly diminished, particularly in recent years.

Initially, however, the position of the region's 65,000 inhabitants was a difficult one. At the end of the 1940s and during the early 1950s they were regarded as nothing more than an appendix to the Belgian population, occupying a fringe position in every sense of the word. In the postwar period the suspicion of widespread collaboration with the Nazis led to a witchhunt. A dossier of some 16,000 individuals in the region was compiled; the listed individuals were consequently deprived of their civic rights. As in other countries in the area a clear distinction was not always

over various areas of responsibility including the job of encouraging use of the German language and supporting cultural activities and establishments, tourism, sports activities and the broadcasting media.

The character of this region is predominantly agricultural, but the population is economically buoyant. Some 2,400 Belgians work in the districts surrounding Aachen and Düren and many others commute to the north. In addition, attractively low rents and land prices have tempted some 1,600 German nationals to the Belgian border area; some of them are students at the university in Aachen.

A multilingual region: In many respects, this area is a microcosm of what may one day become the United States of Europe. The district around Eupen in particular benefits from a number of advantages; a favourable location, a good urban infrastructure, bilingual or even multilingual inhabitants and a disciplined and diligent approach to work (a virtue that is often attributed to the legacy of its Prussian-German past).

While other minority groups resort to violence to draw attention to themselves, the German-speaking citizens of East Belgium feel no need for such extreme measures. Some 89 percent of them feel themselves to be true Belgians in every respect, regarding

the Netherlands were familiar with the little towns of Gemmennich, Kelmis (La Calamine) or Moresnet (Altenberg) from shopping trips. Nowadays German is very much a minority tongue in these villages; the dominant language is a heavily accented French. The younger generation can speak virtually no German; their parents and grandparents still understand the language but seldom speak it. And yet visitors will find numerous shops in the area in which German currency is accepted, and where one can expect to be served in German.

According to an estimate prepared during the late 1970s, 30 percent of the inhabitants of the region around the town of Arlon in the

past history as a closed chapter.

At one time, pockets of German-speaking Belgians could also be found in several of the smaller towns and villages in the Walloon region of the country. One area, lying to the west of the Aachen metropolitan area, not far from the Netherlands border, includes some 10 villages in which German was historically the dominant language. Many people living in the bordering area of Germany and

Preceding pages: Walloon balloons. **Left**, "Just you wait". Nationalism in Belgium is inextricably linked with the language. **Above**, the Church also gets involved.

southernmost part of Belgium speaks German; more than 60 percent can speak *Letzebuergisch*, the dialect of Luxembourg. For political and strategic regions the area was separated from the Grand Duchy of Luxembourg and attached to Belgium in 1839. In former times the inhabitants spoke the Luxembourg dialect at home, German at school and learned French as a second foreign language. In the churches, the situation was particularly complex: mass was said in French and the sermon delivered in French or the Luxembourg dialect. Old habits die hard; both languages have retained their influence until the present day.

Liège hit the headlines of the national press in October 1989. Police had occupied the town hall; bridal couples were waiting in vain to be blessed, and firemen were tipping rubbish on to the streets. The third-largest city in Belgium was on the brink of bankruptcy; public servants, anxious that the radical cures being prescribed for the municipal finances shouldn't be at their expense, were striking.

In spite of its excellent productivity figures, Belgium has to cope with the highest level of national debt in the western industrial world. In August 1989 this small country of only 10 million inhabitants had managed to acquire debts of BFr 6,751 billion – a dizzy total of 135 percent of the gross national product. Two years previously, in 1988, the country had had to find some BFr 457 billion to service interest payments alone, a sum which represented 24 percent of the national budget.

Government efforts to get productivity back on its feet were rather more successful. In 1988 an exceptional growth rate of 3.9 percent enabled the country to achieve its best returns for 11 years. In 1989 the rise was of the same order. Happily for the Belgians, the upward trend seemed to be continuing into the 1990s; at the start of the decade, exports, investment and profits all achieved record levels for the third year running.

Apart from the national debt the only other dark cloud on the otherwise bright economic horizon has been the level of unemployment, which has been unacceptably high for quite a few years. At one point in 1989, nearly 350,000 Belgian citizens had no regular employment. Women have been particularly badly hit by the shrinking job market; they represent 60 percent of the jobless. There are also marked differences between the various regions. In Flanders the number of new jobs available has been rising much faster than in Wallonia.

Preceding pages: the Stock Exchange remains one of Brussels' most imposing edifices. **Left**, *The Banker and his Client*, a painting by Quentin Massys, *circa* 1520. **Right**, rather less personal, the Belgian Ministry of Finance in Brussels.

The problems experienced in Liège were symptomatic of the general national malaise. During the 19th century Wallonia, with its coal mines, blast furnaces, glass factories and metal-processing plants, was one of the richest industrial regions in Europe. Today, this former heart of Belgian industry has declined beyond all recognition, a fact which has provoked envy among the once economically buoyant Wallonians and exacerbated the language dispute. Nowadays the tune is called in Flanders, which was able to

use its previous lack of development as a trump card in the regeneration programmes after World War II. Low wages and a large pool of available labour attracted increased investment capital to the north during the 1950s and '60s.

In addition, the proximity of Flanders to the North Sea was to provide it with an enormous geographical advantage over the rest of the country. As the regional capital and largest city in the province, Antwerp, benefited most. Traditionally a port, it has raised its turnover from 18,000 tonnes to 96 million tonnes during the past 40 years. Antwerp has now become the country's most important economic centre after Brussels, though stiff competition is offered by Zeebrugge. At the end of the 1970s Zeebrugge, primarily a trade centre for Algerian natural gas, a container port and the most important port for cross-Channel ferries to England, was boosted by the extension of its harbour.

The death of the collieries: The chimneys in Liège, Namur (Namen) and Charleroi are still smoking. Without massive government subsidies from Brussels, however, the steel industry of Wallonia would have died long ago. The iron and steel industry clung on to old practices and organisation for too long and missed the appropriate time for mod-

of Europe, although since considerably reduced in size, laid the foundation for an unprecedented expansion of heavy industry in Wallonia. In later years, as Belgium's raw materials became inadequate for industries purposes, additional supplies were imported from abroad. A range of successful metal processing industries also developed here, forming one of the pillars of the Belgian export market even today.

Other concerns crucial to Belgium's industrial development were the companies Gevaert and Solvay. Gevaert – now merged with the well-known German firm Agfa – is a multi-million-dollar concern specialising in the manufacture of photographic materi-

ernisation. The worldwide crisis in the steel industry hit the so-called "Sheffield of Belgium" particularly hard.

The declining steel industry dragged the collieries in its wake. Coal production has shifted from its traditional area on the River Meuse to the Flemish region surrounding Kempen. Today, production in Wallonia totals a mere 5 million tonnes; in 1952, the figure was six times that: 30 million tonnes. The industry's heyday was during the last century. In 1818, John Cockerill – an Englishman – constructed the first modern blast furnace in Seraing near Liège. The Cockerill-Sambre Steelworks, one of the largest in all

als. Solvay initially based its industrial empire on the production of artificial soda; in 1988 the company celebrated its 125th anniversary to great applause.

Founded in 1822 by King William I, the Société Générale also played an important role in the transformation of Belgium into a modern industrial nation. Although its influence has diminished of late, this massive concern nevertheless still controls some sections of the Belgian economy.

One of the few traditional industries that failed to flourish in Wallonia is textile manufacture. Cloth weaving reached its zenith in Flanders and Brabant in the Middle Ages.

Faced with increasing competition from England, however, the industry was in danger of declining. The Flemish maintained their position in the forefront of the industry by re-channeling their skills into the production of luxury goods such as tapestries and lace. Nowadays, after withstanding a crisis during the 1980s, the textile and clothing industry has adapted to modern conditions and requirements to become one of the country's prime growth areas.

The automobile industry of Belgium is firmly in foreign hands. At the end of World War II production plants were set up in Antwerp, Brussels and Ghent. Today they represent one of the most important industrial

employers in the country. Of the 1.2 million cars manufactured in Belgium by Volkswagen, Opel, Volvo, Renault and Ford during 1987, 95 percent were destined for the export market.

The chemical industry has reported record growth figures of late. For many years overshadowed by coal and steel manufacture, it now exports 65 percent of its production of paints, fertilisers, medicines and primary chemicals. The industry benefits from Belgium's relatively lenient environmental pro-

Left, a diamond cutter at work. **Above**, the lady prefers gold.

tection laws; in the face of growing unemployment the protection of people's jobs is seen as more important than avoiding ecological damage.

The lack of a powerful environmental lobby is also evident in the national nuclear power policy. The risks attached to atomic energy are as disregarded in Belgium as they are in neighbouring France. Since the increase in oil prices at the beginning of the 1970s an enthusiastic policy of expansion has been persistently pursued.

The environment: Belgium's farmers also contribute to the pollution of the country's rivers. By using massive quantities of fertilisers and crop sprays they are able to achieve yields per hectare which are among the highest in the world – a fact which, as in other countries, has nonetheless failed to prevent the decline of the agricultural industry. Today fewer than 3 percent of all Belgians earn their living by livestock or arable farming; in 1920, this figure was 23 percent.

The principal crops are wheat, barley, sugar beet and potatoes; during recent years, vegetables, fruit and flowers have increased in importance. Livestock production centres mainly on beef cattle and pig farming, poultry, eggs and dairy products. As in agriculture, progress here has been largely in the shape of increased mechanisation.

The service industries sector is expanding rapidly. Today, two out of three Belgians already work in this sphere, and 68.2 percent of the gross national product lies within the tertiary sector. This figure is well above the average within the European Community (58.5 percent), and just ahead of the United States (67.8 percent). The public sector is the main service industries employer; its 28.2 percent contribution to the gross national product makes it a close second to industry as a whole (29.4 percent).

Much to the regret of many Belgians, tourism still plays a relatively small role even though the country can offer a wide range of attractions to the visitor, from historic towns such as Bruges and the North Sea coast to the picturesque scenery of the Ardennes. Short-stay package trips to the principal towns and cities – Brussels, Antwerp, Bruges and Ghent – have enjoyed increased popularity amongst visitors during the past few years, and such breaks are being heavily marketed.

EUROPE IN MINIATURE

The drama at the court of European diplomacy was like a scene from everyday domestic life: after decades of relatively harmonious partnership a big quarrel broke out in early 1982. One of the two warring parties thought seriously of divorcing the other and forming a new liaison with a wealthy neighbour.

Purely material reasons account for the fact that, in the end, the dispute was patched up. If the divorce had gone through, at least one of those involved would have been forced to pay large sums of money.

the currency union had developed into the most important aspect of their partnership. It was not just that the Brussels government had failed to consult them on their decision; for Luxembourg the devaluation meant that its flourishing economy was put at grave risk. It could become the victim of rapid inflation.

The Luxembourg government retreated to lick its wounds and consider what could be done to protect themselves. Not a few members cast furtive glances eastwards, towards the Federal Republic of Germany. In their view the stable Deutschemark would be the ideal currency for their prosperous economy.

The bankers soon became privy to these considerations and called the injured parties to order. The

During carnival week in 1982, whilst most of Belgium was lost in riotous celebration and nobody really wanted to think of politics or the economy, Brussels – the stronger half of the monetary union between Belgium and Luxembourg – decided on a bold step. Much to the surprise of its central bank, and without so much as informing its weaker partner, the Belgian government suddenly announced a drastic devaluation of the Belgian franc. A correction by two digits was considered to be the best possible answer to problems with the national economy.

The citizens of Luxembourg, whose country had formed a single economic unit with their Belgian neighbours since 1 May 1922, felt they had been humiliated by Belgium. Over the years

Luxembourg bankers were worried that their deposits in Belgian banks (they totalled some BFr 15 billion) would be severely damaged by separation. Agreement was quickly reached. The Luxembourg prime minister, Pierre Werner, persuaded parliament that it was more appropriate to talk of reinterpreting the marriage contract than to contemplate divorce.

If both parties still remember this hitch in their relationship, then it is probably because prior to this event cooperation between Belgium and Luxembourg had functioned perfectly harmoniously for almost 70 years.

Despite being the second-smallest country in the European Community, Belgium has always regarded itself as forming the vanguard in the fight for European integration. The common internal market – Europe with open borders and free passage for persons, goods, capital and services – is nothing new for Belgium. The mid-term goal of economic and monetary union within the European Community has been a feature of Belgian and Luxembourg relations for many years.

The basis for the monetary union remains complete parity between the two currencies whilst maintaining a dual system. The Belgian franc is universally accepted as valid currency by Luxembourg, since its value is identical to that of the Luxembourg franc. That said, Luxembourg francs are not legal tender in Belgium, although they can be exchanged at any bank or currency exchange bureau at a rate of 1:1. Since the Luxembourg

bourg agreed to the creation of a customs union – in other words, to the abolition of existing customs barriers between the three countries and the introduction of common external duties with effect from 1 January 1948.

During the years which followed the Benelux region developed into an economic zone without trade barriers, with free transfer of capital and goods and freedom to establish branch offices for all employers. It was, so to speak, an internal market in miniature. Many years passed before the scheme was actually put into practice; the treaty elaborating the economic union between the three member states was not made effective until 1 November 1960.

The Benelux Union has a decided advantage for

franc is not quoted on the international currency markets, its value is taken to be identical to that of the Belgian franc. The monetary union removed all barriers between the two countries.

The Benelux Union has since served as role model for European cooperation, which is basically merely an extension of the partnership established between Belgium and Luxembourg. The foundation of this close economic cooperation was in place even before World War II had come to an end. In September 1944 representatives of Belgium, the Netherlands and Luxem-

Left, the imposing Ministry of Finance building. **Above**, the three heads of state of the Benelux countries adorn their currencies.

the visitor to Belgium; you can travel to the Netherlands or Luxembourg without having to undergo passport formalities of any kind.

Three years after the end of World War II, Belgium – along with the other Benelux countries, France and the United Kingdom – concluded the so-called Brussels Pact, a mutual defence agreement. The Brussels Pact gave way in 1955 to the West European Union, which also included West Germany and Italy. In 1949 Belgium was also one of the founder members of NATO.

"We were always instrumental in the move towards European integration," commented one leading member of the Belgian Foreign Ministry, "a small cog in the wheel, but one which has never stopped turning."

LITERATURE AND MUSIC

Strictly speaking, Belgian literature has no individual identity of its own; in the north, the Flemish-speaking writers tend to orientate themselves towards the literary traditions of the Netherlands; in the south, the French speakers identify with the literary traditions of France. It is therefore not surprising that even internationally famous Belgian writers should be taken for French by many of their readers – an error which the Walloon writers, in particular, are slow to correct, since they tend to regard themselves as French writers of Belgian origin.

Formerly the identification with French culture went so far that even Flemish-speaking authors chose to write in French. The most famous example is Charles de Coster (1827–1879), a journalist born in Munich who subsequently became professor of literature in Brussels and who wrote his most successful picaresque novel *La Légende d'Ulenspiegel* – published in 1867 and featuring northern Europe's most famous folk anti-hero – in French. Paradoxically, it was de Coster's satirical work describing the Flemings' fight for freedom from the Spanish oppression in the form of Philip II and the Duke of Alva which helped to establish an independent French school of literature within Belgium. Until the publication of de Coster's book, Walloon literature had been stylistically and thematically merely a pale imitation of French literature.

Franco-Belgian cooperation: A further milestone was marked by the foundation of two literary journals: Max Waller's *La Jeune Belgique* in 1881 and Albert Mockel's *La Wallonie*. The two publications provided a platform for authors searching for new forms of content and expression.

Maurice Maeterlinck (1862–1949), to date the country's only Nobel prize laureate (1911), was one such writer. He was the creator of a number of volumes of exquisite lyrical poems – *Les Serres Chaudes* (1889) and *Quinze Chansons* (1896) – as well as dramas such as *L'Oiseau Bleu* (The Bluebird), a fairy tale of great charm and freshness, and *Pelléas et Mélisande*, on which Claude Debussy based his famous opera.

One school of Belgian French literature

searched for its own radical means of expression: the school of visionary writers. Its most notable representatives are Franz Hellens (1881–1972), Jean Ray (1887–1964), Gérard Prévot (1922–75), Michel de Ghelderode (1898–1962), Monique Watteau, Guy Vaes, Jacques Sternberg and Gaston Compère.

Among the country's contemporary Belgian French authors, Georges Simenon, Marguerite Yourcenar and Pierre Mertens have achieved most international fame. Simenon is by far the best known and most prolific of the three writers. In his early years of writing he was sometimes able to complete a book in just one month. His particular skill is in revealing his characters from within and

literary award, for his fictional biography of Gottfried Benn, *Les Eblouissements*.

The Flemish tradition: Belgium's Flemings can look back over a longer literary tradition. It was they who gave the impetus to Flemish literature during the Middle Ages. During the 12th century Hendrik van Veldeke, born near Hasselt, wrote his famous ballad; during the 13th century, Jacob van Maerlant edited his highly-regarded socio-critical works in Bruges, and a Brabant nun named Hadewijch wrote mystic plays which are today celebrated as precursors of feminist literature. The most famous poem to emerge from the Netherlands at this time was the animal fable *Van den vos Reinarde*, a satire

without. His character Inspector Maigret has become one of crime fiction's best-loved and enduring detectives.

Marguerite Yourcenar (1903–87), perhaps best remembered for her novel *Le Coup de Grâce*, a tragic love story set in the turmoil of the Russian Revolution, is also popular well beyond the borders of her native land. In 1980 she achieved the distinction of being the first woman to be elected to the Académie Française. She has also been awarded a number of literary prizes.

The novels of Pierre Mertens are especially highly regarded in France. In 1987 he won the Prix Medicis, the most famous French

on the misgovernment of the Netherlands during the 13th century.

Following the wars with Spain and the mass exodus of Flemish intellectuals to the independent Netherlands during the 16th century, the literature of Flanders declined. It underwent a renaissance in 1840 with the establishment of the Flemish Movement, which aimed to curtail the predominance of French in Belgian public life. The struggle for greater linguistic and political autonomy was closely linked with the name of the Romantic writer Hendrik Conscience (1812–83). In his successful novel *De Leeuw van Vlaenderen* (The Lion of Flanders), published in 1838, he portrayed with undisguised anti-French sentiments the uprising of the citizens of Flanders against the French knights at the beginning of the 14th century. Out of the lyric poetry of the time the work of Guido Gezelle (1830–99) is best known; his fervently pious works did not achieve recognition until after his death.

The Walloon naturalists: At the turn of the century a group of young writers attracted considerable attention. Interested in stylistic experiments, they found a literary platform in the periodical *Van Nu en Straks*, the Flemish counterpart to the Walloon publication *La Jeune Belgique*. The naturalist writers achieved most fame, especially Felix Tim-

Nothing could have been further from the aims of the two most successful Flemish writers after World War II, Louis Paul Boon and Hugo Claus, than the exaltation of their native land. Boon, who died in 1979, was a committed Socialist who tackled the themes of social disadvantage and the hypocrisy of the Catholic church and the petty bourgeoisie. His best known novels include *De Kapellekensbaan* and *Zomer in Ter-Muren*.

The works of Hugo Claus, the most prominent contemporary Flemish writer, also contain a ruthless examination of his fellow-countrymen. Considered to be the *enfant terrible* of the Belgian literary scene, he gained international recognition for his novel

mermans (1886–1947), whose works have been translated into many languages. His novels *Pallieter* and *The Christ Child of Flanders*, both of which were published shortly after World War I, represent a monument to Flemish national consciousness. Since his work includes a strong nationalist element it was widely quoted by the National Socialists to enlist support during the period of German occupation.

Preceding pages: the ballet company *Compagnie Incidence* performs at the Botanique in Brussels. **Left,** Walloon popular theatre. **Above,** on tonight: the Big Kaai Bigband.

The Tragedy of Flanders, in which he denounces the widespread collaboration between his compatriots and the German forces of occupation during World War II. Boon and Claus have both been seen as potential Nobel laureates.

Courtly music: The Franco-Flemish division within Belgium is also evident in the country's musical tradition, although its influence here is rather less marked and more recent. At the end of the Middle Ages the colleges of Cambrai and Antwerp influenced the musical life of the whole of Europe. Orlando di Lasso (*circa* 1532–94), a native of Mons, perfected the vocal polyphonic style, already highly developed in Belgium; his name was mentioned in the same breath as that of the great Italian master Palestrina. Di Lasso was a cosmopolitan artist who studied in Italy and travelled extensively through France and England. For more than 30 years before his death in 1594 he directed the music at the court of the Dukes of Bavaria in Munich. His compositions are noted for the combination of elements from both the Netherlandish and the Italian tradition.

Towards the end of the 17th century, Belgian music was divided between the Walloon tradition, orientated along French lines, and a more provincial Flemish tradition. The only composers to achieve any degree of

today, his organ concertos form part of the standard concert repertoire in churches and concert halls.

The violin concertos of Henri Vieuxtemps (1820–81), a contemporary of César Franck, are frequently performed in France and the Anglo-Saxon countries. Vieuxtemps, himself a gifted violinist, is considered along with Charles de Bériot (1802–70) as a founder of the famous Belgian violin school which produced the virtuoso Eugène Ysaye (1858–1931). Ysaye achieved fame not only as a composer but also as a violinist; probably his greatest service to music in the country was the establishment of the Queen Elisabeth of Belgium Music Competition. Initially open

fame during this period were those from the south – although the Flemings are wont to boast about Ludwig van Beethoven's slight connection with Mechelen: the fact that the grandfather of the famous composer was born in the town.

For almost 200 years, however, the Walloons played first violin on the Belgian musical scene. André Modeste Grétry (1741–1813) from Liège, who moved to Paris in 1762, is regarded as one of the founders of the Opéra Comique. César Franck, born in Liège in 1872, acquired French citizenship in 1871; his remarkable organ compositions won him rapturous acclaim in Paris. Even

to young violinists, the prestigious international contest has been extended to include pianists and composers. One of the competition's first prizewinners was the famous Soviet violinist David Oistrakh.

Belgium also enjoys international success in the field of the *chanson*, in particular through the internationally admired lyrical ballads of the singer-composer Jacques Brel, whose stirring songs are frequently played in the country's bars and restaurants.

Above, student pastimes. **Right**, old favourites: the perpetually-surprised looking Tintin, his dog Snowy and one of the Thomson twins.

BELGIAN COMIC TALENT

The real history of the comic strip begins in pre-historic times with the cave paintings in Lascaux and Altamira, progressing through the pictorial stories of Ancient Egypt and Assyria and the scenes depicted on Greek and Roman vases. It continues via the medieval cartoons in paintings and on icons (and the largest comic strip of all time, the Bayeux Tapestry) to the many leaflets, picture stories and tales of Wilhelm Busch.

Comics in their present form evolved in Britain and the United States, where there have been comic cartoons, the so-called Funnies, for a very long time. The US is undoubtedly a world power when it comes to cartoons, but little Belgium is a good match. Any hit-list of world comic figures will be bound to include such stars as Tintin, Lucky Luke, Gaston and the Marsupilami. Cartoons have become the Ninth Art, and Belgian cartoonists can claim much of the responsibility.

The story of Tintin: Hergé (1907–83), whose pen-name is based on the French pronunciation of the initials of his real name (Georges Rémi) reversed, published his first story about the youthful reporter Tintin and his dog Snowy in 1930. By 1946, after the end of World War II, Tintin's adventures were being published in a new comic of the same name, *Journal de Tintin*. The comic *Spirou* had first been published in 1938. The two detectives *Blake and Mortimer,* who appeared in the first edition of *Tintin,* were created by Edgar-Pierre Jacobs, now a classic cartoon artist equally famous for *The U-Ray* and *The Secret of the Great Pyramid.*

In 1947 another artist, Morris (Maurice de Bévère) had invented for *Spirou* a hero by the name of *Lucky Luke.* The adventures of the lonesome cowboy were later written by René Goscinny (of *Asterix* fame) and drawn by Morris for the French magazine *Pilote.*

Other founder members of *Pilote* included Albert Uderzo (the other co-inventor of the most famous Gaulish warrior of all time and his henchman Obelix) and the Belgian Jean-Michel Charlier, who had previously worked for *Spirou* and *Tintin.* Charlier, who died in 1989, was the author of a number of famous series which were then illustrated by great artists: Victor Hubinon drew *Buck Danny* and *The Red Corsair*, Jijé (Joseph Gilain) – who had initially worked as illustrator for *Spirou* and *Jerry Spring* – drew *Valhardi* and *Mick Tanguy* for Charlier. Gir (Jean Giraud) illustrated the excellent Western cartoon *Blueberry.*

Another famous Belgian story-writer was Greg (Michel Regnier), for whom Hermann (Hermann Hupen) created the character of *Andy Worgan.* Among Hermann's other series were *Comanche*, *Jugurtha* and *Jeremiah.* The emigration of many artists to France led to the establishment of a strong Belgian-French cartoon culture.

The list of Belgian illustrators is still not complete. Bob de Moor created *Barelli* and *The Lions of Flanders*; Jacques Martin was the father of *Alix,* hero of a series of adventures set in ancient Rome. Maurice Tillieux gave fans of all ages *Jeff Jordan* and *Harry and Platte*; André Franquin created *Gaston* and *Spirou and Fantasio,* the story of a wicked super-monster, the one and only *Marsupilami.*

The number of cartoon characters is still increasing: old favourites have been joined by the *Smurfs* by Peyo (Pierre Gulliford), and *Boule & Bill* by Jean Roba. William Vance (not an American, but a Belgian whose real name is William van Cutsen) was the author of *Bruno Brazil* and *Bruce J. Hawker.*

Amongst Belgium's newest talents are Arthur Piroton (*Jess Long*), François Walthéry (*Little Nickel* and *Natasha*), and Eric Warnauts and Guy Raives (*Congo 40*). One day they will all take their places in the Hall of Fame – the Belgian Comic Museum, the *Centre Belge de la Bande Dessinée.*

The picture on the facing page of a prosperous burgher and his bride exchanging marriage vows in a room that is the epitome of bourgeois taste tells us much more about the times (mid-15th century) and the people who lived in them than any document on the subject might.

Contrary to what the 20th-century observer might imagine, the bride is not in the late stages of pregnancy; her convex abdomen and tiny, tightly laced breasts correspond to the Gothic ideal of beauty. Her virginity is symbolised by the clear reflection of the mirror in the background. The presence of Christ as a witness to the betrothal is indicated by the single burning candle. The husband is a member of the bourgeoisie, albeit a wealthy one – a fact revealed not only by the furnishings but also by the wooden pattens; such shoes were only necessary for those who had to walk along the dirty, often muddy streets; the nobility of the time always rode on horseback or in a litter.

For many years it was maintained that the artist who created this worldly portrait which contains all the symbolism of a religious painting, and who self-confidently wrote above the mirror *Johannes de Eyck fuit hi* (in effect, Jan van Eyck was here) was – along with his brother Hubert – the discoverer of oil painting. It is certainly true that the van Eyck brothers played a vital part in the development of panel painting. *The Betrothal of the Arnolfini* (1434) by Jan van Eyck (*circa* 1390–1441) marked the beginning of the tradition of bourgeois art. The artist, who was also court painter to the Count of Holland and Philip the Good, created with his brother the magnificent Ghent Altarpiece, the polyptych of the *Adoration of the Holy Lamb* – installed in the cathedral of St Bavon in 1432 and universally acclaimed as one of the Seven Wonders of Belgium.

Before the advent of panel painting, the only pictures were murals or illustrations in books. The Limburg brothers, who since 1411 had painted for the Duke of Berry the Book of Hours known as the *Très Riches Heures*, were the most famous illustrators of the period. The van Eyck brothers, who also began as illustrators, later used similarly realistic techniques their paintings.

But the world was changing. The Middle Ages were giving way to modern times. This is the period in which Gothic art gradually gave way to the Renaissance. Whilst subscribing superficially to medieval precepts, Jan van Eyck had painted on a wooden panel a bourgeois couple in a bourgeois setting. *The Betrothal of the Arnolfini* initiated a whole new chapter in the history of art. From that time onwards, paintings reflected the tastes and prosperity of their bourgeois owners. Panel painting spread rapidly across Flanders. The artists were highly esteemed (and paid) by society; many became official town painters.

One of these was Robert Campin (1375–1441), for many years known only as the anonymous Master of Flémalle. He was the town painter at Tournai under whom Rogier van der Weyden (1397/1400–1464) had studied. As the town painter of Brussels, van der Weyden exerted considerable influence on Hugo van der Goes, Dieric Bouts and Hans Memling, and on the whole gamut of European art, from Germany to Spain. Hugo van der Goes (1440–82) became a master artist in Ghent. Dieric Bouts (1415–75) introduced landscapes into his paintings, not merely as a decorative detail, but as an independent yet integral element.

Hans Memling (1433–94) was an innovator in the Flemish school. His travels along the Main and Rhine rivers took him to Cologne where, it is thought, he became a pupil of Stefan Lochner. Completing his training under Rogier van der Weyden in Brussels, Memling continued to Bruges where he became the "personification of the spirit" of the wealthy little Hanseatic town; he was the most popular Flemish painter under Charles the Bold. Other notable artists in Bruges included Pieter Christus (1410/20–1472/3), a pupil of Jan van Eyck, and Gérard David (1460–1523).

The first industrial painting: David's influence is much in evidence in the works of Joachim Patinier (1475/80–1524), a landscape specialist who is regarded as the creator of the first industrial painting: *River Landscape with Furnaces*. His nephew and pupil Herrie met de Bles (1510–50) further developed the art of landscape painting.

The works of Bouts taught Quentin Matsys (1466–1530) the art of realistic portraiture. He painted religious scenes and scenes from business life.

In Antwerp, painting was becoming progressively more stylised. Joos van Cleve (Joos van der Beke, *circa* 1485–1540/41) stood between the Mannerists and the late Romance artists. Jan Mabuse (Jan Gossaert, 1478–1533/36) was the founder of the new style; he had accompanied Philip of Bur-

Pieter Breughel (1525/30–69) began his artistic career drawing drafts for etchings in the style of Bosch. Later, in Brussels, he and the other artists in his family were to become popular and famous. Pieter Breughel the Elder – widely known as "Peasant" Breughel – was the father of two artist sons. Pieter Breughel the Younger (1564–1638), who frequently copied the works of his father, became known in particular for his demonic scenes, influenced by the works of Hieronymous Bosch, and earned the nickname "Hell Breughel".

Jan Breughel the Elder (1568–1625) was known as "Velvet Breughel" or "Flower Breughel" because of his predilection for

gundy on a journey to Italy and was profoundly influenced by the work of artists south of the Alps.

Master of fantasy: Hieronymus Bosch (or van Aken, since his ancestors came from Aachen – 1450/55–1516), learned to paint in his father's workshop. He created a world of pictorial fantasy using realistic forms. Some consider him to be the greatest master of fantasy that ever lived. Bosch's world is a mixture of paradise and hell, dominated by sensory impressions, lust and love transformed into sin. Religion and faith were linked with alchemy, arcane knowledge and obscene jokes.

painting highly detailed pictures of flower arrangements against a background of richly-coloured velvet. He became court painter to the Spanish stadholder and produced a number of works in collaboration with his friend Rubens. His son Jan Breughel the Younger (1601–78) became a landscape painter in Antwerp.

Peter Paul Rubens (1577–1640) was born in Siegen in Germany. Painter and freedom fighter, self-confident citizen and servant of warring monarchs, Rubens was the embodiment of the baroque era of universal reason and limitless exuberance. He was nominated court painter in 1609. Sir Anthony van Dyck

(1599–1641), a pupil and assistant of Rubens, also became a court painter; he spent the last nine years of his life in England, where he painted numerous equestrian paintings of Charles I.

In spite of the plunderings of the Spanish, Antwerp remained a conducive environment for artists. Joost de Momper (1564–1635) was a landscape painter. Frans Hals (1581/5 –1666) became a realistic portraitist of the bourgeoisie. In the studios of Jakob Jordaens (1593–1678), scenes of popular life were created alongside mythological and Biblical scenes. Adriaen Brouwer (1605–38) also painted scenes from everyday life. The realistic pictures of David Teniers the Younger

In the end, it was a revolutionary seeking asylum in Brussels who helped propel painting in Belgium to new heights. Jacques-Louis David (1748–1825) was a leading exponent of the neoclassical school. His pictures celebrated republican civic virtues in a classical setting. He became a leading functionary of the French Revolution, falling from power along with Robespierre. Napoleon was one of his biggest patrons; when the emperor was eventually overthrown, David fled into exile.

Jacques-Louis David was a big influence on Belgium's young artists. His most famous pupil was François Joseph Navez (1787–1869), also a painter of historical and mytho-

(1610–40), son and pupil of Teniers the Elder, reveal the influence of Rubens and Brouwer. In 1651 Teniers became court painter in Brussels and in 1665 he founded an Academy of Art in Antwerp.

After this long period in which Flemish and Dutch painters dominated the artistic scene of Northern Europe, many years were to elapse before art was to regain its former glory in the region.

Left, a work by Pieter Brueghel the Elder, and, **right**, a quite different work by his son, Pieter Brueghel the Younger, also known as "Hell" Brueghel.

logical scenes; but his influence is also evident in the works of Gustave Wappers, N. de Keyser, Edouard Bièfve, H. Leys and even Ferdinand Pauwels.

Antoine Joseph Wiertz (1806–65) is famous for his vast canvases depicting gruesome scenes of haunting beauty. He was highly popular during his life but subsequently forgotten, only to be celebrated later as the precursor of the symbolists and surrealists. Another forerunner of these movements was Guillaume Vogels (1836–96), who influenced Rops and Ensor and was one of the co-founders of the artistic association known as Les Vingts (XX). Félicien Rops

(1833–98) was notorious for his erotic fantasies. His critics, incensed at the themes depicted in his paintings, failed to recognise their artistic merit.

Vincent van Gogh paid a short visit to Belgium, attending the Methodist School in Laeken in 1878 before becoming a preacher amongst the workers in Le Borinage and living in poverty amongst the poorest of the poor. Having been dismissed from his post as preacher, he went to the Academy in Brussels in 1880 and remained there until April of the following year. He returned to Holland but went back to study at the Academy of Fine Arts in Antwerp from March 1885 until February 1886.

van Rysselberghe (1862–1926), the leading Belgian Impressionist.

James Ensor (1860–1949), a contemporary of van Rysselberghe's who had studied in Brussels, marked the beginning of the modern period. Although a friend of Khnopff and protégé of Rops, Ensor remained very much a loner whose painting *Christ's Entry into Brussels* (1888) shocked critics and public alike. His pictures are full of terrifying demons, skeletons, and masks painted in strong colours. Although Ensor's works did not achieve recognition until the 20th century, they paved the way for the Expressionists and Surrealists.

Paricles Pantazis (1849–84) was one of

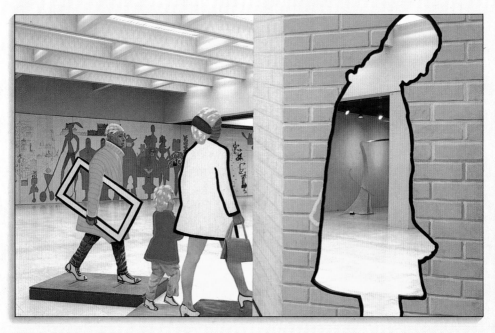

The Realists: Constantin Meunier (1831–1905) was famous for his sculpture of a man carrying a heavy burden as well as for his paintings. Charles de Groux (1825–70) chose similar themes. Another Realist painter was Jan Stobbaerts (1839–1914), who turned his back on established artistic circles in Antwerp and went to Brussels.

Léon Frédéric (1856–1940) painted peasants and workers; he was the most popular Belgian painter during the 1920s. Alfred William Finch (1854–1930) was a fellow-student of Ensor at the Brussels Academy and a co-founder of Les Vingts. Another prominent member of the group was Theo

the few artists whose works Ensor admired. Like the Symbolist Fernand Khnopff (1858–1921), Pantazis was a member of Les Vingts. Without his mysterious paintings the achievements of the Belgian Fantasists would have been unthinkable. Degove de Nunques (1867–1935) and Jean Delville (1867–1953) were two further representatives of the Reality of Fantasy.

The most famous Fantasist of all is René Magritte, often classified (quite wrongly) as a Surrealist; his pictures are the result of an uninhibited imagination which has been allowed to run riot, often to the confusion of the observer. *The Man in the Bowler Hat* may enchant by virtue of its poetry or strike the spectator as amusing. (One of Magritte's paintings shows a pipe; underneath it the artist has added the comment "This is not a pipe." – correct, for the picture is merely a representation of a pipe.)

Paul Delvaux (born 1897) destroyed all his earliest works after seeing the anatomical peepshow of the Spitzner Museum at the Brussels Fair. From that point on, his work was peopled by naked bodies and skeletons.

The fantastic paintings of Félix Labisse (born 1905) are also characterised by naked figures, often depicted in iridescent tones of blue. Labisse was influenced by Ensor, Magritte and Delvaux.

(1924–76), Pol Bury (born 1922), Corneille (Cornelis van Beverloo, born 1922), John F.G. Delogne (born 1933), Panamerenko (born 1940), Raoul Ubac (born 1910) and Georges Vantongerloo (1886–1965).

One Belgian artist whose fame is as widespread as that of Ensor and Magritte is Frans Masereel (1889–1972). He was famous for his paintings, drawings and, above all, his woodcuts. He became the most famous 20th-century exponent of this particular art form. His picture series – *My Book of Hours, The Sun, The Town, The Passion of a Man, The Ages of Life* – are instantly and universally comprehensible. His woodcuts expressed his opposition to war, exploitation and fascism,

Gaston Bogaert (born 1918) arrived in Brussels as an actor, became a graphics artist for an advertising agency, and finally began to paint. He presented his first exhibition, strongly influenced by the Belgian Fantasists, in 1965.

The contemporary art scene: Contemporary Belgian art is not just the preserve of the Fantasists and the Surrealists. It has achieved world fame through the works of Pierre Alechinsky (born 1927), Marcel Broodthaers

Left, the entrance hall of the Museum of Modern Art in Brussels. **Above**, Keith Haring in the Museum of Modern Art in Antwerp.

and his struggle for a world in which all men have a right to happiness. They also served to adorn important works of literature, including the novel *Ulenspiegel* by the Belgian writer Charles de Coster.

Masereel was the kinsman of all Belgian and Flemish painters. He portrayed people and their lives, like van Eyck; he personified the universal spirit, like Memling; he recorded the cruelty of his times, like Bosch; he revealed the joys of love, like Rubens, initiated a revolution in art, like Ensor, and gave fresh impetus to our imagination, like Magritte. He gave us all the ability to recognise the world in which we live.

TOWNS FULL OF TREASURES

The flowering of Belgian art and culture has continuously enriched the country over the centuries. Each of the towns has its own history, traditions and treasures.

As well as being the largest port in Belgium – and one of the biggest in the world – Antwerp is a lively city of baroque elegance. As the handsome Renaissance town hall and guildhalls on its marketplace testify, its increasing prosperity from the 14th century onwards was reflected in its buildings.

Antwerp's churches are of particular interest; in the cathedral of Our Lady hang various masterpieces by Rubens, including an *Assumption* (1626), *The Erection of the Cross* (1610) and, in the south transept, the magnificent *Descent from the Cross* (1612) – generally considered to be one of the Seven Wonders of Belgium. The oldest building in the city is the Steen, today the National Maritime Museum. The Butchers' Guildhall is a museum of history, arts and crafts. The Royal Museum of Fine Arts contains an exceptional collection of works by Rubens.

The town hall of Binche (Hainaut) is surmounted by an onion tower. Binche is famous primarily for its pre-Lenten carnival celebrations as well as for the International Carnival and Costume Museum.

Bouillon is dominated by the castle of Godfrey of Bouillon, one of the leaders of the First Crusade (1096–99). It is one of the oldest feudal fortresses in the country; a magnificent panorama across the castle, the river and the roofs of the old town is to be had from the Austrian Tower.

The entire centre of Bruges is a living museum. The bell tower soars 82 metres (262 ft) above the market place of this town of canals. Dominating the Castle Square are the Gothic town hall and the Basilica of the Sacred Blood. The church of Our Lady contains a statue of the Virgin by Michelangelo. Among the town's museums, those which deserve close attention are the Memling Museum, containing the Shrine of St Ursula – another of the so-called Seven Wonders of Belgium – and the Groening Museum, hous-

Left, the Museum of Fine Arts in Antwerp.

ing masterpieces by Jan van Eyck, Hugo van der Goes, Hans Memling, Gérard David and other works of art from the Flemish primitives to modern times.

Brussels boasts the loveliest marketplace in the world, the Grand' Place. Each of its buildings is an architectural masterpiece, but the real jewel is the town hall. And no visitor should fail to pay his respects to Brussels' Manneken Pis, Belgium's most famous statue. Other sites which shouldn't be missed include the Parliament building and the Palais Royal, the Stock Exchange and the Palais de Justice. The city also boasts the country's best art collections: the Museum of Art contains paintings from the Flemish primitives

Gothic-vaulted town hall houses the Municipal Museum.

Dinant in the Ardennes has a fine collegiate church and a citadel rising 100 metres (320 ft) above the river Meuse.

Eupen is the centre of the German-speaking community in Belgium. Its magnificent churches and houses reflect the town's traditional prosperity.

Ghent is the historic capital of Flanders, where the Emperor Charles V was born. The Weavers' Hall pays tribute to this famous son with an audio-visual display entitled *Ghent and the Emperor Charles*. Ghent's cathedral of St Bavon houses another of the Seven Wonders of Belgium, a polyptych

to works by Breughel and Rubens; next door, the Museum of Modern Art includes collections by Magritte and Ensor. Other interesting art museums include the Wiertz Museum, containing the grotesquely beautiful pictures of the 19th-century visionary, and the Horta Museum dedicated to Victor Horta, the art nouveau architect.

Damme, once the port of Bruges, is the home of Tyl Ulenspiegel, the hero of *The Legend of Tyl Ulenspiegel* by Charles de Coster (1827–79); De Grote Sterr house has a museum dedicated to the folk hero.

Diest, in the Hageland, is sheltered by the remnants of the city's ancient ramparts. Its

altarpiece *The Adoration of the Holy Lamb* by the van Eyck brothers. Other sights include the town hall, the guildhalls on the Graslei, 's Gravensteen (the castle of the Counts of Flanders) and the museums.

Ypres was one of the most important towns in Flanders during the Middle Ages. After being completely destroyed during World War I it was rebuilt in the original style. Its Weavers' Hall is one of the finest examples of secular Gothic art in the country. The biennial Cats' Festival is held here.

Leuven, the former capital of Brabant, is the seat of the oldest university in Belgium. In addition to the ancient academic buildings, attractions include the town hall and the churches.

Liège, on the river Meuse, is the native town of Georges Simenon. The town's landmark is the Perron, a fountain dating from 1698. Notable amongst its plethora of churches is the Romanesque church of St Bartholomew. It contains another of the Seven Wonders of Belgium: the early 12th-century copper font by Renier von Huy.

Mechelen is the capital of Catholic Belgium. The tower of St Rombout's cathedral is one of the finest in the country. Also famous are the two carillons; there is a Carillon Museum and a Carillon School. The churches of St John and Our Lady Across the

painter Felicien Rops. The Convent of the Sisters of Our Lady houses another of Belgium's Seven Wonders: a work of the 12th-century goldsmith Hugo von Oignies.

The town of Saint-Hubert lies in the heart of the Ardennes. St Hubert, a huntsman, was canonised in 683 after seeing a vision of Christ between the antlers of a stag. On the first Sunday in September, the International Huntsmen's Festival begins with a service in the basilica. The saint's festival is celebrated on 3 November.

Stavelot, also in the Ardennes, is characterised by its lovely old houses, churches and museums. Its most notable treasure is the collection of vintage cars and motorbikes on

Dyle house paintings by Rubens.

Mons in Hainaut is surrounded by castles. Its marketplace and museums are worth a visit. On the Sunday after Whitsun the relics of St Waltraud are carried through the town in a golden carriage. The highlight of the Trinity Fair is the fight between St George and the dragon.

Namur, the "gateway to the Ardennes", is dominated by its vast citadel. One of the town's museums is dedicated to the famous

Left, Peter Paul Rubens: a self-portrait. **Above**, Rubens House in Antwerp is today a museum concerned with the life and works of the artist.

the Ardennes racing circuit.

Tongeren, on the former military road from Bavay to Cologne, is the oldest town in Belgium. The Basilica of Our Lady houses the richest church treasury in the land; dominating the square in front of the church is a statue of Ambiorix, who led the resistance to Caesar's invasion.

Tournai stands on the Franco-Belgian border. The cathedral of Our Lady, one of the loveliest Romanesque churches in Europe, is adorned with exquisite reliefs and paintings.

Zoutleeuw, in the Haspengau, was once one of the seven largest towns in Brabant. It is worth visiting today for its church.

PLACES

If you are looking for peace and unspoiled nature, for art and culture, festivals and folklore, for beaches and mountains, for medieval splendour and modern living, good food and drink, and for open-minded, friendly people, the nine Belgian provinces have a great deal to offer.

Our book begins in Brabant with the four-fold capital city of Brussels, leading you through the elegant upper city and the distinctive lower city to what many have called the most beautiful square in the world, the Grand-Place, and sharpening your appetite for the so-called "Stomach of Brussels", domain of some of the world's best chefs. And if you enjoy raking through markets – whether for kitsch or art, books or flowers, bric-a-brac or exotic spices – you cannot go wrong in Brussels – every day is market day somewhere in the city.

Those with more than a few days to spare will want to venture further afield. Within easy reach of Brussels lie Terveuren, with its Central African Museum, and Waterloo, site of the historic battle that defeated Napoleon. A trip through Flanders should begin in Bruges. First, climb the bell tower to get an overall view of this famous medieval city, then explore by boat along the canals and Dyver river. From Bruges, follow us to the coast of Belgium, to Ostend, the Deauville of Belgium, and the family-oriented resorts of Knokke-Heis.

Ghent, with its canals and ancient architecture, has been compared to Venice by more than a few famous travellers. Take time to explore its nooks and crannies. After that, we'll lead you to Damme, the city of Tyl Ulenspiegel, northern Europe's famous prankster.

Antwerp beguiles the visitor with its harbour, its art, and its glittering reputation as a diamond centre. "Antwerp has God to thank for the Scheldt, and the Scheldt to thank for everything else." Does this also apply to Peter Paul Rubens, who created his world-renowned masterpieces in this city?

In the course of a week, the visitor can get to know a great deal about Belgium, including its quieter, wilder spots; the best of its heaths, moors, dunes, forests and lakes lie in the Hautes Fagnes and the Ardennes.

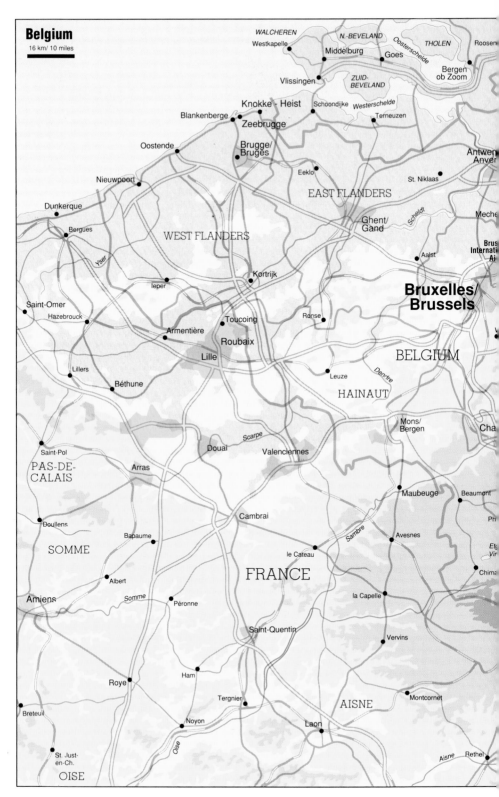

Belgium

16 km/ 10 miles

WALCHEREN
Westkapelle
N-BEVELAND
Middelburg
Goes
Oosterschelde
THOLEN
Roosen
Bergen
ob Zoom

Vlissingen
ZUID-
BEVELAND
Westerschelde

Knokke - Heist
Schoondijke
Terneuzen
Blankenberge
Zeebrugge
Brugge/
Bruges
Antwer
Anver

Oostende
Eeklo
St. Niklaas
Meche

Nieuwpoort
EAST FLANDERS

Dunkerque
Ghent/
Gand
Scheldt
Brus
Internati
Ai

Bergues
WEST FLANDERS
Aalst

Yser
Kortrijk
Bruxelles/
Brussels

Ieper
Ronse

Saint-Omer
Toucoing
Leuze
BELGIUM

Hazebrouck
Armentière
Roubaix
Dendre

Lillers
Lille
HAINAUT

Béthune
Leuze

Mons/
Bergen
Cha

Scarpe
Douai
Valenciennes

Saint-Pol
Arras
Maubeuge
Beaumont

PAS-DE-
CALAIS
Cambrai
Sambre
Avesnes
Ph

Doullens
Bapaume
le Cateau
Et
Vir

SOMME
Albert
FRANCE
la Capelle
Chima

Amiens
Somme
Péronne

Saint-Quentin
Vervins

Roye
Ham

Tergnier
Montcornet

Breteuil
Noyon
AISNE

Oise
Laon
Aisne
Rethel

St. Just-
en-Ch.

OISE

122

123

Kobbegem

Hamme

Hammebrug

Maalbeek

Bever

Ring 0

Haneveld

Rasselhoek

Schaliënhof

Relegem

Wemmel

Palais
du Centenaire
Eeuwfeestwijk

Strombeek-Bever

Koningslo

Neder
Heembe

Heysel/Heizel

Pavillon Chinées
(Chinese Pavilion)

Atomium

Château Royal
(Royal Palace)

Zellik

BOIS DU LAERBEEK
LAARBEEKBOS

Autoroute E 40

Ring 0

Laeken

Ave

Jette

Helmet

Ganshoren

Groot Bijgaarden

Port
(Haven)

PARC ELISABETH
ELISABETH PARK

Gare
du Nord

Koekelberg

Ossegem

Dilbeek

St. Joost-Ten-N
St. Josse-Ten-N

Moortebeek

Pl. de
Broukère

Chaussee de Ninove

Grand' Place
(Grote Markt)

Bruxelle:
Brussel:

Gare
Central

Itterbeek

Bon Air

Maison
d'Erasme
(Erasmushuis)

Gare
du Midi

Neerpede

la Petite Ile/
klein Eiland

Vlasendael/
Vlazendaal

Het Rad
la Roue

PARC
DUDEN
DUDENPARK

Abbaye
de la Cambre
(Abdij ter Kameren)

Université
Libre de
Bruxelles

Ring 0

Canal de Charleroi

BOIS
DE LA
CAMBRE

Bo
Bo

Langeveld

TER
KAMERE

Rattendaal

Klein Bijgaarden

Zuunbeek

Neerstalle

PARK VON
WOLVENDAEL

Observatoire
(Observatory)

Grote
Bempt

Stalle

St. Job/
St. -Job

Drogenbos

Zenne

Ruisbroek

Calevoet/
Kalevoet

Institut
Pasteur

N.D.-de la Paix /
O.L.V van de Krede

St.-Pieters-
Leeuw

Greater Brussels

1600 m/ 1,0 miles

COSMOPOLITAN BRUSSELS

"If only Brabant were nearer!" lamented the Dutch theologian and humanist Desiderius Erasmus in the 16th century. In the modern age of international travel, Brabant isn't far from anyone in Europe. It lies at the centre of Belgium, which itself is at the heart of Europe. The border between Germanic and Romance language territories runs diagonally through Brabant. The Flemings are in the north, the Walloons in the south; Brussels is officially bilingual.

In general, the Belgians are not so much proud of their nation as proud of their civil liberties, customs and culture. In Brussels, the "capital" of Europe, of Belgium and Brabant, nearly a million people live together under the motto: "We are citizens of the world; in our city, the whole world feels at home." About one-quarter of the city's 1 million inhabitants are non-Belgian

Occupied by every nation: Brussels is said to be the most European of cities. The presence of the various EU institutions has cemented this reputation. But long before the advent of the EU, the citizens of Brussels were used to a strong foreign presence in the city – albeit an unwelcome one when it was in the form of an occupying army. At different times Brussels has been ruled by Burgundy, Spain, France and the Netherlands. The Flemings and Walloons did not win their independence until the revolution of 1830.

Manneken Pis (called Menneke Pis by natives of Brussels), the bronze statue of an insolent-looking urinating child at the junction of Rue de l'Etuve and Rue de Chene, embodies the mild disrespect and ungovernable spirit of Brussels' citizens. Their determination to go their own way, to cock a snook at authority, is manifested most noticeably in the struggle of ethnic groups to win respect for their cultures, a struggle felt most keenly in the linguistic dispute.

In Brussels, only a few miles to the north of the Walloon language boundary, the mixture of Flemish and Walloon cultures can be felt more keenly than anywhere else in the country. Here every street sign and the names of every neighbourhood are printed in both languages. This practice disregards the fact that there is a third official language in Belgium: namely German. Every government agency is supposed to uphold the right of all German-speaking Belgians to be understood in their native tongue.

International organisations: Brussels' geographical location is interesting in itself: the city lies at the heart of western Europe. If one draws two lines diagonally through the continent, one from Scotland to Greece and the other from Spain to Denmark, the lines will converge at Brussels. In recent years, the city has been internationalised by three important supra-national institutions based here: the European Commission, the Council of Ministers of the European Union and NATO.

t, another sterpiece. ht, sitting side on Grand-ce.

In March, 1957, the European Coal and Steel Community, Euratom and European Community combined to form the European Economic Community. Brussels was the most likely seat of operations, as the contracts for the founding of the European Economic Community and the European Atomic Authority had been negotiated in the city in 1956. Centrally located and easy to reach, the city was also able to provide sufficient office space for the Community's extensive and growing network of officials.

At the time, Brussels was already preparing for the World Exhibition of 1958 with ambitious building projects. The city saw its chance and seized it, becoming the permanent home of the European Community administration.

At first, the offices of the various EC branches in Brussels were located in several buildings in various parts of the city. Since 1967, the EC building has stood in the Palais Berlaymont at the eastern end of Rue de la Loi, which stretches from the city centre to the Palais du Cinquantenaire.

In 1967, the Community was made up of only six countries. It has since expanded to include 12 member states; this has enhanced Brussels' cosmopolitan flavour still further.

NATO: In 1966, the French President Charles de Gaulle, who was working to achieve his country's withdrawal from the military system of the North Atlantic Treaty Organisation, ejected all NATO forces from France. The NATO military command was accordingly transferred to the area of Mons, in Belgium, while its administrative arm (the NATO Council, the Military Command, and the international staff) moved to Brussels. The city soon saw an influx of thousands of foreigners, all working for the EC and NATO.

There are, moreover, some 200 embassies in the city – for a country is only properly represented in Belgium if it has three legations. As well as some 100 ambassadors accredited to the royal **Ice-cream vendor.**

court, there are representatives of each country for NATO and the European Union (formerly the EC). Politicians and businesspeople from around the world flock to Brussels to represent their lobbies in these European institutions. As a result, Brussels houses some 800 branches of worldwide trading organisations, as well as numerous offices of international companies. Its restaurants and hotels reflect their international clientele; every visitor feels at home, and you can even expect to find your favourite national dish on the menu.

A high price: Diplomats and international officials receive expatriate allowances and tax advantages through living here. This contributes to Brussels' high cost of living and escalating rents. Brussels is ranked as one of the top 10 most expensive cities in the world. Yet, in spite of the hordes pouring in from all over the world, it remains one of the few major European cities where flats are still available to rent.

Nearly every country has its own local community in Brussels. As a general rule, such communities also maintain their own churches and schools. In addition to international schools, the so-called European schools, there are German, French, Dutch, Japanese, British and American schools catering mainly to families who expect to remain in the city for only a short time.

More and more workers are moving into Brussels from the surrounding countryside, impelled in part by the closure of the Walloon coal mines and the resulting unemployment. This flight from the country is responsible for a rise in the city's own rate of unemployment.

As a direct consequence of this migration there has been a flight in the opposite direction, to salubrious neighbourhoods on the city's outskirts, by wealthier citizens. They have been joined by rich foreign residents. In the past 30 years, some 100,000 people have moved from the centre of Brussels to its periphery; this migration has considerably altered the character of the

city. Many of its original residents mourn the passing of the pre-1958 lifestyle; as the Belgian capital grows increasingly international, the provincial elements which once characterised this historic city have become virtually extinct.

Guest-workers, employed in low-skilled manual sectors, form a sizeable part of Brussels' foreign community. Traditionally Spaniards have comprised the largest population of such workers. In recent years they have been joined by workers from further afield, in particular the Maghreb and central Africa. African students, business people and dissidents from the countries of Rwanda and Burundi (former mandated territories of the Belgian state) and Zaire (formerly Belgian Congo) in Brussels add to the cultural mix.

Most residents of Brussels view this influx of people with traditional Belgian nonchalance; but others warn that with the rate of unemployment continuing to rise the level of immigration is stoking trouble for Belgium's future.

A STROLL THROUGH THE UPPER CITY

Our path through the Upper City begins at the **Botanical Garden** (Jardin Botanique National de Belgique/ Nationaal Plantentuin van Belgie) at the intersection of the Boulevard du Jardin Botanique/Kruidtuinlaan and the Rue Royale/Koningsstraat. The handsome iron and glass greenhouses date from 1826 and the garden was completed in 1830. When, in 1944, the Botanical Garden's premises were deemed too small to serve the city's growing horticultural interests, most of its plants were transferred to the park in the area of Bouchout, north of Brussels. Since 1984, the Botanical Garden, though still containing a wealth of exotic plants, has been first and foremost the "Centre Culturel de la Communauté Française" (French Community Cultural Centre). This includes a library, a cinema, various smaller theatres and a number of exhibition rooms in the buildings where the nurseries used to be housed.

Delicious confections: Turning off the Boulevard du Jardin Botanique on to the Rue Royale, in the direction of the city, you come to one of the oldest hotels in the city: the Pullman-Astoria, built in 1909. Diagonally opposite, you can pick up provisions for your tour in the world-renowned Confisery Mary, confectioners to the Belgian Royal Family. Continuing in the direction of **Place Royale/Koningsplein**, we leave the neighbourhood of Notre-Dame-de-la-Neige (Our Lady of the Snows) behind us on the left. Virtually all the houses in this area were badly damaged or destroyed in the 19th century; many have been restored in the style of the period.

Looking right from the Place Royale, you can see the **Column of Congress** (Colonne de Congrès/Kongreszuil). Designed by the architect Joseph Poelaert and built between 1850 and 1859, the column commemorates the founding of the country of Belgium in

An oasis of green: the Botanical Gardens.

1830. Important dates in Belgium's history and the names of men and women who made significant contributions to the Revolution are inscribed in gold letters. Enthroned on the top of the column is a statue of the first King of Belgium, Leopold I of the house of Saxe-Coburg-Gotha.

The four oversized female figures seated at the pedestal at his feet symbolise the human rights which had hitherto been denied to the people of Belgium: freedom of education, freedom of religion, freedom of the press and freedom of assembly. At the base of the column an eternal flame burns over the grave of the Unknown Soldier, a memorial to the victims of both world wars.

The Place Royale is bordered to the east by a wall, over which you can view the lower city. In the background, the tower of the Town Hall on the Grand-Place/Grote Markt rises up like a giant pencil. In the foreground, you can see the buildings of various ministries, the National Bank, the Philips Tower and, some distance to the left, the imposing St Michael's cathedral, which stands on the boundary between the Upper and Lower City.

Dedicated to the two patron saints of the city, Saint Gudula and Saint Michael, the cathedral (**Cathédrale Saint-Michel/Sint-Michiels-Kathedraal**), built between the 13th and 15th centuries, stands a little way back from the Rue Royale. Inside, you can enjoy the fine stained-glass windows from the 16th and 17th centuries, some of which are by the artist Bernard van Orley. Other notable features included the carved chancel by H. Verbruggen and the paintings by the school of Rubens.

From the Place Royale we turn into the Rue de la Loi/Wetstraat and the **Parliament Building** (Palais de la Nation/Paleis de Natie), with its neoclassical facade. The twin chambers of the Belgian parliament, the House of Deputies and the Senate occupy the main building; the surrounding buildings house various ministries.

Laid out with geometrical precision, the **City Park** (Parc de Bruxelles/Park van Brussel) lies opposite the Palais de la Nation. The park, which served as a royal hunting ground as early as the 14th century, was given its formal layout between 1776 and 1780. The path leading directly through the middle of the park from the Theatre du Parc leads to the **Royal Palace** (Palais du Roi/Paleis van de Koning).

Although the royal couple spend most of their time in the palace in Laeken, this is where King Albert conducts his official business. The building houses the Royal Chancellery, as well as conference chambers for representatives and offices. If the flag is flying from the roof, His Majesty is in residence.

Quenched by beer: A fortress used to occupy the site where the palace now stands. In February 1731, however, the building burned to the ground. Due to severe winter weather the city's water supply was frozen, and hardly any was available to quench the flames. In des-

e Brasserie
aterloo in
e Avenue de
ison d'Or.

peration the citizens attempted to put out the fire with beer, but their efforts were in vain. In the 19th century, Leopold II had the castle rebuilt in the style of Louis XV. It was further renovated and enlarged at the beginning of this century. Opposite the palace, amid the greenery of the park, you'll find a bust of **Peter the Great**, the legendary Tsar of Russia.

The **Palace of the Academies** (Palais des Académies/Academienpaleis) stands to the east of the palace square. This building, which was originally conceived as a residence for the Prince of Orange, was built in 1829 in the style of the Italian Renaissance. Today, it houses the Academy of Science, the Academy of Literature and Fine Arts, as well as the Academy of Medical Sciences.

A few minutes' walk past the palace returns you to the Rue Royale. Turning left, you immediately come to the edge of the **Place Royale/Koningsplein**, built in the 18th century.

Fine arts: Especially noteworthy here

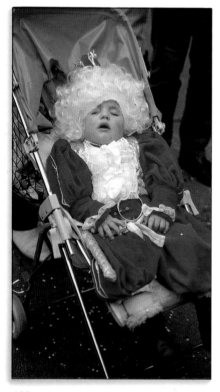

are the classical facades of the houses on the square. One fine example, a row of columns supporting a pediment in the style of a Roman temple, conceals the 18th-century **Royal Chapel of St James on the Coudenburg**. The statue of **Godfrey of Bouillon**, a famous crusader, occupies the middle of the square. Godfrey led the First Crusade in the 11th century, and took Jerusalem by storm in 1099.

By proceeding a little further north along the Rue Royale, you will find, located between the Rue Royale and the Rue Ravenstein/Ravensteinstraat, the **Palace of Fine Arts** (Palais des Beaux-Arts/Paleis voor Schone Kunsten), with its exhibition and concert halls. The palace was designed by the famous art nouveau architect Victor Horta, and built in 1928.

Before turning to the Grand Sablon, take a quick look at one of the city's most beautiful churches: the **church of Our Lady of the Chapel** (Eglise Notre-Dame-de-la-Chapelle/Kapellkerk) on the Boulevard de l'Empereur/Keizerslaan. There's something here from every architectural era: the church was begun in the 12th century, its nave dates from the 15th century, and the tower is largely 18th century. Notice the confessionals, which date from the 16th century, and the carved chancel from the 18th century.

Modern art: From here, we wend our way over the Place de Petit Sablon/ Kleine Zavel to the **Musical Instrument Museum** (Musée Instrumental), whose 5,000 exhibits span the history of music, from the Bronze age, to the present day. The **Museum of Modern Art** (Musée d'Art Moderne/Museum voor Moderne Kunst), containing paintings, drawings and sculpture from the 19th and 20th centuries, is just a few metres down the road; you won't be able to see it from here, however, as its eight storeys are stacked underground. The collection includes the works of many internationally known artists, including Stevens, de Braekeleer, Dubois,

A sleeping beauty.

Khnopff, David, Courbet, Gauguin, Delacroix, Corot, Ensor, Delvaux, Dalí and Magritte

Opposite the museum is the former **Palace of the Counts of Flanders**, now home of the Belgian Auditing Office. A bank is located to the right of **St James**, while to its left is a branch of the Foreign Ministry and the **Congo Library**.

Turning right on to the Rue du Musée/ Museumstraat, you will find yourself in front of the impressive square of the **Place de Musée**, looking up at the composite facade of the residence of Charles of Lorraine. This extensive complex, which includes museums for modern and classical art, also houses the **Royal Library of Albert I** (Bibliothèque Albert Ier/Koninklijke Bibliotheek Albert I).

The Royal Art Galleries: Since extensive renovations in 1984, the Royal Art Galleries (Musées Royaux des Beaux-Arts de Belgique/Koninklijke Musea voor Schone Kunsten van Belgie) have been numbered among the best in the world. The **Museum of Classical Art**, containing works of the 15th, 16th, 17th and 18th centuries, in particular paintings by Brueghel, Rubens, Jordaens, Tintoretto, Bosch, Hals and Rembrandt, is also located here.

The **Royal Library of Albert I** (Albertinum) contains among its many sights the reconstructed workrooms of Emile Verhaeren and Michael de Ghelderode. The **Museum of Books** (Musée du Livre et Cabinet des Donations) has plenty to fascinate bibliophiles; many of its treasures were donated by prominent families in the city. The **Museum of Sound** presents an interesting collection of audiovisual recordings, including recordings of nearly 6,000 famous voices.

The **Museum of Printing**, with its machines for typography, lithography, bookbinding and mechanical typesetting from the 19th and 20th centuries, is also worth a look. You can see examples of wooden and copper type in its Prints Collection (Chalcographie). The Albert-

endly
ants at the
eyboom
rade.

inum was built in the middle of this century in memory of Albert I.

The **Monte des Arts** is an extensive modern complex lying between Place de l'Albertine/Albertinaplein and the Place Royal/Koningsplein, which was designed in the 1950s by the architects Ghobert, Houvoux and van Steenberghen. Its buildings include the **Palace of Congress** (Palais des Congrès) and the **Palace of the Dynasty** (Palais de la Dynastie). The Dynasty Museum (Musée de la Dynastie/Museum van de Dynastie), which is situated behind the Royal Palace, contains an exhibition documenting the history of the Belgian royal family.

Churches and fountains: Returning to the Place Royale, and continuing into the Rue de la Régence/Regentschapstraat, you come to the **Zavelkerk**, also known as the Eglise du Sablon. Its proper name is Eglise Notre-Dame-des-Victoires (church of Our Lady of the Victories). The church was commissioned in the 15th and 16th centuries by the Brussels guild of archers and is sumptuously appointed. Especially noteworthy are its splendid chandeliers, the wall paintings in the choir and the carved wooden chancel. Because of its stylistic harmony, the Eglise du Sablon is regarded as the most beautiful example of high Gothic church building in Belgium. Entrance to the building is via the main portal on **Place du Grand Sablon/Grote Zavel**.

This square is graced by the **Fountain of Minerva**, a gift of the Earl of Aylesbury. He presented it to the citizens as a token of his thanks for the asylum they granted him during his enforced exile from England. The Place du Grand Sablon is lined with bijou restaurants and antique shops.

Returning to the Rue de la Régence, cross the road to the Place du Petit Sablon/Kleine Zavel. This small, well-tended park is surrounded by an intricate grille of wrought iron which merits notice for its 48 bronze statues, each of which represents a craftsman's guild.

Some like it hot, some prefer the shade.

The first statue is a self-portrait by Henry Beyaert, whose image also appears on the Belgian 100-franc note. The entire ensemble is dominated by a bronze portraying the dukes Egmont and Horn, the two heroes of the resistance movement against the bloodthirsty Duke of Alba in the 16th century.

Behind this square stands the noteworthy **Palais d'Egmont** (Egmont-paleis). Built in the 16th century, this building was renovated in the classical style in the 18th century. Famous past residents of the palace include Louis XV and Voltaire. Today, it's the home of the Belgian Foreign Ministry. It was here, in 1972, that Denmark, the United Kingdom and Ireland signed the contracts officially admitting them into the European Economic Community.

When biggest is best: From here, visitors have a choice of two routes: either to return to the Rue de la Régence or to take the Rue aux Laines/Wolstraat, which runs in front of Egmont Palace. Both routes eventually lead to the magnificent **Palace of Justice** (Palais de Justice/Justitiepaleis). A section of the Marolles quarter, Brussels' oldest district, had to be pulled down in order to make room for it. The architect, Joseph Poelaert, was commissioned to design a monument to the Belgian constitution; in other words, it had to be bigger than any other building, either sacred or military. In the end the project developed into a symbol of Belgium's burgeoning industrial and colonial power.

The building is one of the most colossal edifices in the world. Located on the hill where the gallows once stood, the Palace of Justice looks majestically out over the European city. The dome is 104 metres (340 ft) high, and the building occupies 25,000 sq. metres (30,000 sq. yards) of ground. There are 27 conference rooms in the palace, and a further 245 smaller rooms; in addition, there are offices and prison cells. The entrance hall measures an impressive 3,600 sq. metres (4,300 sq. yards). The building was constructed between 1866 and 1883; Poelaert did not live to see its completion, as he died in 1879. In conceiving his design for the building, he took something from virtually every period of Belgian architecture.

Just below the Palace of Justice you'll find the poorest neighbourhood in the city: the **Marolles**. Many feel this to be the true heart of Brussels. The unique and unmistakable Brussels dialect, a mixture of Flemish, French and Spanish, with smatterings of Hebrew and German, originated in this ancient quarter of the city.

South of this neighbourhood there's a remnant of the original medieval city fortifications, the **Porte de Hal/ Hallepoort**. With the exception of a slight structural modification to its north side in the 19th century, this stone structure is preserved in its original condition. The museum which bears its name, the **Musée du Porte de Hal**, presents displays which trace the progress of Belgian military history from the Middle Ages to the 18th century.

Line-up of celebrities at Place du Sablon.

THE MAROLLES

Standing on the terrace on the west side of the Palais de Justice you may fail to spot the district closely stacked at your feet – the Marolles. To see it, you must cast your gaze downwards and then look out towards the south. At the end of the 19th century a considerable section of the Marolles had to be demolished to make way for the massive Palais de Justice.

The district developed in the 17th century as a residential area for the craftsmen working on the palatial homes of the Upper City. It remained a thriving working class district until the 1870s when, with the paving over of the Senne, the wealthier artisans moved out to the city's suburbs. From then on the district declined, eventually becoming a refuge for the poor.

The survival of the Marolles and its inhabitants is due purely to their dogged determination to hold on to their district; they have taken up a common and yet highly individual fight against their wretched living conditions and intruders alike. The traditional appearance of the entire district is perpetually threatened by urban redevelopment and property speculation. An even more insidious enemy, however, is the deterioration of the fabric of the buildings, for the inhabitants have no funds available for essential repairs. Many of the historic builings are crumbling; some are literally falling down.

The district has no clearly defined boundaries; it lies beneath the Palais de Justice, from the Boulevard de Waterloo, the Porte de Hal, the Boulevard du Midi and the Avenue de Stalingrad as far as the Chapelle des Brigittines on the edge of the aristocratic Grand Sablon district. The principal through roads, running side by side from one end of the Marolles to the other, are the Rue Haute and the Rue Blaes.

The district's inhabitants, some 10,000 in all, lead lives largely independent of the outside world. The daily round and the passing of the seasons have retained their original significance here. A clear boundary exists between life in the Marolles and the rest of the city, despite the periodic incursions of outsiders. The original inhabitants are gradually dying or moving away and being replaced by newcomers. Maghrebis and other immigrants from Mediterranean countries make up 50 percent of the present population. Most share one characteristic with the original residents – poverty.

However, as the members of various action groups for the preservation of the Marolles are well aware, in recent years property developers have acquired ambitions in the area. The community of immigrants and indigenous residents has been joined by high-earning yuppies, and independent traders have opened a succession of boutiques, jewellers, galleries and restaurants.

And yet, the drab little snack bars are

The Marolles is slowly being taken over by yuppies.

still found on almost every street, hawking mussels, watery stews, soggy chips and thin draught beer. Also typical are the large, dilapidated tenement blocks containing council flats. One of the city's largest hospitals, the Saint-Pierre, lies within the Marolles – as does the former fire brigade barracks at the Place du Jeu de Balle, where a series of shops – mostly art galleries and antiquarian booksellers – have set up next to expensive modern houses.

Early each morning the cafés surrounding the Vieux Marché opposite the Fire Station attract their first customers; as many of these establishments are open until the small hours, some of them do not bother to close at all. Each has its own individual character and its own type of clientèle.

The outsider may well react with consternation at such evident despair, particularly in the La Samaritaine district which lies cheek by jowl with the art galleries, antique shops, gourmet restaurants and luxury flats of the prosperous Grand Sablon. Here, the contrasts are too marked for comfort.

In some corners, however, the visitor will notice successful attempts at restoration. The numerous action groups are attempting to breathe fresh life into the district and encourage the residents to renovate their homes. But public funds are available only sporadically. For many years they allocated no money at all for the rebuilding of this socially deprived district, finding it easier and more lucrative to encourage private investment by collaborating with builders and property dealers. Private investment, however, is not a realistic proposition in the Marolles, for the deprivation of its inhabitants is so severe that they are unable to finance any restoration work themselves.

The only real chance for the survival of the traditional countenance of the Marolles lies in the collective organisation of its residents. It remains to be seen whether the people who live here can save their district.

g Turks.

THE LOWER CITY

The centre of Brussels is characterised by the striking contrast between the Upper and Lower City. In the former you will find the city's government and business infrastructure. The Flemish Old City, the so-called "Lower City", situated on the Ilôt Sacré, on the other hand, is one of the most lively districts in the capital, well known for its restaurants.

The Royal Decree of 1960 proclaimed that all rebuilding work should preserve the historic facades of the buildings. The city subsidises such projects with a 25 percent grant; this applies in particular to the Grand-Place.

Close to the Grand-Place is **Rue du Marché aux Herbes/Grasmarkt**, a narrow street housing a number of small shops and, at No. 61, the Tourist Information Office (TIP), where visitors can obtain news of events, exhibitions and trade fairs and maps.

Southwest of the Town Hall, at the junction of the Rue de l'Etuve/Stoofstraat and the Rue du Chêne/Eibstraat, stands the city's landmark, the celebrated **Manneken Pis** – a bronze fountain in the shape of a naked boy. On 13 August 1619 Jérôme Duquesnoy the Elder (*circa* 1570–1641) was commissioned to produce the likeness. He was the head of a Brussels family of sculptors whose works were influenced by the style of Rubens (a contemporary).

Speculation on the sculptor's inspiration for the statue includes a number of theories. The best known maintains that during the battle of Ransbeke the son of Gottfried of Lorraine was hung in his cradle from an oak tree to give the soldiers courage. At some stage in the fighting he got out of his cradle unaided and was discovered urinating against the tree. He thus demonstrated his courage even as a child.

Yet another story tells of the son of a Brussels nobleman who, at the age of five, cheekily left a procession in order to relieve himself. According to a variation on this tale, a wicked witch put a spell on the child because he dared to urinate against the wall of her house. She turned him to stone, thus condemning him to urinate for ever.

The statue escaped damage during the bombardment of the city in 1695, but it was stolen on a number of occasions after this. In 1745 it was captured by the British and two years later the thieves were the French. But Manneken Pis was always recovered. By way of compensation for the French theft, Louis XV, who was in Brussels at the time, gave the statue a costume of precious gold brocade. The king had the culprits arrested and honoured Manneken Pis with the title "Knight of St Louis".

In 1817 a newly released convict stole the statue. When it was found, it was in several pieces. These were used in the casting of the present bronze replica. On 6 December 1818 Manneken Pis was returned to its original site, where it can still be seen today. On high days and

ft, this rpet of wers is led out ce a year the and- ice. low, miring the tails of the wn hall.

holidays the statue is dressed in costume. On 6 April, for example, he wears the uniform of an American military policeman to recall the anniversary of the involvement of the United States in World War I. On 3 September every year Manneken Pis is dressed in the uniform of a sergeant of the Regiment of Welsh Guards to celebrate the liberation of Brussels in 1944; and on 15 September it is the turn of the uniform of a British Royal Air Force pilot – in remembrance of the Battle of Britain during World War II.

In all, the statue possesses 345 uniforms and medals, which are stored in the Municipal Museum on the Grand-Place (most of the time he doesn't wear anything at all).

Religion and capitalism: Leaving Manneken Pis and going down the Rue des Grands Carmes/Lievevrouwbroersstraat, the visitor soon arrives in front of **Notre-Dame-de-Bon-Secours/Onze-lieve-Vrouw van Brjstand** (Our Lady of Succour). The church was built in 1664 by Jean Cortvriendt in the 17th-century Italian manner. Another church in the vicinity, **Notre-Dame-aux-Riches-Claires/Rijkelklavenkerk**, dates from virtually the same period. It is the work of Luc Fayd'herbe (1617–97), a pupil of Rubens known above all for his colossal statues adorning the pillars of church naves. The ornate gables represent the typical Brussels interpretation of the Italian Renaissance.

Also near the Grand-Place, in the Rue Henri Maus/Henri Mausstraat, stands the Brussels **Stock Exchange** (La Bourse/de Beurs). This is the most important foreign exchange market in the country.

The Stock Exchange was founded on 8 July 1801. It changed locations several times after its original foundation. When the city councillors became aware of the importance of such an institution they decided to erect a more imposing building on the site left vacant by the demolition of the "Récollets" monastery, which had had to make way for the

The Grand-Place is regarded as one of the world's most elegant squares.

new boulevard crossing the city from north to south. Léon Suys, one of the capital's most distinguished architects at the time, supervised the construction of the magnificent building between 1871 and 1873.

Before leaving the area the visitor should not fail to cast a glance inside the little **Church of St Nicholas** (l'Eglise Saint-Nicolas/Sint-Niklaaskerk). Dedicated to the patron saint of shopkeepers, the building has a colourful history reaching back to the founding of the city. It was originally constructed as a market church during the 11th–12th centuries, and rebuilt in the Gothic style in the course of the 14th–15th centuries. Having suffered damage during the Wars of Religion which dominated the 16th century, as well as during the terrible bombardment of the city in 1695, the church was subsequently rebuilt.

The interior walls are lined with wood panelling and decorated with notable paintings. A classical-style high altar, carved wooden confessionals and the pulpit date from the 18th century. The altar in the left aisle is adorned with a 15th-century Madonna. The pillar on the right-hand side of the choir supports a Spanish figure of Christ dating from the 16th century. A copper shrine in front of the pulpit recalls the martyrs of Gorcum, who were put to death in Brielle (near Rotterdam) in 1572 after suffering unspeakable torture at the hands of the Gueux. The painting of the *Virgin and Child Asleep* is attributed to Rubens.

Streetlife: Leading away from the Stock Exchange to left and right is the **Boulevard Anspach/Anspachlaan**, one of the city's busiest commercial thoroughfares. It is lined with specialist shops of every kind. The avenue opens on to the spacious **Place de Brouckère/De Brouckereplein**, where it meets the Boulevard Adolphe Max and the Boulevard Emile Jacqmain. The middle of the square used to be occupied by the Anspach Monument, a 20-metre (64-ft) high fountain in memory of Jules Anspach, mayor of Brussels between

flower
rket.

THE COMIC MUSEUM

If you want a museum that absorbs children for hours and offers something for adults too, head for the Comic Museum, occupying the house at 20, Rue des Sables/Zandstraat. Allow plenty of time for your visit (the museum is open to the public every day except Monday, from 10 a.m. until 6 p.m) and take your time over the hands-on exhibits; whoever complete first – you or the kids – can take advantage of the reading room, comfortably strewn with cushions and comics.

This treasure-chest of picture stories is a gem in itself, for the building in which it is housed is a prime example of Flemish art nouveau architecture. Known as the Magazins Waucquez, it was built in 1906 for a fabric merchant named Waucquez by the famous Belgian architect Victor Horta (1861–1947).

In those days, customers of the fabric shop entered through a fine portal and then mounted the sweeping staircase. Today these same stairs serve as the launching pad for the red-and-white checked rocket which Tintin and Snowy used to reach "Destination Moon" long before the Americans managed it.

Tintin – who outflanks even Manneken Pis in fame – and his faithful terrier are omnipresent in the museum. Their artist-creator Hergé (Georges Rémi) first introduced them to the newspaper-reading public in 1929. They are his most popular cartoon characters, followed by the twin detectives Thomson and Thompson, Captain Haddock and the absent-minded Professor Calculus. For 60 years their adventures have entranced the whole world in every imaginable language. The museum contains sketches, drawings, relief plates and many other items.

Incredible though it may seem, the lovely Horta-designed building was at one stage poised for demolition. The Magazins Waucquet had closed its doors in 1970 and the building was threatened by the same fate that befell many other buildings in the city centre, including the "House of the People", mentioned in every account of the city's architecture. The capital of Europe needed more

space to house its increasing numbers of politicians and businessmen. The demolition was shortsighted and ruthless. No account was taken of the loss to Brussels' cultural heritage.

However, Horta's Magazins Waucquez was saved from the same fate. Artists and architects managed to persuade the Belgian Minister of Housing and Construction that the house in the Rue des Sables should be saved and restored. The ingenious idea of turning it into a comic museum was widely supported by Brussels' citizens. The plan was to create a symbiosis between art nouveau and the "Ninth Art" – cartoon drawing. The new museum was inaugurated in the autumn of 1989.

On the ground floor, to the right, lies the brasserie-restaurant, "Horta"; to the left, there is a bookshop named Slumberland after the art nouveau comic strip about Little Nemo. Also on this floor is a permanent exhibition commemorating the life and work of architect Victor Horta, and two libraries – one for leisurely reading and the other for more serious study.

On the mezzanine floor, the visitor enters the Saint-Roch Treasure House, where original manuscripts are preserved. Also here are a cinema, a video library, and an exhibition explaining how cartoon films are made, including drawings at every stage of development.

Ascending the staircase, the visitor passes Tintin's rocket and arrives at the first floor. Here, the auditorium of the King Baudouin Foundation is reserved for special events.

Also on the first floor is the Museum of the Imagination, the place to meet all those old friends. In the room dedicated to the journal *Spirou* visitors find the cunning bellboy himself, and in the Vandersteen Room you will find Professor Barabas's time machine. In the room housing the Jacques Martin collection you can experience a thunderstorm by night in ancient Rome, and in the Tillieux Room you will find Jeff Jordan's favourite saloon. Entering Gaston's office in the Franquin room, it seems as if Marsupilami cannot be far away; and in the Hubinon Room you can stand on the aircraft carrier next to Buck Danny. In the Morris room you encounter the shadow which shoots faster than Lucky Luke.

1863 and 1879 and the prime mover behind the construction of the city's broad avenues. Today the Anspach Monument stands on the Fishmarket between the Quai aux Brigues/Bazsteenkaai and the Quai au Bois Brule/Brandhautkaai.

Not far away is the **Place Sainte-Catherine/Sint-Katelijneplein**, at the centre of which stands the church of the same name. It was built in about 1850 by Joseph Poelaert in the eclectic style, a blend of Romanesque, Gothic and Renaissance elements. **St Catherine's** occupies the site of the original church, which was destroyed in 1850. The old tower, known as the Tour Ste-Catherine/Katelijnetoren, still serves as a belfry.

Within the triple-naved church, a painting of St Catherine by G. de Crayer hangs above the altar in the right aisle. In the left aisle stands the **Black Madonna** (Vierge Noire), dating from the 14th–15th centuries.

Behind the church you will come across remains of the first city wall,

dating from the 12th century: the **Black Tower** (Tour Noire/Zwarte Toren). The Place Ste-Catherine is another place to find street traders, their portable barrows laden with ready-to-eat delicacies such as oysters, mussels, snails and pickled herring.

Within easy reach of the square is the Rue du Cyprès/Cipresstraat, which leads to the church of **St John the Baptist** in the **Beguine Convent** (St-Jean-Baptiste-au-Beguinage/Begijnhofkerk van Sint-Jan). The basilica, originally Gothic in style, was rebuilt during the 17th century and became one of the masterpieces of Belgian rococo architecture. Inside, the technique by which the baroque features were superimposed upon the original Gothic structure can still be seen. The entablature rests on a row of angels' heads. The Beguine community itself, which was flourishing with 1,200 members in its heyday, was dissolved in the 19th century.

The well-known **Petite Rue des Bouchers/Kleene Beenhouversstraat** ("Little Butchers' Street") crosses the city centre on its way from the Stock Exchange to the Galeries Saint-Hubert and the Galeries Royales. The street, which is closed to traffic, is also known as the "Stomach of Brussels", as it is lined with good but cheap restaurants.

A fun place to dine: In a narrow cul-de-sac leading off the Petite Rue des Bouchers lies the **Museum Toone**, one of the most famous marionette theatres in the world. The theatre first came to public notice in 1830 under Toone I, who invented the "Woltje", the Little Walloon, who is seen as the epitome of the typical Brussels street urchin. Dressed in a checked jacket and with his cap set at a jaunty angle, he acts as the narrator and speaks all the parts.

In 1911 a grim fate befell Toone III; he was discovered hanging dead between his puppets. Under José Géal, the seventh generation of the Toone dynasty, the marionette theatre experienced a new upsurge. In the 1960s he purchased an old house in the Schuddeveld

Street and turned it into a puppet theatre cum restaurant. An antique pianola dominates the entrance; if you put a five-franc piece into the slot, it will tinkle old tunes.

The plays are performed in the local dialect, which originally evolved in the Marolles, the historic district at the heart of the old city. Though based on the French language, it also includes a mixture of Flemish words and Spanish expressions adopted from the soldiers of the Duke of Alva. The dialect is used for every performance in the Toone theatre repertoire of 500 plays.

Shopping in style: From the end of the bustling Petite Rue des Bouchers, it is only a stone's throw to the Royal **Galeries Saint-Hubert**. In 1830 the city, embracing its new role as the capital of the Kingdom of Belgium, dedicated the exclusive shopping arcades to its new royal family.

The glass-roofed streets, lined with shops, are divided into the **Galerie du Roi**, the **Galerie de la Reine** and the

Galerie des Princes. The galleries, which are 2,133 metres (7,000 ft) long, were designed in 1845 by the Brussels architect Jean-Pierre Cluysenaer, then only 26 years old.

King Leopold I laid the foundation stone on 6 May 1846. One year later, on 20 June 1847, the official opening of the galleries took place.

Leaving by the northern exit of the Galerie du Roi, the visitor can cross the Rue de l'Ecuyer and reach the Place de la Monnaie/Muntplein, the focal point of which is the **Théâtre Royal de la Monnaie/Muntschouwburg**, the Brussels opera house.

Belgium's first musical stage was elevated to the rank of National Opera (Opéra National) in 1963. The name of the square, and that of the theatre, are derived from the building which originally stood on this site – the Hôtel de la Monnaie (the National Mint), which was constructed here during the 15th century and which minted the coins for the Duchy of Brabant.

Call to arms: Brussels opera house was the scene of one of the most important historic events in the city. It was here, on the night of 25 August 1830, that the revolution leading to the country's independence was triggered.

The opera *Masianello* (also known as *La Muette de Portici*), by Daniel François Esprit Auber and based on the Neapolitan Revolution of 1647, had been scheduled to be performed at the Opera some time previously. However, following unrest in the city, the authorities had postponed its run.

The première was finally held on 25 August before a packed house. Its effect on the members of the audience was electrifying. As the opera progressed they became increasingly disturbed and when, in Act IV, the call to arms rang out, they could not be contained. With patriotic cries on their lips they streamed out of the auditorium to the municipal park. The revolution had begun.

The Brussels Opera rates among the best opera houses in Europe. One man

The facade
the "Fox" o
the Grand-
Place.

in particular is associated with its success: Maurice Huisman, who took over the direction of the opera house in 1960 and who breathed new life into the theatrical world.

For many years the Brussels opera house was the headquarters to the Twentieth-Century Ballet under Maurice Béjart. His principal contribution to the contemporary ballet scene was the infusion of a much more masculine approach to dancing. This contrasted starkly with the classical tradition, which was dominated by the feminine style.

Another popular shopping street, the **Rue Neuve/Nieuwstraat**, leads off the Place de la Monnaie. It is a bustling pedestrian area packed with modern stores and a shopping complex called **City 2**. Tucked away amongst these palaces of Mammon is the baroque **Finistère Church/Finisterakerk**, built in 1708 and worth visiting for its elaborate interior decorations.

By taking a side street off the Rue Neuve the visitor will arrive at the **Place des Martyrs/Martelaarsplein**, which was formerly known as the Place Saint-Michel. Its symmetrical layout was devised by the architect Fisco in 1755. In the middle of the spacious square stands a monument by G. Geefs recalling the 450 heroes of the Revolution of 1830 who died fighting the Dutch.

St Michael's Cathedral rises majestically on the hillside between the Upper and Lower City. It is an important example of the Brussels Gothic style. Previously occupying the site was the Carolingian baptistry, dedicated to the Archangel Michael. After the relics of St Gudula were placed here in 1047 the two saints came to be regarded as the joint patrons of the church.

Although work was begun on the present cathedral at the beginning of the 13th century, it was not completed until the end of the 15th. The building thus exhibits a number of different architectural styles. The dimensions are impressive: the main body of the cathedral, 108 metres (345 ft) long by 50 metres (160

THE ATOMIUM – A NATIONAL SYMBOL

The Atomium, a gigantic model of an iron molecule, can be seen from many districts of the city. It dominates the Heysel Plateau, the leafy suburb lying to the north of Brussels (Boulevard du Centenaire/Eeuwfeestlaan)), looming over the bourgeois houses of Laeken. For motorists, access is easiest via the motorway ring; those without their own transport can get there by the Metro (stop Heysel).

The futuristic-looking monument was built for the 1958 World Exhibition. It was originally designed to symbolise in concrete form the potential of Belgian industry. The decision to build the Atomium resulted from a cooperation agreement between the Belgium metal industry and the Commissioner General responsible for the overall planning of the World Exhibition. In November 1954 André Waterkeyn, a professional engineer and director of the Association of Metal-Working Industries, developed the plans for the unusual structure.

It was Waterkeyn's idea to represent the concept of the atom, which forms the basis of all sciences concerned with investigating the constitution of matter. His ambition was to portray in monumental fashion the processes which take place in the microcosm.

With the opening date of the exhibition a strict deadline, it proved possible to construct the Atomium within a period of only four years. It was a huge success among the population of Belgium. After the Exhibition, the City of Brussels placed a formal request that its new landmark should not be dismantled. The striking moument had become a new symbol for the city, almost as well-loved as Manneken Pis.

André Waterkeyn had chosen to represent an iron molecule, at a magnification of 165 billion times, as a symbol of the metal industry. In crystal chemistry, it is customary for the structure of crystals to be represented by spheres, whose central point indicates the central position of the atom within the network of crystals. The forces linking the atoms are represented by rods joining the spheres with each other.

The Atomium is based on this fundamental concept of a metal crystal. It consists of nine large spheres, represented in the basic constellation of a symmetrical three-dimensional system; each of the spheres is linked to the others by pipes measuring 3 metres (10 ft) in diameter.

All told, the Atomium is 102 metres (326 ft) high; each of the nine spheres or balls has a diameter of 18 metres (58 ft). Six of them can be visited by the public, who are transported from one sphere to the next by escalators – some of the longest in Europe at 35 metres (112 ft) and housed in the diagonal connecting pipes. Travelling these escalators is a disorientating experience. The lift linking the bottom sphere with the top one is the fastest in Europe (it travels at 5 metres/16 ft per second), enabling the visitor to ascend in just 23 seconds.

From the topmost sphere there is a spectacular view of the entire surrounding area. In the foreground are the buildings of the exhibition centre in the Parc du Cinquantenaire, and Brupark, a popular amusement park.

The Brupark contains – among its many attractions – a "Mini Europe", featuring the Continent's best-known monuments, constructed on a scale of 1:25 (including the Channel Tunnel); a cinema, with a total of 14 auditoriums; a tropical swimming pool, and the Heysel Sports Stadium. After learning about the peaceful uses of atomic power in the museum occupying the lower sphere of the Atomium, you can adjourn to the restaurant in the top sphere.

The Atomium is a prominent landmark in Brussels, mainly because of its size but also because of its gleaming aluminium coating. At night it is truly spectacular. The nine spheres are illuminated by a succession of circular light fittings positioned about 1.5 metres apart. The lamps are switched on alternately by means of revolving switches, thus giving the impression that points of light are revolving around the spheres. The illumination was conceived as a means of illustrating the revolution of electrons around the centre of each atom of an iron molecule.

ft) wide, is flanked by twin 69-metre (220-ft) towers.

A staircase erected in 1861 leads to the triple doors of the cathedral. The nave impresses above all by its clarity of form, characterised by 12 round columns and ribbed vaulting. The pillars of the nave are formed by life-sized statues of the Twelve Apostles dating from the baroque era. They were carved by Jérôme Duquesnoy the Younger (Paul, Bartholomew, Thomas and Matthew), Luc Fayd'herbe (Simon), Jan van Milder (Philip and Andrew) and Tobias de Lelis (Peter and John).

A typically Belgian baroque wooden pulpit, carved in 1699 by Henri F. Verbruggen, portrays the banishment of Adam and Eve from Paradise. In 1937, excavations between the pulpit and the organ loft revealed the remains of foundations of a 12th-century Romanesque vestibule.

Situated to the left and the right of the high altar are three monumental tombs: two are dedicated to Duke Johann of Brabant and his wife, Margaret of York, who died in 1312 and 1322 respectively. The third is in memory of Archduke Ernst of Austria, who died in 1595; the brother of Emperor Rudolf II, he also held the office of Governor-General of the Netherlands.

Of particular note are the 17th-century tapestries (only occasionally on display). They were woven by van der Borght, who appears to have drawn his inspiration from Rubens. They depict various scenes from the legend of the Miracle of the Sacrament. According to the story, a group of Brussels Jews stole the Holy Sacrament in 1370 and desecrated it with their fists. It is claimed that the Holy Christian Sacrament began to bleed at this, a phenomenon which was taken as proof of the Jews' guilt. They were condemned to be burned at the stake.

Behind the choir lies the **Chapel of St Mary Magdalene**, built in 1282 and remodelled in the baroque style in 1675. It contains a 16th-century statue of the Virgin with Child, which is thought to be the work of Konrad Meyt. The Italian alabaster altar stood originally in the Abbey of La Cambre, which was destroyed during World War I by invading German troops.

The Gothic-style **Chapel of Our Lady of Redemption** lies to the right of the choir. The 17th-century sketches for the stained-glass windows are attributed to van Thulden, a pupil of Rubens. They depict scenes from the life of the Virgin Mary, together with donors and their patron saints.

The cathedral, dedicated to St Michael and St Gudula, the twin patron saints of Brussels, is the city's principal place of worship. For centuries it has hosted the country's official ceremonies. In 1960 it was also the stage for the marriage of King Baudouin of Belgium and the Spanish Countess Fabiola Fernanda de Mora y Aragon. In 1962 the cathedral was officially named "St Michael's Cathedral" when it became the seat of the Archbishop of Mechelen.

t, one of e land-rks of ussels: the omium. ght, ussels' st famous nbol – the nneken .

CHATEAU ROYAL TO THE PALAIS CINQUANTENAIRE

The **Royal Palace** lies in the outlying district of Laeken, to the north. It was built by Montoyer during the second half of the 18th century; during the reign of Leopold II it was rebuilt in the style of Louis XVI. It was here, in 1812, that Napoleon Bonaparte signed the declaration of war against Russia.

Exotic plants: The famous **Royal Greenhouses** (**Koninklijk Domein van Laeken**), a series of 11 interlinked greenhouses were erected on the orders of Leopold II. The **Chinese Pavilion** and the **Japanese Tower** lend the park an exotic air. They were built for the World Exhibition in Paris in 1900. Planned to serve as a restaurant, today the pavilion houses a priceless collection of 17th and 18th-century oriental porcelain, displayed as part of a rotating exhibition. The exotic *objets d'art* are seen to good effect in a baroque interior.

The **Port of Brussels** extends right into the park at Laeken. It stretches from the Avenue du Port/Havenlaan to the Allée Verte/Groendreef. As early as 1434, the city had received from Duke Philip the Good the right to canalise the Senne, since the river was in grave danger of silting up. In 1477 a better solution was found to the problem: Mary of Burgundy gave permission for the construction of a lateral canal alongside the Senne, to link up with the Rupel near Willebroek. Afterwards three harbour basins were added in Brussels itself.

The **Church of Our Lady of Laeken** stands at the junction of the Avenue de la Reine and the Avenue du Parc Royal. It was built by Poelaert in the neo-Gothic style on the orders of the first Queen of the Belgians, Louise-Marie. The sarcophagi of the country's deceased sovereigns lie in state in its crypt. The tombs and chapels are decorated **The bandsmen play.**

with numerous works of art, the most famous of which is undoubtedly the statue *The Thinker* by Auguste Rodin. The church is only open during services.

Home of the EU: Also within easy reach of the city centre is the **Europe Centre**. The present building was constructed between 1963 and 1969 in accordance with plans drawn up by de Westel.

Near the European Union Headquarters lies the **Parc du Cinquantenaire**. It covers an area of 37 hectares (90 acres) and, as the name indicates, was created in 1880 as part of the celebrations marking the 50th anniversary of Belgian independence. Situated at the beginning of the Avenue de Tervuren, the park contains one of the largest museum complexes in Europe.

Around the periphery stand eight female statues symbolising the nine Belgian provinces (the twin provinces of Flanders are represented by a single statue). A **Triumphal Arch**, 60 metres wide (192 ft) and 45 metres high (144 ft) is visible from a distance. The openings in the colonnades on each side are 10 metres (32 ft) wide. The structure was designed by Charles Girault. The four-horse chariot on top of the main arch is the work of the Belgian sculptor Thomas Vincotto; it portrays a victorious Belgium, confidently facing the future.

Inside the park's palace the **Royal Army Museum and Museum of Military History** display weapons, equipment and war posters from the past three centuries of Belgian history. Exhibits include sabres and cannon from the Brabant Revolution, as well as weapons used in both world wars. A separate section contains items tracing the history of the air force.

The **Museum of Art and History** is devoted to the history of civilisation. The highlights of the museum are the famous 5th-century Apamea mosaic from the Syrian town destroyed by the Persians in 612, and a bronze of the Roman emperor Septimius Severus. There are also sections dedicated to Belgian folk art. Especially worth seeing are the

sections covering Decorative Arts and Art Nouveau, and a department devoted to non-European civilisations. Of particular interest here is the 13th-century Civa Nataraja bronze from India, and a collection of painted Tibetan banners.

Classic cars: A further attraction within the Parc du Cinquantenaire is **Autoworld**, an impressive collection of vintage cars, within the Palais Mondial. Some 450 top models from 12 different countries makes Autoworld the finest museum of its kind in the world.

Visitors wishing to move on to a higher plane – metaphorically speaking – should include a tour of the **Air and Space Museum**, also within the Parc du Cinquantenaire. The exhibition provides a summary of flight from its earliest beginnings until the present day.

Outer space: In the north of the metropolitan area, above the royal district of Laeken, lie the **Heysel Heights**, dominated by the Atomium (see *page 146*). This was the site chosen for the 1958 World Exhibition.

BRUSSELS' MARKETS

If you can't find a particular item on the market stalls of Brussels, it probably doesn't exist at all, for you can buy virtually anything here. Brussels' markets are some of the best places to find local colour; and every day of the week is market day somewhere in the city.

One of the most interesting of the city's various markets is the **Antiques Market** which takes place every weekend (Saturday 9am–3pm; Sunday 9am–1pm) on the Place du Grand Sablon; you may even find a bargain here, though you will probably have to search for it amongst a good deal of junk. As elsewhere, the line between art and kitsch is a thin one.

Not many tourists come to Brussels to buy a horse. Nonetheless, a stroll to the **Horse Fair** on Place de la Duchesse de Brabant/Hertogin van Brabantplaats on Friday morning is entertaining even for those with little knowledge of horses or riding (it takes place from 5am to noon). The powerful quadrupeds named after Brabant Province, also known as Pajottenland, are still used as draught horses on many Belgian farms, so the fair still performs an important function. Racehorses are also sold.

One of the most interesting aspects of the market is the bargaining process. Even local residents may fail to understand a single word.

Any self-respecting town has a weekly market, but in terms of kaleidoscopic colour and multi-faceted variety few can compare with the market at the Gare du Midi). It resembles nothing as much as a superb supermarket in the open air; known as the **Exotic Market**, it takes place every Sunday morning.

The range of goods on offer is overwhelming: clothes for every season of the year; food of every kind, from fish to gâteaux. In between are mounds of exotic fruits, almonds and nuts, piles of pots and pans, pictures, jewellery, leather

The Bird Market is a special attraction of the Grand' Place.

goods and books. The noise can be deafening: polyglot cries in Flemish, French and Dutch add to the general din. As Jean Cocteau once maintained, "the city of Brussels is one big stage." The market is no exception.

Some of the city's markets are more tranquil. One of these, the daily **Flower Market**, is held every day apart from Mondays and during the winter months on the Grand-Place/Grote Markt (8am – 6pm).The function of the large umbrellas, in the traditional local colours of red and green, is not merely to provide protection from sun and rain. When they are tipped at a right-angle to the pavement it is a sign by the stallholders that business is bad on the Grand-Place.

On a few days each year the blooms and blossoms are not for sale at all, but form part of a magnificent display. On these occasions the city's gardeners and florists spread a gorgeous carpet of flowers right across the square. The best view of the spectacle is from a window of one of the surrounding houses.

Another relatively peaceful market is the **Bird Market**, where only the twittering of the birds disturbs the peace. Every Sunday, from 7am to 2pm, breeders arrange their cages in front of the Grand-Place. The contents of these cages range from brightly coloured songbirds to game.

Not every visitor to the bird market comes with the intention of purchasing. Many of the enthusiasts merely want to chat with the breeders or to discuss the merits of the latest bird seed for their pet canary or budgie. It is a place where experiences are exchanged and hobbies are nurtured.

Sunday best: Lovers of flea markets will want to visit the **Vieux Marché** on the Place du Jeu de Balle/Vossenplein. Here, in the very heart of the old Marolles district, stalls of some 20 traders or more can be found on any day of the week. The best day to visit, however, is on Sunday (7am–2pm when the number often rises to 200.

Another Sunday market is to be found in the Rue Ropsy Chaudron/Ropsy-Chaudronstraat), where between 8am and 1pm new and used cars are offered for sale. Car dealers can also be found in the Rue du Paruk/Paruckstraat; those operating here, however, are generally considered to offer fewer bargains.

Another favourite Sunday morning stroll takes the visitor to the Place de la Reine Astrid/Koningin Astridplein, where there is a market for records, paintings, secondhand books, toys and jewellery. In recent years a number of food stalls have also sprung up.

In addition to these regular markets, it is common to see clusters of stalls occupying the various squares dotted across the city. Some of these, however, vanish as quickly as they spring up, or disband without warning for weeks or even months at a time. When winter frosts set in, the number of people willing to man an open-air stall declines. Fair weather traders don't bother to emerge again until Brussels is enjoying the first warm days of spring.

BRUSSELS LACE

Brussels lace is famous the world over. Developed during the mid-19th century and initially used to adorn the shirt collars and cuffs of the nobility, it was soon being used extensively. At one point, in fact, it was fashionable to wear gowns made entirely of the precious fabric.

Brussels lace was particularly sought after at the royal courts in Paris and London. Queen Elizabeth I of England reputedly owned 3,000 lace dresses; it is said that Empress Eugénie years of age. During the 17th century 22,000 women and girls worked as lace makers; during the 19th century, the total reached 50,000. In Brussels alone, the capital of lace production, the figure was some 10,000.

Brussels lace was unsurpassable as regards both the fineness of the thread and the beauty of the motifs. The capital's churches and museums are full of examples of the delicate work produced. A particularly fine specimen of the lacemaker's art can be found in the Royal Museum of Art and History: a bedspread which Albert I and his wife Isabella received as a present upon the occasion of

of France owned a lace gown which 600 women had toiled over for 10 months using a total of 90,000 bobbins.

By the second half of the 16th century, women throughout Belgium were engaged in the craft and lace was being exported to prosperous families all over Europe. At the end of the century there was scarcely a young girl, even in the most rural areas, who was not employed by the lace merchants.

The labour-intensive industry posed unforeseen problems, namely a shortage of serving maids in the homes of the wealthy. Eventually a decree was passed prohibiting the manufacture of lace by girls of more than 12 Albert's elevation to Duke of Brabant.

Other masterpieces include the Virgin Mary's veil, on display in the church of Notre-Dame-du-Sablon, and a lace bedspread, carefully preserved in the Museum of Costumes and Lace, which belonged to Emperor Charles VI. The bedspread is decorated with the imperial eagle, symbolising the pomp and circumstance of monarchy.

The production of large covers and entire robes was only made possible when the technique of lace-making moved away from the use of a single continuous thread towards knotting. Until this point it had only been possible to produce small pieces of lace, the size of which was determined by the length of the thread wound on to the bobbin. The technique of joining together individual motifs to produce a single large piece revolutionised the industry. This method permitted the creation of large-scale items with highly imaginative patterns within a relatively short time.

Following this method of production many women produced the same motif time and time again, often over a period of several years. The creative aspect of the craft was thus gradually lost in a sort of mass production. Other workers were allotted the task of joining the individual pieces together.

lution lace-making in Belgium was in decline. The craft experienced a brief renaissance during the 19th century but was never able to regain its previous fashionableness or degree of skill.

Today, the craft attracts only a modest following in its country of origin. Very few women possess the requisite skills. Two schools, in Mons and Binche, train young women in what was once a world-famous art. Unfortunately, nowadays too few Belgian women want to learn the intricacies of lace-making to satisfy the rapidly increasing demands for hand-made lace. Much of that on

None of the lacemakers ever became famous or rich. Their reward for their arduous work was determined by the lace merchants, few of whom were generous; the lacemakers were often forced to work in badly lit, damp cellars where the thread would be less likely to break.

Until well into the 18th century, Brussels lace remained a popular symbol of luxury for the rich. Inevitably, however, fashions changed and by the time of the French Revo-

sale in Brussels today was actually made in China. The Asian product is considerably cheaper but inferior in quality.

One of the largest lace merchants in Brussels is the Manufacture Belge de Dentelles, whose shop can be found at 6-8 Galerie de la Reine. A wide variety of antique and modern lace is on sale. Those who prefer simply to look at fine Belgian lace should visit the Museum of Costumes and Lace just behind the Town Hall at 6, Rue de la Violette. There is also an excellent lace collection in the Royal Museum of Art and History in the Parc du Cinquantenaire; the entrance can be found in the Avenue des Nerviens.

Left, *The Lacemaker* **by Jan Vermeer van Delt (1665). Above, even expert lacemakers can't produce more than a few inches per day.**

Shopping And Nightlife

After a sightseeing tour, a stroll through the city's shops makes an invigorating change, whether you're after typical souvenirs such as Brussels lace or handmade chocolates or prefer to scour the city's antique shops in the hope of finding a more unusual gift to take home.

Where to shop: Brussels' main department stores are on a par with equivalent establishments in other European metropolises. The entire length of **Rue Neuve/Niewstraat** has been turned into a pedestrian zone, and contains a colourful array of elegant boutiques.

Brussels proudly claims to possess more shopping arcades than any other city in Europe. Among the best-loved are the long-established **Galeries Saint-Hubert**, whose elegant classical facade is decorated by columns and a central Renaissance-style motif proclaiming *Omnibus omnia* – "everything for every-one" – and ultra-modern shopping centres such as **City 2** in the Rue Neuve.

Even nobler in appearance are the Royal Arcades, which form part of the Galeries Saint-Hubert: the **Galerie du Roi**, the **Galerie de la Reine** and the **Galerie des Princes**. The elegant glass roofs are supported by a steel-framed vault; the shopping galleries, dating from 1847, house mainly luxury boutiques. Here you will find everything the well-heeled Brussels bureaucrat might need, from jewellery to Brussels lace, but don't expect it to be cheap.

The Grand-Place/Grote Markt is where art lovers tend to head first; but music lovers, too, will find plenty to interest them here. In the **Rue du Midi/Zuidstraat** there are numerous music shops. Musicians can purchase excellent second-hand items or have a damaged instrument repaired. This street also contains shops devoted to philately.

The **Boulevard Anspach/Anspachlaan** in the neighbourhood of the Stock Exchange is a lively thoroughfare. Lin-

Window shopping along the Avenue Louise.

ing the section as far as the Place de Brouckère/De Brouckereplein is a succession of boutiques, newsagents, chocolate shops and electrical stores.

The new galleries near the Grand' Place invite the visitor to browse at leisure. Even the tourist whose wallet is not particularly fat will find items to his taste and pocket here: jeans, leather goods, fashion items and jewellery, souvenirs and records. It is tempting to soak up the atmosphere of the galleries in the many little cafés, a number of which are fronted by a terrace. Particularly worth visiting are the **Galerie Agora**, the **Galerie du Centre** and the **Galerie Saint-Honoré.**

The famous Grand-Place is always full of tourists and as a consequence the neighbouring side streets are riddled with souvenir shops. If you want to purchase some genuine Brussels lace it's a good idea to avoid the shops here and make a short detour to the **Rue du Marché aux Herbes/Grasmarkt**.

Top shops: The district housing the

most attractive luxury boutiques and jeweller's shops lies in the Upper Town. Here, along the **Boulevard Waterloo/ Waterloolaan** and in the **Avenue Louise/Louizalaan** between the **Place Louise/Louizaplein** and the **Porte de Namur** you will find branches of every well-known fashion designer.

The shopping arcades in the Upper Town also rate among the most elegant and expensive in the city. They include the **Galerie Espace Louise**, the **Galerie Louise** and the **Galeries de la Toison**.

Antique lovers should head for the district surrounding the **Place du Grand Sablon** where a market is held every weekend. It's worth having a good rummage through the goods, especially the stamps, crystalware and weapons.

Flea market traders attempt to sell anything and everything. Their shops and stalls can be found above all on the Marché aux Puces, the flea market in the Marolles district.

Also worth a look on the Place du Grand Sablon is the **Sablon Shopping**

ps with
rything.

Garden; it's the longest art gallery in the country.

Since business hours for shops are not controlled by law, shops open late into the evening. On Fridays all shops and supermarkets are open until 8 or 9 p.m. and on the remaining weekdays they are open until 6 or 7 p.m. In addition, most bakers, butchers and small retailers open their shops on Sunday mornings.

Time to boogie: In the city's nightlife, too, a clear distinction is drawn between the Upper and the Lower City. The differences are most obvious in the style and prices found in the various bars and discotheques. Whereas in the Lower City casual dress is the order of the day, a tie and jacket are essential for an evening's entertainment in the Upper City. Establishments in the Upper Town are a lot more expensive.

Members only: A typical phenomenon on the Brussels night scene is the city's many private clubs. The preponderance of these establishments came about as a result of a law restricting the sale of alcohol. Passed during the aftermath of World War I, it prohibited the sale of high-proof alcoholic drinks in public places whilst continuing to permit their consumption in private premises. A solution to the problem was found in the transformation of the numerous bars into private clubs accessible only to members. In order to obtain an "invitation" from the landlord it was necessary to buy membership on an annual basis; the fee charged in most cases, however, remained low.

Getting in to some of these clubs and discotheques can be difficult if you are not a member. Many only grant newcomers entry when they are accompanied by a member. In some, however, it is possible to obtain membership for just one evening.

There is a variety of possibilities for an evening tour of the city's pubs and clubs; but since a venue can lose its popularity as quickly as it was gained – almost overnight – only those regarded as classics are listed below.

Singing in the rain.

Many of Brussels' nightclubs/discotheques have been designed around a theme to distinguish them from more run-of-the-mill establishments. **La Papaye,** situated in the Rue des Bouchers/Beenhouwersstraat, for example, offers its customers a jungle atmosphere: a Tarzan swings from the ceiling and a rhinoceros looms over the bar.

It is not only the dance floor which is exclusive at the **Happy Few** on the Avenue Louise/Louizalaan, but it is certainly as much of a talking-point as the club's glitzy clientele – transparent and made of glass, it forms part of an enormous aquarium.

Those whose taste for the aquatic is more extreme can submit themselves to the wide-eyed gaze of live crocodiles behind a glass partition at the **Crocodile Club** of the Royal Windsor Hotel in the Rue Duquesnoy/Duquesnoystraat. Further along the same street is **Le Garage,** another popular haunt.

Talking of haunting, the **Cercueil** in the Rue des Haring/Haringstraat caters for customers with a liking for the macabre: its tables are made from coffins and the drinks are served in skulls.

Those with more traditional tastes should try the perennially popular discotheque **Le Mirano** in the Chaussée de Louvain/Leuvensesteenweg or a jazz club. Amongst the city's best jazz clubs are the **Brussels Jazz Club** on the Grand-Place, the **Bierodrome** on the Place Fernand Cocq/Fernand Cocqplein, and the **Chez Lagaffe** found in the Rue de l'Epée/Zwaardstraat.

Those who decide to start their evening pub tour early may well find themselves facing locked doors. As in most major cities in Europe, the majority of Brussels' clubs and discotheques do not open until 10 pm. In the meantime, a stroll to the Place de Brouckère will help to pass the time. The square is one of the centres of the city's nightlife and a good place to meet up with friends and enjoy a beer

Food first: Brussels is a bastion of gastronomy. Some of the best restaurants are in the neighbourhood of the **Grand-Place** and the **Old Fishmarket** between the Quai Bois à Brûler/Brandhoutkaai and the Quai aux Briques/Backsteenkaai. In general, the quality of the specialities on offer in the city's 1,800-plus restaurants is of a consistently excellent standard. Belgian cuisine includes meat, fish and poultry dishes; typical examples are Brabant-style pheasant (cooked with braised chicory) and beef stewed in Gueuze beer.

For late revellers, there are some 50 restaurants offering a wide range of specialities late at night. They include **Le Houchier** on the Place du Grand Sablon serving Slavic specialities to the sound of gipsy music, and for those looking for a restaurant that is typically Belgian, the **Poechenelle** in Rue de la Samaritaine/Samaritanessestraat.

And if you don't want a full meal when you emerge from a nightclub, head for a *frittüren* – a snack bar serving chips with everything, including delicious mussels and chips.

ng in the erie St ert.

BRUSSELS
A LA CARTE

Some gourmets maintain that the best chefs in France originally came from Belgium. It is certainly true that the country's cuisine, and in particular that of the capital itself, has a decidedly French accent.

International specialist gastronomic publications provide the latest reviews of the Belgian capital's restaurant scene. In addition, a team of experienced restaurant critics produces an annual guide entitled *Restaurants Gourmet*, obtainable from the local tourist office (TIB) in the Town Hall on the Grand-Place/ Grote Markt. It provides an excellent and up-to-date introduction to the best eating establishments in Brussels. The critics employ a fleur-de-lis rating system to guide readers in their choice. A maximum of five fleurs-de-lis may be awarded to the most distinguished restaurants in Brussels.

In this city where culinary excellence is taken for granted it seems almost invidious to single out individual establishments for praise. The top restaurants in Brussels are world famous; and many of the gourmet places listed here are representative of other less famous establishments (*for further recommendations see Restaurants section of Travel Tips,* page 322).

Top nosh: Almost next door to each other in the vicinity of Koekelberg Basilika (Brussels, 1080) are a pair of celebrated restaurants bearing the names of their owner-chefs. **Bruneau,** owned by Jean-Pierre and Claire Bruneau (73– 75, Avenue Broustin) is one of only three restaurants in the Brussels area to have been awarded the ultimate accolade – the coveted three Michelin stars. **Dupont,** run by Claude Dupont and his wife (46, Avenue Vital-Riethuisen), has two. The specialities on offer in both these restaurants vary according to season and reflect the chefs' daily visits to the local market: fresh game, fine poul-

Smoked ham from the Ardennes..

try, vegetables and salads and herbs. Since neither restaurant is very large, would-be diners are advised to reserve a table well in advance.

Dine in style: If you want divine style as well as superb cuisine head for **Comme Chez Soi** (23, Place Rouppe). Here Pierre Wynants, its owner-chef serves three-star nouvelle cuisine specialities in an exquisite dining room with a belle-epoque atmosphere recalling the decorative style of Victor Horta, the famous Brussels architect of the 1920s and '30s.

Alternatively you might like to try **La Maison du Cygne** on the Grand-Place/Grote Markt 91 lying at the very heart of the city. The entrance is discreetly tucked away in the Rue Charles Buls. It is a charming and elegant establishment and the perfect venue for a celebration dinner. To make your meal a real occasion, be sure to take an apéritif in the **Club Ommegang** beforehand. One impressed restaurant critic commented thus on his most recent visit to the restaurant: "To

sum up, we should rejoice that establishments like this one still exist here in Europe which are not casual meeting places for the jet set but the focal points of a well-established tradition of *les plaisirs de la table*."

At **L'Ecailler du Palais Royal** (18, Rue Bodenbroeck), René Falk and Attilio Basso are renowned for their exquisite seafood delicacies: nowhere is the fish fresher or more skilfully prepared than here.

Near the Bois de la Cambre stands the **Villa Lorraine** (75, Avenue du Vivier d'Or), for many years a favourite gourmet rendezvous. The setting is immaculate. Among Freddy van de Casserie's specialities are the incomparable *Ecrivisses Villa Lorraine* – freshwater crayfish served with a sumptuous sauce of white wine and cream.

Pierre Romeyer serves particularly light, meticulously prepared dishes at his restaurant **Romeyer** (109, Chaussée de Groenendaal in Hoeilláart, 11 km/7 miles from Brussels). He has been

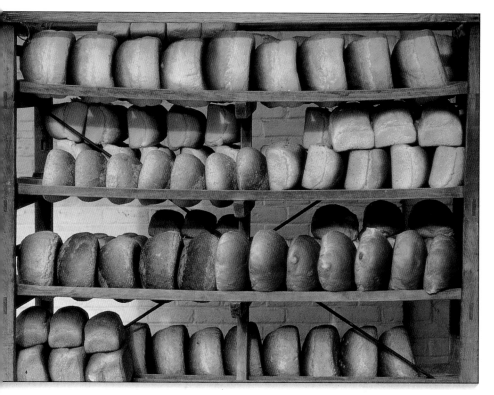

awarded three Michelin stars – the highest mark of excellence – for his culinary achievements.

But it isn't just the food which makes a visit to his restaurant so memorable. There can be few more idyllic spots on a summer evening than the terrace in front of Romeyer overlooking its own gardens and private lake. Romeyer's philosophy, refreshingly self-effacing, is that a chef should adapt what he serves to meet the wishes of his customers, and not vice versa. The presentation, harmony of taste and variety of his specialities are equally highly commended. Of particular note are the home-made pâtisseries.

The outskirts of Brussels are also blessed with a number of first-class restaurants, including **De Bijgaarden** (20, I. Van Beverenstraat) in Grand-Bigard (7 km/4 miles northeast of the capital), **Le Trèfle à Quatre** in Genval (87, Avenue du Lac) and **Barbizon** in Jezus-Eik (95, Welriekendedreef).

Gastronomy on a budget: No city is complete without a wide-ranging choice of cafés, bistros and bars; Brussels is no exception. The district surrounding the Grand-Place/Grote Markt is particularly well endowed with places serving good food at inexpensive prices. In some of the narrow alleys hereabouts it seems as if every house has been converted into a restaurant of some kind. A typical example is Rue des Bouchers/Beenhouwersstraat where, in many cases, polished antique barrows and shelves laden with the ingredients of house specialities are placed in front of the restaurants to tempt passers-by. When business is slack, waiters and chefs often come out and stand in front of their restaurants to drum up trade. Don't be shy of accepting their invitations. Such fare is typically Belgian and reasonably priced.

One of the most atmospheric places to eat in town is **Toone VII** (located at Impasse Schuddevelt 6, Petite Rue des Bouchers) – an old inn containing a puppet theatre, which is reached via a claustrophobically narrow passageway

There are nearly as many different types of sausage as beer.

between two houses. The theatre (go up the rickety stairs) stages performances of classical plays such as *Hamlet* and *Faust*, interspersed by personal comments on the plot by Toone, a true Brussels character. His remarks – profound, sometimes witty – lighten the tragic action on the stage. The puppet theatre/restaurant has been a feature of Brussels for several generations.

The majority of bars and bistros cannot provide such original entertainment, but most of them offer at least a welcoming atmosphere. The décor, usually of a rustic nature and bearing the patina of age, radiates a relaxing ambience.

In such a setting the city's local specialities taste particularly good. Typical of Brussels are poularde, and chicory – with minced beef, stuffed or rolled in ham. A variety of national dishes – Flemish *carbonade* or Mecheener asparagus – are nearly always available. They are all served with the national drink of Belgium – beer.

Like the French, the citizens of Brussels enjoy sitting at a table on the pavement in front of the restaurant or bar. Even in the sheltered, air-conditioned shopping galleries customers display a marked preference for outside tables. Here you will usually find coffee and a selection of tempting cakes and pastries on offer.

Elsewhere in the city cafés cum pâtisseries tend to be thin on the ground. There are some excellent cake shops – **Wittamer**, on the Place du Grand Sablon, is one of the Continent's best – but hardly any are attached to an attractive café of the type common in Germany or Austria.

The Boulevard du Midi/Zuidlaan is an exception. Here, in the **Café Strauss**, you can enjoy excellent Black Forest gâteau or an apple cake which tastes as though it had been made in Berlin.

Another excellent pâtisserie is in the Upper Town in the Avenue Louise/Louizalaan: **Nihoul** has a salon serving a wide variety of cakes, as well as a range of snacks and salads.

"stomach Brussels" located in old city.

To try at home: Finally, for those who would like to try their hand at some of the specialities that are offered in the city's 1,300 restaurants, here is a selection of recipes:

Brussels-style chicory: Chicory is served as a vegetable, a salad or stewed with potatoes and onions, seasoned with lemon and nutmeg. Experienced cooks recommend that when cooking chicory you should add half a lump of sugar in order to reduce the bitter taste. The vegetable will retain its attractive white colour if a few drops of lemon juice are added. **Brussels chicory with cheese and ham** (*recipe below*) is a particularly popular dish.

Ingredients: 1 kg chicory; one slice of cooked ham per plant; 50 gm butter; 50 gm flour; ½ litre liquid (chicory stock and milk); 100 gm grated cheese; salt and pepper; breadcrumbs; a few knobs of extra butter.

Method: Wash the chicory thoroughly and boil it in lightly salted water; drain, reserving some of the stock. To make a sauce, melt the butter in a pan, and add the flour to make a roux. Cook for a few minutes, then gradually add the stock and milk. Thicken the sauce slightly over the heat, then stir in the grated cheese and season with salt and pepper.

Wrap each chicory plant in a slice of ham; lay the rolls side by side in an ovenproof dish. Cover with the cheese sauce, sprinkle with breadcrumbs and dot with knobs of butter. Bake in a preheated oven until well browned.

Brussels sprouts: The classic way of preparing sprouts is to boil them in salted water and then toss them in butter or pork dripping. They are also delicious when puréed in a blender and seasoned with a little nutmeg.

Brussels-style mussels: In Brussels, mussels are usually eaten with chips.

Ingredients: small piece of celeriac; one onion; a little finely chopped parsley; approximately 1 kg mussels (clean them thoroughly in cold water and discard any which refuse to close when tapped); half a lemon.

Preparation: Finely chop the celeriac, onion and parsley. Fry gently in the butter in a covered pan for 10 minutes. Add the cleaned mussels, salt, freshly-ground pepper and the juice of half a lemon. Replace the lid and continue to cook gently for a further 10 minutes, until the mussels have opened. Serve immediately with freshly fried chips or warm French bread.

Brussels waffles: No meal is complete without a dessert and waffles are a perennially popular choice among the people of Belgium.

Ingredients: 1 kg flour; 250 gm butter; 4 eggs; 50 gm yeast; ½ litre water; ½ litre milk; ½ vanilla pod; 1 pinch salt

Method: Warm the milk and water slightly. Melt the butter in a saucepan; add the egg yolks and, beating steadily, gradually mix in the warmed milk and water. Add the salt and the contents of the vanilla pod, and beat in the flour.

Dissolve the yeast in a little warm milk and stir into the dough. Allow to rise in a warm, draughtless place for 30 minutes. Shortly before the end of the rising period whisk the egg whites until they are white and fluffy. Fold into the risen dough. Bake the waffles one at a time in a preheated waffle iron. Serve hot with sugar, cream or jam.

To take home: Two other sweet specialities deserve a mention here: firstly, **pain à la Grecque** ("Greek bread"). It has no connection at all with Greece; it was invented over 500 years ago by a Belgian monk living in an abbey located next to a ditch. At first it was known simply as "bread from the ditch" (in Flemish: *Gracht*), but the French-speaking inhabitants gradually corrupted the name into "Grecque".

The second sweet speciality worth looking out for are *speculoos*, the Belgian equivalent of the German *spekulatius*, the popular spicy Christmas biscuits, but darker and available all the year round. A delicious variation on this type of biscuit, rectangular in shape and containing almonds, is **pain d'amandes** (almond bread).

THE ANCIENT ART OF BREWING

A Latin inscription found on the gable of the Maison des Brasseurs, the Brewers' House, overlooking Brussels' Grand-Place, translates as follows: "Thanks to St Arnold, the divine brew was created from the gifts of heaven and earth and human science."

The Benedictine monk commemorated by the inscription was responsible for spreading the art of brewing across most of Belgium. How a holy man acquired such expertise and felt it right to promulgate his discoveries has been the subject of conjecture. It is said that Arnold was trying to find out why prosperous citizens and noblemen had a considerably higher life expectancy than the common people. After studying the matter, he attributed the reason to the fact that the better-off were able to quench their thirst with beer, whilst those whom fate had treated less kindly had no choice but to resort to water, which was often contaminated by harmful bacteria.

The barrels in his home abbey of St Peter at Oudenburg, near Ostend, were always filled to the brim. Father Arnold exhorted his flock to avoid water and to drink instead beer (in moderation, of course). Arnold was canonised after his death, and has been the patron saint of brewers ever since.

For centuries afterwards, the art of brewing beer remained firmly in the hands of the various religious communities. Their craft, which they took seriously, enabled them to develop a continuous succession of new processes and flavours, spread as far as the court of Spain.

The craft has now become a major industry. Today, Belgium has no fewer than 400 breweries scattered across the country. The experiments of the god-fearing recluses were developed further, and today the country produces more than 200 different kinds of beer; their colours range from light golden through every shade of brown to a deep reddish hue.

One of the most unusual beers is the *Lambic*. This also forms the basis for a number of other beers: the *Gueuze* (pronounced Göse), the *Faro*, the *Kriek* and the *Framboise*. These are yeastless beers where the fermentation occurs spontaneously. It is set into motion by bacteria which enter the liquid from the air. It is claimed that the necessary microbes exist nowhere except in the atmosphere of the capital.

In the Gueuze Museum (*Musée de la Gueuze*) in Brussels the visitor can see the brewers at work as they process the raw ingredients in accordance with methods developed by their ancestors. (The museum is in the Rue Gheude/Gheudestraat; tel: 2-520 28 91; visits can be made by appointment Monday–Saturday between 15 October and 15 May, and there are guided tours on Saturdays at 11am, 2pm and 3.30 pm)

A "young" beer must mature for three to six months and a "mature" one for two to three years. Fermentation takes place in both bottles and casks. The bottle method is used for so-called "Brussels champagne". If cherries are added to the *Lambic* before the second fermentation, the resulting beer is known as *Kriek* (a Flemish word meaning cherry). *Framboise* results from the the addition of raspberries to the basic brew – 150 kg of fruit to 450 litres of beer.

Another interesting variation is *Faro*, which is sweetened after fermentation with rock candy. Since beers of this type are subject to an uncontrolled fermentation, they may, like wine, taste different from one year to the next. Gueuze is produced only during cooler months; the outdoor temperatures are ideal between October and April.

An unusual type of beer is brewed in West Flanders. The Rodenbach Brewery stores 10 million litres in oak barrels. Brewed from winter and summer barley, best quality hops, caramel and malt, a dark brown full-bodied beer is manufactured and subsequently filled into champagne bottles. It is known as *Dobbelen Bruinen*. The *Goudenband* was nominated by beer writer Michael Jackson as the best brown ale in the world.

Most of the 12 million hectolitres of beer which leave the filling plants of Belgian breweries every year are destined for export. Within the country, the per-capita consumption is roughly on a par with that of Germany.

THE GLASS CITY

The Domain of Laeken was created under Marie-Christine and Albert of Saxe-Teck, the Governors General sent to rule the country on behalf of Emperor Joseph II of Austria. They looked around for a suitable site for a palace and in 1781 gained possession of the "Schoonenberg" in Laeken, a district just outside Brussels. Within just three years their magnificent palace had been completed.

The two governors were well-known connoisseurs of art and acquired during their years of tenure a magnificent collection of paintings. It is claimed that the Archduke himself, a keen amateur architect, drew up the initial sketches for the palace and its extensive gardens. At the end of the 18th century the Domain of Laeken was considered to be one of the loveliest estates in the whole of Europe.

Austria did not have long to enjoy its new possessions, however. In 1794, France annexed Belgium. The Austrians left the country, transferring their works of art to a place of safety. They later formed the basis of the famous "Albertina" collection in Vienna, an exhibition of paintings and drawings which still bears the name of its founder, Archduke Albert.

The French forces of occupation intended to transform the palace into a public hospital. Although the scheme was never executed, the plans of the next purchaser, a surgeon, were fatal. He wanted to have the palace demolished and to sell the building material.

In 1804, Napoleon Bonaparte rescued the palace from total ruin – but not before some sections of the building had already been carted away. The palace became his residence until his defeat at Waterloo in 1815. The King of the Netherlands, William I of Orange-Nassau, became the next owner. He, too, had only a brief period to revel in the splendours of his new stately home,

for a few years later, in 1830, the country became independent and Laeken became the residence of Leopold I, the first King of Belgium.

The second King of Belgium, Leopold II, who reigned from 1865 to 1907, had a good understanding of architecture. His aim was to increase the international prestige of his country by means of brilliant and unusual schemes. One of his most successful projects was the development of Ostend into a seaside town. He was also responsible for the creation of the fine park at Tervuren. His most important and attractive scheme was his plan to develop the Domain of Laeken into a National Palace for international congresses. However, Leopold's death in 1909 and the outbreak of World War I shortly afterwards meant that his ambitious project was never completed

But a number of other significant new improvements were undertaken during his reign. The king had magnificent avenues built from the Domain to the

*t, the late
*g
*duoin
*Queen
*iola
*ing a
*oll
*ough their
*ourite
*k where
*enhouse
*aniums
*ht), grow
*high.

capital; the palace itself was extended, and the park was embellished with a Chinese Pavilion and a Japanese Tower, relics of the World Exhibition of 1900. The crowning glory was the construction of the greenhouses.

This remarkable complex has remained virtually unchanged since it was first erected – a fact proved by a study of old photographs.

Leopold II's predecessors had toyed with more modest concepts. A Chinese tower with adjoining orangery had been built during the governorship of the Austrian archdukes. Napoleon, too, entertained grandiose plans for modern glasshouses – but these came to nothing as a result of his separation from the Empress Josephine. The orangery as it stands today was built on the instructions of William I of the Netherlands. Leopold I also had a number of greenhouses erected nearby to supply the palace with orchids and pineapples.

But the so-called "glass city", was built at the behest of Leopold II. He commissioned one of the most important architects of the 19th century, **Alphonse Balat**, to execute his project. The resulting "city of glass" was to become an artistic masterpiece.

Balat made good use of recent technological innovations. During the second half of the 19th century, the techniques required to build metal-framed glass buildings had reached new heights of complexity and perfection, permitting the construction of fairy-tale palaces which combined a romantic enthusiasm for the exotic with a longing for unspoilt nature. The greenhouses represent one of the greatest and best-preserved forms of expression of this typical 19th-century phenomenon.

For the principal extension of the Domain of Laeken, Leopold II engaged the French architect Girault, who had achieved fame by virtue of his buildings for the World Exhibition in Paris. He was responsible for the spectacular "theatre" hothouse.

The Royal Greenhouses consist basi-

Orchids and ferns in the Diana hothouse.

cally of the palm-tree plateau and the winter garden complex. The two sections are linked to each other by a large gallery. The palm-tree plateau is a playful succession of passages and galleries full of unexpected perspectives. The winter garden complex, however, is constructed according to a strict formal pattern. It consists of a row of large hothouses laid out along a central axis. The *pièce de résistance* of the complex is a dome-shaped hothouse which is 25 metres (80 ft) high and with a diameter of 60 metres (192 ft). All the greenhouses are interlinked and allow the visitor to stroll from one end to the other – a total distance of a kilometer.

The plants in the greenhouses are rare and precious, and harmonise perfectly with the architecture. Many species are of historical importance: most of the 44 species of orange tree in the orangery are more than 200 years old. Bananas and different varieties of palms grow between wall ferns, overshadowed by broad palmyra palms. Ferns and orchids of indescribable beauty flourish beside camellias which are almost 200 years old, and which formed part of the hothouses' original 19th-century planting. Today they constitute the most valuable collection of their kind in the world.

At the end of the 1970s a face-lift for the "glass city" was embarked upon. The restoration work is now almost complete, and soon the entire complex will shine forth in its original glory once more, to the delight of the royal family and the millions of visitors alike.

It was the wish of Leopold II that the greenhouses should be opened to the general public once a year. For more than a century now, this tradition has been honoured. Each year, at the beginning of May, when thousands of flowers bloom in rainbow colours, the royal greenhouses are opened to the public. More than 100,000 visitors from all corners of the world come to stroll through the sunlit world of plants, enjoying the hospitality of the king and queen of Belgium.

rding the
hsias.

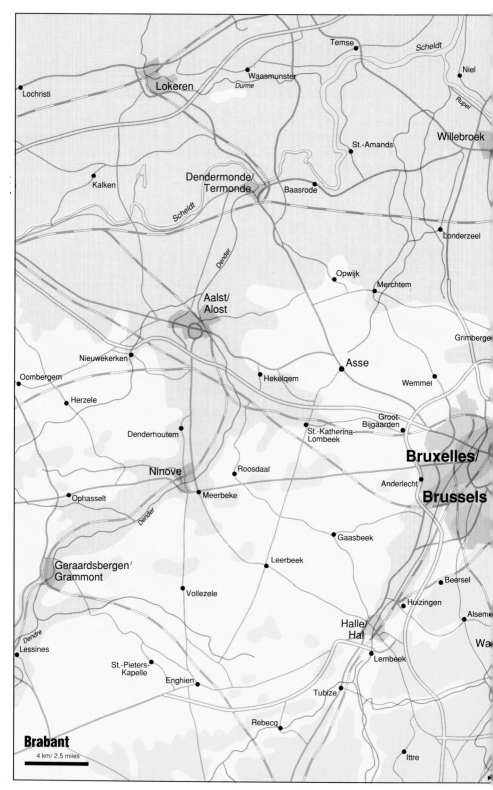

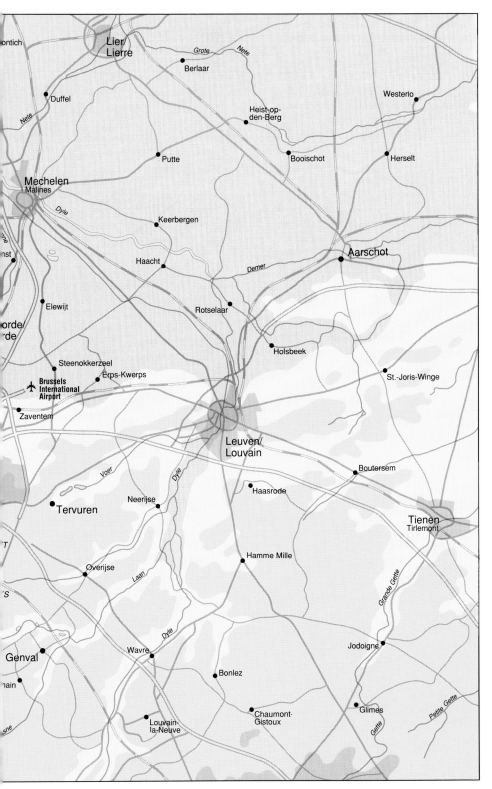

ontich

Lier/
Lierre

Grote Nete

Berlaar

Duffel

Westerlo

Nete

Heist-op-
den-Berg

Mechelen
Malines

Putte

Booischot

Herselt

ne

nst

Keerbergen

Dyle

Haacht

Aarschot

Demer

Elewijt

Rotselaar

orde/
de

Holsbeek

Steenokkerzeel

St.-Joris-Winge

Erps-Kwerps

Brussels
International
Airport

Zaventem

Leuven/
Louvain

Boutersem

Voer

Haasrode

Dyle

Neerijse

Tervuren

Tienen
Tirlemont

Overijse

Hamme Mille

Laan

Grande Gette

T

S

Dyle

Genval

Wavre

Jodoigne

hain

Bonlez

Louvain-
la-Neuve

Chaumont-
Gistoux

Glimes

Petite Gette

sne

Gette

AROUND BRUSSELS

There are a number of worthwhile excursions that can be made from the capital. One of the most popular is to the historic town of **Tervuren**, only a stone's throw to the southeast of Brussels. It can be reached by taking the Avenue de Tervuren/Tervurenlaan, a boulevard constructed by King Leopold II.

During the 17th and 18th centuries **Tervuren Park**, with an area of more than 200 hectares (500 acres) of gardens and lakes, was the setting for many a glittering court ball. Its original palace was rebuilt by Albert and Isabella at the beginning of the 17th century but was demolished in 1781 upon the instructions of Emperor Joseph II; only **St Hubert's Chapel**, built in 1617, and the **Palace Stables**, dating from the 18th century, are still standing. Near the chapel you can rent boats for sailing.

Encounter with Africa: Nowadays Ter-

vuren is principally famous for the **Royal Museum of Central Africa** (Musée Royal de l'Afrique Centrale/Koninklijk Museum voor Midden-Afrika) on the edge of the spacious gardens. The core of the exhibition was provided by Leopold II's Congo Collection. Exhibits on display include a variety of Central African ivory carvings, dancers' masks, weapons, everyday tools, cult objects and sculptures.

The most popular attraction in the museum is a huge pirogue – a boat carved from a single tree trunk – housed in the right wing. The zoological, geological, mineralogical and botanical sections provide a wealth of information about Central Africa. Some sections of the building are devoted to displays of beetles, insects, snakes and birds. Children of all ages love the dioramas displaying stuffed crocodiles, antelopes, water buffaloes, rhinoceroses, zebras, lions, giraffes and elephants set in mock-ups of their natural habitats.

After visiting the museum it's worth wandering round the town of Tervuren. The historic centre contains some fine examples of 18th and 19th-century townhouses, in particular those in the **Kasteelstraat**. The famous art nouveau architect Henry van der Velde lived in **Het Nieuwe Huis** (Albertlaan 3). It was built according to his own designs.

Capuchin monastery: A stroll in the **Kapuzinenbos** makes a refreshing change. Leopold II had a little footpath laid between Tervuren and Jesus-Eik; it's a lovely woodland route, skirting the domain of a former Capuchin monastery. An **Arboretum** was planted here in 1902, harbouring a collection of trees from the temperate zones as well as a number of more exotic specimens.

The university town of **Leuven** (Louvain) lies some 25 km (16 miles) from Tervuren. Its university, the oldest in the Low Countries, adds to the town's medieval character.

During the 12th and 13th centuries, the town's weaving industry made it one of the most important cloth manu-

Gorillas at the Museum of Central Africa in Tervuren.

facturing centres in Europe. Until the end of the 13th century it was the seat of the Counts of Leuven; in 1190 they were made Dukes of Brabant. The monasteries and churches still bear witness to their tremendous wealth.

Leuven's **Town Hall** was built by Mathieu de Layens between 1448 and 1463 for the ruling Duke of Burgundy, Philip the Good. The three-storey building has 10 pointed-arched windows per floor and six exquisitely carved octagonal turrets, making it a masterpiece of Brabant Gothic architecture. The niches in the facade house statues of famous local personalities and reliefs illustrate themes from the Bible.

Within the Town Hall itself, visitors may tour the jury room, once furnished by paintings by Dieric Bouts, a powerful influence on German 15th-century painting, who died in Leuven in 1475.

Directly opposite the Town Hall stands the late Gothic church of **St Peter** (St-Pieterskerk). The cruciform basilica with ambulatory and chapels was never finished because the foundations proved too unstable.

The exuberantly baroque pulpit, dating from 1742, is adorned with reliefs depicting Peter's denial and the conversion of St Norbert. Three arches completed in 1488 separate the choir from the nave. The church's most valuable treasures are two paintings by Dieric Bouts. The triptych illustrating the *Martyrdom of St Erasmus* is also of note.

The tabernacle is 12 metres (38 ft) high and contains the *Altar of the Last Supper*, in which the Apostles are shown gathered round a table, listening to the words of Christ.

The **University** of Leuven has a venerable tradition. The "Studium Generale Louvaniense" was founded on 9 December 1425 by Pope Martin V at the request of Duke Jean IV of Brabant. The 12 teachers were summoned from Cologne and Paris.

Pope Adrian VI, Erasmus of Rotterdam and Justus Lipsius, who founded the discipline of classical and antiquar-

f man,
beast.

ian studies, all had close links with the University of Leuven. The University printers produced the first Latin edition of Thomas More's *Utopia* (1516).

When the German troops invaded during World War I the entire archives, consisting of over 300,000 books, went up in flames. In May 1940 the new university library – a gift of the United States, and containing 1 million books – was also destroyed.

For many years the University of Leuven was at the centre of the bitter feud between the Flemings and the Walloons. The problem was solved in 1962, when the Catholic university, founded in 1425, was split into two sections: a Flemish section ("Katholieke Universiteit Leuven") and a French-speaking one: ("Université Catholique de Louvain"). The books in the university library were shared out between the two universities by allotting those with an even catalogue number to the one, and the odd numbers to the other.

One of the most popular attractions in the entire province of Brabant – visited by approximately 1 million tourists from all over the world every year – is the battlefield of **Waterloo**, situated some 18 km (11 miles) from the capital. It was here that in June 1815 Napoleon suffered a crushing defeat at the hands of the united forces of Prussia and England (*see page 175*).

The best view of the site on which the fighting took place can be gained from the famous Lion's Hill, the Butte du Lion. The visitor must first climb the 226 steps to the top of the artificial mound. This was created in 1825 on the spot where the Prince of Orange was wounded whilst commanding an army of Dutch-Belgian troops. The hill takes its name from the cast-iron statue of a lion with its right forepaw placed symbolically on a globe. The statue, 4.5 metres (14 ft) long, 1.5 metres (5 ft) high and weighing 28,000 kg, was erected on a stone pedestal on the mound built of soil scraped from the battlefield.

The Belle Alliance, the inn in which

Brick facad on the Grar Place in Leuven.

Napoleon established his quarters, and the lodgings taken over by the Duke of Wellington are still standing. The village church dates from 1855; the numerous inscriptions on its walls recall the fallen multitudes.

Walking country: The region to the south of Brussels is ideal territory for taking extensive country walks. Nestling at the heart of this magnificent landscape lies the town of **Nivelles**, some 35 km (22 miles) from the capital. The town's history is closely linked to that of the **Abbey of St Gertrude**.

Founded in the 7th century, the abbey is the oldest monastery in Belgium. According to legend, following the death of the Frankish ruler Pepin the Elder, his widow Itta retired with their daughter Gertrude to a villa on the hillside over the Thines valley. After the death of her mother and after an unsuccessful marriage to Dagobert I, Gertrude founded the monastery, at the instigation of Amand, Bishop of Maastricht.

Nowadays, the abbey church is regarded as one of the finest Romanesque church buildings in Belgium. The porch is flanked by two small towers, the "Tour Madame" and the "Tour de Jean de Nivelles". The Tour de Jean de Nivelles contains a bronze statue which has become a symbol of the town and which was donated by the Duke of Burgundy, Charles the Bold.

Inside, a silver reliquary contains the remains of St Gertrude. Each year, on the Sunday following the Feast of St Michael, the bones of St Gertrude are carried in procession along a 12-km (8-mile) route through the town and its immediate surroundings. The tradition has been observed since the 12th century.

The village of Nivelles grew up around the abbey and developed into one of the country's most famous weaving towns. It prospered until well into the 17th century, but fell into economic eclipse after the Weavers' Uprising and subsequent emigration.

To the east of Nivelles, the visitor will soon arrive at the ruins of the Cistercian Abbey of **Villiers-la-Ville**, founded in 1146 by St Bernard of Clairvaux (1090–1153). Under his guidance the order blossomed and became known as the Order of St Bernard.

Further to the west, 15 km (9 miles) south of Brussels, lies the pilgrimage town of **Halle**. The **Basilica of Our Lady**, formerly known as the church of St Martin is a fine example of Brabant Gothic dating from the 14th century. The tower recalls the fortified towers of many Belgian town halls and weavers' halls. Inside, above the high altar is a wooden statue of Our Lady, carved during the Middle Ages and thought by some to possess miraculous powers. Processions of pilgrims visit the statue of Our Lady at Whitsun and at the beginning of September each year.

In nearby **Huizingen**, the extensive park covering an area of 91 hectares (225 acres) provides an excellent place for recreation. The magnificent gardens display more than 1,200 species of flowers and plants.

**town hall
sts more
cate
gns.**

THE BATTLE
OF WATERLOO

About 10 km (6 miles) south of the Belgian capital lies Waterloo, where Napoleon, following his period of exile on Elba, attempted to return to the political arena of Europe. It was here in June, 1815, in an area of peaceful countryside just 2 kilometres square, that 45,000 men died in agony or were seriously crippled and 15,000 horses were slaughtered.

From half-past two during the night of 15 June 1815, the French army could be seen marching northwards in two columns – a total of 125,000 men and 25,000 horses. The next day, at noon, Napoleon, mounted on his dainty grey, rode through Charleroi. Leaving the town behind him, he rode on to a rise where the road forked left towards Brussels and right towards Fleurus. Here the Emperor came to a standstill. Back on the road, the seemingly endless winding procession was veiled in dust; the heavy tramping sound of thousands of foot soldiers mingled with the rhythmical beating of drums, the shrill blasts of bugles and the echoing cries of *"Vive l'Empereur!"*

Battle tactics: A short time later, Napoleon explained his war strategy to his field marshals and commanders. The English soldiers, under the command of the Duke of Wellington, had stationed themselves around Brussels; the Prussian troops, under Field Marshal Blücher, were approaching from the Rhine. It was essential to French success, Napoleon told them, that these two armies should be prevented from joining forces.

It was not until 26 February 1815 that Napoleon had been able to leave his place of exile of the island of Elba. But he didn't waste much time in re-establishing his power. On 20 March he had entered Paris in triumph. Within five days, an alliance had been formed by Austria, England, Prussia and Russia with the aim of waging war against him.

On Friday, 16 June 1815, Marshal Blücher set up his command post in the windmill at Brye. Only a few kilometres to the south as the crow flies Napoleon had installed himself in a windmill near Fleurus, from which point he could observe the troop movements of his opponent through a telescope. At 3 p.m. he gave the signal to attack.

The Prussian army had lined up a force of 84,000 men and 216 cannon, and were dug in at Ligny; they hoped that Wellington's troops would reach them during the course of the afternoon. Napoleon had assembled 67,500 men and 164 cannon.

Ligny was soon engulfed in a sea of flames under the carefully aimed gunfire of the French. The Prussians waited in vain for reinforcements from the English, and by 10 o'clock that night it was clear that the French, though fewer in number and less well equipped than their opponents, would emerge from the bloodbath victorious. Prussia, having lost the battle but not the war, beat an ordered retreat. That same night they marched off in a northerly direction with the intention of joining forces with the English in the final struggle against Napoleon. It is estimated that some 20,000 dead and wounded were left behind on the field of battle.

Napoleon failed the next day to reinforce the advantage he had gained at the battle of Ligny. Wellington and his troops, who had left Brussels the previous night, took up battle positions on the hill known as Mont St-Jean on the road between Brussels and Charleroi. Their plan was to ward off the French army until Blücher arrived. Wellington himself established his headquarters three kilometres to the north, in the old posting station of the village of Waterloo. During the afternoon of 17 June there was a sudden thunderstorm which turned the ground into a quagmire.

Napoleon reached the Belle Alliance inn, 9 km (5 miles) south of Waterloo on the Brussels road, shortly after 6 p.m.

He watched Wellington's troops setting up camp across the valley on the Mont St-Jean, only 1.5 kilometres away, then took up quarters himself in the dairy farm called La Caillou.

The rain looked as if it would never cease. The cavalry soldiers sat huddled in their saddles trying to snatch some sleep. The foot soldiers searched in vain for dry patches in the trampled fields of corn. The camp fires had to be stoked continually with wood. They produced clouds of acrid smoke, but very little warmth. It had been a wasted day, a day for reflection.

The protagonists: The three leading players in the battle of Waterloo were no strangers to each other. For 20 years, Europe had acted as a stage for their posturings. Napoleon Bonaparte, a native of Corsica, was the most famous of the three. He had become consul, emperor, ruler of the Continent and beneficiary of the Great Revolution of 1789. But Arthur Wellesley, since 1814 First Duke of Wellington, and Gebhard

Leberecht Blücher, a Pomeranian landowner and field marshal, were both revered military men.

Wellington, a tall, slim Irishman, was a typical product of the British aristocracy. Cool, almost phlegmatic, he regarded soldiering merely as a job, not a matter for emotional involvement. He rarely wore a uniform; his tailor was considered one of the finest in England. He had been commissioned in 1787, and from 1796 to 1805 had served as a soldier and administrator in India. In 1808 the British government had sent him to Portugal to support the local citizens' guerilla war against the Napoleonic forces of occupation. In defeating the French, he had allowed their forces to withdraw, a concession for which he was court-martialled but later exonerated. In 1812 he had marched into Madrid, driving Napoleon's forces back into France; two years later, he had reached Toulouse.

What drove Blücher on to the battlefield was hatred; his hatred of Napoleon and his destructive power. The longer Napoleon's rule lasted, and the more oppressive it became, the more Blücher's view was shared by his compatriots. With every battle which Napoleon won, and with every corner of Europe he seized, the more Prussia yearned for freedom and unity.

The Germans proved apt pupils when it came to learning the lessons of the French Revolution. The twin ideas of nationhood and democracy were born together. During the struggle against Napoleon, a pan-German patriotism arose for the first time, spreading across the frontiers of the many individual German states.

There was a basic difference in the motives of the English and the Prussians. The English were determined to defy Napoleon, but their enmity remained basically dispassionate: they already lived with a confident national identity. However, Napoleon's territorial aspirations had destroyed Prussia, the one state on which German hopes of na-

Climbing Lion's Hill

tional unity were based, and the Prussians wanted their revenge. Shrill voices of protest were to be heard from the intellectual élite, whose violent resistance to Napoleon echoed the missionary-like fervour of the French revolutionaries. When, in 1813, the French tyrant had been defeated near Leipzig by an alliance between Prussian and Russian forces, with the assistance of Sweden, the nationalist movement in Germany – which had been gaining steady support – had been fired with new hope.

But the diplomats at the Congress of Vienna in 1814 were divided as to the best way of resolving the most pressing problems in Europe. The majority remained determined to reinstate the feudal conditions of 1789 and to prevent the rise of a powerful Germany. The Congress of Vienna attempted to set out the framework for the restoration of order in post-revolutionary Europe, but for the Germans it signalled the beginning of a long period of frustration, of

French ntry takes osition.

the failure of national democratic hopes. Blücher, by this time 73 years old, shouted to the soldiers as they set off westwards from Berlin in June 1815, "Now we soldiers can put right the diplomats' blunders!"

The campaign to defeat Napoleon represented a combined strategy by the Allied Coalition – the seventh formed against France between 1792 and 1815. A total of five armies was involved: an Anglo-Dutch force under Wellington and Blücher's Prussian regiments were to meet near Brussels and converge on France; the Austrians under Karl Philipp zu Schwarzenberg were to operate along the Rhine, with the Russians led by Barclay de Tolly in reserve; and an Austro-Italian army commanded by Johann Maria Frimont were to block a retreat from northern Italy.

During that June of 1815, the English and Prussian forces spearheaded the attack. Refusing to be discouraged by the defeat at Ligny on 16 June, during which Blücher was wounded, the Prussians

broke camp at Wavern at dawn on 18 June to continue their westward march. Blücher was in good spirits. He was confident that once they had joined forces with the English army, his soldiers would have no difficulty defeating Napoleon.

Napoleon and his troops also rose early that Sunday morning. The breakfast table was laid before 5 a.m. But, as fate would have it, bad rain impaired visibility and the attack – planned for 9 a.m. – was delayed. The gun crews could hardly move the cannon on the muddy ground, even with teams of 15 men and 12 horses per gun. But, despite such unpromising conditions, Napoleon was sure that the final victory would be his: "Gentlemen, if you carry out my orders well, we shall sleep tonight in Brussels," he said.

Napoleon's defeat: At 11.30, from his command post south of the Belle Alliance inn, the emperor gave the signal to attack. The English troops were engulfed in the fire from 120 French cannon. Opposite, in his headquarters at Mont St-Jean, Wellington took shelter under an elm tree, from where he could direct his army.

In the valley between Mont St-Jean and the Belle Alliance lay the ancient manor of Hougoumont to the west and the farmstead of La Haie Sainte to the east, on the road to Brussels; both were occupied by English troops. It was evident that if the French wanted to storm the Mont St-Jean they would need to take both strongholds first.

The attack on Hougoumont had started shortly after 11 a.m; it was a long and bitter battle. At 5 p.m. the French gave up their attempt and retreated. Piled up in front of the manor's perimeter wall was a gruesome heap of corpses – almost 3,000 French soldiers lost their lives in the assault.

In the meantime, at 1 p.m., Napoleon took a risky decision and ordered his men to attack the centre of the valley. He had already been informed that the Prussian forces were at last approach- **But the British wo the day.**

ing, but their imminent arrival did not alter his plan.

The French infantry charged down into the valley in columns of 4,800 men in 24 rows of 200 soldiers each. The English forces waited behind the embrasures of La Haie Sainte or behind the hills. A deadly rain of cannon fire engulfed the manor; to the amazement of the French, thousands of English soldiers suddenly rose up from the crest of the hill and fired their muskets.

The French, even more than their opponents, fought as if in a drunken frenzy. Some of their columns did actually manage to reach the top of the eminence, but the task of killing the enemy became progressively more difficult as the growing mountains of dead soldiers and horses hampered their advance. At 6.30 that evening the French Tricolour was hoisted above La Haie Sainte. Wellington's front at the heart of the Mont St-Jean began to waver. He had no more reserves left. Hopes for the arrival of Blücher and his troops or nightfall was the only comfort he could offer his generals when they demanded fresh supplies.

But Napoleon, too, had only one more reserve battalion when, at about 7.30 p.m, the first brigades of Prussians reached the battlefield. The emperor sent his personal guard charging down the hill of Belle Alliance. The well-aimed fire of the English marksmen hit them fatally at short range. By 8.30 p.m, Blücher and his entire army had arrived. Shortly afterwards there was no holding the French; they knew they faced defeat. The battle cry went up: "Run for your life!", as the Prussians and British careered down the hillside in pursuit of the fleeing soldiers.

Victory and repercussions: At 9.30 p.m, Wellington and Blücher embraced each other in the courtyard of the Belle Alliance inn. It was a hard-won victory. The Prussian band played "God Save the King" and *"Grosser Gott, wir loben Dich"*. In Wellington's words, the outcome of the battle had been "the nearest run thing you ever saw in your life".

News of the French defeat reached Brussels at about 10 o'clock. Just four days afterwards, Napoleon dictated his second document of abdication in Paris. From there he was sent to the Atlantic island of St Helena.

It is the Duke of Wellington who in most British minds was the key figure in the victory at Waterloo; but in Germany Blücher became an equally popular hero and an important symbol of German aspirations. But such aspirations were thwarted at the Congress of Vienna, and for the German peoples 1815 signalled the beginning of a long period of frustration, of the foundering of national democratic hopes, which would be repeated in the Revolution of 1848.

Re-play: On 18 June 1990, the 175th anniversary of the battle was celebrated in colourful costumes on the battlefield of Waterloo (as the pictures in this chapter record). Visitors travelled to witness the occasion from England, France and Germany.

iving the its with a beer.

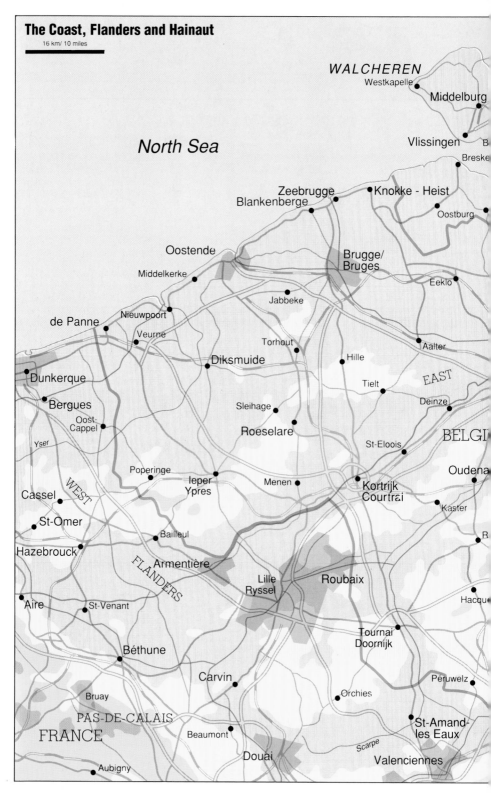

The Coast, Flanders and Hainaut

16 km/ 10 miles

WALCHEREN
Westkapelle
Middelburg

North Sea

Vlissingen B

Breske

Zeebrugge
Blankenberge
Knokke - Heist

Oostburg

Oostende

Brugge/
Bruges

Middelkerke

Eeklo

Jabbeke

de Panne
Nieuwpoort

Veurne

Torhout

Aalter

Diksmuide

Hille

EAST

Dunkerque

Tielt

Bergues

Oost-
Cappel

Sleihage

Deinze

BELGI

Yser

Roeselare

St-Eloois

Poperinge

Oudena

Cassel

Ieper
Ypres

Menen

Kortrijk
Courtrai

St-Omer

Kaster

Hazebrouck

Bailleul

R

Armentière

WEST

FLANDERS

Lille
Ryssel

Roubaix

Aire

St-Venant

Hacqu

Tournai
Doornijk

Béthune

Carvin

Peruwelz

Bruay

Orchies

PAS-DE-CALAIS

St-Amand-
les Eaux

FRANCE

Beaumont

Scarpe

Valenciennes

Douai

Aubigny

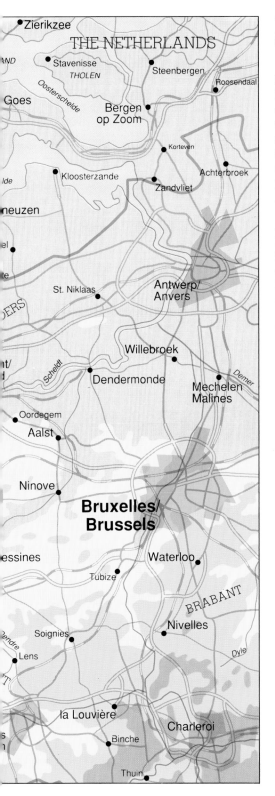

BRUGES AND DAMME

For most people, a trip through Flanders has to begin in the city of Bruges, the capital of West Flanders. Bruges is one of Europe's best preserved medieval cities. Unfortunately, this makes it a major attraction for tourists and as a consequence it has been somewhat over-prettified in an attempt to please them. As Arnold Bennett said as long ago as 1896: "The difference between Bruges and other cities is that in the latter, you look about for the picturesque, and don't find it easily, while in Bruges, assailed on every side by the picturesque, you look curiously for the unpicturesque, and don't find it easily."

Despite being a favoured destination for tourists, this city enjoys no more than a shadow of its former glory. In the 14th and 15th centuries, when the grand dukes of Burgundy, the heirs to the Counts of Flanders, held their court in Bruges, it was the last word in pomp and splendour. Some thought it the last really princely court of the Middle Ages. At the time, Charles the Bold was reaching out to grasp a royal crown, to make Burgundy the third major European power after France and Germany. Bruges, his capital, was a radiant nucleus and, since the founding of the guilds, the largest, richest and most powerful merchant city north of the Alps.

Only after seeing **Bruges** (Brugge), the grande dame of the cities of Flanders, can you understand Flanders, or begin to grasp and recognise the many-faceted heritage which the Burgundians and French, the Austrians and Spanish, the Germans and English have left in this city between the North Sea and the Ardennes. Perhaps this sounds exaggerated, not to say unkind to the other Flemish cities, but whoever has got to know Flanders knows that it's true: Bruges is Flanders. Flanders would be a

Preceding pages: early morning in Bruges.

very different place without this city.

A view of the city: Because the most exciting first impression of Bruges is to be had from above, our visit to Bruges begins by climbing stairs. Not just a couple of steps down to the waters of the omnipresent Reie, which flows around the old city, crisscrossing it with its canals, but the really difficult, steep flight of stairs up to the **Bell Tower**. This mighty tower, nearly 88 metres (300 ft) high, is a landmark of the city. It is located next to the medieval **Cloth Hall**, where the merchants of Bruges used to store their textiles. Bruges' wealth stemmed from fabric production and trade. The towers of the **church of Our Saviour**, the **church of Our Lady**, and the Bell Tower comprise the triumvirate of Bruges towers which makes the city visible from so far away. There are 366 steps leading to the observation deck; here, one is high enough to get a real perspective on this unique city.

Cut off from the sea: In the midst of the city is the broad marketplace, the **Grote Markt**, with its memorial to the two liberation fighters Jan Breydel and Pieter de Coninck, who distinguished themselves in the Battle of the Golden Spurs in 1302. The splendid neo-Gothic edifice of the county administration building dominates the right-hand side of the marketplace; to the left and in the background are the guild houses, their narrow gables looking as neat as pickets in a fence. Sitting on the terrace of one of the Markt's many restaurants, you can listen to the bells pealing out from the bell tower; folk melodies played on a carillon of 47 bells echo over the city.

One building on the Grote Markt which is particularly worthy of note is the **Cranenburg**, which like so many of the houses here is now a restaurant. This was where, in the Middle Ages, the knights slept and ate with their ladies. The Cranenburg has often played a significant historical role, notably in the 15th century when Maximilian of Austria was incarcerated here for 100 days. By then the fortunes of Bruges had

The town h testifies to past prosperity.

started to decline. With the silting up of the Zwin, Bruges was cut off from the open sea, and the city was in danger of losing access to its trade routes. Furthermore, the reign of the Dukes of Burgundy had come to an abrupt end through the tragic death in a riding accident of the young Mary of Burgundy in 1482.

The citizens were incensed at certain tax increases which had been forced upon them by their rulers. They captured their sovereign, Mary's widowed husband Maximilian, and locked him up in the Cranenburg. The audacity of incarcerating the Crown Prince of the House of Habsburg, later to become Emperor Maximilian I, called the "last knight", caused a stir across the whole of Europe. Eventually Maximilian's father, Frederick III, demonstrated his imperial power by sending in warships. Maximilian was set free, but not before swearing to respect the rights of the proud burghers of Bruges in the future.

Maximilian paid no attention to his oath and immediately took his revenge on the citizens of Bruges. He moved the Ducal Residence to Ghent, and transferred Bruges' trading privileges to Antwerp. This sealed Bruges' fate; the death sentence had been pronounced and executed. For nearly 500 years Bruges was "*la ville morte*", the dead city. Not until the final years of the 19th century was the city, by then badly dilapidated, rediscovered with all its original charms.

Gothic beauty: Today, one has to say that the city's economic death after 1488 was a blessing in disguise. During the ensuing centuries, the city simply couldn't afford to reconstruct or alter its Gothic character. One of the most beautiful parts of the Gothic city lies just under the bell tower: **Burg Square** with its town hall, Holy-Blood Chapel, Office of the Town Clerk, and justice buildings. The **town hall** is considered to be the square's *tour de force*: built in 1376, this Stadthuis resembles nothing so much as a stone copy of one of the reliquaries one sees in Flanders' churches and museums, on a larger scale. The Stadthuis in Bruges is the oldest and perhaps the most beautiful town hall in Belgium.

Originally, the facade was ornamented with brightly painted statues of important personages, male and female, in the history of Flanders. The painting was the work of the great artist Jan van Eyck, who worked for a period in Bruges. Unfortunately the sculptures were destroyed in the wake of the French Revolution. Replacements for them have gradually been erected over the course of the past few decades, although today's sculptures are a sober white.

Particularly lovely is the figure of the Virgin to the outer left in the bottom row, just where the narrow Blinde-Egels-Straat begins. This is the *Madonna of Ourdenaarde*, also called Madonna with the Inkwell. The highlight inside the town hall is the vaulted ceiling, carved entirely of oak, which used to be described as the eighth wonder of the world. The walls are painted with relatively "new" frescoes, dating from the

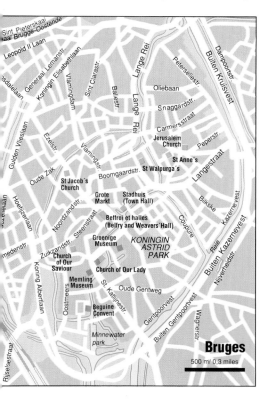

19th century and depicting important events in the city's history.

The Renaissance edifice next to the town hall is the former office of the Town Clerk, the **Oude Griffie**; next to this, on the site where the castle of the Counts of Flanders once stood, is the building housing the **Law Courts**. In the jurors' court, you can see a splendid ebony and black marble chimneypiece dating from the Renaissance. The alabaster frieze depicts the victory at Pavia over Francis I of France, and the subsequent Peace of Madrid, in 1529. This treaty was particularly important, as it was through it that Belgium finally managed to separate itself from France.

Holy blood: To the right of the town hall, you'll find the **Heilig Bloed Basiliek** (Basilica of the Holy Blood). The lower part houses the Romanesque Basilica of St Basil, while the upper part documents the history of Bruges' veneration of the Holy Blood. Returning from a crusade to the Holy Land in 1149, Count Dietrich of Alsace brought a small phial containing a drop of blood said to have been washed from the body of Christ by Joseph of Arimathea. It was given to him in recognition of his bravery during the Second Crusade. To commemorate the return of the victorious army with this relic, a **Holy Blood procession** is held every year on Ascension Day; it is the most important folk festival of Flanders.

The reliquary can be seen in the **Museum of the Holy Blood** in the Holy Blood Chapel; it is one of the finest pieces of medieval goldsmithery in existence. One of the most valuable components of this shrine is a diamond which is supposed to have belonged to the English queen, Mary Stuart. The crown which tops the reliquary once belonged to the young Mary of Burgundy who was so beloved in Bruges.

The small, narrow Blinde-Egels-Straat leads to the **Fish Market**. If you like seafood, you should sample the delicious lobster stew in the fish restaurant called De Visserie. A few steps

The strong Catholic influence i Belgium...

further along, past the delightful Café Mozart, where you can hear good classical music, you come to the **Huidevettersplein**, which boasts some of the best eating establishments in the city. The view over the waters of the **Burgundian Cross** is stunning and painters often set up their easels here. Winston Churchill was one of those who painted the scene.

The **Dyver**, the branch of the Reie which flows from here in the direction of the mighty church of Our Lady, is the place to find water pursuits. Its banks are punctuated by berths for motor launches. The sight-seeing tours of the waterfront and canal network of Bruges are highly recommended.

Flemish primitives: Some of the old patrician houses of Dyver still have windowpanes made of valuable Venetian glass; **House No. 7**, in particular, is worth noting. Right next to these is Bruges' municipal painting gallery, the **Groeninge Museum**. This gallery, located in a former Augustinian monastery, is small both in terms of physical size and in terms of its collection; yet in terms of the quality of what you can see here, the gallery deserves to be ranked with the Hermitage in Leningrad or the Prado in Madrid. The collection concentrates on the work of the Flemish Primitives, the term used to describe the artistic trend of the 15th century, instigated by Jan van Eyck, for painters to depict real people in their paintings.

The works of Jan van Eyck feature strongly: they include his famous *Canonicus van der Paele* and a portrait of a woman which is taken to be his wife. Hans Memling is represented with a painting of St Christopher. The work of Gérard David, Pieter Pourbus, and Rogier van der Weyden are also displayed in the museum.

The Gruuthuse Palace, situated next to the Groeninge Museum, dates from the 15th century. Its owners, the Lords of Gruuthuse, had the right to impose a tax upon the grain (*gruut*) used in the brewing industry: hence the name of the

family and their residence. The English kings Edward IV (1471) and Charles II (1656) both found asylum within its walls. Today, the building houses a museum dedicated to life in 16th and 17th-century Bruges.

The **church of Our Lady** close by is the largest Gothic church of the Low Countries; it was built in the 13th century. During the reign of the Grand Dukes it served as Royal Chapel to the Dukes of Burgundy. It was here that the magnificent wedding of the wealthy Burgundian heiress Mary, daughter of Charles the Bold, and the impoverished but handsome Crown Prince of Habsburg, Maximilian of Austria, was held.

Maximilian made a triumphant entry into the city, his armour gleaming in silver gilt, a garland of pearls and precious stones instead of a helmet on his blond head and the black cross of Burgundy emblazoned on his breast-plate. Formal introductions in the ducal palace were inhibited by neither bride nor groom speaking the other's language and by courtiers milling about to witness the Flemish custom of finding a flower concealed on the bride's person.

The tombs of Mary of Burgundy and her father (which were fully restored only a few years ago) and several Old Master paintings are among the chief highlights of the church; another sight not to miss is the Michelangelo *Madonna and Child*. The sculptor executed this piece for the cathedral of Siena, but when it was completed he found that the cathedral had no money to pay him. Thus the Madonna came to Bruges; it was the only work by Michelangelo that left Italy during his lifetime.

The other major church in Bruges also houses masterpieces from the time of the Burgundians. The Gothic choir stalls in the **church of Our Saviour**, the city's diocesan church, founded by Saint Elegius in 646, still bear the crest of the Knights of the Golden Fleece. Philip the Good, Mary of Burgundy's grandfather, established this order on the occasion of his marriage to Isabella of Portugal. Jan van Eyck, incidentally, had sued for Isabella's hand by proxy on behalf of his Duke (in such marriages the proxy groom was required to lie next to the bride on a bed with one leg bare). When Isabella came to Bruges, she brought her private secretary. She allowed him to build an enchanting brick house; today, this is home to one of the finest and most atmospheric restaurants of Bruges, the Vasquez.

Bruges museums: The **Memling Museum** has pride of place among Bruges' museums. It is housed in the medieval **St Jan's Hospitaal**, built in the 13th century. The only evidence of the museum's former role is the dispensary, which dates from the 15th century, and some wards. The ward nearest the entrance contains a large picture of what the hospital looked like when it was in operation. In the adjoining room, originally where terminal cases were kept, hang some of the most important works of the German-born painter Hans Memling: note in particular the *Mar-*

The man in the moon.

riage of St Catherine and the *Shrine of St Ursula.*

This shrine, on which Memling depicted six scenes from the life of the saint, is numbered among the seven most important art treasures in Belgium,

Beguine Convent: One of the most enchanting nooks in Flanders is the **Beguine Convent**, the Prinselijk Begijnhof Ten Wijngaarde, founded in 1245. The convent incorporates elements of every architectural style, starting with Gothic and working forward. Right next to the entrance gate, one of the little cottages is set up as a museum.

The women of the convent are not Beguines, but Benedictine nuns. The order of the Beguines was founded in the 13th century, to give unmarried or abandoned woman a chance to join a respectable and secure society without having to take the strict holy vows of a monastic order. Although their life was far from comfortable, the Beguines were allowed priviliges not granted to *bona fide* nuns – they were, for example,

allowed to have personal property. Traditionally, members of the order devoted themselves to the care of the sick, or earned their bread by making lace; the Benedictine nuns who live here today prepare and maintain the costumes for the participants in the annual Holy Blood procession – all 2,000 of them.

There are few places in Flanders which radiate such an aura of peace as the Beguine Convent in Bruges. Concealed behind white walls, the small houses are arranged over a broad expanse of greensward dotted with poplars. When the bells of **St Elisabeth's** ring out in the morning and evening, the small doors of the cottages open and the black-clad Benedictine sisters scurry over the grass toward the church.

The Beguine Convent lies in the area where lace-making, the most famous craft of Bruges, is still practiced. On warm days, you can see old women and young girls sitting in the alleyways around the Beguine Convent, their fingers deftly working the fine threads.

You can buy "Kanten", the fine lace of Bruges, virtually anywhere in the city. For those especially interested in lace, there's a **Lace Centre** in Baalstraat, open every afternoon.

Wandering around the streets and alleyways north of the market, you stumble over the past at literally every turn; in the Middle Ages some 35 European cities, countries and republics had business outlets and embassies in Golden Bruges, as it was known in Europe. Spanjardstraat leads to the oldest bridge in the city; there, one sees the Spaanse Looskai, the Oosterlingeplein and the Natiehaus (Nation House) of Genoa. Today, this last building is known as the "Saeyhall" after the serge fabric once traded here. The headquarters of the Florentines were located at the corner of Vlamingstraat and Academiestraat; the Venetian residence was a little further along the street.

Between the Florentines and the Genoese lies a particularly handsome Gothic house, now home to the Bank of Roselare and Westvlaanderen. In 1257, this building belonged to a family of prosperous brokers named Ter Beurse. The businessmen of the city used to meet each other in front of the house, to negotiate their business in the open air; they called this "going Ter Beurse", to the Bourse. "Bourse" (and variations thereupon) is the word for stock exchange in many European languages; most of the people who use this word are no more aware than those of us who use the word "exchange" that such a vital part of international economic life originated in Bruges.

A few steps down the Academiestraat, you'll find the **Poorterslogie**, the Porters' Club, which was a meeting place for the well-to-do citizenry in the 14th century. The white bear which you can see on the facade outside is the emblem of a jousting club, which used to hold its tourneys in the marketplace.

Diagonally opposite this building is the old **Customs House**, one of the most beautiful and most richly

As if time h stood still: medieval Bruges viewed fro▶ the Bell Tower.

ornamented Gothic buildings of Bruges. Next to this, the **Ghent Courtyard** contains a memorial to the painter Jan van Eyck; a similar memorial to Hans Memling can be seen in the nearby **Woendsdagsmarkt**.

Only two important buildings in Bruges fell victim to the troops of the French Revolution. One of these was the cathedral of St Donatus, which stood in Burg Square; all that remains of it today is an outline on the pavement. The other was called Prinsenhof, the residence of the Dukes of Burgundy. Remnants of its walls were incorporated into the building of what is today an old people's home.

Before you leave the medieval city of Bruges, drive along the Reie on the Ring Street which runs around the city, and look at the medieval city gates: the **Gentpoort**, the **Kruispoort**, the **Ezelpoort** and the **Smedepoort**. And don't forget to visit the wonderful old **windmill** which rises above the Kruisvest.

There's only one way to take your leave of a city whose past greatness was based on overseas trade: go out by the **Canal Road**, which leads you beneath the poplars along the Bruges-Sluis Canal towards **Damme**.

If you're lucky, you'll be able to get a seat on one of the small launches which run along the canal between Bruges and Damme. Or you could rent a *fiets* (bicycle) and ride along the canal, lined with fishermen and windmills. It's only a few miles to Damme, an enchanting, sleepy town where time has stood still ever since the ship-bearing, life-giving Zwin silted up.

Damme has one of the most beautiful marketplaces of Flanders. It is dominated by the late Gothic **town hall**, which, although simpler than the one in Bruges, can still be counted as one of the most impressive Gothic town halls in Flanders. It is a telling memorial to the city's glorious past. The statues in the niches of its facade are of the great figures of Flanders and Burgundy: Philip of Alsace, the founder of the city;

Johanna and Margarete of Constantinople and Charles the Bold. The quality of the sculpting is superb. The tenderness of Charles the Bold as he offers the graciously smiling Margaret of York a wedding ring in his outstretched right hand is movingly captured. The wedding of this noble couple took place in the town in 1468, in the house of the ducal administrator, Eustaas Wyts, which is still extant. The interior of the town hall contains a museum of the city's history. On the other side of the street, you can see the oldest house in the city: **De grote Sterre**, a charming brick house with two gables, of a kind one seldom sees in Flanders. Built at the beginning of the 15th century, it now houses the **Ulenspiegel Museum**.

The misreading of a phrase carved in stone at the entrance to the church of Our Lady was responsible for the mistaken 17th-century belief that the well-known fool Tyl Ulenspiegel was born or buried in the Flemish town of Damme. The story of Ulenspiegel, who in fact came from Kneitlingen in Saxony and who is buried in Mölln, was then a best-seller in the Netherlands, so the figure of Tyl Ulenspiegel was thoroughly familiar to the citizens of Damme. The belief that the man on whom the character Tyl Ulenspiegel was based actually came from Damme was so widely held that the Flemish poet de Coster even mentioned it in his famous epic novel *Thyl Ulenspiegel and Lamme Goedzack*, an error which lent further credibility to this piece of misinformation.

Guided by nuns: Diagonally opposite the Ulenspiegel Museum is **St Jan's Hospitaal**, which was founded in the 13th century by Margarete of Constantinople. To gain access to this building, which has been converted into a museum, pull the bellrope by the entrance and wait. The sound of shuffling footsteps will announce the approach of a nun, who will silently accompany you on a tour of the museum. It houses a collection of old furniture, documents, and sacred objects.

Touring the canals by boat is a popular excursion visitors to Bruges.

If a prize were awarded to the city which has best preserved its medieval appearance, Damme would be one of the hardest to beat, above all because of its exquisite **Marketplace**. Upon this square stands a statue of Jakob van Maerlant, a 13th-century writer who was the first author to write in Dutch, and who has been dubbed the Father of Dutch poetry. The marketplace is lined by restaurants of all kinds, offering all manner of Flemish culinary delicacies. The Flemish have always known how to eat well, a trait that has been admirably illustrated by the still-lifes of the region's artists, from Pieter Breughel to Felix Timmermanns.

If you go from Damme to the coast, you'll come upon the Boudewijnkanal. From there, take the road through **Lissewege**, which is one of the most beautiful Flemish villages. Located virtually in the shadow of the towers of Bruges, Lissewege seems to embody the adjective "meditative". The town lies among broad fields of cultivated land, dominated by the Gothic church of Our Lady. This church deserves mention as one of the great Gothic brick churches of what used to be the Netherlands (the term Netherlands denoting the entire linguistic and cultural area of the Low Countries).

A few minutes distant from the church lie the remains of the monastery **Ter Doest**, which flourished in the Middle Ages. All that is left of it are the enormous buildings which were used to store tithes, in which, so it is said, one could store the grain harvest from 100 acres of farmland. Today, this impressive edifice, with the noteworthy oak timberwork in its interior, looks just as it did when it was built in the year 1275.

One inhabitant of this former monastery was a monk called Willem van Saeftelinght who, returning to Ter Doest after an absence of several days, informed the abbot that he had just taken part in the Battle of the Golden Spurs and had single-handedly killed 20 or more French knights.

ing the of day by amme 4.

FRANS VAN IMMERSEEL
TILL "SLA DE KRIJGSTROM"

ULENSPIEGEL IN DAMME

Tyl Ulenspiegel is one of the most famous characters in northern European story-telling. He is the rogue who takes everything anyone says literally; the scamp who plays pranks on all and sundry. He is the character who tries to teach a donkey how to read and begins the lesson with "E and AW"; he is the joker who throws the baker's flour into the moonlight instead of into the sieve; he is the quack doctor, who can cure his patients through pure fear, without using medicine at all. This rascal's adventures have been appearing in books all over Germany, Holland and Belgium since the early 16th century.

Virtually omnipresent Ulenspiegel is at home everywhere; and he is, by a corollary, never really at home in any one place. Some stories claim that the original Ulenspiegel was born in Kneitlingen, on the Elm river in Saxony, and died in the city of Mölln in Germany, but such details have little to do with the facts and several other cities claim him as their own. The only fact that is known for sure is that the original flesh-and-blood Tyl Ulenspiegel upon whom all the stories are based lived some time in the 14th century. His name has been associated with legends and unlikely anecdotes ever since.

Freedom fighter: But *The Legend of Tyl Ulenspiegel,* published in 1866 (translated in 1918) by the Flemish author Charles de Coster (1827–79) elevated Ulenspiegel to an entirely different plane. De Coster took the well-known stories of the country's most famous folk character and gave them a new, heroic dimension. He depicted the trickster as a Belgian freedom fighter, a valiant hero of the bloodiest epoch in Flemish history. De Coster's story opens with the words: "In Damme in Flanders, as the May moon opened the flowers of the hawthorn, Ulenspiegel, the son of Claes, was born." The book is an heroic epic in which history and legend are interwoven.

De Coster's purpose in the book was to inspire confidence and national pride in the Belgian people. The Belgian declaration of independence had taken place scarcely 40 years before, in October, 1830, bringing with it the clear need for national regeneration.

The political reorientation of a folk hero proved an extremely popular device among the Belgian people. Tyl Ulenspiegel was torn from the timeless, episodic realm of the folk tale and given a specific birthplace and an exact date of birth: 1527, the same year as King Philip, Infante of Spain, the son of Charles V.

De Coster wasted no time in conveying his political purpose in the book. "Two children have been born," prophesies the good witch Katheline near the start; "one in Spain, Philip, the Infante; and the other one in Flanders, the son of Claes, who will later be known as Ulenspiegel." As soon becomes evident, the former is destined to become the executioner of the country; the other, its liberator.

Medieval setting: The city of Damme flourished in the Middle Ages as a harbour of Bruges. The city lay on the Zwin, at the end of an inlet of the sea, and was situated on a dyke – the "dam" from which it took its name. With a city charter and trade rights and basking in the reflected splendour of Bruges, the city continued to flourish and when Philip-Augustus, the King of France, had Damme burned to the ground in 1213, it was quickly rebuilt, lovelier than ever. However, by 1527 the town had passed its prime. When the Zwin became clogged with sand, the harbour choked to death and the city's fortunes foundered.

Relegated to a backwater, Damme changed little over the centuries. Visitors entering the town today are always delighted by its unspoilt character. The marketplace is still dominated by the beautiful town hall with its stepped gables and the old warehouse where the goods that were traded in the city were stored. Pretty fishermen's houses, the imposing buildings of merchants, and the stately St Jan's Hospital add to the city's architectural charm.

Towering high above it all is the church of Our Lady. In the wake of the city's decline, parts of this church have been dismantled over the years, but it remains huge. The church tower, which has been without a steeple since 1725, is 45 metres (147 ft) in height. A narrow staircase, with hairpin turns and 206 steps, leads to the top of the tower and a magnificent view over Damme, reaching as far as the eye can see: on the one side, from Knocke-Heist to Bruges; on the other, over 10,000 hectares (25,000 acres) of Damme land.

From here, the city looks like a seven-pointed star stretched over the earth. The canals with their attractive borders of poplars are a century younger than the rest of Damme; but the city was always fortified. Today, the fortifications chiefly serve as an abode for bats.

Damme was a fitting place for Coster's Tyl Ulenspiegel to grow up in; in the book, he plays all manner of crude pranks on its citizens, "creating all kinds of nonsense with all his heart and soul," as Katheline observes. Meanwhile, as the tale repeatedly reminds readers, in Spain there was a child who never laughed. If anything at all amused this Spanish infante, it was cruelty.

De Coster's Ulenspiegel is driven out of his homeland for heresy. For three years he wanders through the country, playing his well-known tricks on his fellow countrymen, just like his counterpart in the folk tales. But this Ulenspiegel has a serious side to his character, a political consciousness which gathers strength as his journey progresses and he sees more and more evidence of social injustice. Above all, he is horrified by the senselessness of religious conflict. "Pikes with heads on them; young girls stuck in sacks and thrown alive into rivers; men, naked, broken on a wheel or beaten with iron rods." But, continues De Coster, "the confessors of all these deeds had so regretted them beforehand that they pocketed 12 kreuzers for each act" – in other words, the clergy were making a tidy profit out of the perpetrators' confessions. When Ulenspiegel finally returns to his home in Damme, he learns the ultimate horror – that Claes, his father, has been burned at the stake in front of the town hall.

Charles de Coster's evocation of the countryside and villages in the tale is extremely vivid; reading this adventure story, readers have the sense that they, too, are travelling through 16th-century Flanders, guidebook in hand. The language in which the book is written – an archaic, artificial-sounding Old French – is another device used to great effect by the author; the tale thus resounds with echoes of the past, as if it had been handed down from a more exciting, dangerous age.

Enraged by his father's murder, Ulenspiegel decides to dedicate his life

The great Tyl: an illustration for De Coster's novel by Félicien Rops.

to political change. De Coster sets at his side a Sancho Panza-like friend, Lamme Goedzak, gentle as a lamb and a committed Epicurean. "Don't you know," he tells Ulenspiegel, "that our soul, which you say is the breath of life, needs, in order to breathe, beans, beef, beer, wine, ham, sausage, pickle, and plenty of rest."

The good witch Katheline's opening prophesies assign allegorical roles to all the book's characters: "Claes is your valiance, you noble people of Flanders, Soetkin is your brave mother, Ulenspiegel your spirit; a fine lovely maiden, Ulenspiegel's lady love, immortal as he, will be your heart; and a mighty glutton, Lamme Goedzak, will give you your stomach."

The "fine lovely maiden" is Nele, Katheline's daughter, Ulenspiegel's beloved. The young couple travel together through war-torn Flanders, looking for the "Seven" and the "Magic Belt". The "Seven" in the book are the new virtues which will take the place of the old vices; the number is also a reference to the northern "Seven Provinces", the once-united Low Countries, whose declaration of independence in 1579 was the beginning of war with Spain. The magic belt is a symbol of the unity which both Ulenspiegel and de Coster sought to achieve.

A national epic: Despite the book's initial popularity, when de Coster died in 1879 he was quickly forgotten by the Belgian people and by 1892 it was difficult even to locate the author's grave. It was only after the tribulations of World War I that the novel came to be truly appreciated. Today, Flanders celebrates Charles de Coster as much as Ulenspiegel himself.

Two memorials in Damme pay tribute to the pair: in the churchyard is a monument to Tyl; and near the water, on the Speystraat, you will find a sculpture of Ulenspiegel characters (erected in 1979 on the 100th anniversary of de Coster's death). In the house called Die Groote Sterre (the Big Star) there is a museum dedicated to Ulenspiegel, where you can see translations of the book in Hebrew and Chinese.

Other, less formal, memorials to the epic tale have materialised over the past few years. Steamers on the canal bear the name *Lamme Goedzak*; Bij Lamme Goedzak is a restaurant on Kirkstraat, not far from Ulenkotje and from the Bistro Soetkin, which offers a "Menu Prestige van Lamme Goedzak". You can buy delicious Ulenspiegel marzipan and gâteaux in the pastry-shops of Damme. The restaurant In de drie Zilveren Kannen, which bears the Ulenspiegel coat of arms, offers a special dinner which is called "Festival d'Ulenspiegel".

"When," asks Lamme in the novel, "is that longed-for peace ever going to come, so that a man can roast a partridge without being bothered, so that he can fricassee his chickens and let his sausages sing in the pan with his frying eggs?" As any modern-day visitor to Damme can testify, that time has most definitely come.

said that
spiegel
ed on his
ks and
his fight
amme.

WEST AND EAST FLANDERS

A soldier said to an old lady: "So when we got to Wipers…"

"*Ypres*," said the old lady.

The soldier resumed: "So when we got to Wipers…"

"Ypres," said the old lady.

The soldier heaved a sigh and began again: "So when we got to Wipers…"

"*Ypres*," said the old lady.

"Cor," said the soldier, "you aint't 'arf got 'iccups."

This anecdote, repeated in James Agate's *Ego 7,* is one of the lighter stories that came out of this region during World War II. More usually, the name is associated with total devastation. Flanders was central to the bitter trench warfare of World War I and was heavily bombed during World War II. Nevertheless, it has emerged as a prosperous region of modern Belgium.

Early history: The land between the city of Bruges and the coastal town of Het Zoute was formed less than a millennia ago. In the Middle Ages the waves of the North Sea splashed in the inlet of Zwin and the waters reached to the city gates of Bruges. Sailing ships floated where today low whitewashed farmhouses nestle under their red roofs.

The inlet had been created by a terrible storm in the 5th century. But what the ocean gave, it was gradually to take away by depositing increasing quantities of sand. Eventually the Zwin silted up altogether.

However, the salt marshes hereabouts still acknowledges the area's aquatic past. Formerly an upmarket resort, **Het Zwin**, lying on the edge of Knokke, Belgium's most cosmopolitan seaside town, is now best known for its reserve for waterfowl and saltwater flora.

An imaginatively arranged complex of aviaries, open-air enclosures and specially constructed water sites enable visitors to examine a multitude of waterfowl at close range. Children in par-ticular enjoy the reserve's amenities. Visitors can stroll along the dyke and survey the breeding-grounds of thousands of resident and visiting birds, some of which are extremely rare, or walk along the narrow paths through the salt marshes, where sheep graze and geese waddle about fearlessly. Guided tours of the reserve are given every Thursday and Saturday between Easter and the end of September.

Zwin belongs to the municipality of **Knokke-Heist**, located on the Belgian seacoast. This coast, over 70 km (40 miles) long, contains Belgium's best loved family resorts. There are plenty of opportunities for safe bathing and sandcastle building (the two gaming casinos in Knokke and Ostend lure those interested in more adult pursuits). This fact is reflected in the great efforts that are made to cater to children's needs: hotel staff are pleased to set up children's beds in their parents' rooms free of charge and go to great lengths to provide baby-sitting services and spe-

*, Het
1, a
derful
re
serve
Knokke.
t, the
ument to
founder
e
in",
nt Léon
ens
1–
6).*

cial entertainment. The 15 towns between Het Zoute and De Panne, west and east of Ostend, comprise a holiday zone which is far better known and more popular than size alone would seem to indicate.

The posh resort: Knokke and its suburbs Heist and Het Zoute is the epitome of an elegant, well-kept resort nestling in the dunes. Nearly 12 km (8 miles) long, the beach here bears no traces of the massive hotels and high-rise apartments which mar so many seafronts. Strict zoning regulations forbid any building to be higher than two storeys, so the sun falls evenly everywhere along the beach.

Knokke has always been a resort for guests with high expectations (and incomes); located near the Belgian-Dutch border, it's the number one bathing resort in Belgium today. Nowhere else in the country, not even in Brussels, are the shops so exclusive: many of the boutiques are branches of world-famous designer stores.

With its casino, international exhibitions of modern sculpture, annual *Cartoonale*, an exhibition of caricatures from around the world, and its cosmopolitan beach life, Knokke is up among the most renowned, most elegant beach resorts in Europe, on a par with Deauville or Biarritz. The attractions of Knokke are rounded off by its 18-hole golf course set among the dunes; it is considered to be one of the most beautiful golf courses in Europe.

Things are less pretentious, quieter, more family oriented in the beach resorts lying to the west of Knokke, such as **Heist**, a suburb of Knokke, **Duinbergen**, and **Zeebrugge**. But however peaceful Zeebrugge seems to be as a bathing resort, it's busy in its function as a harbour. It's the second largest fishing town in Belgium and consequently an excellent place to eat freshly caught fish (try any one of the little restaurants clustered around the harbour). Visitors to Zeebrugge can also take a special kind of walk out to sea by strolling along

A dash of colour.

the harbour breakwater; this extends for more than one-and-a-half miles into the North Sea.

Zeebrugge is becoming increasingly important as a port for ferries to and from Dover, Felixstowe and Hull. The town shot to international fame in 1987 when a British-owned ferry, the *Herald of Free Enterprise*, sailing towards Dover, sank in Zeebrugge's harbour, still within sight of the coast – the bow doors of the ferry had not been closed properly on departure. More than 150 people perished in the disaster.

Blankenberge is a more traditional bathing spot, which is today known as the Festival Bathing Resort. The most important festivals held here are the Carnival in February, the Harbour Festival in June, the Ocean Festival in July and the large, bright Flower Parade in August. These festivals, like nearly all festivals in Belgium, are rooted in ancient traditions. One of the largest festivals is held on Whit Monday in nearby **Wenduine**; an integral part of the event is a special blessing invoked for all those whose livelihoods are connected with the sea.

For a quiet, elegant beach resort with a residential air visit **De Haan**. The dunes of nearby **Vosseslag** have been incorporated into a splendid 18-hole golf course. These forested dunes are the pride and joy of foresters, who have managed to persuade the sand to support plant life. The little train which goes along the Belgian coast, the Dune train, stops in De Haan at one of the most enchanting art nouveau railway stations in Europe.

With its 28 campsites, **Bredene** is a coastal paradise for camping and caravan enthusiasts. In addition, there are many fine hotels dating from the turn of the century.

At the other side of the inlet is **Ostend**, situated right in the middle of Belgium's coast. The city suffered greatly as part of the Spanish Netherlands in the 17th century. It valiantly tried to hold out against the Spanish and won the admi-

ding the
s at Het
1.

ration of Protestants all over Europe. One siege lasted from 5 July 1601 to 15 September 1604. Some 70,000 people lost their lives before the city was eventually stormed.

William Beckford, an 18th-century English visitor to Ostend, expressed his dislike for the place in no uncertain terms: "Were I to remain ten days in Ostend I should scarcely have one delightful vision; 'tis so unclassic a place! Nothing but preposterous Flemish roofs disgust your eyes when you cast them upwards: swaggering Dutchmen and mungrel (*sic*) barbers are the first objects they meet with below."

By the 19th century Ostend was being called the "Queen of the Belgian Coast". Both Leopold I and Leopold II endeavoured to turn the former village into a presentable bathing and health resort for the upper classes of 19th-century Europe.

Ostend is perhaps no longer Belgium's most stylish bathing resort, but it still has a fine sandy beach; the international

jetset, or those who would like to be thought of as such, continue to meet in the elegant gaming casino and the spa. The carnival festivities held in the Ostend casino are some of the most spectacular to be held in any part of Belgium.

Art connoisseurs will know Ostend as the abode and workplace of the painter and engraver **James Sydney Ensor**. He was born in Ostend of Anglo-Belgian parentage in 1860, and died here in 1949. Although he trained at the Brussels Academy he rarely left Ostend and was neglected by the art world for much of his life. His imaginative, often macabre, carnival paintings of fighting skeletons and masked revellers have led to his being described as the heir of Hieronymus Bosch and Pieter Breughel and a precursor of Expressionism. His fiercest work was probably his *Entry of Christ into Brussels* (1888).

The artist's first home, Vlaanderenstraat 27, has been turned into a museum dedicated to the artist. The paintings on its walls are not originals; anyone interested in seeing the real thing should visit the **Museum of Fine Arts** in Ostend.

Sailing museum: Ostend has a long maritime history. Today it is the most important port for ferries to and from England. Children, and anyone else interested in sailing ships, will probably go aboard the *Mercator*. Once the ship for the sailing school of the Belgian merchant marine, it now lies at anchor in the harbour of Ostend, and is open to visitors as a floating museum of ships and sailing. Another draw for children is the **North Sea Aquarium**, located in the former auction rooms of the crab fishermen on Visserskai.

The Royal Villa: This villa is famous far beyond the borders of Flanders. It was originally built on the dike as a summer residence for Leopold II and commanded an unparalleled view of the beach and the sea. It was destroyed in World War II, but subbsequently rebuilt by the city.

The royal couple, however, preferred to holiday in Spain, so the former summer residence of kings was rented out.

Cooling th toes in the briny.

Today the building has been converted into a hotel and one of the most famous restaurants in Belgium, Au Vigneron, famous for its gourmet fish and shell-fish dishes. It is said that Leopold II, by all accounts an amorous man, had a tunnel built between the palace and the city so that he could conduct his various affairs undetected.

The neighbouring towns of **Westende** and **Lombardsijde** are known for their folk markets and shrimp fishing, for rustic farm festivals and antique markets; **Nieuwpoort** (Nieuport), on the other hand, is a renowned centre for sailors and sailing craft. Its modern European marina has berths for 2,600 boats. The harbour restaurants are well known for their excellent fish. The **Fish Market**, held early every morning after the boats return, is an experience worth catching. Even if you don't understand a word of what the auctioneers are shouting, you are bound to enjoy all the bustle and excitement.

Ostduinkerke has preserved a unique

Belgian tradition: "crab-fishing on horseback". What's special about this event is that it is an integral part of the lives of the crab fishermen and not something merely laid on for the tourists. Clad in oilcloth and sou'westers, the fishermen mount their heavy Belgian horses and ride out into the sea to snare crabs and shrimp in their trawling nets, just as they have been doing for centuries. When the weather is fine, spectators – young and old alike – follow them into the water.

In Nieuwpoort, a visit to the **National Belgian Fishing Museum** is an absolute must. This museum presents the visitor with a summary of the development of fishing on the North Sea coast from 700 BC to the present day. **Koksijde's** main sight-seeing attraction is **St-Idesbald**, better known as the Dune Monastery. In the 12th century, St Idesbald was the most important monastery in Flanders. But the monks who founded it had not reckoned on the destructive force of the shifting dunes.

ndy day
nokke.

Eventually the encroaching sands proved invincible and the monastery was buried. St Idesbald was rebuilt, but again the sand destroyed everything and the monks were obliged to move away from St Idesbald. Today, the dunes have been cleared from a section of the ruins and are restrained by a protective wall. The museum displays artefacts which have been rescued from the sand.

The claim that one can swim in the North Sea and then, half an hour later, wander through the dunes of the Sahara may seem a bit far-fetched, even in this jet-age, but in fact it's perfectly possible in **De Panne** (La Panne), Belgium's westernmost beach resort, right on the French border. The largest dune area in Belgium, located just behind the last apartment houses of De Panne, has been called Sahara for as long as anyone can remember. So wild and wide are these sand dunes that numerous cinema directors have used them as a location for desert scenes.

On 17 June, 1831, Belgium's first king, Leopold I, who had been living in England, set foot on his kingdom for the first time in De Panne. Today, this beach is a paradise for beach sailors, whose narrow, wind-powered carts reach speeds of no less than 75 miles an hour as they zoom over the broad, firm sands. About 2 miles (3 km) away lies the town of **Adinkerke** with its well-known amusement park, **Meli**.

Blood-drenched Flanders: De Panne's Sahara is part of a large wildlife preserve called **Westhoek**. This name, which roughly translates as "Western corner", has come to denote the entire western part of the province, the area along the French border. No other area in the country of Belgium, today so peaceful and quiet with its canals and bell towers, its windmills and grazing cows, is as drenched in blood as this one. Westhoek was the most horrible battleground of World War I. Tens of thousands of young men from England, Germany, France, Canada and Australia met their deaths here.

Hibiscus blossom i **Knokke's** **butterfly** **garden.**

Even so long after the event, places such as Ypres and Langemark evoke strong emotions, and not just among the dwindling number of old soldiers who come to relive old memories and pay tribute to their dead comrades. It is not possible to hike through the woods and countryside at Kemmelberg as light-heartedly as in the Ardennes.

Even today, 75 years after the atrocities of the war, it is hard to "enjoy" Flanders' fields. Watching the farmers of Poperinge harvesting hops, admiring the stately farmhouses, encountering trucks laden with sugar beets in the autumn, or seeing the newly-built, almost artificial looking facades in the marketplace at Diksmuide, you might be lulled into thinking the area much like any other in Belgium – until you see children playing in the abandoned trenches and sheep chewing their cud in tumble-down bunkers.

The past begins to take over as soon as you come to the city limits of **Ypres** (Jprès/Jeper). From a distance, the

Menin Gate looks like a Roman triumphal arch. In fact, it is a memorial arch to the 54,896 soldiers who were listed as missing in action after the battle of Ypres. Some 150 British cemeteries in and around the city are testimony to the bitter, four-year-long struggle for the contested city of Ypres and the devastating English losses.

Contemplating the staggering death toll as one surveys the rows of graves, one is inevitably reminded of the words of Rupert Brooke: "If I should die, think only this of me:/ That there's some corner of a foreign field / That is for ever England. There shall be / In that rich earth a richer dust concealed, / A dust whom England bore, shaped, made aware… A body of England's, breathing English air, / Washed by the rivers, blest by suns of home". Brooke himself was killed in action on his way to the Dardanelles in 1915; he was 28.

Today, Ypres is an attractive city with a picturesque **marketplace**, a **Bell Tower**, and a **Weavers' Hall** to attract

for the

the visitor. Ypres was, along with Bruges and Ghent, among the most important Flemish weaving centres of Europe's Middle Ages.

One part of the 13th-century Weavers' Hall is given over to a museum of World War I. None of what you see is original medieval architecture. When the war was over, not one stone of Ypres was left standing. The city was a wasteland, a field of death; it was the Stalingrad or Hiroshima of World War I. The memory of the worst four years in the history of the little city is kept alive still: every night a policeman stops traffic before the Menin Gate at 8 p.m. and four men on the street perform the bugle call of the last post.

Height 62 near Ypres bears the great memorial for the fallen soldiers of Canada. The Canadian front line ran along here in 1916. Between this elevation and the nearby English cemetery you can find the **Sanctuary Wood Museum**, one of the many museums dedicated to the war. It contains various relics, including bayonets, shells, rifles and bully cans. Some critics are unhappy about the way war and death have been exploited by the tourist industry; for example, in front of the small Café Sanctuary Wood, where British, Australian, and Canadian flags wave, you can buy souvenir grenade shells, steel helmets and bayonets. Inevitably the relationship between war memorial and tourist attraction is an uneasy one.

A pretty face: Passing through an apparently peaceful landscape, which a painting by Breughel couldn't have made prettier, you come to the village of **Langemark**. From a distance, it looks like any other Flemish village, but in fact this was the battlefield where tens of thousands of young Germans were killed between 1914 and 1915. The German cemetery bears the inscription which was the battle-cry of so many of these young soldiers: "Germany must live, even if we have to die for it." Commonly known as the Students' Cemetery, it holds the bodies of 44,294

A storm gathers ov the Blankenbe pier.

206

fallen Germans, 25,000 of them in a mass grave. The cemetery of **Vladslo** contains another 20,000 German graves; at the edge of this graveyard you can see one of the most powerful anti-war sculptures in existence, *Grieving Parents*, by the German graphic artist and sculptor Käthe Kollwitz, whose own son Peter lies in Vladslo. The small cemetery in **Hoogleda** contains 8,247 fallen Germans, the large one in **Menin**, 47,864. Altogether, over 210,000 Germans met their deaths in Flanders.

On the once infamous **Height 60**, near Zillebecke, there's a monument at the edge of the road to the fallen Australians. Behind this is a plot of fenced-in land. A few sheep roam among rabbits darting to and from their holes. This field, many acres in area, was created entirely by bombs. Shell crater by shell crater, every cubic centimetre of land here was torn up by exploding shells. Here and there you can see the remains of bunkers, torn apart by the grenades. The front of the British cemetery **Tyne Cot** is almost a mile long. Altogether, 11,856 soldiers are buried here; only some of the 11,856 headstones, arranged in seemingly endless rows, are inscribed with a name; others simply bear the words: "A soldier of the Great War known unto God". The names of the missing – 34,959 of them – are carved upon the surrounding wall.

The drive along the winding roads of the so-called Flemish Ardennes to **Kemmelberg** is a pleasure, especially in autumn. Kemmelberg itself was an important strategic site in the Great War. It was captured by Bavarian mountain hunters in August, 1918, and held for a total of four days.

Today, the crest of the hill is occupied by one of the best restaurants in Flanders (in the woods a little way from the road), which enjoys spectacular views of the Flemish hop-growing country below. Only 100 metres away, a large monument commemorates the many French soldiers who died at Kemmelberg and who were buried in the cemetery at

ermen in brugge.

the foot of the hill. There are cemeteries everywhere. Their crosses and headstones are as much a part of the landscape of Westhoek as the 6-metre (18-ft) high hop trellises, whose cover helped the little town of Poperinge to escape the death and destruction of neighbouring villages.

Poperinge is a pretty little town with a tranquil **marketplace** which, unusually for towns and villages hereabouts, is the original, old square. One of the village's oldest houses is the **Talbot House** of the British Army. Today this house provides accommodation for a modest charge to any British citizen who travels to Flanders to visit the graves of relations or former comrades.

The Hops Route: The three churches of Poperinge are every bit as worthy of note as the **Belgian Hops Museum**. Poperinge lies in the middle of an extensive hop-growing area. The town's annual **Hops Festival** takes place on the first Sunday in September. A leisurely drive along the **Hops Route**, through the hop fields, is definitely worthwhile, particularly in summer.

Veurne on the river IJzer is another town that was largely spared in World War I. The little town lies on reclaimed land, some 4 metres (13 ft) below sea level. It is associated with the period in history when Flanders was ruled by the Spanish line of the House of Habsburg, for Veurne served as headquarters of the Spanish officers. The **Old Landhouse**, the **Bell Tower**, the rebuilt **Meat Market** and the **church of St Walburga** in the town centre are worth a quick stop, but the town which served as the Belgian Army Headquarters in 1914–15 and was the provisional residence of the king, has more to offer. Of special note are the so-called **New Town Hall** on the picturesque **marketplace**, built in the 16th century, containing priceless leather wall-coverings of Spanish origin, and the 16th-century inn called **Nobele Roze**, where the Austrian lyric poet Rainer Maria Rilke once stayed.

The city's old town hall, which quartered Spanish officers, is known as the **Spanish Pavilion**. The 17th-century **Hoge Wacht** at the edge of the marketplace also housed Spaniards for a time. Veurne's best-known folk festival, the **Atonement Procession** on the last Sunday in July, hearkens back to Spanish austerity with its cross-bearing participants shrouded in dark hoods and robes.

It's not only Route 14–18 that allows access to the battlefields of Flanders; you can also visit them by boat from Nieuwpoort. Boats sail along the IJzer to Diksmuide. The name of this river was given to one of the war's most terrible battles.

Diksmuide, like Ypres, had to be completely rebuilt after 1918 and it was decided to reconstruct the original village as faithfully as possible. Unfortunately this has resulted in something of a stage-set atmosphere; the houses, facades and gables, the **town hall**, the copy of the 13th-century **Beguine Convent** with its idyllic nooks and crannies were all built in the 20th century.

Fishing for shrimps.

208

Less beautiful, but impossible to overlook, is the **Cross of Diksmuide** which commemorates the Battle of IJzer, and its museum of the battle. The cross-shaped building affords a broad view of the countryside around the IJzer, which was flooded in 1914 when the dikes were opened. This was done to prevent, or at least hinder, the invasion of German troops.

Flemish against French: Flanders has always been a contested land. Yet again it was a battle – albeit a much more ancient one – which thrust **Kortrijk** (Courtrai), in the south of West Flanders, to fame: the Battle of the Golden Spurs in 1302. Against all the odd, the Flemish weavers, armed with only spears and catapults, managed a resounding victory over French knights, who were armed to the teeth. One of their most cunning battle tactics was to disguise an expanse of marshy ground outside the town with brushwood. The French, anticipating an easy victory over their amateur opponents, failed to take due precautions and fell into the swampy mud. The triumphant Flemish took more than 600 golden spurs from the fallen French, and preserved them in the **church of Our Lady**, which dates from the 12th century. Unfortunately, these spurs are no longer to be seen; but the church does contain a terrific *Descent from the Cross* by van Dyck.

There are several paintings from the Rubens school in **St Martin's church** in Kortrijk. Although it contains many beautiful old buildings and was ranked as one of the great cloth producers of medieval Flanders, this town does not endeavour to present quite the same image of an old Flemish city as Bruges, Ghent or Ypres. On the Grote Markt you'll find the **Bell Tower**, or as much as remains of it today. The statues on the facade of the high Gothic **town hall** next door to the Bell Tower are of the Counts of Flanders – introduced when the building was renovated in 1962. There's a **Municipal Museum of Fine Art** in one of the city's most lovely

patrician homes. It contains many fine examples of lace and damask, some 18th-century Delftware and paintings by Roelandt Savery. Nearby are the **Broel Towers**, remnants of the medieval city's fortifications.

However, the most noteworthy sight in Kortrijk is the **Belgian Flax Museum**. Even today, flax continues to be produced in large quantities in the area surrounding Kortrijk.

Another enchanting sight is the **Beguine Convent**, the largest of its kind in Belgium. Forty little cottages form a small "town within a town". Its picturesque streets afford a wealth of fascinating insights into this self-chosen world of seclusion and solitude. The Beguine Convent was founded in 1241 by Joanna of Constantinople.

On your way to Ghent, it's worth while making a short stop in the small town of **Oudenaarde** (Audenarde). In the Middle Ages the town on the upper Scheldt was renowned for two things: for its masons, who worked on the con-

struction of many famous Flemish buildings, such as the Town Hall in Bruges; and for its tapestry-makers, the weavers who created the beautiful and world-renowned wall tapestries.

The **Town Hall** on the Grote Markt is an ornate edifice in the style of Brabant Gothic, built in the 16th century. In the **Weavers' Hall,** which dates from the 13th century, you can visit the **Museum of Oudenaarde Tapestries**. Other noteworthy sights are the **church of Our Lady of Pamele**, the **church of St Walburga**, the **Beguine Convent** and the **Our Lady Hospital**.

Perhaps it's not merely by chance that the Emperor Charles V is depicted so often in Oudenaarde, above all in the public room of the town hall. As a young man, the monarch had a love affair with a middle-class girl from the town named Joanna van der Gheynst. Joanna bore a daughter on 7 July 1522, and had her baptised Margaret. The illegitimate daughter of the mighty man played an important role in the history

A haven of tranquillit the Begui Convent a Kortrijk.

of Flanders and the Netherlands under the name of Margaret of Parma. In her role as regent of the Low Countries under her half-brother Philip II, Margaret proved herself an able politician.

Ghent (Gand) is the capital of the province of East Flanders and has a population of 250,000. For centuries it has been the focal point of the Flemish nationality. As is the case with other major Flemish cities, Ghent owes its historical importance to the cloth trade. The city flourished during the Middle Ages, and there was even a period, around the turn of the 14th century, when it was the second largest city north of the Alps, after Paris. Today it is the third largest industrial region in Belgium and the country's second largest port; its harbour is connected to the North Sea by canal. The city's economy revolves around the chemical, steel and automobile industries, as well as publishing and banking.

Many visitors have likened the city to Venice. One of the first was the diarist John Evelyn; in 1641 he records: "The Ley and the scheld meeting in this vast Citty divide it into 26 Ilands which are united togethere by many bridges somewhat resembling Venice." Thackeray noted this common comparison – rather more damningly – in his impression of the city, recorded in 1844: "Ghent has, I believe, been called a vulgar Venice. It contains dirty canals and old houses that must satisfy the most eager antiquary, though the buildings are not in quite so good preservation as others that may be seen in the Netherlands. The commercial bustle of the place seems considerable, and it contains more beershops than any city I ever saw."

It had evidently improved since William Beckford's visit in 1783: "To one so far gone in the poetic antiquity, Ghent is not the most likely place to recall his attention... it is a large, ill-paved dismal-looking city, with a decent proportion of convents and chapels."

As in Bruges, the visitor should first ascend the **Bell Tower** and survey the

layout of the city, which spreads over 13 islands at the confluence of the Scheldt, Leie and Lieve rivers. One advantage which the bell tower here has over the one in Bruges is that you don't have to climb stairs; you can take an elevator to the top. This 90-metre (300-ft) tower, a symbol of the freedom of the citizens of Ghent, has been crowned with a gilded dragon since the 14th century.

The Ghent altarpiece: If you want the most beautiful view over the city, there's only one place to go: **St Michael's Bridge** over the Leie. From here, the view extends from **'s Gravensteen**, the fortress of the Counts of Flanders, across the Romanesque, Gothic and baroque facades of the warehouses and guild halls on Korenlei and Graslei, all the way to the towers of St Bavon, St Nicholas and the bell tower.

Where should you begin your exploration of this city, which Albrecht Dürer described as "large and wonderful" in the course of his trip through the Low Countries? Your best bet is probably to follow in Dürer's footsteps. No sooner had the painter arrived in the city than he set out to see the most important sight of Ghent: the famous Ghent altarpiece. From the outside, Ghent's main church, **St Bavon's cathedral** (also known as St Baaf's), has a somewhat eclectic appearance. Visitors with an interest in art history can trace the development of architectural styles from late Romanesque to late Gothic. But the undisputed highlight of this church, where Emperor Charles V was baptised in 1500, is first and foremost Jan van Eyck's most famous and admired work, the Ghent altarpiece, known as the *Adoration of the Holy Lamb,* located in one of the cathedral's 20 side chapels.

It is not certain whether Jan van Eyck painted this 12-panelled work alone in 1432, or whether he was assisted by his brother Hubert; the latter is not mentioned in any other documents but is cited on a somewhat enigmatic inscription on the frame of the altarpiece itself. Today's art historians tend toward the

The fields
Flanders:
memory o
the fallen

view that Jan painted the piece by himself. This altar which, like Hans Memling's *Shrine of St Ursula* in Bruges, belongs to the so-called "Seven Wonders of Belgium", is regarded as the greatest masterpiece of early Flemish art and is one of the most famous paintings in the world. The use of light in the canvas is such that the viewer has the impression that the sunlight from the cathedral's windows is continually illuminating the altarpiece's 284 figures. The work depicts the Adoration of the Lamb of God, an allegorical glorification of the death of Christ.

This masterpiece wasn't always so revered. At the end of the 18th century, Emperor Joseph II of Austria took exception to the nakedness of Adam and Eve; as a result, the panel depicting Adam and Eve was replaced by a new painting of two clothed figures and the original panel was hidden away in the sacristy. Today, the original Adam and Eve have been restored to their rightful place in the altarpiece; the panel with the clothed figures hangs near the exit, on the left wall.

During every major European conflict the altarpiece has been looted from Ghent; Napoleon Bonaparte took it to Paris and it was stolen by the Germans during World War II. But it always found its way back to the city – except, alas, for the panel depicting the wise judges, which had to be replaced by a copy after it was stolen in 1934.

Ghent contains more historical buildings than any other city in Flanders. It is therefore difficult to choose which to include in your sightseeing itinerary. Between the cathedral and **the church of St Nicholas**, where you can study the development of the Scheldt version of Gothic architecture, you'll find the Weavers' Hall and the Bell Tower. In the Middle Ages, the bell tower represented the power of the various guilds. The alarm bell, which called the citizens to arms, was proudly called "Klokke Roeland". At the foot of the bell tower, you'll find the "Triomfante", the suc-

cessor to the "Roland Bell", cast in 1660: this bell cracked in 1914.

Imperial city: The Gothic Weavers' Hall once housed the inspection commission for the cloth weavers who were responsible for Ghent's economic well-being. Today, a visitor to the hall can watch the audiovisual documentary *Ghent and the Emperor Charles V*. This film celebrates the fact that Charles V was born and raised in Ghent. The Emperor was, thanks to the South American territories which his mother, the Infanta of Spain Joanna of Castille, brought to the House of Habsburg, able to boast that the sun never set on his empire. He was supposedly more fluent in Dutch than in any other language. Nonetheless, Ghent rose up against him in 1639; the following year Charles marched into his native city in a six-hour triumphal parade.

Near the Weavers' Hall, you'll find the 16th-century town hall, the **Stadhuis**, which is built partly in the style of Flemish late Gothic and has features in the style of the Renaissance. The building's dark, ornate facade is an impressive sight, embellished as it is with countless sculpted figures and various ghoulish ornaments.

In accordance with medieval tradition, the town hall housed two city parliaments. One of Ghent's particular characteristics was that the parliament of the *Keure* and the parliament of the *Ghedele* were set side by side. The Keure was made up of 13 judges from patrician families; it was responsible for the judicial and financial sides of the city administration. The first member of the Keure was also the mayor of the city. The parliament of the Ghedele, on the other hand, had a somewhat subsidiary function. The 13 judges who belonged to this commission functioned more as referees in disputes between individual citizens or patricians.

However unified the massive block of the town hall may appear from without, its interior is segmented and convoluted, in part as a result of building **Some hav easy.**

additions and modifications carried out over the course of the centuries. The loveliest feature of its interior is the rectangular Gothic spiral staircase in the corner between the "Collatiezolder" and the Throne Room. In 1576, the Peace Treaty of Ghent was signed in one of the building's most beautiful rooms; this treaty officially brought to an end the disputes between Catholics and Protestants.

Opposite the Town Hall, on the **Botermarkt** (the Butter Market, of which Dorothy Wordsworth said, "I can hardly endure to call a place so dignified by such a name"), you can find **St Jorishof**, built in the 13th century and one of the oldest hotels in Europe. In the Middle Ages the archers of Ghent kept their practice ranges here. Both Charles V and Napoleon have been guests in St Jorishof, but its biggest moment was when it hosted celebrations for the engagement of Maximilian of Austria and Mary of Burgundy.

If you cross Limburgstraat and head

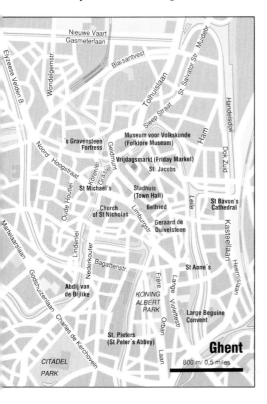

Ghent
800 m / 0,5 miles

south, you pass a modern memorial to the brothers Jan and Hubert van Eyck, and one to Geraard de Duivelsteen. The **castle of Gerhard the Devil** is a fortified knight's castle dating from 1245; it contains a remarkable Roman crypt not open to the public.

Gloomy castle: Visitors are welcome to visit **'s Gravensteen**, Ghent's other major castle, much larger and more important than the first. This fortress of the Counts of Flanders is perhaps the most gloomy medieval building in Europe. The castle is encircled on one side by the waters of the Leie; it was built on the model of the castles of the Crusaders in Syria and the Holy Land. Philip of Alsace encountered these buildings when he himself undertook a crusade to the Holy Land.

At first, 's Gravensteen served as a residence and a fortress; after the 14th century, however, even the Counts of Flanders themselves became a little uncomfortable in the sinister surroundings, and the building was turned into a dungeon, its inner courtyard used as a place of execution. Even the crypt was used as a torture chamber. Today, the torture chambers, with their gruesome collection of exhibits, are the most popular of the castle's attractions

But there was plenty of torture and execution going on outside the walls of the castle, as well; medieval Ghent could boast of many institutions which were empowered to "interrogate painfully" and execute suspects. At the foot of 's Gravensteen, there's a bridge with the grisly name **Ondhoofdingbrug** (Bridge of the Beheaded).

Before the castle gates lies pretty **Veerle Square** with its many beautiful old gabled houses. Once the square contained a wheel of torture and a gallows; here, murderers and thieves, magicians and witches, forgers and heretics, vagabonds and robbers were strangled, beheaded, hanged, flayed on the wheel or, bound hand and foot, thrown into vast vats of boiling oil.

The Counts' former quarters now

house a museum documenting the medieval system of criminal justice. It's a harrowing collection of all the horrible things that people thought up in order to hurt others, either to force a confession out of them or to kill them in the grisliest possible manner. There's only one bright spot in the fortress and that's the top level of the castle's main tower. If it weren't for the captivating view from St Michael's Bridge, the panorama from the tower of the castle would be the best view of the city of Ghent.

Korenlei and **Graslei**, the rows of houses to the left and right of the Leie between St Michael's Bridge and Gras Bridge, comprise the architectural heart of the residential Ghent of centuries past. Here are the loveliest groupings of city buildings that you'll encounter in all of Flanders. Take special note of the houses in Graslei; the best view of them is from the Korenlei, looking across the water. Ghent schoolchildren are brought here to draw or paint, not to the Bell Tower or to St Bavon's Cathedral or even to 's Gravensteen. Although Bruges offers a more unified image of a medieval city, it does not offer the wealth of ornament and intricacy which these houses of Ghent possess.

Take, for example, the **House of the Grain Measurer**, a building of red brick and white stone, with decorative stepped gables, built in 1698. Next to it is the narrow **Customs House**, of only slightly more recent vintage. The **Stockpile House** next to that, with its unmistakable Romanesque forms, is 500 years older: it was built in 1130.

The House of the Free Boatmen was built in 1531. The splendid houses line both sides of the river; they are richly ornamented with Gothic stepped gables or rounded baroque gables, false fronts and lavishly decorated cornices. But Ghent's wealth of elaborate old houses isn't confined only to these two streets. A row of houses in the **Oudtburg** really shouldn't be missed. The most famous house here is the pub "In de Hel" ("In Hell"). Also worthy of mention is the

Reflection **Ghent.**

former house of the spice merchants' guild, called **Klein Turkje** (Little Turk). It's part of a hostelry in which Albrecht Dürer stayed when he visited Ghent. The inn still bears the name it bore then: "The Red Hat". Dorothy Wordsworth, visiting Ghent in 1820, was enchanted by Ghent's houses: "The buildings, streets, squares, all are picturesque; the houses, green, blue, pink, yellow, with richest ornaments still varying. Strange it is that so many and such strongly contrasted colours should compose an indiscordant whole."

The visitor shouldn't forgo a visit to the **Sikkel Complex** situated behind St Bavon's cathedral. Some guidebooks list it as the Hoogpoort Complex. This extensive complex was built as a residence for a patrician family between the 13th and 15th centuries, and continued to be rebuilt and expanded; it is reminiscent of similar establishments in Italy. The buildings are arranged around a central courtyard containing a fountain. The Sikkel family, who commissioned

the palace, even included a watchtower in their plans. Sikkel is the Flemish word for "sickle", and you can see the family's emblem, three sickles, on the building's Romanesque facade. Hoogpoort is the name of the Gothic facade of the complex.

Living on credit: It's the interior architecture, particularly its vaulted ceiling, rather than its exterior, which makes the **Old Securities House** worth seeing. Located in Abrahamsstraat, the house was founded as a credit institution under the regency of Albert and Isabella of Austria in 1621. It's a perfect example of Flemish Renaissance architecture. For 300 years, the citizens of Ghent were able to borrow money here at an exorbitant rate of interest.

The wonderful walk along the Leie is cut off by the presence of the imposing **Vleeshuis** building, the medieval meat market, which looks very like a fortified stronghold. Passing this, and crossing the Vleeshuisbrug, you will come to the **Dulle Greet** on Kanonen Square. The

Dulle Greet is a cast-iron cannon dating from the Burgundian epoch.

Going into any one of Ghent's many restaurant to sample a *waaterzoi*, a vegetable stew which is a speciality of Ghent, visitors will gain ample opportunity to get to know the city's residents. The dialect spoken in Ghent is much harder and louder than in Bruges, and to the ears of strangers it may even sound inflammatory. It's still said that the citizens of Ghent are among the most single-minded in the country. In his study of the Burgundian region in the 17th century, Caspar Merian set Ghent alongside Paris and Liège as one of the European cities most easily incited to revolt. (On the other hand, it could be that the loud, excited-sounding voices are simply a result of excessive consumption of the local Trappist beer, which is ranked among Belgium's most popular brews.)

The people of Ghent revolted more often than the citizens of other parts of Flanders. They often staged their political meetings on the **Vrijdagsmarkt** (Friday Market), where the colourful weekly market takes place today. Dominating the Vrijdagsmarkt is the statue of Jacob van Artevelde, the high-born Ghent brewer who, having been elected captain of the city in 1338, made a commercial treaty with Edward III of England to protect the Flemish weaving trade. He continued to support the English when Edward declared himself King of France in 1340, but died in a riot after proposing that Edward the Black Prince should be made Count of Flanders.

No city in Flanders is without its Beguine Convent. Ghent has two: the large and the small Beguine Convents. The **Large Convent**, located in the eastern suburb of Sint Amandsberg, is fitted out as a museum of the Flemish Beguines. Near 's Gravensteen, at the city centre, you'll find the **Small Convent**, which looks like a miniature 17th-century town. Only a few sections of the St Bavon monastery, founded in the 7th century by St Amandus, remain: the cellar, the refectory and a nave. Today it

A fanfare at the Ros Beiaardommegang parade in Dendermonde.

serves as a location for the Ghent Stone Museum, containing mosaics, cobblestones, and old architectural ornamental building elements.

The former monastery of van de Bijloke has been converted into the city's **Archaeological Museum**, although this name is a little misleading. The former convent – erected in the 14th century, and worth a visit in itself, for architectural interest – houses implements of daily life in the Middle Ages: weapons, pieces of clothing, porcelain and glass, as well as a fine collection of Chinese art. The most interesting object in the museum is a mechanical Jenny-loom, which the Mayor of Ghent, Lieven Bauwens, smuggled out of England, breaking the strict export laws, at the end of the 18th century. With his help, and with further looms modelled on this one, a new era of economic prosperity dawned in the city of Ghent, after a long period of decline.

In the former Hospital of Alyns, the **Museum for Folk Culture** is housed in 18 small, typically Flemish houses; the museum conveys a picture of life in Ghent around the year 1900.

There isn't much left of **Prinsenhof**, the castle where Charles V was born, except for an entrance gate. Prinsenhof was once a large castle complex with a well-tended garden, fountains, and 300 rooms. Today, a memorial plaque on a house in Mirabelklostraat is the sole reminder that the room in which the emperor was born was located here. The birth of the future emperor was celebrated in great style: it was deep winter and the authorities even went to the trouble of flooding the Vrijdagsmarkt so that the children could ice-skate.

Not far from this rises the **Rabot**, one of the few remnants of the medieval city fortifications, built in 1489. In fact, the Rabot is nothing more than a large river-lock, flanked by two round towers. It stands at the place where the canal of Lieve lapped the former city walls.

Artists' colony: Ghent is a good city to walk around; although the notable sights

may not lie quite as close together as they do in Bruges, they're all accessible on foot. If you want to sight-see in style take a carriage ride through Ghent. The horse-drawn carriages stand under the bell tower, ready to take on passengers.

You may also choose to take a half-hour tour of the city by motor launch; or, if boats appeal, a tour of several hours up the Leie to **Deurle**. This unusual village is one of the most interesting places in the area surrounding Ghent and has attracted many craftsmen and artists. Expressionist Flemish painters, are particularly well represented. Visit the **Gustaaf de Smeets Museum** or the **Dhondt-Daenens Collection** to see examples of their work.

The neighbouring village of **St-Marterns-Latem** is another area renowned for its artists. Its charming setting, with its whitewashed houses, bright flower gardens, windmills and the picturesque banks of the Leie, was home and working area for the painters of the internationally known Latemer School.

Those particularly interested in Flemish painting may be interested in stopping off in the Ghent suburb of **St Amandsberg**, or rather, at its cemetery, **Campo Santo**; countless Flemish figures from the worlds of art, science and culture are buried here.

Further along the road to Antwerp you come upon **Lochristi**, where you are brought face to face with the culture of the Low Countries.

On the green outside the church there's a monument to Reinaart; the author of the great Netherlands animal epic *Van den Vos Reinaarde* (Reynard the Fox) who set the activities of his animal characters in the area between Ghent and the town of Hulst, which is located in the Netherlands.

Lochristi is also the centre of the flower industry, which has come to play such an important role in the economy of East Flanders. From the end of July until well into October, Lochristi is perfumed with the begonias which carpet its vast fields. In 1157, Dietrich of Al-

A cosy café

sace had his **Castle Laarne** built on land enclosed by a bend in the river Scheldt, only a few miles from Ghent. This was the same Dietrich who brought the Sacred Blood to Bruges and who had 's Gravensteen built in Ghent. Laarne shares none of the Ghent castle's dark gloom.

One of the most beautiful castles in East Flanders which is open to the public is **Castle Ooldonk**, located in the enchanting Lys Valley; the castle's foundation walls date from the 12th century. Originally the castle was a defensive fortification of the city of Ghent. For nearly 200 years it belonged to the Montmorency family; Philip II of Montmorency spent his youth within its walls. He was to become famous as Count Horn who, together with his father, Count Egmont, was beheaded on the Grand' Place in Brussels at the command of the Duke of Alva.

A visit to **Leeuwerghem Palace**, south of Ghent between Aalst and Oudenaarde, is also strongly recom-

official
tographer?

mended. The palace isn't usually open to the public, as it is still privately inhabited; visitors must content themselves with a stroll through the palace grounds, which contain one of the most unusual theatres in Flanders. This park is laid out in the style of Le Nôtre, the famous French landscape designer of the 18th century. The theatre has a seating capacity of 1,200 in its two-level balcony, its circle and its orchestra level.

Aalst (Alost), halfway between Ghent and Brussels, on the southwest border of the province of East Flanders, is perhaps not one of the great cities of Flanders, but as the former capital of the county, lying between the Scheldt and Dender, it can boast a number of noteworthy old buildings. In addition, Aalst – which for many years belonged to the province of Hainaut – is interesting in any case from a standpoint of cultural history and population.

The **Schepenhuis**, the Gothic town hall, dominates the old town. In 1469 the bells in the **Bell Tower** rang out over the Flemish town for the first time. In a corner of the town hall lies the **Beurs van Amsterdam**, or Barbara Chamber, a building from the early baroque period. Richly ornamented, and notable for an arcade on the first floor, this building once housed a rhetoricians' guild, a type of guild common in Flemish cities in the past. The Walloon influence on the town is especially visible in the annual Carnival, when one of Belgium's most splendid parades takes place. Many of the participants wear high, waving ostrich feathers in their hats, a custom shared by the Carnival in Hainaut.

Aalst, like Poperinge, lies in countryside characterised by its fields of hops. During the hop harvest, the villages of **Moorsel**, **Baardegem**, **Medert** and **Herdegsem** hold harvest festivals, at which plenty of Lambieck (French: *lambic*), a traditional strong beer of Belgium, which is produced according to an extremely specialised process of fermentation, is consumed.

ANTWERP

If you ask Antwerp residents what they thinks is special about their city, they'll probably mention the port, the diamonds and the art, not necessarily in that order. Art and business, the beautiful and the useful, coexist in total harmony in Antwerp, a relationship its residents, who call themselves *Sinjoore*, have been keen to foster since the time of Peter Paul Rubens, its most famous son.

Antwerp/Anvers, the capital of the province of the same name, which also contains the cities of Mechelen/Malines and Lier/Lierre, isn't that easy to characterise. Brussels is the European capital; Liège/Luik a steel centre; Bruges is nicknamed La Morte (because time seems to have stood still there!); but Antwerp is many things at once: a major port, a diamond centre, an industrial nucleus, the city of Rubens, a cultural metropolis, a haven for gourmets and an elegant shopping centre. In Antwerp, medieval charm and modern industry are located side by side. The city's proverbial tolerance is balanced by a healthy dose of chauvinism, and the provinciality of some aspects of life in the city by an insouciant, cosmopolitan air.

They say that "Antwerp has God to thank for the Scheldt, and the Scheldt to thank for everything else." The Scheldt has always been Antwerp's lifeline: a rise, followed by a fall, followed by another rise – the Scheldt has brought this city, which lies 88 km (55 miles) from the coast, into its own rhythm.

According to legend, even the name Antwerp is inextricably linked with the river. A giant named Druon Antigon was said to demand high tolls from every ship that passed his castle on the Scheldt. Anyone who refused to pay this fee had a hand chopped off. Eventually, Silvius Brabo, a Roman soldier, mustered the courage to kill the giant. As a final act of good riddance he chopped off Druon Antigon's hand and

threw it in the Scheldt. The site where this all took place was called "Antwerpen" – hand-*werpen* (hand-throwing) – by the people of the region. (A modern reminder of the legend is the Brabo Fountain in front of the town hall, built by Jef Lambeaux in 1887.)

In reality, the naming of Antwerp is much more prosaic. The name refers to the city's foundation on an arm of land reaching into the river: *aanworp* or *aanwerpen* means "raised ground".

History: The oldest testimonials about Antwerp date from Gallo-Roman times. Frisians settled on the Scheldt in the 2nd and 3rd centuries AD; Salic Franks followed, building their houses in the north of the city; in the 7th century, they erected a fortress, which was destroyed by the Normans in 836. After the fall of France, Antwerp became a possession of Lorraine in 843, and then, in 963, of Germany. At the beginning of the 12th century, the Duke of Brabant took over power in Antwerp. As protection from Flanders, which continued to expand

without interference from its French rulers, and from which the city was only protected by the Scheldt, the Brabanters had a wall built around Antwerp. But neither this nor further fortifications built in the 13th century were able to prevent the city from being annexed by Flanders in 1357.

The Flemish had had their eye on Antwerp, which had received its city charter at the end of the 12th century, for a long time. The city on the Scheldt couldn't hold a candle to Bruges, then at the optimum point of its flowering, but its port was experiencing a new phenomenon – the arrival of increasing numbers of ships from Venice and Genoa. With the birth of the Flemish weaving industry, the city became a vast warehouse for English wool and prospered accordingly. The church of Our Lady, which was begun in 1352, reflected the city's pride and well-being. The cathedral, finished 170 years later, is one of the largest in the world.

In 1406, under the Dukes of Bur-gundy, Antwerp was reunified with Brabant and was on its way to becoming the major port of western Europe. Protected by its new rulers, and with the silting up of the port of Bruges benefiting Antwerp still further, the city entered a golden age. By 1560, the city could boast a population of 100,000. More than 100 ships entered and left the port every day; more than 1,000 foreign businessmen conducted their business from Antwerp. Booming trade was reflected in a corresponding growth of industry: textile factories, sugar refineries, soap-makers, breweries, diamond-cutters and book publishers all prospered. In 1532, the city opened a stock exchange. Many of the guilds built splendid houses on the marketplace to display their wealth and status.

Drawn by Antwerp's wealth, famous artists and scientists settled along the Scheldt. They included Christoph Plantin, the greatest book printer of his time; painters such as Otto Venius, Quentin Massys and Pieter Breughel;

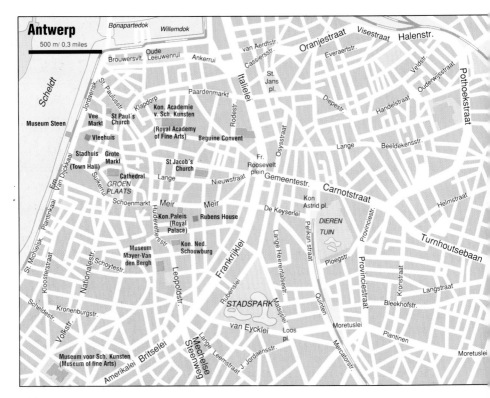

Gérard Mercator and Justus Lipsius; the writer Anna Bijns; and sculptors Pieter Coecke van Aalst and Corelis de Vriendt.

The new belief: Antwerp's flowering came to an abrupt end with the advent of Protestantism. Under William the Silent the city became the centre of the revolt against the Catholic Church and Spanish political authority. Spanish forces under Charles V's fanatical son, Philip II, attacked the city in 1576, killing, looting and burning all around them. The episode, which became known as the "Spanish Mutiny" cost 8,000 lives. The Spanish forces were driven out in the following year but they returned; in 1585, Alessandro Farnese forced the city to its knees in a siege which lasted seven months.

The punishments which the Spaniards meted out to adherents of the new belief were so ghastly that the residents of Antwerp left the city in droves. To top it all, the navigation of the river Scheldt fell into the hands of the Dutch, starting a mass exodus from Antwerp.

In 1582, there were still 83,700 people living in the city; by 1589, the number had fallen to just 42,000. The city's role as an economic centre of Europe was abruptly terminated.

The city entered a long period of depression. James Howell writing "Letter to Sir James Crofts, 5 July 1619" described the changed character of Antwerp vividly. "This goodly ancient City methinks looks like a disconsolate Widow, or rather some super-annuated Virgin, that hath lost her Lover, being almost quite bereft of that flourishing Commerce wherewith before the falling off the rest of the Provinces from Spain she abounded to the envy of all other Cities and Marts of Europe."

Legendary artists: Despite the economic decline, the fine arts continued to flourish. In the first half of the 17th century, the chief painter of the baroque, Peter Paul Rubens, painted his masterpieces in Antwerp. The artist, who managed to achieve fame and fortune in his own lifetime, had a house

built for himself on the Wapper. Today the **Rubens House**, containing paintings by Rubens and a reconstruction of his apartment, is a place of pilgrimage for fans of baroque painting.

As well as Rubens, both **Antonis van Dyck** and **Jakob Jordaens the Elder** lived and worked on the Scheldt. The city has immortalised all three of these artists in stone: Rubens' statue stands on Groen Square, van Dyck's on the Meir, and Jordaens' on the bank of the Scheldt. Two other artists who were inspired by Antwerp's cosmopolitan character were the sculptor Artus Quellin and the well-known woodcarver Christoffel Jegher. Many of their works can be seen in the churches and museums of Antwerp.

Economic well-being didn't return to Antwerp until the 18th century. The French, who after a brief interval of Austrian rule became masters of the city in 1792, opened up the river Scheldt; under Napoleon Bonaparte, they built up the port as a base for the French navy.

For Napoleon, Antwerp was a prized possession, "a pistol aimed at the heart of England."

The docks and jetties which Napoleon built proved extremely valuable to the city. Antwerp's trade with overseas colonies was stepped up, particularly under the Dutch, who took over from the French.

The port grows: In 1830, the Belgian Revolution put an end to this economic upswing. Belgium had won its independence, but the mouth of the Scheldt still lay in the hands of the Dutch. Only when the Scheldt Tax was lifted in 1863 was it possible to continue the expansion of the port begun by Napoleon.

In 1881, the former city centre had to give way to the expanding port. More than 800 houses and the old landing-place were demolished. To compensate, brand-new buildings, streets, alleys and squares were erected elsewhere. The Palace of Justice, the National Bank, the Royal Gymnasium and the former **Antiques** City Theatre are examples of the archi- **junk?**

tecture typical of this period. In the course of the expansion, Antwerp was provided with running water, gas and electricity.

With this expansion, the city's finances and its fine arts experienced a renaissance. Artists such as Leys, de Keyser, Verlat, Wappers and de Braekeler comprised a famous school of Antwerp painters. Peter Benoit, Jan Blockx and Emiel Wambach gave new impetus to music, while authors such as Willems, van Rijswijck, Snieders and Conscience (who, it is said, taught the people how to read) wrote their greatest works in the city. In 1885 and 1894, Antwerp was the location of major world exhibitions.

Even the two world wars didn't leave an appreciable scar on the growth of the metropolis. They merely postponed the city's development. After World War II the city experienced an unprecedented economic boom. Capital from overseas streamed into the city on the Scheldt.

Today, in the north of the city, refineries, chemical and petrochemical plants, shipbuilders and automobile factories crowd together. The port stretches to the Dutch border. Its half a million inhabitants and 520-sq. km (200-sq. mile) area make Antwerp Belgium's second largest city.

The city's sights: First-time visitors should begin their sightseeing in the **Old City**. The heart of the historical centre is the **cathedral of Our Lady.** With its seven aisles, 125 pillars and 123-metre (400-ft) high tower, this cathedral is the largest and most beautiful Gothic church in Belgium. Its construction took from 1352 until 1521. The finishing touch was the slender, neatly designed tower. On Monday evenings in summer its beloved carillon of bells attracts crowds of listeners.

Inside the cathedral, you can see a wealth of masterpieces by Rubens: in the transept, you will find the *Crucifixion* to the left and the *Descent from the Cross* to the right. The altarpiece in the choir depicts the *Assumption of the Vir-*

gin, also by Rubens. Although a fire in 1533, a spate of iconoclasm in 1566, and the French occupation were responsible for the loss of a whole group of irreplaceable ornaments, the cathedral still houses many artistic treasures: as well as valuable paintings, it contains magnificent tombs, marvellous sculptures, fine woodcarvings and impressive examples of stained-glass painting.

The old alleys and squares around the cathedral are interesting places in which to wander. Residents are particularly proud of the **Vlaaikensgang**, a street which has been restored in the style of the 16th century. It can be reached from the **Oude Koornmarkt**, a square containing a wide range of restaurants, pubs and cafés. Gourmets take note: the entire Old City is full of excellent eating establishments. Sample the local specialities: mussels, prepared in a number of ways, stewed eel in chervil sauce or meat casserole. You'll find a number of characteristic Antwerp pubs selling good local beers in the **Sukkerei** and on the

Handschoenmarkt, at the foot of the cathedral.

Creating a strong architectural contrast to the venerable cathedral is the nearby **Tourengebouw** bank building, a soaring modern edifice. It is 100 metres (more than 300 ft) and 27 storeys high. Built in the 1920s, it was the first skyscraper in Europe. There is a wonderful view of the city centre from the top floor.

Turning northwest from the church of Our Lady, you'll come to the **Grote Markt** and the Brabo Fountain, town hall and guild houses. The stately Renaissance **Stadhuis** (Town Hall) with its marble facade and richly decorated rooms was built between 1561 and 1565, according to plans by Cornelis de Briendt; it combines Flemish and Italian stylistic elements. Most of the guild houses, which have been painstakingly restored over the last few years, also date from this period. With these splendid buildings, influential guilds, such as the archers, grocers, carpenters, and tailors, erected monuments to their respective trades.

On Gildekamersstraat, behind the town hall, you will find the **Museum of Folk Culture**, presenting the customs and traditions of old Flanders. Only a few steps away, the **Vleeshuis**, built at the beginning of the 16th century as a butcher's market and guild house, today accommodates a museum of arts and crafts and local history. The house of the butchers' guild, its "bacon streaks" of red brick and white sandstone carefully restored to their original glory, is one of the most remarkable secular buildings in all Antwerp. What is particularly notable about its interior is an extensive collection of musical instruments. If you would like to hear what these sound like, investigate the dates of the concerts which regularly take place in the museum.

Less centrally located, but no less interesting, is the **Brouwershuis** on Adriaan Brouwerstraat, near the port. This was where, in the 16th century,

For vesse
large and
small: the
river Sch

FLANDRIA 20

water was drawn for the breweries in the area. In the lowest storey you can still see the horse-mill with the aid of which the complicated machinery was set in motion. Forty metal buckets scooped up water and transported it to the upper storey, from where it was piped to the various breweries. It is worth looking in on the ornately decorated conference room in which the brewers continued to hold their annual meetings until relatively recently.

Halfway between Vleeshuis and Brouwershuis stands the magnificent 16th-century **church of St Paul**, in which elements of the Gothic, the Renaissance (tower) and the baroque (interior) are harmoniously juxtaposed. The former Dominican church contains many paintings by Rubens, Jordaens and van Dyck. Further attention is warranted by Artus Quellin's statue of St Rosa of Lima and his wonderful *Stations of the Cross*.

Southwest of St Paul's church, where the Venetian and Genoese ships once anchored, you'll come upon the oldest building in Antwerp: the **Steen**. Built in the 12th century, this castle is now the location of the **National Shipping Museum**. Model ships, old land maps and sea charts and historical instruments of navigation document Antwerp's centuries-old connection with the sea and shipping.

Right next to the Steen the white excursion steamers of the shipping company Flandria put to sea. Interested visitors can take a tour of the Scheldt of either 50 or 80 minutes' duration. Alternatively you can opt for a 2½-hour tour of the port or choose one of the various day excursions available. Day trips to the mouth of the Scheldt, to the river Rhine or through the coastal delta area prove particularly popular, especially as Flandria is well known for its first-class service.

Harbour economy: Other than this, there's not much happening along the Scheldt's docks. Along the promenade north and south of the Steen, you can

full
tment.

THE GLITTER OF PRECIOUS STONES

It is not certain when diamonds were first discovered. It is, however, known that until the 18th century, diamonds were mined only in India. Today, diamonds are mined primarily in Australia, Zaire, Botswana, the Soviet Union and South Africa.

The precious stones made their way to Bruges in the 13th century. They came via Venice, which at the time had a monopoly on trade with India. Soon the diamond trade was flourishing in the city. By the end of the 15th century the trade had spread to Antwerp. The city on the Scheldt became the leading economic and diamond centre of Europe. After the Dutch War of Independence, Amsterdam controlled the diamond monopoly for a time; but Antwerp recovered its position in the 19th century. Since World War II, this city has led the world in this glittering business.

Nowhere else can you find so many different diamond cutters, exchanges and shops in such a small area as in the "Diamond Quarter", less than one-fifth of a square mile in area, at the edge of Antwerp's old city. Some 2,000 diamond companies and 450 diamond cutters are based here. More than 30,000 people work in this field, which had a turnover of US$12.5 billion in 1988, and which accounts for 7 percent of Belgian exports. Only 20 percent of the diamonds produced here are used for jewellery; the rest is used in industry. More than half of the diamonds produced in the world – be they raw, cut or for industrial purposes – pass through Antwerp.

The Belgians are keen to augment the city's fame as a diamond centre. Relaxed import and export laws and various tax concessions make the diamond trade in Belgium particularly lucrative. There are six schools devoted to teaching the skills and secrets of the industry and a special research centre is devoted to developing even better technology for diamond working.

The "High Diamond Council" (HDR), a leading organisation in the field, ensures the maintenance of quality standards. Here, all the stones are checked and provided with certificates. Quality depends on the four Cs: carat, colour, clarity and cut.

Carat is a measurement of the stone's weight. The term harks back to the time when the weight of diamonds was measured against carob beans; "carat" is the Arabian word for carob. As for colour: most diamonds have a yellowish tinge, but it's the white stones which are most prized by dealers. However, there are also brown, green, black, blue and pink diamonds. Clarity has to do with purity. There are faults in every diamond: the smaller and less visible these are, the better the quality of the stone. The most valuable diamonds are classed as "lens-pure": even under 10-fold magnification, no faults are visible. Cut is judged on the basis of symmetry and clean intersections of facets. In the most popular type of cut, the brilliant full cut, proportion also plays a determining role. Other popular cuts include the emerald cut, the marquise, the heart, the drop and the oval.

Two museums and numerous guided tours offer the visitor the chance of a closer look at Antwerp's diamond world. In the Provincial Diamond Museum (Lange Herentalsstraat 31), the visitor can admire copies of the world's most famous diamonds and learn about the process of diamond manufacturing. The Grobbendonk Diamond Museum (at Bovenpad 3a, Grobben–donk), near the gates of the city, shows the processes a diamond must undergo on its way from the mines to the jeweller.

The guided tours that are offered by the High Diamond Council are extremely informative, but have to be requested in writing and scheduled at least three weeks in advance (write to HDR, Public Relations Department, Hoveniersstraat 22, 2018 Antwerp).

If your curiosity will be satisfied by a somewhat briefer glimpse into the world of diamonds, there are numerous private exhibitions, such as Van Moppes Diamond Exhibition Centre (Maarschalk Gérardstraat 2), Diamond Showroom Diamondland (Appelmanstraat 33a), Steigrad (Hoveniersstraat 16–20) or Dilady (Lange Herentalsstraat 29), which are also very interesting. Here, diamonds are also offered for sale.

see, aside from the steamers, an occasional warship, or a freighter waiting to be loaded; the real life of Antwerp's port is carried on in the north of the city, where the new harbour basin and the main industrial facilities are located.

If you want to go on a tour of exploration around the **port**, pick a weekday for your visit: it's then that the hustle and bustle on the jetties, in the dry dock and on the water are at their height. You don't have to take your tour by ship; you can also go by car. There is a well-marked route 65 km (40 miles) long which takes in the most significant points of the harbour area. You can pick up a brochure containing detailed and specific information about the port from the Tourist Office.

Some 75,000 people work in and around the port. Hundreds of cargo freighters, container ships and tankers pass through it on a daily basis. The docks measure a total of 127 km (79 miles) in length. A tangle of tracks (949 km/588 miles) and streets (337 km/209 miles) surrounds the harbour area, which itself measures some 336 sq. km (130 sq. miles).

Seven water-locks connect the port to the Scheldt. The newest, the **Berendrecht Lock**, has only recently been completed. At 500 metres (1,625 ft) long, 68 metres (222 ft) wide and 17.75 metres (58 ft) deep, it is the largest river-lock in the world.

An absolute must for bibliophiles is the **House of the Plantin-Moretus Family**, a handsome Renaissance building on Vrijdagmarkt, only a few hundred metres from the Steen. The house has been turned into a museum celebrating the golden age of Antwerp. You can see the original printing presses (still functioning) and typesetting equipment, stroll through an old Flemish patrician apartment and browse over old manuscripts and books, copper-plate engravings and woodcuts. Particular gems of the collection are the 13 copies of the 36-line Gutenberg Bible and the *Biblia Regia*. If you schedule your visit to this

museum on a Wednesday or Friday, you can also visit the Friday **Market** (Vrijdagmarkt). Twice a week, antiques and knick-knacks are auctioned off to the highest bidder.

Another jewel in the old city is the **church of St Charles Borromeo**, built between 1614 and 1621 in the so-called Jesuit baroque style after plans by Huyssens and Aguilon. Rubens is said to have been responsible for the design of the main facade. Thirty-nine ceiling paintings by Rubens were destroyed in a fire in this church in 1718. Three of his altar paintings, however, have been preserved, as well as carved-wood confessionals from the 18th century and some magnificent statues of angels. The Chapel of Our Lady is every bit as splendid as it was in Rubens' day, having, like the graceful tower and the facade, survived the fire unscathed.

Several hundred metres to the east of the Jesuit church towers the Gothic **St Jacob's church**, where the foremost families of the city used to lay their loved ones to their rest. Rubens is among those buried here. His altar painting of the Holy Family was originally designed for his funereal chapel. Containing as it does paintings by virtually all the great Flemish masters, valuable sculptures and ornate items of gold and brass, St Jacob's church outdoes even the cathedral in artistic wealth.

Chips and beer: Proceeding south from St Jacob's church, you'll come to the **Meir**, which divides the old city, surrounded by broad avenues, into two parts. The Meir and **De Keyserlei**, which leads to the main railway station, are Antwerp's two leading shopping streets. The people of Antwerp love to stroll along the "shopping mile", and then relax in one of the streets' excellent cafés. Order a *handje* (sandwich) and one of Antwerp's famous beers: a light Pintje, a strong Bolleke, or a dark, heavy Trappist beer.

On the other side of the Meir, you can follow in Rubens' footsteps to the **Rubens House** on Rubensstraat. The **The bustle the city centre.**

painter had the house built in 1610. It was not acquired by the authorities until the middle of the 20th century, by which time it was virtually derelict. Now it has been turned into a museum devoted to the artist; the studio where he worked and taught and the living apartments have been carefully restored. The apartment in the left wing of the house is soberly decorated in the old Flemish style, but the studio demonstrates the more lively spirit of the baroque. Ten Rubens works are on display in the house, including *Adam and Eve in Paradise*, a work painted in his youth.

Don't neglect to take a look at the garden. The imposing portico which divides the inner courtyard from the garden makes an appearance in many of Rubens' pictures. It's assumed that the artist designed this portal himself.

You can enjoy more art in the nearby **Museum Mayer van den Bergh** on Lange Gasthuisstraat. Located in a former patrician home, the museum bears the name of a wealthy Antwerp citizen who bequeathed his unique art collection to his native city. High points of the collection are two paintings by Pieter Breughel: the *Dulle Griet*, one of his most striking works, and the *Twelve Sayings*, an early piece.

Just next door, you'll find the **Maagdenhuis**, once an orphanage, today a museum with wonderful faience pieces from the 16th century and valuable paintings, sculptures, and other ornaments from the 15th century. A few steps further on, you come to the **St Elisabeth Hospital**, which is supposed to have been founded in the year 1204. If you go a little further down the Lange Gasthuisstraat with its attractive, historical facades, and then bear left, you'll come to the **Oude Vaartplaats**, where Antwerp's most famous market, the **Bird Market**, is held every Sunday morning. Everything from animals and plants to food and clothing and art and kitsch change hands at this market. In the evening this area is a popular meeting-place: its many cafés, bars and pubs

have earned this neighbourhood the nickname of *Quartier Latin*.

The **Beguine Convent**, on Rodestraat, is rarely visited by tourists. This 16th-century group of alleyways, cottages and gardens is an oasis of peace and quiet in this bustling city.

For fans of fine porcelain, the **Museum Ridder Smidt van Galder**, in an 18th-century patrician house south of the City Park on the Belgelei, is a real treat. Contemporary paintings, wall tapestries and furniture are displayed side by side with fine porcelain from Europe and East Asia. The garden is also well worth a look.

The **Royal Museum of Fine Arts** on Leopold de Waelplaats spans the complete history of art. The collection of Flemish painting takes up a considerable part of the museum. The first floor is taken up by more than 1,000 works by old masters, including such famous works as *The Adoration of the Magi* by Rubens, the *Entombment of Christ* by Quentin Massys, and the *Seven Sacra-*

ments by Rogier van der Weyden. With some 20 paintings by Rubens, reflecting virtually every period of his creative output, this museum can boast the most remarkable collection of Rubens works in the world. Contemporary painting is also well represented in the museum. Some 1,500 paintings and sculptures in the collection date from the 19th and 20th centuries. As well as well-known works by international artists, the surrealistic pictures of the Belgians René Magritte and Paul Delvaux are particularly worthy of note.

Those interested in modern sculpture will find something to their taste in the **Middelheim Park** in the east of the city. Here, some 300 famous works of contemporary sculptors from Rodin to Moore can be viewed in the open air. Every two years, between June and September, this open-air museum is also the site of the Sculpture Biennial, which is well regarded in the international art world. Jazz festivals also take place regularly in Middelheim.

Left, the entrance to the Rub House. Ri it isn't on the British who have pillar-box

If you're in the mood for something completely different after seeing so much art and architecture, a visit to the **Antwerp Zoo**, with its aquarium, dolphin house, reptile house and planetarium, could be just what you need to revive. Located next to the main railway station, this zoological garden is one of the most beautiful in the world. More than 6,000 animals of 950 different species live in conditions as near to their natural habitats as possible. The socalled Nocturama, dedicated to nocturnal animals, is of particular interest.

A special Children's Zoo opened in 1984; the antics of the young raccoons, nimble squirrels and other animals seem to divert even the most fractious children. In the winter, the zoo allows visitors to take a look behind the scenes.

East of the main railway station, the **Jewish Quarter** stretches between the Avenue Frankrijklei, the zoo and the Koning Albert Park. Antwerp, which is sometimes nicknamed "the Jerusalem on the Scheldt", has the largest Orthodox Jewish community in Europe. Fifteen thousand Jews in the city live in observance of strict religious laws; there are 22 synagogues in Antwerp. Men with long black coats, broad-brimmed hats, long beards and side curls are a common sight on the streets around the railway station. When the sabbath begins on Friday evenings a host of candles illuminate the windows of this district. In Pelikanstraat and the streets around it, there are many small shops which sell kosher groceries, Hebrew books and menorahs.

One of Antwerp's four diamond exchanges is also located on **Pelikanstraat**; only registered members are allowed to enter. The Jewish community is extensively involved in Antwerp's diamond trade, and in its diamond industry in general.

Outside the city centre: Like so many other major cities, Antwerp has expanded its boundaries at the expense of surrounding towns. Today, the city is made up of 10 boroughs which still bear

taurant
Jewish
ter.

the names of the autonomous communities they once were. **Berchem** is well known far beyond the city limits. Here, at the turn of the century, lay the **Zurenborg Quarter**, where art nouveau and all manner of subsequent derivatives originated.

The district of **Hoboken** is highly respected in Japan. Nearly every Japanese child knows the sad story of Nello and his faithful dog Patrasche, who drove their milk-cart from Hoboken to Antwerp every day.

The children's book *A Dog of Flanders*, written by the English author Marie-Louise de la Ramée in 1871, was a best-seller in Japan long before its discovery and subsequent rise to fame in Belgium. Apart from Nello and Patrasche, who have since been immortalised with their own memorial opposite Hoboken's tourist information centre, the visitor can admire the borough's four palaces – among them the rococo castle **Sorgvliedt** – the city's parks and its late Gothic church of Our Lady.

Ekeren's main sights are a moated castle from the 16th century and the 500-year-old church of St Lambert with its towers of white sandstone. Local legend has it that many years ago a heavy hailstorm struck Ekeren and after the storm the hailstones in one area instead of melting remained lying on the ground in the shape of a cross. The population interpreted this as a holy sign and renamed the place "hail-cross". Every year a festive parade is held on the site of the miracle, today marked by a stone cross.

The borough of **Merksem** earned its name not as a result of its four majestic castles, but because it was once the property of a "majesty", or lord. For years residents of **Wilrijk** have been known as "goatheads", a nickname which sprang from the long tradition of goat-raising in the town. This is not to say that Wilrijk, originally a Roman settlement, is without any architectural interest: there is, for example, the magnificent 15th-century Iepermann

The processio
Our Dear
Lady in
Mechelen

castle and the Gothic St Bavon's church.

The giants of Deurne: One of the main attractions in the town of **Deurne** is the museum, in which 19th-century workers' apartments have been faithfully reconstructed; but the town is best known for its "giants". Every September, giant puppets are carried through the streets. A similar festival takes place in nearby Borgerhout, where the giants, slightly smaller than in Deurne, dance to the music of a band.

Geese are the centre of attention during the legendary "goose riding" held during Carnival and on Easter Sunday in **Zandvliet** and **Berendrecht**. The festivities attract thousands of visitors to these two cities, which, despite the continuing expansion of the port, have managed by and large to preserve much of their local character.

Lillo, which was incorporated into Antwerp at the same time as Zandvliet and Berendrecht, doesn't retain much of its former character. The erstwhile village centre has become the site of massive industrial and harbour buildings. Squeezed between the Scheldt and legion factory buildings, only the little port, the old fortification wall (Lillo-Fort) and the Eenhoorn Windmill, which was moved stone by stone from its original location and rebuilt, have been able to withstand the encroachment of the modern port.

The villages of Oosterweel, Oorderen and Wilmersdonk, which were incorporated into Antwerp in 1929, have altogether vanished from the map. They were razed to the ground in 1962 to make more room for the port. Occupying the site where Oorderen once stood, is a General Motors assembly plant. All that remains of Wilmersdonk is a single church tower rising, like an eternal reproach, from the warehouses of the Churchill Basin.

Tall stories: Only 23 km (14 miles) from the gates of Antwerp lies Mechelen (Malines). Mechelen can look back on a glorious past; today, it is known as the city of the bells and has made a name for

itself as a carpet producer and a centre for market gardening. The Emperor Charles V grew up in this city, which was an enclave of the diocese of Liège in the Middle Ages. After 1356, it belonged to Flanders. In 1473, Mechelen became the base of the highest court in the Low Countries, the Great Council; shortly thereafter, it was made the capital of the Burgundian Low Countries, and was the epitome of splendour and glamour. The Emperor Charles's guardian in the Netherlands, Margaret of Austria, resided in Mechelen from 1507 to 1530. In 1559, Mechelen became the religious centre of Belgium. The primate of the Catholic Church resides in Mechelen.

Mechelen's main symbol is the mighty Saint Rombout's cathedral, the construction of which began in the 13th century, but was not completed until 200 years later. The church tower was to have been 167 metres (546 ft) high; in the end, construction stopped at 97 metres (317 ft). Anyone who climbs this tower can enjoy a wonderful view over the city. The citizens' pride in their tower may be responsible for a story that they once tried to reach the moon – their aim being to put out its light (they have been known as *maneblussers* – moon-extinguishers – ever since).

Inside the cathedral you will find a wealth of marble altars, ornate tombs, paintings by Flemish masters – van Dyck and Quellin among them – and baroque decoration. But the church is best known for its carillon. Since 1981 the tower has had two sets of bells; the new carillon, with 49 bells, is not only the heaviest in Europe, it is said to be the richest in tone, as well. You can judge for yourself during the Monday evening concerts in the summer, when the bells of the cathedral, the **church of Our Lady Across the Dyle**, and the **Hofes van Busleyden** ring out.

Mechelen is said to be the cradle of the Flemish carillon. In Russian, the word for carillon translates as something like "bells from Mechelen". The

Men in a house for women: the Beguine Convent in Lier.

Internationaal Hoger Instituut voor Beiaardkunst is unique here, would-be bell-ringers from around the world are trained to become masters of their profession. Mechelen's enthusiasm for bell-ringing is such that the city even has a mobile carillon for processions.

The cathedral is not the only souvenir of the city's glory days: there are also the **Palace of Margaret of Austria**, today's Palace of Justice, built in 1520; the old **Assizes** (today the City Archive); the late Gothic Hof van Busleyden, now the city museum; and many splendid churches. The city's town hall is located in the former Cloth Hall (14th century) in the Palace of the Great Council. Its construction lasted nearly 400 years, until the beginning of this century. A statue of Margaret of Austria stands on a pedestal in the square in front of the building. The impression that she is giving the building the cold shoulder rather than standing sentinel is explained by the fact that the council used to meet on the other side of the marketplace, where the main post office stands today.

Timmermans's homeland: On the border of Kempenland, where the Great and Lesser Nethe intersect, the town of **Lier** lies only 17 km (10 miles) away from Antwerp. Local wisdom has it that Lier's residents declined a university in favour of a cattle-market. This story is said to have resulted in their nickname "sheepheads". But Lier isn't devoid of culture. The birthplace of the Flemish author Felix Timmermans, it gained worldwide renown under the pseudonym "Lierke Plezierke". The writer erected a literary monument to this city and to the Flemish way of life in his works. The **Timmermans-Opsomer House** in the old manor of van Geertruyen is dedicated to him and to other artists who were born in Lier.

Opposite this, on the other side of the Lesser Nethe, stands the main sightseeing attraction of Lier: the **Zimmer Tower**, named after the clockmaker and astronomer Louis Zimmer. The tower, which once belonged to the medieval fortifications of the city, has housed the astronomical studio with planetarium and Zimmer's Jubilee Clock since 1930. The clockwork of Zimmer's timepiece is a masterpiece of human precision. Its 13 dials are clearly visible on the building's facade.

Lier became a city as early as 1212. The one-time clothmaking community still retains much of its original plan. Its chief attractions are located close together: the Gothic Saint Gummarus church (1425–1520) with its imposing tower and many artistic treasures; the **Grote Markt** with its rococo **Town Hall** and the **Bell Tower** from the year 1369; the **Vleeshuis**, from 1418; and the medieval **Beguine Convent**.

Founded in the 13th century, expanded in the 17th, and still in an extremely good condition, the Beguine Convent is a town unto itself. A stroll through its narrow alleyways, past the low houses and picturesque corners, transports the visitor from the modern day to the fictional world of Felix Timmermans.

whom the tolls: the astronomical clock on the Zimmer Tower in Lier.

BELGIAN LIMBURG

The province of **Belgian Limburg** lies in the Flemish part of Belgium, bordering on the Netherlands and Germany. Limburg belonged to the territory of the bishopric of Liège until 1784, and didn't become an independent province until 1815. Since 1839, Limburg has been divided into a Dutch section and a Belgian one. The core of the former duchy, containing the town of Limburg, is today still part of the province of Liège.

In the past, Limburg was more a place for passing through than lingering in for any length of time; tourists from Holland and northern Germany cross the area when heading to the west and southwest. Of late, however, the region has managed to establish itself as a holiday area in its own right. Limburg offers weary city dwellers relaxation for both body and soul.

The region is traversed by three major motorways: the 100-km (60-mile) long Haspen route leading through the hilly country in the south of Limburg; the Teuton route running for about 140 km (90 miles) and connecting Limburg's Kempenland with Dutch Brabant; and the Demer and Mergel route leading for over 100 km (60 miles) through Bilsen, Hoeselt and Riemst.

The area where tourists are made so welcome today was once far from hospitable. It was the Romans who built the area's first roads, to link up with their established settlements on the Rhine: the old Roman cities of Cologne, Koblenz, Aachen and Trier are not far away. But they probably wouldn't have gone to such lengths had they envisaged that from the 3rd century AD those same roads would be used by marauding Germanic tribes intent on attacking their empire.

Physically, the province is remarkably attractive. Its landscape is made up of areas of heath, fen, dunes, forest, and lake, one giving way to another. The

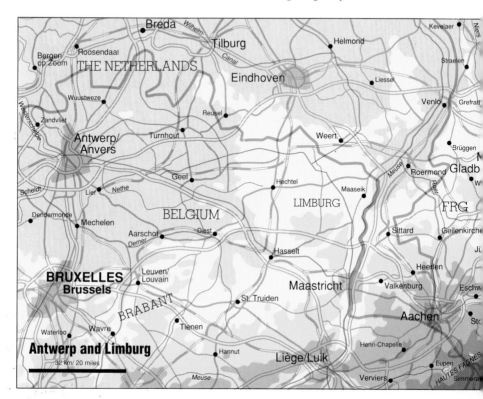

flat, agrarian countryside, with a liberal sprinkling of camping sites, recreation and holiday centres, as well as nature preserves and well-marked trails, is ideal for lengthy walks and bicycle tours, particularly as the gradients are never too steep. There are special cycle paths everywhere, often well away from the main roads and always well maintained. Because most car drivers in these parts also use their bikes quite a lot, they are a good deal more considerate towards cyclists than elsewhere. Exploring Limburg by bike is a viable option even for the whole family.

Our tour begins in the southeast, in Tongeren, and proceeds counter-clockwise around the province, along the Dutch border.

Belgium's oldest town: The region of **Hesbaye** lies in the southwest of the province of Limburg. The rolling land rises to 70 metres (230 ft) above sea level in the north, and 230 metres (750 ft) in the south. The fertile countryside is characterised by fruit trees, fields and farmhouses. It's here that the most important old towns of Limburg can be found. **Tongeren** (Tongres, population 35,000), for example, is the oldest town in Belgium. To make sure that the visitor doesn't forget this fact, there are signs advertising its venerable age along all roads going into town.

Belgium's first Christian town was founded in the 1st century AD; at that time, it bore the name Aduatuca Tungrorum. In Roman times, Tongeren occupied a position of strategic significance on the road from Bavai to Cologne. The town became the first bishop's see of the country in the 4th century. In the Middle Ages, Tongeren saw the flowering of a prosperous weaving and linen industry.

Tongeren is so clean that it reminds the visitor of one of those spic-and-span Dutch towns which look more like model villages than real life communities. The modern-looking window displays in the shops offer a sharp contrast to the relative poverty of Belgium's industrial

urg's
agrarian
tryside.

areas and to the old-fashioned looking shops in the Ardennes. It's as though the visitor had entered another world, a different country. Here hair is worn in the latest styles and skirts are worn with considerably shorter hemlines. The town and its residents are thoroughly stylish. You can't buy simple, inexpensive tennis shoes here: they have to be Airwalks, Reeboks or Converse. Shopping streets are dominated by international products sold in shops with names like "Charisma" or "Xylos-Fashion".

Gallic uprising: The town contains a wealth of historic sites worth seeing, even though many of its very oldest buildings were destroyed by the Norman invasion of 881. Most of the buildings which one can see today are products of the Romanesque or Gothic architectural periods.

A statue of **Ambiorix** stands proudly at the centre of the marketplace. The chieftain of the Eburon tribe, he was the first citizen of Tongeren. The memorial is a reminder of the year 54 BC, when Ambiorix plotted an uprising in Belgian Gaul in order to annihilate the legions of the occupying Romans, with the result that the latter were forced temporarily to abandon their attempts at conquering this part of the country of the Belgae. It should be added that this collective term would never have been welcomed by the fiercely independent tribes operating in this part of the world at the time.

Towering over this figure is the **Basilica of Our Lady**, which, with its 90-metre (294-ft) high tower, presents an impressive sight. This basilica stands on the foundation of a 4th-century sanctuary to the Virgin Mary. While its choir, transept and main aisle date from the 13th century, the building's western pillars and tower are products of a later time. The old windows from the middle of the 16th century have been preserved. The church's wealth of treasures is one of the richest in the country. One noteworthy item among the many wonderful objects is the *Head of the Dying Christ*, a woodcarving from the 11th

century. Major concerts are given in the basilica every year as a part of the well-known Festival of Flanders.

Roman fortifications: Tongeren was fortified by the Romans in the course of the 2nd century AD with a double wall which ran around the town; the original outer wall was some 5 km (3 miles) in length. These Roman protective walls served as a basis for the medieval fortifications. Access to the town was facilitated by the many gates in the walls; in the west of the town, you can still see some remnants of these fortifications.

Only the 14th-century **Moerenpoort** among the gates survived. Its three storeys house the Museum of Military History. The old town hall fell victim to a fire in 1677, when the French troops of Louis XIV set the town ablaze. The **New Town Hall** replaced it in the early 17th century. As well as containing a collection of 18th-century furniture from Liège, the town hall boasts a collection of excellent paintings. It's also home to the **Municipal Museum and Archive,**

documenting the history of the town.

The **Beguine Convent**, with its charming crooked streets and picturesque corners, is one of the largest and most beautiful in Belgium. We have already mentioned that the Beguine order was created for women who wanted to live in a religious community without taking strict religious vows; it was founded during the Crusades to provide for the widows of the many aristocrats who lost their lives in the battles. Later, middle-class women were also accepted. The Tongeren Beguine Convent was founded in 1300, but the buildings and small church which you can see today weren't built until the 17th century.

The **Gallo-Roman Museum** tells the story behind the Asterix comics; it's also the Archaeological Museum of the province of Limburg.

Along the Meuse: As you proceed toward the Dutch border, which is only marked by a sign, you come to **Lanaken**, which provides enthusiasts of watersports with a place from which to launch

, church anaken. ht, a brisk ll in seik.

canoe trips down the Meuse. The large brick buildings which make up the groups of tidy farmhouses along the road are always being cleaned. Even the cows in the meadows look as though they have been scrubbed.

Heavy bicycle traffic on the road north toward Maaseik demands a car driver's undivided attention. There are, of course, well-tended bike paths on either side of the road, sometimes even separate bike roads; nonetheless, it's sensible to exercise caution.

Decorating windows with flowers, copper kettles, pots, figures, and small frilly curtains is a whole folk art in itself in these regions (perfectly clean window panes are a prerequisite). Modern chemical cleaners are in fierce competition with more traditional methods. When the cashier at the petrol station polishes the counter after you've picked up your change, you can be sure you're in Limburg. The windmills in the little villages off the road are no longer of any economic importance. Research into renewable energy is now concentrated on solar technology.

Maaseik: The countless old patrician buildings of the town of **Maaseik** (population 20,000) give an idea of the architectural style of the Meuse area. The "eik" in the village's name refers to the oak forest which used to surround the town. A monastery was founded here in the year 725 and it was from this that the present town developed. The square **marketplace** is bordered by two rows of tall lime trees and surrounded by all the important buildings of the village: the registry office, the banks, hotels, the town hall with a typical stoop and, quite nearby, the **church of Saint Catherine**. This church contains some interesting ecclesiastical vestments which were made in England at the beginning of the 9th century. Art historians believe the brothers **Jan and Hubert van Eyck** were originally from Maaseik; a memorial to them has been erected in the marketplace.

Among the 30 or so Renaissance fa-

The van Eyck brothers dominate marketplace of their birthplace Maaseik.

248

cades which have been preserved in the Meuse valley one of the most interesting is the facade of the oldest apothecary in the country, which dates from the year 1704. Three museums shelter under one roof, in a complex known as **Museactron**. Here, you can see the Apothecary Museum; its sales rooms, where countless containers, scales and jars are on display, lead to the local Archaeological Museum, which has an extraordinary collection of items from prehistoric, Roman, medieval and modern times. The Baker's Museum contains a reconstructed bakery, complete with equipment.

Yachting on the Meuse: Due to the relative dearth of public transportation, hitchhiking is common hereabouts. Even those of more advanced years rely on their thumbs and the brotherly love of passing drivers. The area past **Kinrooi**, which is the northernmost community of the Meuse region, attracts primarily water-loving tourists, due to its plethora of water-related facilities, including two yacht marinas with capacity for about 1,300 boats.

Going west on Route 73, you can visit four windmills near **Tongerlo**. One of these is a restored watermill with a restaurant, which also houses two museums: a **Forest Museum** and a **Pipe Museum**. The **Premonstratensian Abbey** of Tongerlo was founded in the 12th century. The avenue leading up to the wall surrounding the abbey's buildings is lined with lime trees which are over 300 years old. It was from this abbey that Father Waerenfried van Straaten led a relief programme for the starving population of Germany after World War II. The abbey buildings include mission houses and workhouses, a church with neo-Byzantine ornamentation, the bishop's residence, and a refectory, as well as farm buildings and a printing press.

Art exhibitions are regularly held in the monastery's 16th-century granary buildings. The **Leonardo da Vinci Fantasy Museum** also belongs to the ab-

ical
for the
ns of
urg.

bey. It includes a copy of Leonardo's *Last Supper* executed by Leonardo's student Andrea Solario shortly after the original had been painted.

Passing through the cosy town of **Bree**, whose **church of St Michael** contains impressive woodcarvings, you come to the first major holiday spot on our route: **Peer**. A notable tourist attraction is the **Pony Express Station**, named after the famous mail route of the American West. It offers a broad range of country & western activities, a saloon, stables and workers' barracks. The most popular attractions are the tours, either on horseback "Western style" or in a covered wagon.

In the forested holiday area which lies to the north, around **Lommel**, an attractive bungalow park, **De Vossemeren,** stretches between dunes and heath. This holiday resort offers a subtropical swimming pool, called "Aqua Sana", and various other tourist attractions. By following the road further west you come to Mol, which as well as

being well-known in Belgium for its export of containers for radioactive waste, is famous for a centuries-old library housed in the Norbertine Abbey.

Coal and heath: Kempenland, Limburg's northernmost region, does not, according to strict administrative divisions, belong to the province of Limburg itself, but rather to Antwerp. Limburg's share of Kempenland consists of a single large evergreen forest and broad expanses of heath. Only if it is sufficiently irrigated can the flat, rather sandy soil be used as pastureland, or for growing grain and feed. The forests, idyllic moors and purple-coloured heaths of Kempenland conceal numerous small lakes, home to a rich variety of birdlife, including crested grebes, rare kinds of woodpecker and pochards. The moors are known for their flora, including pipeweed and carniverous sundew.

Visible traces of industrial buildings serve as reminders of the natural veins of coal underlying the area. For a time these veins were responsible for a rush

The lamb **season.**

of prosperity and a rapid increase of population in the region. But the coal was exhausted as early as 1910 and the industrial landscape was reclaimed to form holiday and hiking areas in the 1960s. In the mining town of **Beringen**, the **Mining Museum** (Mijnmuseum), located directly at the entrance to the pits, is devoted to the history of Limburg's coal mines.

In the region east of Beringen, particularly around **Houthalen-Heichteren**, there are numerous recreation parks – such as Hengelhoef, Kelchterhoef and Molenheide – all well endowed with hotels, vacation houses and campsites. In addition, they include a wildlife park and a hiking park, a waterslide complex, paddle-boat rentals, fishing ponds, and De Plas, a centre offering all manner of water sports.

In the community of **Heusden-Zolder**, southeast of Beringen, the most important tourist attractions are the **racetrack of Terlaemen** and the holiday estate of Bovy. The racetrack, 4.2 km (2.6 miles) in length, is a meeting-place for the international racing car and motorcycle elite, but you are welcome to drive along it with your own vehicle. In the domain of **Bovy** the chief attractions are the goatyard and "herbal path", a restaurant serving typical farmhouse dishes of the region and a pancake house. Throughout the year Bovy provides a rich variety of traditional Flemish folk pastimes. A historic train with a steam locomotive offers a chance to take an excursion through the forests and meadows to the coal mines of Zolder.

Central Limburg: Between Beringen and Hasselt, you can see the **Albert Canal**. This important waterway connects the Meuse to Antwerp and the sea: it can accommodate ships of up to 9,000 tons.

Hasselt (population 65,000), the capital of the province, lies in the middle of extensive fruit orchards reaching south as far as St Truiden. As well as many fruit-related businesses, the town contains the seat of the province's adminis-

tration. Hasselt is the third-largest business centre in Flanders, the sixth largest in Belgium; it is a bustling, flower-filled shopping centre for the neighbouring communities. A market is held every Tuesday and Friday on Kolonel-Dusart Square. Every Saturday afternoon in summer an art market is held behind the town hall.

The construction of **Saint Quentin's cathedral** was begun in the 11th century, but the work continued until well into the 19th century. As well as a Renaissance choir, a baroque chancel and many splendid paintings, the cathedral contains the oldest monstrance (1287) in the world. The cathedral tower houses the 42 bells of the famous **Hasselt Carillon**. Now restored, the bells regularly ring out in concerts during the summer months. In June campanologists from around the world rendezvous at the International Festival of Bell-Ringers held in the town.

The **church of Our Lady**, near the marketplace, was built in 1730, and restored in 1951. Among the church's many art objects, the one which particularly stands out is the image of the **Virga Jesse**, the Black Virgin, from the 14th century. A festival is held in her honour every seven years.

Hasselt has been the headquarters of the *jenever* (gin) industry since the 17th century and many folk customs have grown up over the years around this regional liqueur. The "Witteke" of Hasselt is most commonly served as an aperitif or with coffee but it is also valued as an essential ingredient in many local dishes. The **National Jenever Museum** offers the visitor a closer look into the long and rich jenever-making tradition of Hasselt. Here, you can see the entire process by which the clear liqueur was produced in the early 19th century. The visitor can learn about the construction of the original steam distillery and follow the entire manufacturing procedure, step by step.

There many exclusive clothing boutiques in Hasselt, but much more inter-

Typical residentia architectu in Hasselt

esting for most visitors is the **Fashion Museum**, tracing the development of men's, women's, and children's fashion from 1830 to the present day.

The **Stellingwerff-Waerdenhof Museum** offers a perspective on the County of Loon and contains some interesting art nouveau ceramics.

The **Carillon Museum**, located in the tower of Saint Quentin's cathedral, is devoted to the function and history of carillons in general, and the carillon of Hasselt in particular.

Next to the **Minorite church**, in the **Museum of Saint Paterke**, you can see the funeral chapel and the confessional of Father Valentinus Paquay, as well as the room in which he died on 1 January, 1905. The **National Museum of War and Peace** displays an impressive collection of weapons, war machines, posters and documentary material concerning the two World Wars. The extensive collection, which is divided into four departments, deals with the origin and history of Belgium, the period up to the end of World War I, World War II and its consequences, and the situation in Belgium today.

There are nine **nature trails** which lead through the various communities of Hasselt. Hasselt strikes pedestrians first and foremost as a town of flowers; it has been awarded numerous national and international prizes for its gardens and floral decorations. If one is interested in taking an excursion into the outlying area, the **Hazelaarroute**, a 65-km (40-mile) long tourist route for motorists or cyclists, is recommended. This route leads to the most beautiful spots in the communities of **Kuringen**, **Kermt**, **Stevoort**, **Sint-Lanbrechts-Herk** and **Wimmertingen**.

To the east of Hasselt, on the road to Genk, you'll find the region's principal tourist attraction: the **Provincial Domain of Bokrijk**. The town's open-air museum is one of the largest and most scientific in Europe; it's also an important centre of folk culture in Belgian Limburg. The museum presents a fascinating picture of the lifestyle of a typical Flanders farmer living between 1500 and 1920.

The idea of building an open-air museum was first conceived in 1953, when a farmhouse from Lummen was moved to the area, at that time an unremarkable stretch of woodland. When the museum opened in 1958, and for a few years after that, it comprised a group of 20 houses. Today the museum covers some 1,375 acres and includes exhibits covering rural and urban themes. The museum's rural division depicts the daily life of the people in the different regions of Flanders. It's not only the houses which are reconstructed: the entire environment in which people of earlier times lived and worked, including their barnyards, interiors, furniture, kitchen utensils and equipment, has been recreated.

Among the buildings are mills, chapels, a Romanesque church from the 12th century and a village school. Highlights include a bakehouse from Oostmalle, a peat-storage barn from Kalmthout and a

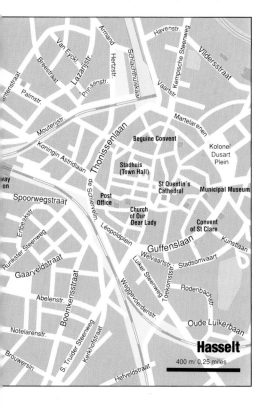

blacksmith's from the village of Neeroeteren. The museum's urban division is a replica of part of the old city of Antwerp.

The three distinct sections of the museum are divided from one another by stretches of greenery. Approximately 100 buildings rescued from various villages and towns comprise this open-air museum; most of these buildings would have been ruthlessly torn down during the process of modernisation had they not been transported here. They have been carefully brought stone by stone and faithfully reassembled.

As well as these structures, the grounds also contain an **arboretum** (containing over 3,000 species of shrubs and trees), a rose garden (**rosarium**), a deer park and a chicken yard, numerous ponds and, to the delight of all children, a first-rate playground. Each year, this open-air museum is visited by some 100,000 tourists from all over the world.

Industry and administration: Administrative buildings and industrial structures dominate the skyline of the city of **Genk** (population 61,000). Genk is the geographic and economic centre of Limburg. Founded by the Celts, Genk was, at the beginning of this century, a village of 2,500 inhabitants: today, its coal industry, first developed at the beginning of the 20th century, has transformed it into a modern city with a wealth of shopping centres and stores.

More than 30,000 people in the area are employed in the automotive, chemical or energy industries. The **Limburg Zoo** in Zwartberg, which contains more than 3,000 animals, has the largest bear population of any European zoo, and also boasts a white rhinoceros.

Fruit gardens: Going back through Hasselt and diagonally through the surrounding orchards, you will come to **Sint Truiden** (population 37,000) in the southwest of the province. This city grew out of a Benedictine monastery, which was founded in the 7th century by St Trudo.

The slender **Bell Tower**, near the

Between Genk and Hasselt: the "Queen of the South" restaurant

marketplace and the town hall, is visible from a long way off. While its pedestal dates from the 12th century, the bell tower itself was built in the 17th century. Its carillon is made up of 41 bells. The city's spacious **marketplace** is the second-largest in Belgium. The elegant town hall was given its classical facade in 1750.

Right next to this, you can see the remains of the former **benedictine monastery**. The steeple of the Romanesque tower burned down in December 1975, but the monumental entrance gate and the abbot's house with the Imperial Chamber have been preserved. The buildings of the **Beguine Convent** date from the 17th and 18th centuries. The 35 wall paintings in the early Gothic **Collegiate Church of Our Lady**, which date from the 14th and 15th centuries, depict legends of the saints. The **Astronomical Clock** of K. Festraets opposite this church is made up of more than 20,000 individual parts. At 6 metres (20ft) high and 4 metres (13 ft) wide, it is the largest clock of its kind. When the clock strikes the hour, representatives of the 12 medieval guilds appear, followed by Death in the figure of a skeleton.

Halfway between this city and Tongeren, the departure point of our excursion, lies the old town of **Borgloon**. In the Middle Ages, this was the capital of the county of Loon, which is today a part of the province of Limburg. The Renaissance **town hall**, which dates from the year 1680, is ornamented with an open arcade and a polygonal tower; the building contains a treasure chest from the 12th century.

Close to Borgloon is **Henk Palace**, one of the most splendid sights of the whole tour. It stands in the midst of wonderful gardens dotted with exquisite fountains. Unfortunately, this building is not open to the general public. Nevertheless, the view from without is sure to provide the visitor with a lasting impression of the invigorating freshness and undisturbed tranquillity of Belgian Limburg.

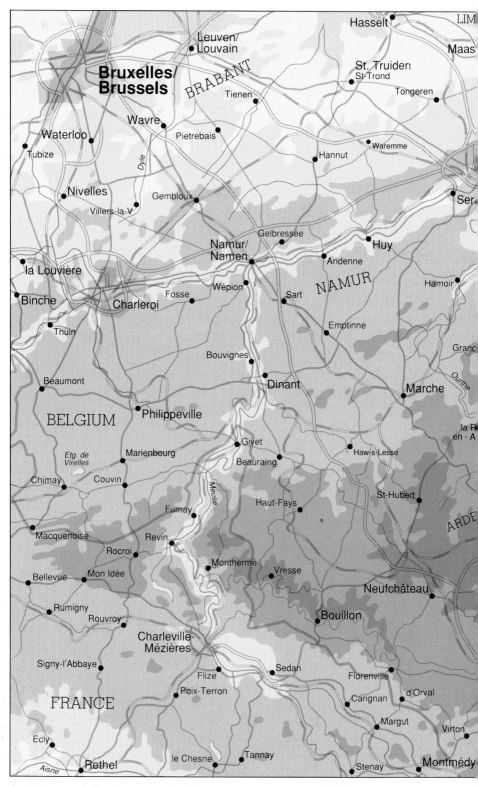

Hasselt

LIM

Maas

Leuven/
Louvain

St. Truiden
St-Trond

Tongeren

BRABANT

Tienen

Bruxelles/
Brussels

Wavre

Pietrebais

Hannut

Waremme

Waterloo

Tubize

Dyle

Nivelles

Villers-la-V

Gembloux

Ser

Gelbressée

Namur/
Namen

Huy

Andenne

la Louvière

Wépion

NAMUR

Hamoir

Binche

Fosse

Charleroi

Sart

Thuin

Emptinne

Bouvignes

Beaumont

Dinant

Marche

BELGIUM

Philippeville

Granc

Ourthe

Givet

Marienbourg

Etg. de
Virelles

Beauraing

Haw-s-Lesse

la R
en - A

Chimay

Couvin

Meuse

Haut-Fays

St-Hubert

Fumay

ARDE

Macquenoise

Revin

Rocroi

Monthermé

Vresse

Neufchâteau

Bellevue

Mon Idée

Rumigny

Bouillon

Rouvroy

Charleville-
Mézières

Sedan

Signy-l'Abbaye

Flize

Florenville

Poix-Terron

d'Orval

FRANCE

Carignan

Margut

Virton

Ecly

le Chesne

Tannay

Aisne

Rethel

Stenay

Montmédy

16 km/ 10 miles

erlen
kenburg
Eschweiler
Düren
Stolberg
Aachen
**FED. REPUBLIC
OF GERMANY**
pelle
Wollersheim
Eupen
HAUTES FAGNES
Rur-Talsperre
Urft
Verviers
Simmerath
Monschau
Schleiden
**NORTH RHINE
WESTPHALIA**
Malmedy
Bullange
Stavelot
Losheim
EIFEL
St-Vith
Prüm
Pronstel
Wemperhardt
alize
RHINELAND - PALATINATE
Clervaux
Sinspelt
Bitburg
Wiltz
Vianden
Sure
Ettelbruck
Diekirch
ange
Echternach
Jseldange
Mersch
Graulinster
LUXEMBOURG
Capellen
Luxembourg
Saarbourg
Remich
gwy
Esch-s-A.
Mondorf-le-B.

FROM EAST
TO WEST

It is easy to cross Belgium from East to West on the motorway which is extremely fast and, at night, brilliantly lit (as mentioned before in this book, Belgium's motorways are so brightly lit they can be seen from the Moon). The alternative is to drive along the Meuse, the Sambre, and the Canal de Centre – that is to say the northern part of French-speaking Wallonia.

Such a trip will lead you from Eupen, near Aachen, through Liège, Huy, Namur, Charleroi, and Mons to Tournai. As this area is heavily industrialised, there aren't as many points of interest as there are in the typical holiday regions of the country. Even such a nature-loving and hospitable land as Belgium can't live exclusively from its tourism.

In the province of Liège, the three Eastern Districts of Eupen, Malmedy and St Vith, with their 70,000 German-speaking inhabitants, form Belgium's 85-km long (53 miles) border with Germany. In 1919, this territory was ceded to Belgium under the Treaty of Versailles; Hitler annexed it to the Third Reich in 1940, and it was liberated by the Allies in 1945.

Since the constitutional reforms of 1970, the Belgian government has formally recognised language communities and language barriers, and they have become offically delineated. The redrawing of county boundaries conferred linguistic independence on German-speaking regions, as well as on French and Flemish ones. In 1984, German-speaking Belgians were officially acknowledged to be a national cultural entity, and a German-speaking government council was created, equal in authority to that of the other two linguistic communities. The council governs state support of the German-language radio station, which can be heard all the way to Brussels; it also administers education, both for children and adults, health,

FIERY ELIJAH

On Sunday, all hell breaks loose in the Raeren railway station. Without fail, some hundred rucksacks, hiking trousers and waterproof anoraks, together with the men and women wearing them, crowd on to the station's narrow platform. They're all waiting for the arrival of what's currently the most popular tourist attraction of Belgium: the Venn Train.

The route gave this train its name. Drawn by a 1,750 horsepower diesel locomotive, the train crosses the greater part of the Hautes Fagnes (Hohes Venn). This area of high moorland in the region near the German-Belgian border, between Aachen, Eupen and Malmedy, is probably the loveliest part of the whole Ardennes.

Every Sunday at 10 a.m. the train starts from Eupen. Shortly before 10.30 it rolls into the little railway station of Raeren. The rucksacks and anoraks begin to move. Those who've had the forethought to reserve in advance (tel: 0032-87-852487) take their seats in the train's beautifully appointed 1930s carriages; those who haven't booked ahead have to rough it on the hard wooden benches located towards the rear of the train.

A short blast on the whistle by the guard and the train begins to move. Somewhat laboriously, it zigzags through the hills of Raeren. Here the Venn Train crosses from Belgium to Germany, and sets its course for the very heart of the Hautes Fagnes.

In Roetgen, a special kind of retail trade awaits the visitor: the border market. Here, on Belgian soil, but before the customs station, cigarettes, tobacco and coffee are sold at cut prices.

When, 106 years ago, the Venn Train first went into operation, things were very different. At that time, the area around Eupen was still administered by the Prussians. The government in Berlin wanted to link the coal veins around Aachen and the iron ore deposits in Luxemburg and Lorraine. Dubbed "Fiery Elijah" by locals, the train was warmly welcomed by residents of the area. Its advent provided what was an economically deprived region with a link to the main rail connections in the north and thus to the world.

An upward economic trend wasn't far behind the introduction of the railway. Factories quckly sprang up along the tracks, and the timber trade also flourished. Where once wood had to be hauled with slow horse-drawn conveyances, it could now be transported via the Venn Train. Furthermore tourism also blossomed. "Out of the grey town walls into the woods and fields" ran the not-very-catchy slogan of the new tourist industry.

Most cities and villages along the line saw the dawn of a whole new way of life. In Monschau which the train reached after an hour and a half, the

locals looked on the train not so much as aiding the area's hitherto untapped industrial potential as a "bringer of guests" to the Eifel region.

At Monschau the first passengers leave the train, with good reason: Monschau has managed to preserve its late-medieval ambience perfectly. Lying in a narrow valley, and not very large, the village seems to have been overlooked by the passage of time.

A German from the Rhineland who has chosen to settle here describes the attitude of people of the Hohes Venn thus. "They advertise for tourists and hope that not too many strangers come."

From Monschau onwards the veteran train really has to work. The climb up to the German-Belgian border village of Kalterherberg is considerable. Children and adults alike wonder how, and if, the train will manage to meet the challenge of the mountain. The conductor reassures the passengers in the local dialect.

Conductors, engineers and any other personnel of the Venn Train are enthusiasts, not professionals. Their weekend work is completely unpaid. On Saturday, they get the train ready for its Sunday journey; on Monday, it's back to their regular jobs in shops, offices and factories.

In Kalterherberg the rucksacks, hiking trousers and anoraks get off. From here, the rest of the journey is by foot.

tourism, sport, and the concerns of pensioners. Other public considerations fall under the jurisdiction of the Walloon part of the country. The German council convenes in Eupen, the largest town of the German-speaking area of Belgium.

Door to the West: Eupen (population 15,000) lies near the German border, at the edge of the nature park Hautes Fagnes (Hohes Venn). In the 14th and 15th centuries, the town experienced flourishing growth thanks to the textile industry, which reached its peak in the 18th century.

Although Eupen suffered considerable damage in World War II, the old town of today is still characterised by numerous patrician buildings dating from the 17th, 18th and 19th centuries. A notable example is the house on the marketplace which houses the *Grenzecho*, the daily newspaper for German-speaking Belgians.

Eupen's most famous church is **Saint Nicholas**, originally a chapel; it is first mentioned in documents of 1213, and became a parish church in 1695. The city planner of Aachen, Laurenz Mefferatis, designed the baroque building which you can see today; construction began in 1721. Ludwig von Fisenne, a well-known architect from Aachen, is responsible for the appearance of the western facade, which was built between 1896 and 1898. The front of the church is "defended" by two towers.

The **Municipal Museum of Eupen**, housed in a building that is worth a look in itself, is devoted to the history of the area, which was compelled to change its political allegiance remarkably often over the years. As well as exhibits demonstrating the developments of Raeren stoneware and regional fashion, the museum offers a complete restoration of a goldsmithy; in this workshop, three generations of Eupen goldsmiths toiled; some of their remarkable handiwork is on display.

The **Museum of Natural History** contains a collection of minerals of the region and an exhibition of stuffed mammals and birds, shown in their natural habitats.

Carnival is celebrated with gusto in Eupen. From the Thursday before Carnival weekend until the parade on the Monday before Lent with which the festivities culminate, the streets are bustling with activity. Another event which attracts crowds of visitors every year is the **St Martin's Parade** held on 11 November, when citzens re-enact the story of St Martin. The saint is accompanied by his goose, Roman soldiers and lantern-bearing children. A huge bonfire concludes the festivities. In the summer, Eupen residents unwind at the **Stau See** (Dam Lake), the largest lake in Belgium. It was created at the confluence of the Vesder and Getz rivers by a dam 63 metres (206 ft) high and 410 metres (1,340 ft) long.

Metropolis in the East: Liège (Luik; population 250,000, or half a million including environs), located at the junction of the Meuse and the Ourthe rivers, is a bishopric, a university city, the centre of the Belgian steel industry, and the capital of the province. The city of Liège grew from a simple chapel, which was erected on the Meuse in 558 at the behest of St Monulphe, the Bishop of Tongeren. One of the Bishop's successors, St Lambert, Bishop of Tongeren-Maastricht, was murdered in Liège in 705. St Hubert later had a church built in Lambert's memory, and transferred the seat of the bishopric to Liège.

The city experienced its first burst of development in the 10th century under Bishop Notker; his reign saw the construction of a cathedral, the Bishop's Palace, two cloisters, and seven monasteries. Liège in the Middle Ages was a city of craftsmen, particularly of goldsmiths, silversmiths and arms manufacturers. At the city limits stood the Fabrique Nationale d'Armes de Guerre, world-renowned for its hunting weapons in particular. Liège was the first city in Europe to mine coal. The roads along which coal and steel were transported have remained, although the coal-mining

eding
s: Liège
dles the
Meuse.
"Fiery
1" on its
ey
gh the
hills.

industry was eventually to come to an end. Liège has the third-largest inland port in Europe, after Duisburg and Paris.

The **marketplace** and the adjoining **Place St-Lambert** form the city's heart. A fountain, symbolising the city's freedom and its autonomous jurisdiction, dominates the marketplace, which is overshadowed by a large pedestal from the 13th century. The two-and-a-half storey baroque **town hall** from the early 18th century, which stands on the Place du Marché, has retained a large portion of its original ornate furnishings: a double staircase, a lobby with eight marble Doric columns, fireplaces, and other artistic treasures.

To the left of the entrance, a bronze plaque commemorates the most famous citizen of Liège: **Georges Simenon**, the creator of Inspector Maigret. The plaque was put up in memory of the policemen who fell during World War II (the real Arnold Maigret was one of these). Rue Léopold 24 is the house in which Georges Simenon was born; he was a personal friend of Chief of Police Maigret, and later used him as the model for his fictional inspector.

The **Archbishop's Palace** on Place St-Lambert, which today houses the **Palace of Justice**, dates back to the reign of Bishop Notker. The parts of the building which have been preserved date from the 17th and 18th centuries.

Museums: One of the most extensive collections of material pertaining to Belgian history is housed in the **Musée de la Vie Wallone**, in the nearby Minorite Cloister, which dates from the 17th century. The museum documents the history of the city's arts and industry and the folk customs, history, language, and heritage of the Walloon peoples. There is even a model of a coal mine.

Dating from 1600, the Renaissance palace in which the **Curtius Museum** is housed was once the residence of the wealthy arms trader Jean Curtius. Today, the museum contains collections of Frankish and Gallo-Roman coins, furniture from Liège and porcelain, stone-

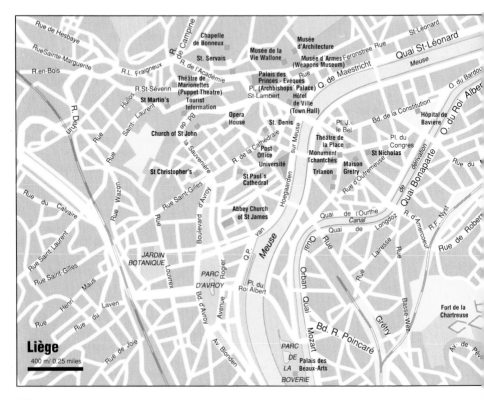

ware and woodcarvings from the Meuse area. Located in the same building, the **Glass Museum** displays works by Phoenician, Moslem, Chinese, Venetian and Belgian craftsmen.

Side by side with the numerous modern industrial administration buildings are the churches of Saint Paul, Saint Jacques and Saint John, all centuries old. Originally a collegiate church, **St Paul**, was elevated to the status of a cathedral by the Concordat of 1801. It was founded in the 10th century, but restored and added to in the middle of the last century. Worthy of note are the stained-glass windows from the 16th century, the *Dead Christ* by Del Cour, and extraordinary furnishings from the 19th century. Other treasures include ivory carvings from the 11th century and a half-length reliquary of St Lambert, which was a present from Charles the Bold.

Of the **abbey church of St Jacques**, founded in the 11th century, all that remains today is the western wing of limestone, with its ribbed vaulting and its medallions, and the famous craftsmen's windows, which date from the 16th century.

The former **Collegiate Church of St John** was built in the 10th century on the model of the Carolingian cathedral of Aachen. According to contemporary sources, the exterior of the original main building had 16 sides, while its interior was octagonal. In the middle of the 18th century a small round building, the side chapels and the choir were altered in accordance with the spirit of classicism. Located in the church is the famous Seat of Wisdom, the *Sedes Sapientiae*, the throne of Christ.

The **church of the Holy Cross** presents the visitor with the relatively rare spectacle of a church with three aisles of the same height; it can be reached from the Place Saint-Lambert by an open staircase. The church contains the keys of Saint Hubert, who was the first Bishop of Liège (he held office in the 8th century). Similar keys were

a
ician in
e. **Right,**
sware is
ditional
uct of the

GEORGES SIMENON

When he created the figure of the pipe-smoking Inspector Maigret, Georges Simenon shaped one of the legendary characters of our time. Indeed Simenon, like Maigret, rose to world fame. Eventually, after 34 years, Simenon decided to forego a further episode of Maigret adventures, to "catch his breath", as he put it. But by the time he made this decision, there wasn't much time left for relaxation: in September, 1989, the author died in Lausanne at the age of 86. In accordance with his last wishes, his death was not made public until after his cremation and interment.

As an author, Simenon broke many records. A total of more than 300 published works make him the most prolific writer since Balzac and the fact that 500 million copies of his books have been sold makes him the most read author in the world. His many stories and novels have been translated into more than 50 languages. Some of his works also made it to the screen, where they met with similar success.

In the 1950s, Simenon selected Switzerland as his preferred country of residence. Here, after the suicide of his beloved daughter Mari-Jo, the former extrovert spent the last 10 years of his life as a recluse, withdrawn from society. At the same time, in keeping with his taste for the paradoxical, he exchanged his luxury villa near Lausanne for a modest house in the city.

Before these quiet later years, Simenon had had a reputation for living life to the hilt. In his *Intimate Memoirs* (translated in 1984), he tells of having casual sexual affairs with thousands of different women.

Simenon spent the first 19 years of his productive life in the Belgian city of Liège, where he was born on 13 February, 1903. "All of the feelings and impressions which we retain in later life have been collected by our 17th or, at the latest, 18th year," he was fond of saying. At 17, he was already a reporter for Liège's daily paper, *Gazette de Liège*.

He wrote his first novel when he was 18; and he wasn't yet 20 when he signed a contract with the publishing house Fayard. The signing of this contract was, in effect, the official hour of Inspector Maigret's birth.

By the age of 26, the author Simenon was firmly established on the path of success. He began to lead an extravagant and nomadic life. At one time or another, he owned a ranch in Arizona, a villa in Cannes and a castle in Switzerland; altogether he moved 33 times in his life. Moving from Europe to the USA, from the canals of Belgium to the lagoons of Tahiti, Simenon travelled the world eagerly gathering impressions and recording his adventures in the form of news reports.

The pace which the writer set himself for his daily output was unbelievably quick: he is supposed to have written one of his novels in a span of three days. He generally used to shut himself up with six full pipes for six hours. He filled 100 pages every day.

Inspector Maigret lives on in the popular imagination as a figure comparable with Sherlock Holmes or with Agatha Christie's master detective Hercule Poirot. However, Inspector Maigret has little in common with the other heroes of detective fiction – he is not, for instance, a detective like Holmes who uses pure logic to solve his cases. As Simenon himself said, he didn't believe in stories, only in people. "Even in the Maigret novels, there aren't any good stories; they aren't really proper detective novels," he once said.

Simenon's private life was characterised by crises, scandals and blows of fate from every direction. In 1950, he divorced his first wife, Tigy, to marry his secretary, the Canadian Denise Quinet. But this marriage, too, fell apart. It wasn't until he was fairly elderly that the successful writer found, in his former housekeeper, Teresa, what he was really looking for: love and mothering.

Simenon bad life a quiet farewell, without fanfare. The "phenomenon" of Simenon remains a kind of fabulous literary beast. Paradoxically, it's the intellectuals who are most attracted to him – perhaps because he resembles them so little.

once used in the church to cauterise bleeding wounds.

In 1794, the **cathedral of St Hubert**, located on the square of the same name, was destroyed by Liège revolutionaries. Its foundations are still visible. The work of art which has become the most famous in the city today was, fortunately, rescued from the destruction: the bronze **Baptismal Font** by Renier van Huy, housed in the Romanesque **church of St Bartholomew**, dating from between the 10th and the 12th centuries, which is also located in the historic city centre. The central image of the five baptismal scenes on the font is a depiction of John the Baptist baptising Christ.

Since 1885, a neoclassical patrician house has been home to the **Weapons Museum**. The elegant building was constructed by the architect Berthelemy Digneffe from Liège. Containing some 12,500 different weapons, the museum is internationally recognised as one of the most important of its kind. Weapons of all kinds – for hunting and fighting – are on display.

The **Aquarium** of the Zoological Institute of the University of Liège has all the latest technical equipment. It presents a fascinating record of the oceans' fauna.

The two buildings in which the **Architecture Museum** is housed are typical of the building style popular in the Meuse valley in the 17th century. Exhibits include doors and woodcarvings (faithfully restored), fine panelling, fireplaces and mouldings. The museum's garden contains numerous porticos, arcades, fountains, statues and bas-reliefs. The museum also houses a photo gallery and regularly holds exhibitions of modern art.

Modern art is more thoroughly addressed in the **Museum of Modern Art**, which contains paintings and sculptures from 1850 to the present day. Among these are some 250 works by Chagall, Ensor, Gauguin, Magritte, and Picasso. The museum is located in the Parc de la Boverie, at some distance from the city centre.

On the other bank of the Meuse, you will find the neighbourhood of **Outre Meuse**, which is steeped in tradition. Every year on 15 August it holds a folk fair, with lively church festivals and folkloric entertainment. The marionette Tchantchès, a figure central to local folklore hereabouts, is said to embody the spirit of the local inhabitants. Tchantchès spoke out plainly every time he saw an instance of injustice. **André Modeste Grétry** (1741–1813), the composer, was originally from Outre-Meuse; the house in which this man, called the "father of comic opera", was born, Rue des Récollets 36, has been converted into a museum in his memory. Another memorial to this artist stands in front of the opera house of Liège.

You can get a good view of the city and the Meuse from the old **Citadel**. It's been destroyed many times, but always rebuilt anew. You can reach it by climbing 407 steps, but there's also a street which leads directly to it.

Liège has one of the largest pedes-

trian zones in Europe. Its total of more than 5,000 shops make the whole city seem like one huge shopping centre. And there are other ways of shopping: the flea market known as **Batte** is one of the largest and most interesting in the country. It's held every Sunday morning on the left bank of the Meuse, between Cockerill Square and the bridge Pont Maghin, between 9 a.m. and 2 p.m.

In the Walloon dialect of Liège, the word *batte* means embankment or river walk. Many such "battes" were erected over the centuries. This Sunday market has appropriated for itself the name used for the road running along the river. It originated in the 16th century, when the city administration decided to build an embankment along the Meuse and to open the land to trade. Cattle dealers and fruit and vegetable salesman began to advertise their wares on the spot; it was here, too, that the first public theatrical performances took place.

Early settlements: South of Liège, in the direction of Spa, the town of **Theux** lies in the valley of Hoegne. Countless archeological finds of Gallo-Roman objects have been made in the area of the former settlement.

For a long time, Theux was the only town in the area, as Louis the Pious forbade his subjects to clear the wood or to build farms. In 1467, Theux received its city charter. Just 11 years later, the town was laid waste by the troops of Charles the Bold; some citizens had revolted against the Burgundian Duke, without success. Theux's **town hall** was built in 1770 by order of the Mayor of Liège, Barthélemy Digneffe.

The hall church of **St Hermès-et-Alexandre**, on the edge of Theux, is first mentioned in documents of 814; today it is a parish church. Excavations have shown that it is built on the foundations of an even older building; the parts of the church which we can see today date from the 11th century. The impressive gable roof spans the three broad aisles. Later additions are the choir, the chapels to the southeast of the main

aisle, the sacristy and the entrance hall.

Along the Meuse: Two roads lead along the **Meuse valley** from Liège in the direction of Huy; even travelling on the motorway, the more southerly of the two, one can glean a perfectly good impression of the region. The landscape which unfolds is not a romantic, castle-filled valley such as one might find along the Meuse tributaries in the Ardennes, but rather a broad, wooded river valley packed with evidence of heavy industry. Metalworking plants, stone quarries, gravel manufacturers and cement factories stand in rows, one after the other. However, if you turn off into one of the many smaller side valleys, the twitter of birds soon drowns out the drone of industry.

First mentioned in 636, **Huy** (population 15,000) is one of the oldest cities of Belgium. In the Middle Ages it was a flourishing trade centre for pewter, copper and cloth. A **cable car** runs 70 metres (230 ft) upwards to Weiler La Satre, from which you can look far out over the town and the Meuse valley; the view, from this perspective, is quite lovely. Its **Citadel** was built in 1818 on the site of a former castle. In the town centre, the **Collegiate Church of Our Lady** has stood on its bridge over the Meuse since 1377; its huge rose window on the west tower is 9 metres (30 ft) in diameter. Destroyed in a fire in 1803, the steeple of the tower has never been rebuilt. A series of 14th-century reliefs in the Bethlehem Portal, flanking the choir entrance to the church, depict scenes from the birth of Christ.

The church treasury contains many valuable reliquaries, two of which come from the workshops of Godfrey of Huy. The **town hall** on the marketplace, which was built in 1799 in the style of Louis XV, was intended to symbolise the town's spiralling prosperity, as its majestic external double staircase demonstrates. The bell tower's complement of 36 bells regularly pealed out in celebration of the town's renown in trade – and, no doubt, the assured taxes to pay the

town council. Another building which contributes to the harmonious appearance of the old town is the parish **church of St Mangold**. It was built as a simple church in the 15th century, but the foundation of its tower dates back from the 13th century.

Some 6 km (4 miles) south of Huy on the N641 one of the most beautiful castles in Belgium is beautifully located in the midst of a nature preserve of 1,125 acres. Perched on top of a high rock wall, **Castle Moldave** commands a view of the valley all the way to the little river of Hoyoux. Containing 20 lavishly furnished rooms (open to the public), complete with sculptures, Brussels wall tapestries, and relief decorations in stucco by Jean Christian Hansche, the castle has, since 1673, been owned in succession by the Count de Marchin, Prince Maximilian of Bavaria, Cardinal Fürstenberg, Baron de Ville, the Duke of Montmorency, and the families Lamarche and Braconnier.

A trade route: Between Huy and Namur, the Meuse landscape is quite beautiful; Namur is a turning point in the course of the river. The Meuse, which flows north out of the Ardennes, is intersected by the Sambre at Namur; from there, it follows the Sambre's original course eastwards. This stretch of the river serves as a shipping route for industry, part of an extensive network of waterways which, along with many canals, connects the west of the country with the Netherlands, and leads to the North Sea.

The Meuse is also a traffic route for barges south of Namur, flowing from the French border through Dinant, but many excursion steamers also ply this route. A trip along the river, passing between the high cliffs, castles and citadels while enjoying cake and coffee, is highly recommended.

Namur/Namen (population 35,000) is the capital of the province; furthermore, because of its position at the confluence of the Meuse and Sambre rivers and among the foothills of the Belgian Ardennes, it is the transportation hub of

Black cats Huy.

the region. Two major European motorways, the E 40 and E 41, intersect north of the city; these are, respectively, the historic link between Brussels and Luxembourg in the south and the East-West connection from Cologne through Aachen to Paris. On the outskirts of the city, high-rise buildings stand shoulder to shoulder, as if strung on a chain.

It's said that the name Namur harks back to a legendary dwarf who dwelt on the mountain where the castle now stands. People came to consult him for advice, and he gave a different answer to each of them. However, following the birth of Christ, the oracle remained mute. Later, the city which lay at the mountain's foot was named after the dwarf ("nain muet").

History offers a different account. The city was known in the days of the Romans as a point of military significance, due to its ideal location; at that time, it was called *Namurum Castrum*. Namur was a fortified city in the early Middle Ages; in 1559, it was made the

seat of a new bishopric. Between the 16th and 18th centuries, its inhabitants were subjected to repeated sieges and bombardments, which were responsible for the destruction of large areas of the well-to-do city.

In 1711, Namur was made the capital of a small, independent country which encompassed modern Namur, Luxembourg and parts of Hainaut. Nine years later, this state fell to the Netherlands; broad boulevards were subsequently laid out within the city. Namur became the capital of the Department of Sambre-et-Meuse in 1794. In 1914 and 1940, the Germans seized the city, destroying substantial sections of it.

The city is dominated by its mighty citadel, which has put in some 2,000 years of military service. The Celts established a fortification here; later, it was the fortress of the Counts of Namur, one of the best-fortified castles of Europe during the late Middle Ages. Its appearance today is largely the responsibility of the Dutch, who ruled here

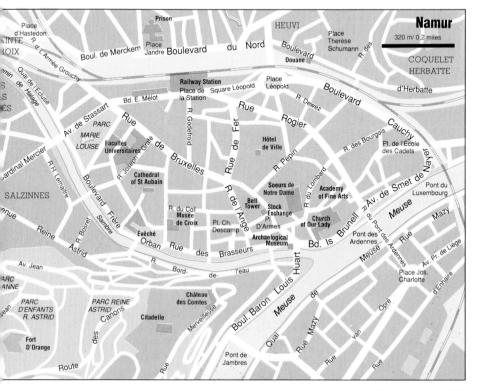

between 1815 and 1830. From Easter until October, a tram runs between the city and the citadel; otherwise, you can take the so-called *route merveilleuse*. Merveilleuse, of course, means marvellous, a name which this winding road richly deserves: virtually every point along it commands a marvellous view of the city.

There's not much left of the original fortress: a square with a small tower and a well 50 metres (163 ft) deep, and the bases of two towers. The citadel was built in 1692. Today, its 200-acre grounds include parks, an open-air theatre, an amusement park, an observation tower and the Château de Namur, visible from afar, now operating as a hotel. A small train takes visitors slowly through the castle's halls.

Located in two of the citadel's towers are the **Weapons Museum** (Musée d'Armes) and the **Forest Museum** (Musée de la Forêt). The Weapons Museum presents an overview of the military history and the most important sieges of Namur, culminating with World Wars I and II. The museum also contains a range of African weapons, as well as some for hunting and fencing. Fauna and flora of the Ardennes are on display in the Forest Museum. Of special interest are the exhibits warning against environmental damage and the magnificent butterfly collection. Around the museum, trees of the Ardennes and other rare kinds of wood have been planted; they include chestnuts, plane-trees, oaks, beeches, birches, aspens, firs, acacias, poplars, limes, willows, maples and walnut trees. With 3,500 seats, the citadel's open-air theatre is the largest in Belgium. The former castle smithy is today a ceramics studio.

Namur's **Old City** stretches along the north bank of the Sambre and Meuse. The **cathedral of Saint-Aubain** was built in the middle of the 18th century by the Italian architect Gaetano Pizzoni. Count Albert II of Namur had founded a collegiate church on the same site as early as 1047; the church's Gothic bel-

The flea market in Namur.

fry is a remnant of this former building. Topped with a classical dome, the cathedral's interior is ornamented with statues by Laurent Delvaux. A plaque behind the main altar commemorates Don John of Austria, whose heart is interred here. This son of Charles V died of the plague in 1578 near Namur; he had beaten the Turks in the sea battle of Lepanto. Since 1579, his remains have lain in the Escorial, near Madrid.

On the right of the church, next to the choir, the **Diocesan Museum**, which contains the treasury of the cathedral, displays a Merovingian reliquary from Andenne, as well as the famous crown of Philip the Handsome. This is supposed to contain thorns from Christ's crown of thorns, which Philip received from his brother, Emperor Henry of Constantinople. In addition, the museum displays treasures from churches and cloisters which were closed or destroyed during the French Revolution.

Near the cathedral, you can see the works of Namur artists and craftsmen in the **Musée de la Croix**, the municipal and regional museum. The City Archive is located in the 17th-century **Palace of Justice**, behind the cathedral.

Opposite the cathedral stands the **Provincial Palace**, which was built as the bishop's residence between 1726 and 1740. The Council of Namur Province meets in the chapel. **Saint-Loup church** was built by the Jesuit Huyssens between 1621 and 1645; the tower of this three-storey building was never finished. Black marble bases and red-brown columns make the interior of this baroque church surprisingly colourful.

The Namur architect J.F. Maljeau drew up the plans for the **church of Our Lady**, which was built in 1750; the three aisles of the church are divided from one another by Ionic columns. One of the city's most important works of art is housed in this church: the treasury of Hugo von Oignes.

The **Place d'Armes**, where the Stock Exchange is located, is the city's most popular square; behind it looms the **Bell**

ing day river.

Tower, "Tour St-Jacques". The base of the tower is actually the remnant of the second city wall, which was erected in the 14th century. The bells in the bell tower's two smaller turrets were once rung to signal the opening and closing of the city gates.

In the city centre, the **Musée Felicien Rops** holds an important collection of the works of this painter, printmaker, draughtsman and illustrator. Built in 1588, the former **Butcher's Hall**, the city's oldest extant secular building and a fine example of Meuse regional architecture, today houses the **Archaeological Museum**, which contains a treasure trove of prehistoric, Roman and medieval finds from the area.

Medieval beer: Some 9 km (5 miles) along the road to Charleroi you'll find the **Floreffe Monastery** of the Premonstratensian order, founded by Saint Norbert in 1121. In the Middle Ages, the influence of its monks extended all the way to the Netherlands. As usual, the church occupies the loveliest spot in the area. The view from the building high above the valley of the Sambre over the broad expanse of forest is wonderful whatever the season.

The monastery is open to the public; once inside, between the agricultural buildings, the aroma of goat and cow is immediately noticeable. These farm buildings were converted in 1819 for the growing numbers of visitors; now you can buy bread, cheese and handcrafted pottery here. The income from the shops goes towards the maintenance of the monastery.

The **Brewery** can be seen as a monument to small business in the Middle Ages. Still operative today, it produces a fine blond beer, as well as several kinds of speciality beer, which you can sample in the adjacent pub. The beers are exported to Italy, France and Canada. The best accompaniment to these beers is the local strong bread, developed by Sister Marguerite at the beginning of the century and which continues to be baked according to her methods. Even

The Abb **Floreffe,** **which b** **still brev** **accordin** **the anci** **recipe.**

in the Middle Ages the monks, with their broad farmlands, didn't worry about going hungry.

Flexibility is the distinguishing characteristic of these monks. Catering to the Belgians' tremendous proclivity for celebration, they organise large private parties on request; weddings at Floreffe, for example, are extremely popular in the region. Sometimes, the monastery itself arranges festivals, and children are particularly well catered for. At Easter they can hunt for eggs in the grounds, be entertained by clowns and devour a gigantic chocolate cake.

A flower festival is held during the first two weeks of July, an open-air folklore festival in the middle of August, and all manner of toys are available at the children's fair that starts in the middle of November.

A city surrendered: Settlements become more numerous along the road to Charleroi; one town gives way to or combines with the next. The architectural homogeneity of this area makes it difficult for anyone, let alone a stranger to the region, to notice the transition from one town to another. All the houses are built using the same type of brick. Charleroi itself has some 26,000 inhabitants; the area immediately surrounding it has a total population of 220,000.

Châtelet, the easternmost outpost of the coal and heavy industry area, contains many small houses of pre-World War II vintage. It is clear to even a casual visitor that the town has fallen on hard times: here, there are no large billboards, and the shops in the town centre don't seem to stock any of the luxury articles which are virtually standard in most Central European cities. You'll look in vain for individuality, for exclusivity: this town has, in effect, been written off. More and more people are leaving; unemployment is steadily rising, especially among the immigrant workers who settled in the town when heavy industry was still going strong.

As the demand for coal declined and competition in the steel industry be-

came more intense, the neighbourhoods inhabited by the North Africans expanded considerably; new life was injected into the town. The influence of the Maghrebis is strong. Televisions run throughout the day in bars used by men alone; the city centre is usually ensnared by lengthy traffic jams; there are no pedestrian zones. The selection of goods in the shops, whether groceries or books or underwear, seems aimed at the demands of a simple or rural clientele. It's not a place which is much sought after by the ambitious younger generation; property, therefore, can be had quite cheaply.

Industrial area: The complexes around **Charleroi** are no different from industrial areas in any country, whether England or Germany. Once red, the brick buildings of the former miners' communities, complete with allotments (their vegetables made a vital contribution to a family's table), are laid out symmetrically around the former mine. Near the entrance to the pits are the directors' villas; after them, the foremen's houses, and then the smaller houses. Unemployment in the region is around 15 percent. The city centre is characterised by plain administrative buildings.

Originally called Charnoy, the town was renamed Charleroi in the 17th century in honour of King Charles II. Nearly all the major buildings are of more recent vintage. The **town hall**, with its 70-metre (230 ft) high bell tower, was built in 1935; the 17th-century domed church of **St Christopher** was renovated in 1957, and considerably enlarged in the process. There's a **Museum of Photography** in the erstwhile Carmelite convent of Mot-sur-Marchienne, while the **Museum of Industry** is housed in a former smithy.

Leaving Charleroi, you can follow the N90 toward Mons through the little town of **Binche**, which contains remnants of a 12th-century city wall and whose riotous carnival celebrations are said to have given rise to the English word binge. But if you want to reach the

The fair comes to Charleroi

former royal palace and park of **Mariemont**, 6 km (4 miles) south of Fayt, it's easier to take the motorway E42. A wrought-iron fence 3 metres (10 ft) high surrounds this wonderful park full of trees; its grounds are so extensive that the park has developed its own microclimate, perceptibly contrasting to that of its industrial surroundings.

Doubtless because of the region's developing mining industry and its steel refineries, whose smoke darkened the skys, the king lost interest in his residence here. Nowadays the ruins of the ornate 16th-century palace are overrun by children.

The modern Palace Museum in the park, the region's cultural oasis, offers a wide range of archaeological finds, porcelain, and temporary exhibitions.

Continuing along the route, you can't help but notice the heaps of garbage at either side of the road; they seem to stretch as far as the horizon. It is hard to remember that this dreary region, left out in the cold as the country developed,

lies so close to the beautiful Ardennes.

Industry and history: Billboards are an unfailing indication of a prospering economic development. Things are really moving in **Mons** (Bergen, population 100,000). Warehouses, modern industrial complexes, large automobile dealerships and a gleaming shop for bridal wear let you know you're entering the capital of the province of Hainaut. The visitor is welcomed by a plethora of church towers and factory chimneys. This is an upright, industrious town.

The city is the centre of the **Borinage**, Belgium's largest coal-mining area. Coal was mined here as early as the 12th century, in one of the first coal mines of Europe. The region's economic potential was the reason that the German Empire was so eager to annex Belgium in World War I.

The city of Mons grew grew up around a cloister which was founded by Waltraud, the daughter of a Count of Hainaut, in the 7th century. This cloister developed into a cathedral chapter of

tling in Marie-Park.

canonesses at the centre of what later became the city. Waltraud died in 688; her relics have been preserved and honoured in various buildings. In 1295, Mons became the capital of the County of Hainaut; over the ensuing centuries, it was a key strategic point in numerous wars. The city has been occupied by French, Spanish and Austrians since the 17th century, and has withstood several sieges. The 20th century offered the city no respite from the ravages of war: Mons suffered under bombardment and artillery shelling in World Wars I and II.

Precious relics: However, the **Collegiate Church of St Waudru**, dedicated to St Waltraud, has been preserved. Its architect, Mathieu de Lazens, also built the renowned town hall in Leuven. This edifice has long been admired for its size and beauty: the church is a remarkable 115 metres (376 ft) in length, 32 metres (105 ft) wide, and 24 metres (78 ft) high. Of light grey stone, St Waudru's, which was built between 1450 and 1621, has a choir with four galleries, a choir hall and a dome; the three aisles have seven galleries. The tower was to have been 190 metres (621 ft) high, but only the base of it was ever built. Further building work was forever abandoned in 1669, when the three aisles were finally roofed over. Twenty-nine chapels surround this imposing building, and a mighty staircase leads up to the main portal. A rood screen by Jacques du Broeucq of Mons, which was installed in the 16th century, was largely destroyed in 1797.

The precious reliquary of St Waltraud is housed in the church, as is, in the foyer, the gilded processional coach (Car d'Or) in which the bones of the saint are borne through the city on the Sunday after Whitsun. This famous procession dates back to the plague of 1348. The church treasury contains gold objects from the 13th through the 19th centuries, including monstrances, communion goblets, reliquaries, censers and liturgical books.

Located above the church, **Castle Square** was laid out by the city of Mons on the site of the former castle of the Counts of Hainaut. All that remains of the castle is the **Calixtus Chapel**, which was erected in 1051 by Countess Richilde to house the relics of Pope Calixtus; she had received these as a gift from her Aunt Egberge, the Abbess of Neuss. When Castle Square was constructed, workers uncovered **wall paintings** from the 11th and 12th centuries; these were, however, badly damaged, and eventually disappeared entirely, not to be reconstructed until 1951.

A stone found in 1860 is inscribed with the date 13 April 1293; it was once set upon two vertical pillars. The chapel door is made of heavy oak, four inches (10 cm) thick; the walls are 1.5 metres (5 ft) thick, made of blocks of sandstone. Three reclining figures are housed in the interior. The first of these is a representation of the knight Gilles de Chin, who was interred in the monastery of Saint-Ghislain after his death. When this cloister was destroyed in the

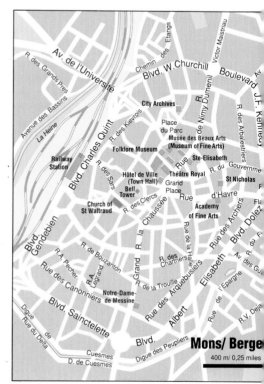

18th century, the figure was brought to a final resting place in Mons. It has been heavily damaged over the years.

The other two figures date from the 14th century and are of Guillaume de Gavre, Lord of Steenkerque and Tongrenelle, Count of the Holy Roman Empire, and his wife, Jeanne de Berlo de Liège, Luxemburg et Westphalie. These were donated to the city of Mons during the 19th century by Baron de Hérissem, who was a city counsellor of Mons from 1849 to 1866.

The seal of Hainaut: To the left of the entrance hang reproductions of significant **charters**, all of which were issued in 1200 by **Baldwin VI** of Hainaut before his departure on the Fourth Crusade. Seals of all the counts and countesses of Hainaut from the 11th to the 14th centuries are displayed in a cabinet on the wall; you can also see the **Seal of Mons** and the seals of the other most important cities of old Hainaut. Casts of two more figures lie in the middle of the crypt. Both of these are of French kings:

Philip VI of Valois, who lived from 1328 to 1359, and Charles V the Wise (1364–80). The originals are preserved in the Basilica of St-Denis-les-Paris and in the Louvre.

An exhibition in the **Museum of Medieval Iconography**, situated close by, enables the visitor to learn more about the history of the county, from its 9th-century beginnings until 1436. Almost 200 photographs depict churches, castles or objects of old Hainaut dating from before 1436. A map helps one to reconstruct the various boundary changes which Hainaut has undergone over the years.

Castle Square is a good observation point: the hill lies nearly at the city centre, and commands a panoramic view of Mons itself and its immediate and more distant surroundings. Looming over the square's southwest side is the **Bell Tower**, built between 1662 and 1672 by the architect Louis Ledoux and the engineer Anthoni. The tower is 87 metres (284 ft) high, and has two ground

gtime in

floors, one on the Rue des Gades and one at the level of Castle Square. In the former guardroom, you'll find large panels explaining the four major battles of World Wars I and II which were fought at Mons. Comprised of 47 bells, of which the heaviest weighs 6,000 kg (13,200 pounds), the carillon was somehow able to survive both world wars. On 11 November 1918 and on 2 September 1944, the same citizen, M.F. Redouté, tolled the mighty bells to announce the liberation of the city.

Battle memorial: North of the square is the British war memorial, 7 metres (23 ft) high, which Lord Alexander of Tunis had dedicated in 1952. It commemorates the two battles of Mons, which marked both the beginning (23–24 August 1914) and the end (9–11 November 1918) of World War I for the British.

Going along the Rue des Clercs, you'll come to the **Grand-Place** with its Gothic town hall and its Renaissance and baroque houses. The tranquillity of the marketplace, devoted mainly to vegeta-

bles and flowers, enables one to forget about the smoking factory chimneys surrounding the city. The **town hall** was built between 1458 and 1467. The two storeys of the facade have 10 pointed window arches and are ornamented with architectural reliefs. To the left of the town hall's main entrance, the **Singe du Grand-Garde**, a little cast-iron monkey, is supposed to bring luck to the unmarried; according to local superstition, anyone who touches him will soon find a partner. The monkey's head has been worn smooth over the years.

Orlando di Lasso: The main entrance of the town hall leads into the mayor's garden, where a monument has been erected to one of Mons' most famous sons, born here in 1532: Roland de Lassus, who is better known by his Italian name, Orlando di Lasso. After Palestrina, di Lasso was the most successful composer of the 16th century. Also located here is the **Musée du Centenaire**, which exhibits a collection of ceramics.

In this pa
the world

Between August 1879 and October 1880, **Vincent van Gogh** lived in the Rue du Pavillion in Cuesmes-Mons. The painter assured friends that the Borinage was every bit as picturesque as old Venice, Arabia, or Brittany.

Some 9 km (5 miles) north of Mons, you can see, in the distance, the headquarters of NATO (North Atlantic Treaty Organization) in Casteau. It's generally known as SHAPE, an acronym for "Supreme Headquarters of the Allied Powers in Europe".

Passing roadside villages and large farmhouses on the N56 going northwest, one comes to **Ath**, which lies at the intersection of the two Denders rivers. Baldwin IV, Count of Hainaut, had a fortress erected on the road from Flanders to Burgundy in 1136; today, all that remains of it is the **Tour du Burbant** (Brabant), with walls 3.7 metres (12 ft) thick. The **Grand' Place** has a number of interesting buildings, including a stepped-gable house from the 16th century, several buildings from the 17th

and 18th centuries and the **town hall**, which was built between 1614 and 1624 by the German architect Michael Somer, after plans by Wenzeslau Coubergher. There's also a monument to the lawyer **Eugène Defacqz**, who was born in Ath in 1747 and took part in the revolution of 1830.

During the last weekend in August, the Grand' Place is the site of the so-called "Wedding of Goliath". The highlight of this folkloric festival is the **Procession of the Giants of Ath** which winds through the town. This festival originated in 1390, at which time it was a purely religious event. In the middle of the 15th century, completely secular figures and vehicles began to be included in the procession: farm wagons decorated with flowers, representatives of the guilds and, in particular, giants, who danced in the street to the music of brass bands. In the course of the festivities, the giantess "Madame Gouyasse" (Goliath) weds the giant "Gouyasse", as she has done since 1715. The couple are

more
ant to
than to
a car.

married in front of the Town Hall every year, after pledging their troth before the mayor and the local magistrate. After the wedding, David challenges Goliath to battle; in the course of the fighting, the giant is felled, and David becomes a hero.

Little Versailles: 10 km (6 miles) southwest of Ath, a narrow road leads to the community of **Beloeil**, the little town is known for its palace which once belonged to the Princes of Ligne. After a damaging fire in the 19th century, most of the original castle was rebuilt and restored; but its oldest sections date from 1511. At first glance, the building looks like a miniature Versailles. Various collections of valuables are housed in the palace's interior, including art objects and coins. Most of the lavish interior decoration dates from the 15th and 16th centuries.

The **Kingdom of Minibel** is laid out over 10 acres of the palace grounds. Built on a scale of 1:25, the model represents the the most famous sites of Belgium. Strolling along the flower-lined paths, the visitor comes upon buildings such as the Bell Tower of Bruges or Brussels' town hall on its Grand' Place, all in miniature.

Some 20 km (12 miles) to the west, **Tournai** (Doornik; population 70,000) is one of Belgium's most important art centres; it is also, along with Tongeren, one of the oldest cities in the country. The original Roman settlement of Turris Nerviorum was a residence of the Merovingians from 440 to 486. Clovis was born here and his father, Childeric, died here in 482. In the 6th century, the town became the seat of a bishopric; it later became well known for its fine porcelain, wall tapestry production and paintings, particularly through Rogier van der Weyden.

In the 17th century the French and the Dutch took turns fighting about who should have dominion of the city. Tournai was spared in World War I, as it lay on the westernmost edge of war activity. However, German air raids from

A room with a view.

280

16 to 22 May 1940 destroyed the city centre in World War II. Nearly 1,300 houses were flattened in the bombing. Nonetheless, one of the oldest residential houses in Europe (1175) survived; it can be seen in the street Barre-St-Brice.

In the 9th century, a new cathedral was built on the site of the earlier Merovingian house of worship; this was, however, destroyed in the wake of Norman pillaging and arson in 881. Its successor didn't last long, either: it caught fire in 1060. Thousands of people made pilgrimages to the image of Mary in the cathedral during the plague epidemic of 1089, praying for protection or salvation from the disease. A procession of relics on 14 September 1090 was dedicated to driving out the plague. The church which we see today dates from the 12th century.

Not for nothing is Tournai's **cathedral of Our Lady**, which rises up majestically over the roofs of the city, called the most beautiful church in Belgium. Made of local blue granite, the building is of tremendous proportions: 135 metres (441 ft) long, with a nave 66 metres (216 ft) wide and a central tower 83 metres (271 ft) high. Yet despite the church's great size, it doesn't strike one as being bulky. Each of its five towers – four outside and one in the middle – is shaped differently. The central lantern tower once allowed daylight to stream into the church over the altar standing at the intersection of nave and apse through its many round-arched windows; however, the addition of the Gothic choir to the Romanesque nave altered the arrangement of the windows.

Pilgrims to Our Lady: On the northern, Scheldt side of the cathedral, one enters or leaves through the **Porte Mantile**, or Mantilius Portal. Its name refers to the blind Mantilius, whom Saint Eleutherius once miraculously healed at this spot. Near the bell tower, the **Porte de Capitole** (Capital Portal) stands at the church's south entrance. Today somewhat damaged, the door is carved with images of the Last Judgment. One of the

ing-gum ensers. t, a re of dom.

images depicts an angel battling with evil at the bedside of a dying man; this is supposed to represent the redemption of the dead. Next to the main portal, the founders of the cathedral and of the first Christian community of Tournai keep watch: **St Piatus** and **St Eleutherius**, the latter holding a model of his church in one hand. Between them, "Our Lady of the Sick" is an object of veneration for countless pilgrims every year.

The cathedral's main facade on Bishop's Square is constantly being altered; the lower half of this facade is overshadowed by a Gothic vestibule from the 14th century. Bas-reliefs depict scenes from the Old Testament.

Once inside the cathedral, you'll be overwhelmed at the sight of the immense central nave. Its sides are four storeys high. Because of the daylight streaming in through the many windows, and the light-coloured walls, the interior of the building is unusually bright. Cruciform vaulting from 1640, which spans the central aisle, the pulpit

and the side aisles, has replaced the earlier wooden ceiling.

Over the **Mantilius Portal** is the Chapel of Mary Magdalene; the Chapel of Saint Catherine is over the Capitol Portal; while the Chapel of Saint Michael is next to the organ. The chapels of Saint John the Baptist and Saint Margaret contain wall paintings from the 13th century. Note that these chapels can only be visited at special request.

The chancel dates from 1759; here, too, stands the revered **Notre Dame la Brune** (the dark-complexioned), who is borne through the city in an annual procession on the second Sunday in September. In the right side aisle, a chapel is dedicated to Saint Louis. Built in the year 1299, it contains remains of stained-glass paintings from the 14th and 15th centuries, as well as baroque panelling from the Monastery of St Ghislain, near Mons, which was destroyed in the French Revolution. Made of marble and alabaster, the rood screen replaced the Gothic choir screen which

Language dispute in Tournai: Flemish masked; car was in Wallonia

282

used to stand here; the present screen dates from 1572, and was built by Corneille de Vriendt of Antwerp. An exploding powder keg was responsible for the partial destruction of the old stained-glass windows in 1745. Off the aisle, the Chapel of the Blessed Sacrament contains an oil painting by Rubens dating from 1635. The picture depicts the Salvation from the flames of Hell.

Bishop's relics: At the entrance to the **Chapel of the Holy Ghost**, you'll also find the door to the Cathedral Treasury, which contains valuable objects such as two late Romanesque reliquaries. A golden shrine of the Virgin Mary from 1205 is shaped in the form of a house; this ornate work is studded with precious stones and small enamel insets dominated by the colour blue. Another masterpiece of the goldsmith's art, the **Shrine of St Eleutherius** dates from 1247, and contains the relics of the first Bishop of Tournai. The treasury also includes crosses set with gemstones, early ivory carvings and tapestries from Tournai. At the south side of the cathedral there's a monument to the renowned painter Rogier van der Weyden, who was born in Tournai in 1399.

Immediately adjacent to the cathedral, a 72-metre (235-ft) **Bell Tower** rises high over the triangular marketplace. Construction work on the tower commenced in 1187, making this edifice the oldest of its kind in Belgium. Since then, the bell tower has been altered and renovated every bit as often as the cathedral itself.

A Renaissance building from 1610, the **Halle aux Draps** (Cloth Hall) also stands on the Grand' Place. Located on the south side of the square, the building reflects the flourishing textile industry which was responsible for the city's economic well-being until the 16th century. A bronze statue commemorates Christine de la Laings, under whose leadership the citizens of Tournai were able to defend themselves during the siege of 1581. The **church of St Quentin** stands on the northwest side of the

marketplace. Originally dating from the 12th century, it has been modified and restored many times since.

To the northwest of the marketplace, the **Pont des Trous** (Bridge of Holes) spans the river Scheldt, which flows through the city. This Bridge of Holes consists of two mighty towers which were part of the original city fortifications, erected in 1290.

Not far from the marketplace, you can find the **Musée des Beaux-Arts** (Museum of Fine Art). Although containing many examples of modern art, the museum also displays paintings by Rogier van der Weyden and Rubens. A famous painting by Louis Gallait of Tournai depicts the plague of 1032. Further paintings by this artist exhibited in this museum are *The Abdication of Charles V* and *The Severed Heads of Counts Egmont and Horn*.

A boating excursion on the river Scheldt is a wonderful way to get one's first impression of Tournai: the boat trips last approximately one hour.

dest ower in um is in ai.

THROUGH THE ARDENNES

There's a prejudice going around that the Ardennes, in the south of Belgium, are dark, cold, and inhospitable. In fact, this mountain landscape is marvellously beautiful, almost Mediterranean in character, with houses of natural stone reminiscent of houses in the south of France. The people are open and talkative and ever ready to dispense information and advice to visitors.

Sparsely populated, with 125 inhabitants per square mile (the national average is about 800), and predominantly agricultural because of its loamy, chalky soil, this region at the heart of Europe seems to have been overlooked by industry; the hilly, peaceful countryside with its friendly inhabitants is an ideal spot for holiday relaxation. However, even when the sun shines, temperatures in the mountains, which rise to heights of between 400 and 500 metres (1,300 and 1,600 ft), can be quite chilly at night. The Ardennes are not particularly well suited to winter sports; like many other mountain areas in Central Europe, they have experienced little snow over the last few years.

Mediterranean mood: The lifestyle and temperament of this region strike the visitor as being similar to those that prevail in the Mediterranean countries. People here live at a leisurely pace. The mentality is evident in their tendency to stop and chat on a street corner rather than rush home to do the housework or gardening. Residents tend to overlook the first signs of rust or peeling paint on their property and, unlike most other inhabitants of these latitudes, are not as obsessed by their work.

About half of the land in the area is used for forestry. A characteristic feature of the region is its many grottos: those in Hotton, Remouchamps, Han, Rochefort, Dinant and Goyet, to name a few. Many of the most popular caves are located directly on the through road (signs indicate where you should turn off). The caves were formed over thousands of years by water containing carbolic acid carving a path through the chalky rocks. The rivers Vesdre, Ourthe, Lomme, Lesse and Semois which flow through the region contributed to the formation of these caves.

Our trip begins in the southeast of Belgium, near the German border, in the little village of Sankt Vith; from there, we move north through Malmedy and the health resort of Spa, and then turn slowly back toward the south, passing through Remouchamps, Hotton and La-Roche-en-Ardenne and penetrating deep into the hills as far as Bastogne and Arlon. Taking the motorway for a brief stretch, we come to the caves of Han, the town of Dinant – hemmed in between the Meuse and a chain of rocky cliffs – and the area around Namur, our final destination. From here, it's not far to Brussels; or you can embark on the East-West route described above.

On first impression, **St Vith** (popula-

tion 2,800) looks very much like a post-war town. The 14th-century "Beech Tower", where customs duties were once collected, is the sole reminder of the city's former historic importance. St Vith is one of those towns which were utterly wiped out in the battles of the Ardennes in World War II. Near St Vitus's church, a stone memorial pays tribute to the fallen heroes of the 99th US Infantry Division. At that time, the region, which was ceded to Belgium in the Treaty of Versailles in 1920, was occupied by the Germans.

Residents of the area still speak German. On the map, the linguistic border is clearly identifiable: simply locate the cities and towns which bear German names. The Belgian radio also broadcasts in German, providing a full programme which includes Top-40 hits, folk music and news. If you ask a local here whether he's a German or a Belgian, he'll probably wrinkle his brow before answering. Although of German origin, they're officially Belgian citizens, with full rights as a minority group. The tension between the linguistic communities was especailly pronounced after the war, when returning soldiers who had served in the army of the Third Reich were met by Resistance fighters armed with cudgels; now such tensions have relaxed almost completely. The region's postwar economic development has been more rapid and easy than that of Wallonia. Today German is the official language in the schools, but students begin to learn French after the first grade. Children are raised bilingually, and often have a good command of Flemish and English, as well.

Passing meadows providing pasture for cows and horses, or sites for turkey farms, the road goes by large, solid houses which are as strudy as the Belgian furniture they contain. Homes in this region are built to last forever.

The road then brings us into the valley of **Malmedy** (population 6,000). Here, small oriels ornament the slate-covered houses. The area has a pleasant relaxed

The river in Malme

ambience. Patrons of the numerous open-air cafés which line the market-place engage in conversation until late into the evenings. Their preferred refreshment is French fries, beer and the local mineral water (most of which is destined for export).

A memorial plaque in front of the cathedral pays homage to the victims of the war, the majority of whom were destroyed in an Allied air attack of 1944; the memorial honours those who died between 1940 and 1945, some at the hands of the Nazis, some through the agency of the Resistance. The decision to install such a plaque must have involved the re-opening of sensitive questions, and a great deal of debate on the part of residents. The history of the town began with St Remaclus, who founded a cloister here in 648.

At the same time, the **Stavelot Abbey** came into being; over the next millennium, this cloister took on a greater spiritual and cultural importance than Malmedy. Remaclus, the "Apostle of the Ardennes" who later became the Bishop of Maastricht, founded the double cloister of Stavelot-Malmedy in the spirit of St Benedict, at the behest of King Sigisbert III. Only the Gothic tower of the former abbey church remains today: originally some 100 metres (330 ft) in height, it now measures a mere 30 metres (98 ft). Its cornerstone was laid in August 1534 by Guillaume de Manderscheidt – laid upon a church which had originally been built in 1040 by the Abbot Poppon.

As a consequence of the secularisation attendant upon the French Revolution, the abbey was converted into a hospital for French soldiers, specialising in sexual diseases. The two-thirds of the tower which are missing today were used as building material to construct the houses in the well-preserved, narrow alleyways of the town of **Stavelot** (population 5,000). An edifice which appears to be a large greenhouse has been built in front of the tower. With a little luck, you'll find Edgar Raskin there. Until

1977, Raskin was a television repairman, pursuing an overly hectic lifestyle until he suffered his second heart attack. Since then, he's devoted his time to archaeological excavations. It would hardly be fair to term Raskin an amateur archaeologist, when it's he, together with other volunteers, who has excavated the old abbey from the area around the church. Actually, Raskin explains, the remains of several churches are to be found here, one within another. In the summer, students and professors from the University of Liège come to help. According to Raskin, there are years to go before excavation work is completed.

At the entrance to the abbey premises, you'll stumble across a shining white monument which depicts a face with an oversized, three-dimensional nose. This memorial also has to do with the monks. In 1499, Prince Abbot Guillaume de Manderscheidt forbade them to take part in the carnival celebrations of the town. The Stavelot monks mocked this order by participating in carnival festivities at

Laetare, three weeks before Easter, dressed as white monks. This is the origin of the **"Blanc Moussis"** who, equipped with long red noses and a ladders, represent the town as guests of honour at carnival celebrations in Düsseldorf, Cologne, Compiègne and Saint-Quentin. Thousands of visitors flock to the town's carnival festivities every year.

Another part of the former abbey, the 1,000-year-old vaults, have been converted into a museum of the **Racetrack of Spa-Franchorchamps**, which is located to the north of the town. It contains more than 80 vintage cars, Formula One racing cars and motorcycles. The ancient vaulted building provides a superb setting for the cars. Housed directly next door is a collection of artistic treasures of the Ardennes, concentrating in particular on the ancient art of leather-working in the region.

A reminder of Remaclus in the church of St Sebastian is the **Remaclus Shrine** of 1268, the product of 18 years of work by three master craftsmen. The ornate sarcophagus is based on the shrine of Mary and Charles in Aachen. On its gable, you can see an image of Saint Remaclus; opposite him is Saint Lambert, while the Apostles are depicted in an arcade of seven arches along the side.

In the town hall there is a small display which recalls the French poet and musician Guillaume de Machaut (1300–77). One of the creators of the harmonic art, he wrote countless songs and ballads, as well as a considerable amount of organ music. Geoffrey Chaucer is said to have been greatly influenced by *Le Livre du voir-dit*, written in the form of letters from the elderly poet to a girl. Machaut stayed in Stavelot for three months, and then made off without paying the bill.

To the north of Stavelot in **La Gleize**, there is a German army tank which recalls the unit of the SS that was forced to halt here in 1944 because supplies of fuel had run out. At a time when the end of the war was already in sight, the SS men terrorised the local population. Almost 100 civilians were lined up and shot. Around Christmas they decided to pack up and go home on foot, leaving their 175 vehicles behind. The Musée Décembre 1944 in Trois-Point, to the south of Stavelot, gives a vivid account of the terrible events of those days.

More than 2,500 soldiers fell on the section of the front between Stavelot, La Gleize and Stoumont in the north; today the distance can be covered by car in only a few minutes.

International resort: Some 12 miles (20 km) to the north of Stavelot, the resort of **Spa** has for centuries been the meeting place of the rich and famous of the European world, who come to take the waters and take precautions – water and mud baths containing alkali and iron – against arteriosclerosis, heart trouble, varicose veins and rheumatism.

Spa has flourished without pause since the 16th century. By the 18th century it was like a modern-day Cannes or Monte Carlo. Philip Thicknesse, visiting in 1786

had this to day: "You may easily imagine that a spot like this, visited by all the world, and where gaming is tolerated, nay, encouraged by the first magistrate of the principality, that it is not only the resort of invalids, and people of real fashion, but of the counterfeit nobility innumberable, and the outcasts, scum and refuse of both sexes, from every nation. So that what with the real, and the assumed badges of distinction, to be seen at Spa, a stranger would be apt to think all the crown heads in Europe had sent their courtiers to drink the Pohoun water".

A *fin du siècle* ambience is still in the air, albeit somewhat antiquated. The **Well-House of Peter the Great** is encircled by a traffic ring; however, able sprinters should have no trouble crossing the busy street to view the building.

In the 20th century, two events in particular have been responsible for the city's remaining in the limelight: on 8 November 1918, the town was the centre of world attention when Kaiser

Wilhelm II, not far from the former German headquarters in Neubois Castle, took leave of his people and went into exile in Holland, to chop wood, as many of his detractors claimed. Two years later, Spa was the site of the conference of the same name, held to discuss the disarmament of Germany and its obligation to repay war debts.

Today, elegant villas in the town centre attest to Spa's former glory as an international resort, as do the baths and the casino. In the **Casino**, only the ballroom and theatre from 1763 are still extant. Once a luxury hotel, the building today houses the town hall. Although its former charms may have faded somewhat, Spa nonetheless continues to radiate a certain morbid attraction.

Making the steep ascent into the Ardennes, passing barren fields and thick evergreen forests, the road comes to Remouchamps (population 2,300) and its famous caves. In peak season, tours into the subterranean caverns start every eight minutes. The first inhabitants of these caves were Paleolithic hunters, who dwelt there some 8,000 years ago. They left behind them the skeletons of animals, thousands of stone tools, bone tools and jewellery, weapons, wall paintings and a calendar. Since 1829, the Stalactite Cave of Remouchamps has been open to the public; in 1912, while systematically developing the cave for visits by tourists, workers discovered the chamber which was to become its greatest attraction: the "Cathedral", 100 metres (330 ft) long and 40 metres (130 ft) high. The boat tour is highly recommended. Following the underground river, it winds through faults in the limestone. At one point it passes a spectacular pillar formed by the joining of a stalactite and a stalagmite. The tour lasts about one hour.

Wilderness safari: To the south, in the direction of Marchen-Famenne, the village of Aywaille offers an entirely different kind of natural experience: a **Safari Park**, which you can visit by car or in an open-top train. Zebras, hippo-

The flow
that bloo
the sprin

potami, gorillas and elephants move freely across the landscape. The zoo houses lions and tigers, jaguars and bears. For children there's a farmyard where domestic animals, such as donkeys, goats and sheep, can be petted and fed. Children will also find plenty to entertain them at the **Toy Museum** in Ferrieres, the next village along. Open on weekend afternoons and during school holidays, it presents more than 1,000 objects from the end of the 19th century until 1950: wooden toys, dolls, dolls' houses and musical toys.

A great many houses are offered for sale along the road, visible sign of the fact that there aren't many jobs available in this area. The young people of the area migrate into the cities as soon as they are old enough. Even the feudal lords of earlier days don't seem to be immune to the ills caused by the lack of an economic infrastructure: a wonderfully situated, medium-sized castle in good condition between Vieuxville and Barvaux has been on the market for

years. You can't miss the sign on the side of the road. **Logne Fortress** in Vieuxville, half a mile further on, was also abandoned by its owners, the de la Marcks, who went by the nickname "the Wild Boars of the Ardennes". Today the fortress is a ruin, but it offers magnificent views over the Ourthe and the forested mountains around. A visit to the castle will lead you to the underground passageways which, legend has it, contain medieval treasure.

Leaving the province of Liège, we enter Belgian Luxemburg. Over the years, the flow of the Ourthe near Barvaux has eroded a broad valley between the chalky cliffs. Not far from rock walls, ideal for climbing and topped by little castles and fortresses, you will find a profusion of campsites and fields. It is a delightful region, in which the trees are in full bloom as early as the beginning of April. Take a river excursion by canoe or kayak; you can rent both in Barvaux or Bomal.

Further to the south, toward Marche,

yllic
e valley.

is the grotto of "A Thousand and One Nights", in Hotton. Thirty metres (100 ft) underground, this cave, with its red, white and pink stone strata, is the most beautiful, if not the largest, underground grotto in Europe.

As you penetrate more deeply into the Ardennes, passing Marche and going on toward La Roche, the country around you becomes more and more sparsely populated and the landscape appears wilder. The roads have barely been graded, the brooks haven't been turned into canals, and the sun streams down into the pine forests with a kind of magical light. This area is a favourite haunt of racing cyclists, so watch out! Families picnic by the river and fishermen park their cars so close to the river that you'd think they'd be able to fish from the driving seat.

However, this idyll also has a more sober side. Standing right by the Ourthe in **La Roche** (population 2,000), a tank is a sober reminder of the devastating consequences of the war. Every town

and every village displays its own tank in remembrance of its liberation. Before the war, La Roche was a flourishing holiday town which had retained its medieval flavour and had over 40 hotels. Two days after the German army had marched into Belgium, on 12 May 1940, the village was occupied. It was liberated by the Americans in September, 1944, but the Germans managed to win it back, albeit briefly, in December. Over 100 citizens were killed, and two-thirds of the houses were destroyed.

Occupying the figurative no-man's-land between the village's attempt to survive by means of tourism and its struggle with a history divided between Resistance fighters and collaborators, amidst ice-cream stores, cafés and billboards, the tank seems to be the forgotten remnant of a long-distant past. Along with the 11th-century castle ruins nearby, it is a favourite photographic subject of local, American and German tourists. Not far off, in the display window of a toy store, a video advertises toy tanks,

In the museum the Battl the Arde in Basto

rockets and space weapons, while an accompanying soundtrack blares through a loudspeaker into the shopping street of the peaceful old town.

The **War Museum**, a small exhibition in La Roche, presents bloodthirsty German soldiers in original uniforms next to French, English and Canadians in their land vehicles. The museum is an impressive collection of puppet soldiers and uniforms, but it doesn't begin to go into the history of the war or its causes.

Devoted to the pottery of the area, and open only in summer, the **Museum Poterie de Grès Bleu** in the Rue Rompré tends to be pushed somewhat into the background by the history of the war. However, it gives one an insight into the serendipity of the locals and their fundamental link with the soil.

Battle of the Ardennes: Further to the southwest, near the border of the Duchy of Luxemburg, the highest town in Belgium, **Bastogne** (population 11,000), contains the **Trier Gate** (Porte de Trèves), a reminder of the area's histori-

cal link with the parts of Germany which were occupied by the Romans. Some of the city's 14th-century fortifications, built by John the Blind of Luxemburg, have been preserved in the town. Sixteenth-century ceiling murals in the church of St Pierre are signs of the region's Catholic heritage.

The town is relatively well preserved. In the marketplace at its centre, lined with lively street cafés, there's a Sherman tank, where young American tourists – striking the victory sign – pose for souvenir photos. Outside the town, and with parking facilities for at least three military companies, the Historical Centre is a monument to the 77,000 American soldiers who fell in the Ardennes. The 7,000 Germans who fell here are buried in the cemetery of Recogne-Bastogne. Bastogne's tourist brochure touts the "wonderful war museum" in which the visitor can look at the battle and the "war collection". In fact, this museum, rendered sepulchral by the darkened skies of its dioramas, seems

en-air
it.

more like a museum dedicated to military fashion. Small models of battle scenes are displayed, with uniformed mannequins standing by. You can see the blue eyes of General "Ike" Eisenhower, who sports a "rare officer's jacket"; or, even more impressive, General Baron Hasso Eccard von Manteuffel, sun-tanned, in a fur-lined winter coat. The "replication of the scene was carried out with his full understanding and according to his description". A beaming US Air Force pilot with an irreproachable set of teeth, holding French bills in his hand, stands by Mrs Lilliam Kirkemo, a nurse who looks like a larger version of the Barbie doll.

In a film and slide-show, the Ardennes battle is presented with commentary by the two opposing generals, discussing the proceedings from a purely military point of view. Next to American flame-throwers and a comic book of the Ardennes offensive sold in the souvenir shop, you can buy books from the right-wing German publishing house Viking, such as *Hitler's Bodyguard*, written by an author who belonged to the "First SS Tank Division".

Continuing south toward Arlon along a well-paved road, you'll see the slate roofs, the church spire, and the smokestack – one of the few along this route – of **Martelange** across the valley. Then, suddenly, an unexpected vista opens out before you. Neon signs along the roadside advertise gas stations: Shell, Elf, FINA, Q8, Texaco. All of the major oil companies, and some of the smaller ones, seem to have got together and bought out the entire left-hand side of the village. Oil wells in the Ardennes? Hardly. The reason is simple: the left side of the road belongs to Luxemburg, where the tax on oil is lower than it is in Belgium.

Southern climes: Seen from the road to **Arlon**, the Ardennes present a broad, level and spacious aspect: here, there are no charming valleys, no steep cliffs. Large fields, and farm vehicle dealers at the side of the road, are indications that

Arlon is
south of
Ardenne

in this area farming, as well as raising animals and forestery, is the major occupation. In Arlon's town centre (population 23,000), red-brick houses alternate with white ones, all fronted with little balconies. There is a plethora of small speciality shops: one window contains only lovely cast- and wrought-iron pumps. Narrow alleyways and flights of steps are again reminiscent of the Mediterranean. The marketplace is used as a car park – an unfortunate custom also common in other countries.

Up a steep staircase, past the statues of Roman legionaries and of Christ carrying his cross, and you come to the Roman Tower, once part of a 900-metre (3,000-ft) stretch of wall which the Gallo-Romans hoped would defend them against the Germanic hordes.

The town has been built on the site of an old Roman settlement. Roman legionaries controlled the roads here as early as the 3rd century. With more than 400 sculptures from tombstones and secular buildings, the Luxembourg Museum contains the largest Roman collection in Belgium. Tools and cult objects of the early Franks are also displayed . Arlon can also boast of having the oldest church in the country, the remains of the Roman **Basilica** in the old cemetery, which has been transformed into an archaeological park (Rue des Thermes Romains). Originally, the building was 125 metres (400 ft) long and some 12 metres (40 ft) wide. In the early Middle Ages, the Franks buried their dead here. Just next to it you can see all that's left of a 1st-century bath house. **St Donatus church** was built by Capuchin monks in 1626, over the remains of the castle of the Counts of Arlon. From the church tower, there is a panoramic view of three countries: Belgium, Luxemburg and France.

You can taste Maitrank, a speciality of Arlon, at any time of year. A slice of orange accompanies this aperitif made from Moselle wine.

At the Hondelange service station on the E411/E25 motorway, near Arlon, a

Arlon
320 m/ 0,2 miles

gigantic building houses the largest war museum in Belgium: the **Victory Memorial Museum**. The Allied victory over Germany, from North Africa to Berlin, is depicted with uniformed wax figures and more than 200 original vehicles, some unique. The brochure informs you that "because it is built on one level, the museum can be visited without difficulty by the handicapped. The guns, uniforms and equipment form the largest and most important collection in the world about this period of history." Veterans receive a reduction.

Grotto of Han: On its path through the Ardennes, the E411 motorway crosses the **Lesse River** twice before Exit 23; the river then hides itself in the chalk hills. The forests are a kaleidoscope of green. Fields tenanted by grazing white cows and level, bald plateaux characterise the landscape. The nearer the motorway gets to the well-marked town of Han, the more picturesque the nature preserve of Lesse becomes. Its stone farmhouses, with their small windows, are like the ones in the Ourthe valley.

Campsites, holiday cottages and an extensive but unobtrusive touristic infrastructure with many hotels and restaurants await the visitor in **Han-sur-Lesse** (population 900). If you've made the long drive here in a single day you can be assured of a relaxing evening in Han. As well as the **caves**, Han offers a **nature park**, part of which is dedicated to the fauna of the Ardennes, and a **wildlife preserve** where you can see the animals which once roamed freely in the region: bison, wild horses, aurochs and brown bears. Treasures from the caves are exhibited in a small museum. The caves of Han, particularly those near the entrance, have provided men with shelter since the dawn of the human race and have been a rich source of archaeological finds.

Kayak tours are offered along the Lesse; to save your muscles the return journey is made by bicycle. Regular bicycles, mountain bikes or tandems can be rented, while for those who want

The magi◄ the Han caves.

to learn about free-style rock climbing, there's a practice climbing wall. All these attractions draw some 300,000 visitors each year. The chief enticement is, of course, the caves, discovered in 1771; you reach them on an old tram which runs from the centre of the village. Han is a place of superlatives: the largest of its many impressive caves, the "Cathedral", is 129 metres (422 ft) high.

Visitors come to the mouth of the caves by boat; from there you embark on a fantastic voyage along the Lesse, led through a forest of stalactites, a journey enhanced by music and special lighting effects. After a two-hour tour, the hungry traveller is met, at the exit, by French-fry stands, a restaurant and a small animal zoo.

Located 4 miles (6 km) further north, **Rochefort** (population 5,000) has its own cave, which is in no way inferior to Han's. Discovered in 1865, and traversed by the Lomme river, this series of raw, wild caves includes the "Sabbath Room", the largest of the chambers, which is enhanced with light and sound effects.

Ardennes' sights are well marked. Signs direct the visitor from one sight to the next; however, there's no need to include them all in your itinerary. The Domaine Provincial in **Chevtogne**, for example, is nothing more than a dull holiday resort with small wooden bungalows and everything necessary for the comfort of a tourist whose principal concern is security: restaurants, a pool, horses, miniature golf, a go-cart track, and a fishpond which guarantees a daily catch to all novice anglers.

Véves Castle: Whether you go via Chevtogne or proceed directly toward Dinant, the road commands an impressive view over the seemingly endless forests of the Ardennes. Rustic inns offering local or French cuisine, often with overnight accommodation as well, welcome travellers. For many the smoke rising from the chimneys of the stone houses is a long-forgotten aroma.

Somewhat off the track, about half a

mile (1 km) from Celles-sur-Lesse, **Véves Castle** is the stuff of which dreams are made. Looking like a fairy-tale castle with its four pointed towers, surrounded by a moat, it perches on top of a rocky hill. It is a truly idyllic spot. A stream rushes through the valley, birds twitter and you almost expect a maiden to appear in one of the lofty windows. In fact this could actually happen, as the castle is still inhabited by descendants of the Countess Liedekerke Beaufort. The elegant early 18th-century interiors are open to visitors.

Dinant: To get to **Dinant** (population 10,000), you go through a rocky gorge so narrow and high you wouldn't think a car could get through it. Built in its present form in 1820, the town is hemmed in on one side between the Meuse and the steep cliffs. The town's outlying suburbs range themselves along this narrow ridge like links in a chain. Communities existed here even in prehistoric times; the town of Dinant proper received its charter in 1152.

Because of its flourishing economy, the town was largely able to defend its independence against the archdiocese of Liège. It suffered greatly in the two world wars. Of its significant buildings, only the citadel and the early Gothic church of Our Lady, with its two incomplete towers, have been preserved. The citadel, which towers atop steep chalk cliffs to a height of 100 metres (330 ft), tells of the long military history of the town. Today, you can reach it by means of a cable car which leaves from the church on the Meuse bridge; there's also a road up to the well-preserved fortification. You can prowl through its secret subterranean passageways into its mysterious past.

Since the Middle Ages, a main pillar of Dinant's economy has been the production of handcrafted objects for church and household use. Brass pulpits and chandeliers in the churches are souvenirs of a time when craftsmen with their Dinanderies travelled along the Rhine to Liège, Leuven, Bruges, Paris, Milan

Dinant is sandwiched between the cliffs and the river Meuse

and London. Today, you can travel along the Meuse in the comfort of a steamer, or discover the Lesse under your own steam, travelling upstream by kayak to the Anseremme. Dinant's **cave**, "La Merveilleuse", lies on the other side of the Meuse, about a quarter of a mile from the bridge. Each cave has its own distinct character; "La Merveilleuse" is notable for its light, fine stalactites and its underground waterfalls.

Gardens of Annevoie: Proceeding towards Namur, you'll see signs for the Gardens of Annevoie. These gardens were created in the 18th century, and are not as severe as the gardens of the baroque period, or Versailles, which was planned in the 17th century. Charles-Alexis de Montpellier began working on Annevoie's gardens in 1758 and they have remained virtually unchanged since 1776.

Using only natural water pressure (no pump), absolutely clear water from four springs feeds the park's many fountains and waterfalls. Some of these were based on Italian and French models, but others were designed specially. Charles-Alexis drew inspiration from garden facilities he'd seen on his travels through the France and Italy.

In bygone centuries, formal gardens didn't contain many flowers; coloured stones and green borders were more common. As contemporary landscape gardeners have different ideas, a compromise has been reached here: Pierre de Montpellier laid out a flower garden, complete with many fountains, at the edge of the formal garden in the 1950s.

These very beautiful gardens, open to the public, are still the private property of the Montpellier family, who emphasise the fact that they want to share with visitors their joy at being able to live in such splendid surroundings. They have taken great care to make visitors welcome; even the car park they have provided is quite pleasing to look at.

After this splendid culmination to this part of your trip, you can proceed along the Meuse to Namur.

SPA WATER

Just as Dom Perignon brought champagne to fame, Bishop Remaclus succeeded in popularising the waters of Spa. The holy man of the Middle Ages had a reputation for performing miracles: he was able to cure seriously ill patients simply by prescribing a drinking cure. Of course, it was the water which was responsible for their recovery; and the water which the Bishop preferred came from the "holy springs" of the Ardennes. Whether one was ailing physically or spiritually, a pint or two of Spa water was sure to wash the problem out of one's system.

But it is not only spiritual advisers who set such store by Ardennes water: purveyors of spirits value it as much, if not more. Bartenders around the world will all tell you that a good whiskey should only be mixed – if mixed it must be – with low-salt mineral water. With the carbonated water, in short, from the Belgian town of Spa.

Spa is tucked away in the forested hills of the Ardennes. The country hereabouts has an austere beauty: expanses of forest give way to meadows and heaths; the moorland landscapes are frequently shrouded by drifting fog.

Most visitors to Spa come for their health and for the world-renowned water, which even Peter the Great found increased his sense of physical well-being (one of the springs is named "Peter the Great"). Of course, not everyone who travelled to Spa was of his sublime rank; but the resort numbered among its guests many consequential figures on the European stage.

In those days, most of the guests seeking rejuvenation or cures came from Russia, Sweden and England. The fame of the springs' healing powers spread far and wide across the globe. In the end, "Spa" became a synonym for healing baths everywhere, and was incorporated into the English vocabulary.

The inevitable outcome of such success was a drive to export the precious water. By the end of the 18th century, some 150,000 bottles were being exported every year. They went to all corners of Europe and even further afield. Today, the company "Spa Monopole", which belongs to the Brussels firm Spadel, fills more than 300 million bottles annually. Mineral water from Spa is especially prized in the neighbouring countries of the Netherlands and Germany, Great Britain and the USA.

Spa comprises a plethora of springs. "One hears everywhere the dull murmur of the fountains," wrote one literary resident of the town. Professor A. Monjoie, of the University of Liège, differentiates between four basic types of Spa water: "Pure", "Brisart", "Source", and the extremely variable "Pouhons". For purposes of export, only the first two types come into question: a bottle of "pure Spa", with a blue label, contains clear spring water without gas and virtually without metallic elements (even someone on a salt-free diet can enjoy this beverage without worrying), while "Spa Brisart", with a pink label, is carbonated and contains some minerals.

Even if you're something of a layman when it comes to water, and do not study the list on the side of a bottle as carefully as you might, you may be surprised at the sodium content of "pure Spa" – three milligrams a litre. In international comparisons, this water stands at the low end of the scale. Perrier contains 14 milligrams a litre; Apollinaris, 500; and Vichy Celestins a staggering 1,265. "Spa Monopole" can claim, without exaggeration, to market the mineral water lowest in salt.

In view of the town's close identification with its water, it's not surprising that its very name hearkens back to the springs: "Spa" derives from the Latin word *spagare*, meaning to bubble up.

Even today, this name is a source of pride (and business) for the town.

INSIGHT GUIDES
Travel Tips

FOR THOSE
WITH MORE THAN
A PASSING INTEREST
IN TIME...

Before you put your name down for a Patek Philippe watch *fig. 1*, there are a few basic things you might like to know, without knowing exactly whom to ask. In addressing such issues as accuracy, reliability and value for money, we would like to demonstrate why the watch we will make for you will be quite unlike any other watch currently produced.

"Punctuality", Louis XVIII was fond of saying, "is the politeness of kings."

We believe that in the matter of punctuality, we can rise to the occasion by making you a mechanical timepiece that will keep its rendezvous with the Gregorian calendar at the end of every century, omitting the leap-years in 2100, 2200 and 2300 and recording them in 2000 and 2400 *fig. 2*. Nevertheless, such a watch does need the occasional adjustment. Every 3333 years and 122 days you should remember to set it forward one day to the true time of the celestial clock. We suspect, however, that you are simply content to observe the politeness of kings. Be assured, therefore, that when you order your watch, we will be exploring for you the physical—if not the metaphysical—limits of precision.

Does everything have to depend on how much?

Consider, if you will, the motives of collectors who set record prices at auction to acquire a Patek Philippe. They may be paying for rarity, for looks or for micromechanical ingenuity. But we believe that behind each $500,000-plus

bid is the conviction that a Patek Philippe, even if 50 years old or older, can be expected to work perfectly for future generations.

In case your ambitions to own a Patek Philippe are somewhat discouraged by the scale of the sacrifice involved, may we hasten to point out that the watch we will make for you today will certainly be a technical improvement on the Pateks bought at auction? In keeping with our tradition of inventing new mechanical solutions for greater reliability and better time-keeping, we will bring to your watch innovations *fig. 3* inconceivable to our watchmakers who created the supreme wristwatches of 50 years ago *fig. 4*. At the same time, we will of course do our utmost to avoid placing undue strain on your financial resources.

Can it really be mine?

May we turn your thoughts to the day you take delivery of your watch? Sealed within its case is your watchmaker's tribute to the mysterious process of time. He has decorated each wheel with a chamfer carved into its hub and polished into a shining circle. Delicate ribbing flows over the plates and bridges of gold and rare alloys. Millimetric surfaces are bevelled and burnished to exactitudes measured in microns. Rubies are transformed into jewels that triumph over friction. And after many months—or even years—of work, your watchmaker stamps a small badge into the mainbridge of your watch. The Geneva Seal—the highest possible attestation of fine watchmaking *fig. 5*.

Looks that speak of inner grace *f*

When you order your watch, you w doubt like its outward appearance t reflect the harmony and elegance of movement within. You may therefo find it helpful to know that we are uniquely able to cater for any specia decorative needs you might like to express. For example, our engravers delight in conjuring a subtle play o and shadow on the gold case-back o of our rare pocket-watches *fig. 7*. If bring us your favourite picture, our enamellers will reproduce it in a br miniature of hair-breadth detail *fig.* The perfect execution of a double h nail pattern on the bezel of a wristv is the pride of our casemakers and t satisfaction of our designers, while chainsmiths will weave for you a ri brocade in gold *figs. 9 & 10*. May w also recommend the artistry of our goldsmiths and the experience of o lapidaries in the selection and settir the finest gemstones? *figs. 11 & 12*.

How to enjoy your watch before y own it.

As you will appreciate, the very nat of our watches imposes a limit on t number we can make available. (Th Calibre 89 time-pieces we are now n will take up to nine years to comple We cannot therefore promise instar gratification, but while you look fc to the day on which you take deliv your Patek Philippe *fig. 13*, you w have the pleasure of reflecting that is a universal and everlasting comm freely available to be enjoyed by all

Should you require information on any particular Patek Philippe watch, or even on watchmaking in general, we would be delighted to reply to your letter of enquiry. And if

fig. 1: The classic face of Patek ...ilippe.

fig. 4: Complicated wristwatches circa 1930 (left) and 1990. The golden age of watchmaking will always be with us.

...g. 2: One of the 33 complica-...ns of the Calibre 89 ...ronomical clock-watch is a ...ellite wheel that completes one ...olution every 400 years.

fig. 5: The Geneva Seal is awarded only to watches which achieve the standards of horological purity laid down in the laws of Geneva. These rules define the supreme quality of watchmaking.

fig. 3: Recognized as the most advanced mechanical regulating device to date, Patek Philippe's Gyromax balance wheel demonstrates the equivalence of simplicity and precision.

fig. 6: Your pleasure in owning a Patek Philippe is the purpose of those who made it for you.

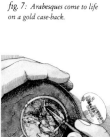

fig. 7: Arabesques come to life on a gold case-back.

fig. 8: An artist working six hours a day takes about four months to complete a miniature in enamel on the case of a pocket-watch.

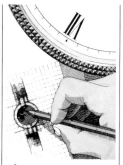

fig. 9: Harmony of design is executed in a work of simplicity and perfection in a lady's Calatrava wristwatch.

fig. 10: The chainsmith's hands impart strength and delicacy to a tracery of gold.

fig. 11: Circles in gold: symbols of perfection in the making.

fig. 12: The test of a master lapidary is his ability to express the splendour of precious gemstones.

PATEK PHILIPPE
GENEVE

fig. 13: The discreet sign of those who value their time.

...ard marked "book catalogue" we shall post you a catalogue of our publications. Patek Philippe, 41 rue du Rhône, 1204 Geneva, Switzerland, Tel. +41 22/310 03 66.

Reality check. Call home.

—— *AT&T USADirect® and World Connect®. The fast, easy way to call most anywhere.* ——

Take out AT&T Calling Card or your local calling card.** Lift phone. Dial AT&T Access Number for country you're calling from. Connect to English-speaking operator or voice prompt. Reach the States or over 200 countries. Talk. Say goodbye. Hang up. Resume vacation.

Austria*††† 022-903-011	Luxembourg 0-800-0111	Turkey* 00-800-12277
Belgium* 0-800-100-10	Netherlands* 06-022-9111	United Kingdom.............0500-89-0011
Czech Republic*.............00-420-00101	Norway 800-190-11	
Denmark 8001-0010	Poland†◆ı ....0◊010-480-0111	
Finland 9800-100-10	Portugal† 05017-1-288	
France...............................19-0011	Romania* 01-800-4288	
Germany...........................0130-0010	Russia*† (Moscow) 155-5042	
Greece* 00-800-1311	Slovak Rep.* 00-420-00101	
Hungary* ....00◊-800-01111	Spain● 900-99-00-11	
Ireland 1-800-550-000	Sweden 020-795-611	
Italy* 172-1011	Switzerland* 155-00-11	

AT&T
Your True Choice

**You can also call collect or use most U.S. local calling cards. Countries in bold face permit country-to-country calling in addition to calls to the U.S. World Connect® prices consist of USADirect® rates plus an additional charge based on the country you are calling. Collect calling available to the U.S. only. *Public phones require deposit of coin or phone card. †May not be available from every phone. †††Public phones require local coin payment during call. ◆Not available from public phones. ◊Await second dial tone. ıDial 010-480-0111 from major Warsaw hotels. ●Calling available to most European countries. ©1995 AT&T.

For a free wallet sized card of all AT&T Access Numbers, call: 1-800-241-5555.

CONTENTS

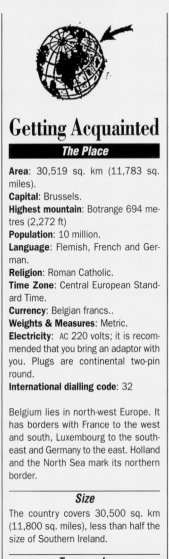

Getting Acquainted

Area: 30,519 sq. km (11,783 sq. miles).
Capital: Brussels.
Highest mountain: Botrange 694 metres (2,272 ft)
Population: 10 million.
Language: Flemish, French and German.
Religion: Roman Catholic.
Time Zone: Central European Standard Time.
Currency: Belgian francs..
Weights & Measures: Metric.
Electricity: AC 220 volts; it is recommended that you bring an adaptor with you. Plugs are continental two-pin round.
International dialling code: 32

Belgium lies in north-west Europe. It has borders with France to the west and south, Luxembourg to the south-east and Germany to the east. Holland and the North Sea mark its northern border.

Size

The country covers 30,500 sq. km (11,800 sq. miles), less than half the size of Southern Ireland.

Topography

Belgium comprises nine provinces: West Flanders, bordering the North Sea; East Flanders, Antwerp and Limburg to the north; Brabant and the capital, Brussels, in the centre; Liège to the east; Hainaut to the south-west; Namur to the south and Luxembourg (not to be confused with the Grand Duchy of Luxembourg) to the south-east. The country is trisected by the Scheldt and the Meuse, both major commercial rivers.

The north of Belgium, including the provinces of West and East Flanders, is mainly flat like Holland. The North Sea coast, site of Belgium's popular holiday resorts, is lined with sandy beaches, dunes and salt marshes.

To the south-east, in the Ardennes provinces of Namur, Liège and Luxembourg, the land becomes hilly and forested with deeply-wooded valleys and high plateaux.

Brussels itself is situated upon several hills along the Senne, a small tributary of the Scheldt river. During the past century the river has been completely built over within the centre of the city. The city centre lies at about 15 metres (50 ft) above sea level and the Forest and Duden Parks at about 100 metres (335 ft). Corresponding to its hilly character, Brussels falls naturally into two parts: the Upper and Lower Cities, the latter of which includes the old part of the town.

Climate

Belgium enjoys a temperate maritime climate with relatively cool summers and mild winters. In summer the average temperature is about 16°C (61°F), in winter about 3°C (27°F).

The People

Belgium derives its name from the Belgae; the first recorded inhabitants, probably Celts. It was conquered by Julius Caesar and ruled in turn by Rome, the Franks, Burgundy, Spain, Austria and France. In 1815 Belgium was made part of the Netherlands and in 1831 it became an independent constitutional monarchy. Today Belgium has a population of 10,022,000; Brussels has 951,000 inhabitants and Antwerp 465,000.

The Flemings of northern Belgium (about 60 percent of the population) speak Dutch while French is the language of the Walloons in the south (40 percent). A German-speaking minority lives in East Belgium. This language difference has been an ongoing source of acrimony and while prosperity has shifted between the regions the French-speakers have traditionally represented the aristocracy and the Flemings the bourgeoisie. In the early 1980s parliament took steps to ease the tension by transferring power from central government to three regions, Wallonia, Flanders and Brussels but the language divide still influences all aspects of working life, education, politics and culture.

The Economy

On the basis of its manufacturing industries alone, Belgium can be counted as a member of the leading European industrialised countries. The first industries to get underway were those based on coal and iron ore deposits. The most important industrial products manufactured in Belgium today include iron and steel, machinery, textiles, motor vehicles and chemical products. Diamond cutting, glass and textile manufacture also play an important role. The chief crops are wheat, potatoes and sugar beet. Belgium's most significant trading partners are France, Germany, Holland and Great Britain. In Europe, the port of Antwerp is second in importance only to the great ports of London and Rotterdam. This harbour is primarily responsible for growing prosperity throughout the whole of Flanders. Tourism also plays a significant economic role along the Belgian coast, in Brussels and in many Flemish cities.

Brussels is the seat of The European Union as well as of NATO. The city is regarded as an international centre of high finance where thousands of multinational corporations maintain their headquarters. Business life is chiefly carried out in the old Flemish part of the city (referred to as the Lower City). The textile industry has enjoyed a special status in Brussels for hundreds of years. Wool, upholstery fabric and the world-famous "Brussels lace" are all manufactured here. International metal, electrical and chemical companies have also been successful in establishing themselves in this thriving capital.

The Government

In accordance to the constitution of February 1831, Belgium is a constitutional monarchy which is passed on through the House of Saxe-Coburg. The legislature is composed of the senate and the house of parliament, members of both being elected every four years. The monarch is the head of state; since 1993 this has been Albert II. The executive branch of government is in the hands of the prime minister and his cabinet.

Constitutional reforms have created a federal state guaranteeing autonomy

e Dutch, French and German cul-
communities of Belgium.
russels is the capital city both of
ium and of the province known as
ant. It is officially bilingual as it is
ated only a few kilometres north of
"language border" between Flan-
and Wallonia. However in every-
discourse French is by far the
t common language used through-
the city. Greater Brussels, the
xelloise", is comprised of 19 dif-
nt districts. Formerly suburbs,
e have expanded and merged to
a single, built-up area.

lanning The Trip

What To Bring

Belgians are quite fashion-con-
us. In large cities especially peo-
pay attention to presenting themes in smart attire. However, visi-
preferring to dress more casually
not feel conspicuous. When pack-
or a visit to Belgium, keep in mind
the weather is variable and select
travelling wardrobe accordingly.

Maps

t good bookshops stock maps on
ium. General maps to look out for
the AA Baedeker Map of Belgium
le 1:250,000); RAC European
d Maps No. 3 Belgium, Nether-
ds and Luxembourg (1:500,000);
tholomew Belgium and Luxem-
rg (1:300,000); Falk Benelux Coun-
s (1:500,000); GeoCenter Interna-
al Euro-Map Belgium-Luxembourg
00,000); Hallwag Euro-map Bel-
n-Luxembourg (1:250,000); Hilde-
d's Belgium (1:250,000); Mich-
Map No. 409 Belgie-Luxembourg
50,000); and Michelin Map No. 51
is-Lille-Brussels, No. 212 Brugge-
terdam-Antwerpen, No. 213 Brus-
-Oostende-Liege (all 1:200,000).
eocart and Falk both produce town
s of the major cities and the Na-
al Geographic Institute publishes
graphic maps of Belgium itself,
Hautes Fagnes, Proven-leper-

Ploegsteert and the Belgium Woods
(Zoniëwoud/Forêt de Soignes) regions.

Entry Regulations
Visas & Passports

All visitors entering Belgium from countries which are members of the European Union or from Switzerland require
a valid personal identity card or passport. Visitors from the United States,
Australia, New Zealand and Japan
need only a valid passport, no visa is
required. Visas are still required for
nationals of certain Commonwealth
countries. Children under the age of
16 must be in possession of a child's
identity card/passport if their names
have not been entered in one of their
parents' cards. For further information
contact the Belgian Embassy, 103
Eaton Square, London SW1W 9AB. Tel:
0171-235 5144.

Animal Quarantine

Travellers bringing in cats or dogs are
required to have an official certificate
issued by a vet stating that their pet
has been vaccinated against rabies.
The vaccination must have taken place
at least 30 days prior to arrival and be
no more than 1 year old (in the case of
cats, 6 months).

Customs

There is no limit to the amount of foreign currency that can be brought in or
taken out of Belgium.

Items for everyday use and those
frequently transported by tourists,
such as cameras and sporting equipment, may be brought into the country
duty-free.

European Union citizens: in addition to
the above, visitors over 17 from European Union nations are not subject to
restrictions on goods and consumable
items for personal use.

Non-EU citizens: citizens from non-EU
nations are permitted to bring the following items into Belgium duty-free:
200 cigarettes or 50 cigars or 250g
tobacco; 2 litres still wine; 1 litre spirits or 2 litres sparkling or fortified
wine; 50g perfume and 0.25 litres toi-
let water.

Health

Visitors from THE UK to Belgium are not
required to produce an international

smallpox vaccination certificate or any
other medical document.

Currency

The unit of currency in Belgium is the
Belgian Franc (Bfr), with 100 centimes
to 1 franc. There are 100, 500, 1,000
and 5,000 Bfr notes and 50 centimes,
1, 5, 10, 20 and 50 Bfr coins in circu-
lation.

Eurocheques can be cashed in for a
maximum of 7,000 Bfr a cheque. As a
rule, the exchange offices located in
the larger railway stations maintain
longer hours than the banks.

Most international credit cards are
accepted in larger hotels, numerous
gourmet restaurants, many shops and
boutiques, and at some banks and car
rental agencies.

If you should lose or have your
Eurocheque card stolen, report the
loss immediately to your bank so that
measures can be taken to freeze your
account. You should also report the
loss or theft of a credit card at once to
the security service in Brussels. It is
open day and night and can be
reached by dialling 539 15 02.

Public Holidays

1 January: New Year's Day
March/April: Easter Monday*
1 May: Labour Day
May: Ascension Day* and Whit
Monday*
21 July: National Holiday
15 August: Assumption of the Virgin
Mary
1 November: All Saints' Day
11 November: Armistice Day
25 December: Christmas Day

If any of these holidays fall on a
Sunday, the following Monday is taken
in lieu.

*Variable dates. The Chamber of
Commerce of Belgium publishes a cur-
rent calendar of festivals each year.
See Festivals.

Getting There
By Air

Brussels' international airport, Zaventem, is 14 km (8 miles) north-east of
the city centre. It has a tourist information booth in the baggage reclaim hall,
and general information is available by

telephoning 02-722 31 11. International air services information is provided by Sabena (Tel: 02-511 90 30). Being the seat of the European Union, Brussels is well served by international airlines. By air, it is one hour from the European cities of Paris, London, Amsterdam and Frankfurt. Sabena, the Belgian airline, has particularly good links with Africa. For the United States, American Airlines flies daily to its gateway cities of Chicago and New York.

A fast and frequent train service (every 20 minutes) connects the airport with Brussels' main railway station from 5.39am–11.14pm. The journey takes 20 minutes.

International airline offices in Brussels:
American Airlines, Rue de Trone 98. Tel: 02-508 77 00.
British Airways, Rue Rogier. Tel: 02-217 74 00.
Lufthansa, Boulevard Anspach 1. Tel: 02-218 43 00.
Sabena, Rue Cardinal Mercier 35. Tel: 02-511 90 30.
Swissair, Place de Brouckére. Tel: 02-219 03 41.

Airlines with offices in the UK operating services to Brussels:
Sabena, Tel: 0181-780 1444.
British Airways, Tel: 0181-867 4000.
British Midland, Tel: 0171-589 5599.
Air UK, Tel: 01345-666777.
City Flyer Express (to Antwerp), Tel: 0181-897 4000.
Loganair, Tel: 01703-651119.
VLM, Tel: 01920-485059.
Sky Service (to Kortrijk), Tel: 01345-666777.

By Ship

Ferry services between the United Kingdom and Belgium are operated by:
North Sea Ferries between Hull and Zeebrugge, Tel: 01482 795141; **P&O European Ferries** between Dover and Calais and Zeebrugge, Tel: 01304-203388; **Sally Ferries between Ramsgate and Ostend**, Tel: 0171-834 2345.

By Train

The Belgium railway system maintains a well-developed railway network. There are a number of international railway lines crossing Belgium, connecting France and Holland, Great Britain and Germany with one another.

The capital's main railway stations are Brussels North (Nord), Brussels Central (Centrale) and Brussels South (Midi). Trains to Paris take 2 hours 27 minutes; to Cologne 2 hours 13 minutes; to Amsterdam 2 hours 55 minutes.

Belgium National Railways, Premier House, 10 Greycoat Place, London SW1P 1SB. Tel: 01891-516444.
P&O Ferries (Tel: 0171-834 2345), is a reliable source of information about boat trains to Brussels from the UK.
Sally Ferries (Tel: 0171-834 2345), train-boat-train services from London to Bruges, Brussels, Ostend, Ghent and Antwerp via Ramsgate.

In Brussels, rail information is available on tel: 02-219 26 40.

The Channel Tunnel, opened in 1994, has shuttle trains with a capacity of 120 cars, which take about 10 minutes to load. From Folkestone to Calais the journey takes around 35 minutes and there are up to 4 trains an hour, tel: 01303 273300 for bookings and information. A direct passenger service of through trains connects London (Waterloo) to Brussels in 3 hours, tel: 01233 617575 for reservations and information.

By Bus

Hoverspeed, tel: 01304-240241, offers coach-Hovercraft-coach travel from London or Dover to Brussels, Mons and Antwerp.
Eurolines European Coach Travel, tel: 0171-730 0202, coaches from London to Antwerp, Brussels, Ghent and Liège.

By Car

Belgium is criss-crossed by international motorways which are toll-free.

Distances from Brussels to other European cities: Amsterdam 232 km (144 miles), Paris 302 km (187 miles), Cologne 220 km (136 miles), Ostend 114 km (70 miles), Luxembourg 216 km (134 miles).

If you are planning on entering Belgium by car, you will need a driver's licence, vehicle registration papers and a nationality sticker fixed to the rear of your vehicle.

You should carry a red triangle to display in the event of a breakdown. It is wise to take out additional insur-

ance (Green Card) for full comprehensive cover.

The minimum age for driving in Belgium is 18 for cars and motorcy, 16 for mopeds. Children under 12 not allowed in front seats if there room in the back. Seat belts must worn.

Like other Continental countr Belgium drives on the right. In to the speed limit is 50 kph (31 m outside built-up areas 90 kph mph); motorways 120 kph (75 m There is a minimum speed on m ways of 70 kph (45 mph). At juncti cars coming from the right have p ity unless otherwise stated. Tr have priority, as do their passen when crossing the road to boar alight.

BREAKDOWNS

Touring Club de Belgique, rue Jos ll 25, Brussels. Tel: 02-512 78 9
Royal Automobile Club de Belgi rue d'Arlon 53, Brussels. Tel: 02-09 11.
Vlaamse Automobilistenbond, Jacobsmarkt 45, Antwerp. Tel: 03-34 34.

INFORMATION AND ROUTE MAPS

Available in the UK from the AA 01256-20123) and the RAC 01800-550 550)

Many city names appear in Flemish and French. The most im tant of these are: Aalst (Flemish)/A (French); Antwerpen (Felmish)/ An (Antwerp); Brugge/Bruges; Brus Bruxelles (Brussels); Tendermor Termonde; Gent/Gand (Ghent); H Huy; Ieper/Ypres; Kortrijk/ Cour Leuven/Louvain; Luik/Liège; M elen/Malines; Bergen/Mons; Nam Namur; Oostende/Ostende (Oste Oudenaarde/Audenarde; Ronse/ aix; Zinnik/Soignies; Doornik/Tou Veurne/ Furnes.

Special Facilities
Travelling with Children

The majority of hotels in Belgium come and cater for babies and s children. Most of them are able to vide facilities such as cots, I chairs, special food and baby-sit services. Simply state your req ments when making reservations

Tour Operators

complete list of travel firms, con-
the Belgian Tourist Office, 29
s Street, London W1R 7RG, tel:
-629 0230, fax: 0171-629 0454.
re follows a selection of tour
tors.

lotoring Holidays, PO Box 128,
n House, Basingstoke, Hants
2EA. Tel: 01256 493878.

France Holidays, 27 West Street,
ngton, W. Sussex. Tel: 01903
45.

um Expressions, 4 Belsize Cres-
London NW3 5QU. Tel: 0171-
.820.

um Holidays, 175 Selsdon Park
, Surrey CR2 8JJ. Tel: 0181-651

um Travel Service, Bridge House,
, Herts SG12 9DG. Tel: 01920
31.

h Airways Holidays, Atlantic
e, Hazelwick Avenue, Crawley, W.
ex. Tel: 01293 572763.

os Holidays, Tourama House, 17
esdale Road, Bromley, Kent BR2
Tel: 0181-464 3444.

line Europe, Greenleaf House,
s Lane, Potters Bar, Herts EN6
Tel: 01707 660011.

reak, 10-18 Putney Hill, London
6AX. Tel: 0181-780 0909.

camp Travel, Canute Court, Toft
Knutsford, Ches WA16 0NL. Tel:
5 650022.

sior Holidays, 22 Sea Road,
emouth, Dorset BH5 1DD. Tel:
2 309555.

ess Travel, 37 Commercial
t, Kenfig Hill, Bridgend, Mid-Glam
6DH. Tel: 01656 740323.

de France, 178 Piccadilly, Lon-
V1V 9DB. Tel: 0171-408 1343.

von Holidays, Halcyon House,
olmlee, Hull HU2 8HT. Tel: 01482
2.

Battlefield Tours, 15 Market
t, Sandwich, Kent CT13 9DA. Tel:
4 612248.

asons Holidays Abroad, Sunway
e, Lowestoft, Suffolk NR32 3LT.
1502 500555.

uttle Holidays, Eurotunnel, PO
01, Folkestone, Kent CT19 4QY.
1303 271717.

Sea Ferries, King George Dock,
n Road, Hull HU9 5QA. Tel:
2 77177.

Pattison World Travel, 5 West View,
Wideopen, Newcastle upon Tyne NE13
6EG. Tel: 0191 236 3304.

P&O European Ferries Holidays,
Travelscene House, 11-15 St Anns
Road, Harrow, Middx HA1 1AS. Tel:
0181-427 8800.

Sovereign Cities, Groundstar House,
London Road, Crawley, W Sussex. Tel:
01293 588432.

Sport Abroad, The Travel Centre, Wix
Hill House, West Horsley, Surrey KT24
6DZ. Tel: 01483 225000.

Sportscene, 163a Victoria Road,
Horley, Surrey RH6 7AR. Tel: 01293
774 1123.

Sports Tours, 19 The Parade, Colches-
ter Road, Romford, Essex RM3 0AQ.
Tel: 01708 344001.

Stena Sealink, Charter House, Park
Street, Ashford, Kent TN24 8EX. Tel:
01233 647022.

Time Off, Chester Close, London
SW1X 7BQ. Tel: 0171-235 8070.

VFB Holidays, Normandy House, High
Street, Cheltenham, Glos GL50 3HW.
Tel: 01242 526338.

Wallace Arnold Tours, Gelderd Roads,
Leeds LS12 6DH. Tel: 0113 636456.

York Tours & Holidays, Town Centre
House, 3 Mercers Row, Northampton
NN1 2QL. Tel: 01604 21014.

Travel Federations

Abito, Cogels-Osylei 36, 2600 Antwerp. Tel: 03-218 45 91.

FTI, Bergstraat 38, 1000 Brussels. Tel:
02-512 27 69, fax: 02-512 2769.

VVR, (Flemish Association of Travel
Agents), Emmaüsdreef 4, 8021
Zedelgem-Loppern. Tel: 50-33 12 15.

Travel Agencies

Acotra World Travel NV, Magdalenen–
st'w 51, 1000 Brussels. Tel: 2-512 86
07, fax: 2-512 39 74.

Albo Comfort Travel, Baasrodestraat
114, 9350 Dendermonde. Tel: 52-21
95 01, fax: 52-22 50 72.

ATI Travel, Vilvoordelaan 153 A, 1930
Zaventem. Tel: 2-720 61 40, fax: 2-
721 36 50.

Babbelbus, Tujastraat 12, 1170 Brussels. Tel: 2-673 18 35.

BBL-Travel, St-Michielswarande 60,
1050 Brussels. Tel: 2-738 45 36, fax:
2-738 61 00.

Belgian Travel House, Louisalaan
526, 1050 Brussels. Tel: 2-648 60
24, fax: 2-640 82 05.

De Boeck, Heuvelstraat 8, Grasmarkt,
1000 Brussels. Tel: 2-513 77 44, fax:
2-513 61 54.

Flanders International, Airport Terminal, Building Room P 290-292, 8400
Ostend. Tel: 59-50 69 56, fax: 59-50
69 16.

Flanders Travel (VTB-VAB), St-Jacobs–
markt 45, 2000 Antwerp. Tel: 3-220
3355, fax: 59-220 32 50.

Ghent Incoming, Rozemarijnstraat 23,
9000 Ghent. Tel: 91-24 40 46.

Grard Link Travel, Stw. op Bergen
495, 1070 Brussels. Tel: 2-521
01 82.

Hasselt Travel Service, Maastrichter-
straat 67, 3500 Hasselt. Tel: 11-22
96 60, fax: 11-24 20 25.

Hebo, Cogels-Osylei 36, 2600
Antwerp. Tel: 3-218 4591, fax: 3-218
85 68.

Panorama Tours, Grasmarkt 105,
1000 Brussels. Tel: 2-513 61 54, fax:
2-513 61 51.

Scheers International, A. Maxlaan
132, 1000 Brussels. Tel: 2-217 77
60, fax: 2-217 57 50.

Transcontinental General Car,
Guldenvlies-galerijen, Elsenesteenweg
2931, 1050 Brussels. Tel: 2-513 64
20, fax: 2-512 69 18.

Travel Partners International, Route
d'Hannonsart 12, 1328 Ohain. Tel: 2-
633 39 90, fax: 2-633 17 03.

Voyages Belges, Doverstraat 17,
1070 Brussels. Tel: 2-523 21 32, fax:
2-520 51 69.

Wagons-Lits, E. Plaskylaan 114, 1040
Brussels. Tel: 2-736 10 43, fax: 2-736
48 11.

West Belgium Coach CY, Archi–
medesstraat 7, 8400 Ostend. Tel: 59-
55 44 91, fax: 59-55 44 18.

Booking Agencies

BTR (Belgium Tourist Reservations),
PO Box 41, 1000 Brussels 23. Tel: 2-
230 5029, fax: 2-230 60 9. Provides
hotel accommodation and will make
any reservation for both single parties
and groups throughout Belgium.

Westtoer VZW, Kasteel Tillegem, 8200
Bruges 2. Tel: 50-38 02 92, fax: 50-38
0292. In the province of West Flanders: reservations for hotel accommodation, boat cruises, guided tours,
evening events and entertainment,
arrangements for conventions and
educational courses.

Toeristische federatie provincie Antwerpen, Karel Oomstraat 11, 2018 Antwerp. Tel: 3-216 28 10, fax: 3-273 83 65. Province of Antwerp: day excursions for groups, weekend and short holidays trips.

Provincial verbond voor toerisme in Limburg, Domein Bokrijk 3600 Genk. Tel: 11-22 29 58, fax: 11-22 60 86. In the province of Limburg: day tours for groups, bicycle excursions.

Practical Tips

Emergencies

Security and Crime

The usual precautions are recommended:

● Don't keep all money, credit cards or traveller's cheques in one wallet or purse; disperse them so one theft won't make you totally penniless.

● Make sure to hold bags closely and keep them fastened. Never leave them unattended.

● Have some form of identification in your wallet, because sometimes the thief will deposit your stolen wallet (minus the money, of course, but with all else intact) in a local mail box or drop it where someone might recover your property and forward it on.

Smoking: Throughout Belgium, smoking is strictly prohibited in enclosed areas.

EMERGENCY NUMBERS

Accident Aid and Fire Brigade, tel: 100.

Police, tel: 101.

In Greater Brussels the **Emergency Service** can be contacted at any time, day or night, tel: 479 18 18 and 648 80 00.

Doctors on emergency call in Brussels, tel: 479 18 18 and 648 80 00.

Red Cross, tel: 649 50 10.

National Telephone Information, tel: 1207.

Time, tel: 1200.

Weather Report, tel: 702

Loss of Belongings

Report any lost belongings immediately to the nearest police inspector's office, or at the police headquarters at Rue du Marché au Charbon in the centre of Brussels city, tel: 517 96 11, and ask for a certificate of loss for insurance purposes. If you lose your passport, contact your local embassy/consulate as soon as possible.

There is a lost and found office at Brussels airport, tel: 755 21 11. For articles lost or left behind on a train enquire at the nearest train station or at the Quartier Leopold Railway Station, Place du Luxembourg, Brussels, tel: 218 60 50. Otherwise items left on trains or buses may turn up at The Public Transportation Lost Property Office, Avenue Toison d'Or, Brussels. Tel: 513 23 94.

Medical Services

Visitors from EU countries should obtain a form E111 before leaving home. This entitles them to some free treatment, but does not cover all eventualities. Medical treatment must be paid for and the cost recovered when you return home. All visitors are, however, strongly advised to take out private medical insurance.

Chemists: After regular hours and during holidays you will find the name and address of the nearest chemist on night-duty posted at all chemists.

Weights and Measures

The metric system is in use in Belgium, which means that units are measured in metres or kilograms and their derivatives.

Some useful conversion rates include:

1 gramme (g) = 0.04 ounces (oz)
1 kilogramme (kg) = 2.20 pounds (lbs)
1 litre (l) = 1.76 pints (pt)
1 millilitre (mm) = 0.39 inches (in)
1 metre = 3.28 feet (ft)
1 kilometre (km) = 0.62 miles
8 kilometres = 5 miles

Business Hours

Banks: All the banks in Belgium will exchange foreign money. Most are open from 9am–noon and again from 2–4pm Monday–Friday. Some banks,

however, do remain open at mid-

Shops: There is no official closing for shops in Belgium. Most shop open 9am–6pm, with grocery st frequently remaining open until ▼ Some shops close for a lunch t between noon and 2pm.

In large cities big depart stores stay open late – until 9 once a week, usually on Fridays will also find a number of shops round the clock, as well as on Sur and holidays.

Post Offices: Generally post of are open 9am–5pm; in smaller c they are usually closed in the a noons.

Museums: Most museums are Tuesday–Saturday, 9am–4pm sometimes on Sunday, closed: day. A number of museums are from Easter–September only.

Tipping

You are not obliged to leave a t cinemas and theatres it is neve less customary to pay a bit mo addition to the price of the progran

In hotels, all service tips ar cluded in the room price, but again it is usual to give a little s thing to the maid, doorman and p when you depart if you've staye more than a couple of nights.

Where there is no charge fo use of a public lavatory, it is cus ary to leave between 10 and 15 B the attendant.

Media

Newspapers and Magazin

As a result of three different lang communities existing simultaneo in one country, there are nume newspapers published in Belgiun

The three most important Fr papers are the Le *Soir*, La Belgique and *La Dernière Heure*.

The three most popular Dutch r papers are *Het Laatste Nieuws Standaard* and *De Morgen*, and most read German newspaper is *Grenz-Echo*.

The weekly English language r paper, *The Bulletin*, keeps the r thousand members of the inte tional community in Brussels info and up-to-date regarding what is g on in Belgium.

reign newspaper and magazines
be purchased at larger bookshops
e major cities.

Radio and Television

ddition to the many local stations
elgium, listeners can also tune into
national radio stations, the RTBF
adcasts are in French), BRT (pro-
mes delivered in Flemish) and the
(for German-speaking listeners).
television monopoly is shared by
RTBF and the BRT; in nearly all parts
e country it is also possible to
ve foreign programmes transmit-
by cable.

Postal Services

offices are generally open Mon-
Friday 9am–5pm; in smaller cities
are usually closed at lunch-time
sometimes in the afternoons. The
office located at the South Rail-
Station in Brussels is open every
around the clock.

st boxes are painted red.

grams can be sent by dialling the
ber 1225 or via your hotel recep-

Telecoms

ll find current calling rates posted
elgian telephone booths. Booths
which it is possible to make inter-
onal calls are designated by inter-
onal flags. To make a call to an-
r country, first dial 00, then the
try code and finally the number of
arty you are trying to reach (omit
) from the dialling code).

elephones take Bfr 5, 20, 50 coins
cards, available from newsagents,
offices and railway stations, for
00 or Bfr 500. Some post offices
telephone booths from which you
call and pay afterwards.

he following is a list of dialling
es for the most important Belgian
s:

Antwerp	03
Bruges	05
Brussels	02
Ghent	091
Liège	041
Namur	081
Ostend	059
Tongeren	012
Tournai	069

Tourist Offices

Belgian Tourist Office, 61 Rue du Marché aux Herbes. Tel: 02 504 03 90. Open: Monday–Saturday (January–May and October–December) 9am–6pm; (June–September) 9am–7pm; Sunday (January–March and November–December) 1–5pm; (April, May, October) 9am–6pm; (June–September) 9am–7pm.

Brussels Tourist Information, Townhall (Hôtel de Ville), Grand Place. Tel: 02 513 89 40. Open: Monday–Saturday, 9am–6pm, Sunday (in summer) 9am–6pm, (in winter) 10am–2pm. Closed: on Sunday, 1 December–28 February.

Provincial Tourist Offices

Antwerp: Karel Oomsstraat 11, 2018 Antwerp. Tel: 3-216 2810, fax: 3-237 8365.

Brabant: Rue Marché aux Herbes 61, 1000 Brussels. Tel: 2-513 0750.

Brabant: Grasmarkt 61, 1000 Brussels. Tel: 2-504 0455.

Hainaut: Rue des Clercs 31, 7000 Mons. Tel: 65-36 04 64.

Liège: Boulevard de la Sauvenière 77, 4000 Liège. Tel: 41-22 42 10.

Limburg: Thonissenlaan 27, 3500 Hasselt. Tel: 11-22 29 58, fax: 11-22 60 86.

Luxembourg: Quai de l'Ourthe 9, 6980 La Roche. Tel: 84-41 10 11.

Namur: Rue Notre-Dame 3, 5000 Namur. Tel: 81-22 29 98, fax: 81-22 47 68.

Oost-Vlaanderen: Koningin Maria-Hendrikaplein, 64, 9000 Gent. Tel: 92-22 16 37, fax: 92-21 92 69.

West-Vlaanderen: Kasteel Tillegem, 8200 Brugge 2. Tel: 50-38 02 96, fax: 50-38 02 92.

Local Tourist Offices

Antwerp: Grote Markt 15, 2000 Antwerp. Tel: 3-232 01 03, fax: 3-255 10 13.

Arlon: Place Léopold, 6700 Arlon. Tel: 63-21 63 60.

Blankenberge: Léopold III-plein, 8370 Blankenberge. Tel: 50-41 22 27, fax: 50-41 61 39.

Bruges: Burg 11, 8000 Bruges. Tel: 50-44 86 86, fax: 50-44 86 00.

Brussels: City Hall, Grand-Place (Grote Markt), 1000 Brussels. Tel: 2-513 89 40, fax: 2-514 01 29.

Dinant: Rue Grande 37, 5500 Dinant. Tel: 82-22 28 70.

De Panne: Gemeentehuis, Zeelaan 21, 8470 De Panne. Tel: 58-41 13 02, fax: 58-41 36 35.

Glent: Stad Gent, Predikherenlei 2, 9000 Glent. Tel: 9-225 36 41, fax: 9-255 62 88.

Hasselt: Lombaartstraat 3 (Town hall), 3500 Hasselt. Tel: 11-22 22 35, fax: 11-22 88 94.

Ieper (Ypres): Stadhuis, 8900 Ieper. Tel: 57-20 26 26.

Knokke-Heist: Stadhuis, 8300 Knooke-Heist. Tel: 50-60 15 16, fax: 50-62 08 13.

Kortrijk: Schouwburgplein, 8500 Kortrijk. Tel: 56-20 25 00.

La Roche: Place du Marché, 6980 la Roche. Tel: 84-41 13 42.

Liège: Féronstrée 92, 4000 Liège. Tel: 41-22 24 56.

Leuven: Naamsestraat 1A, 3000 Leuven. Tel: 16-21 15 39.

Mechelen: Stadhuis, Grote Markt, 2800 Mechelen. Tel: 15-20 85 11.

Mons: Grand-Place 20, 7000 Mons. Tel: 65-33 55 80.

Namur: Square Léopold, 5000 Namur. Tel: 81-22 28 59, fax: 81-22 47 68.

Ostend: Monacoplein 2, 8400 Ostend. Tel: 59-70 11 99, fax: 59-70 34 71.

Spa: Place Royale 41, 4880 Spa. Tel: 87-77 25 10/19.

Tournai: Rue de Marché-aux-Poteries 14, 7500 Tournai. Tel: 69-22 20 45.

Tourist Information Abroad

Denmark: Det Officielle Belgiske Turistbureau, Vester Farimagsgade 7-9, 1606 Kopenhagen V. Tel: 124 777 or 123 027.

France: Office Belge de Tourisme, 21, Boulevard des Capucines, 75002 Paris. Tel: 1 47 42 41 18.

Germany: Belgisches Verkehrsamt, Berliner Allee 47, 4000 Düsseldorf. Tel: 0211 326 008.

Holland: Belgisch Verkeersbureau, Herengracht 435-437, 1017 BR Amsterdam. Tel: 020 251 251.

Japan: Belgian National Tourist Office, Tameike Tokyu Bldg 9 F 1-14, Askaka 1-chome, Minato-ku Tokyo. Tel: 586 7041.

Sweden: Belgiska Turistbyra, Box 19.520, 10432 Stockholm 19. Tel: 341 575 or 314 119.

USA: Belgian Tourist Office, 745, Fifth Avenue, New York 10151. Tel: (212) 758 8130.

Embassies and Consulates

Great Britain: Rue Joseph II 28, Etterbeck, Brussels. Tel: 2-217 9000.

USA: Boulevard de Regent 27, Brussels. Tel: 2-513 3830.

Canada: Avenue de Telvarel 2, Brussels. Tel: 2-735 6040.

Australia: Avenue des Arts 52, Brussels. Tel: 2-213 0500.

Ireland: Rue du Luxembourg 19, Brussels. Tel: 2-513 6633.

Getting Around

On Arrival

Getting from the airport: Brussels National Airport is at Zaventem, 14 km northeast from the centre of Brussels. There is a tourist information desk in the arrivals hall, open Monday–Friday 8am–9pm; Saturday–Sunday 8am–8pm, tel: 2-722 30 00, which can provide details of accommodation and transport, sells metro, bus and tram tickets and will make hotel reservations.

Trains run every 20 minutes to the Gare du Nord and Gare Centrale, with one train every hour going on to Gare du Midi. The journey to Gare Centrale takes 18 minutes. Tickets can be purchased from the train information desk (open daily 6.40am–10pm) before you go through customs, or from the ticket office in the station. The first train from the airport to the city is at 6.09am, the last at 11.46pm.

Arriving by bus: Hoverspeed buses from Britain stop in the Place de la Bourse, Brussels, Eurolines at Place de Brouckère. The main terminal for domestic buses is the Gare du Nord.

Getting from the ports: Distances are fairly short and motorways serve most of the country with the exception of the mountain regions of the Ardennes. Access to all roads is free, there are no toll roads in Belgium.

Ostend: The ferry terminus is at Montgomerydok next to the railway station, within walking distance of the town centre. The information office at the station has details of train services, open Monday–Friday 7am–7pm; Saturday–Sunday 8am–7pm. Trams depart from beside the station heading east to Knokke-Heist and west to De Panne.

Zeebrugge: The ferry companies offer a free bus service from the docks to the railway station to coincide with sailings. Trains to Bruges depart hourly. There is a tourist kiosk on the sea front, open: July–August daily 10am–1pm, 2pm–6pm.

Public Transport

Bus

There is a bus service operated by the European Railway Association and referred to as the Europabus, running from various countries to Belgium during the summer months. It will deposit passengers at any of the larger cities in the country. Belgium has an extensive railway network and there are few long-distance bus services within the country.

Train

For information regarding relatively inexpensive railway journeys within Belgium, consult the brochures available at any tourist information office. The "Benelux-Tourrail", whereby pass holders are able to travel five days within a 17-day period using the complete railway network in any of the Benelux countries is just one of the deals offered.

There are numerous international railway lines which pass through Brussels; many of these connect Belgium to France and Holland, and to Great Britain and Germany.

There are various discount ticket schemes. Three of the most popular are "A Weekend at the Seashore", "A Weekend in the Ardennes", and the popular "A Lovely Day in...". Considerable price reductions also apply to children's fares. Further information is available at the following addresses or directly from any Belgian railway station.

National Belgian Railway Association, Shell Building, Ravenstein 60, Box 24, 1000 Brussels. Tel: 2-219 2880 (Dutch), 2-219 2640 (French).

Germany: Generalvertretung der Belgischen Eisenbahnen, Haupt– bahnhof, Bahnhofsvorplatz 3, 5 Köln. Tel: 0221-13 47 61, fax: 02 13 27 47.

France: Représentation Générale Chemins de Fer Belges, Boulevard Capucines 21, 75002 Paris. Tel: 47 42 40 41, fax: 01-42 09 06 3

Great Britain: Belgian National ways, Presnick House, 10 Grey Place, London SW P 1SB. Tel: 01 233 0360, fax: 0171-233 0360.

Luxembourg: Représenta Générale des Chemins de Fer Bel Rue du Fort Wallis 2, 3 Et Luxemburg (2714). Tel: 352-494 fax: 352-496 420.

Switzerland: Generalvertretung Belgischen Eisenbahnen, Aesch vorstadt 50, 4051 Basle. Tel: 041 23 72 85, fax: 041-61 21 23 84.

RAILWAY TRAFFIC IN BRUSSELS

In Brussels there are four railway tions: **Gare du Nord (North Rail Station)**, Rue du Progrès; G **Centrale (Central Railway Stati** located under the ground at the E evard de l'Impératrice; **Gare du (South Railway Station)**, Boulevar l'Europe; **Gare du Luxembourg (G du Quartier Léopold)**, Place du Lux bourg.

All four railway stations are inter nected by means of a fast un ground train network. Numerous i national railway lines pass thro Brussels; connections are espec good with France and Holland, as as with Great Britain and Germany information regarding timetables a four Brussels railway stations, tel: 26 40. Reservations can be mad advance by calling 525 31 54 or 31 87. Those wishing to trans their vehicle by train should con Schaerbeek Railway Station, tel: 26 40.

Brussels maintains a well-de oped underground system com mented by bus and tram routes. T tables can be obtained at the re tion service, Rue du Marché Herbes/Grasmarkt 61, as well a the TIB (Tourist Information Office cated in the town hall. Undergro stations are easily recognised: loo the sign sporting a blue "M" Metro) on a white background. stops are marked with red and w signs, tram stops with blue and wh At bus and tram stops with signs b he words "*sur demande*", waiting sengers can stop the bus or tram a simple hand signal.

formation and tickets for the Belgian National Railway (SNCB/NMBS), Regional Railway (SNCV/MIVB) and the Brussels Passenger Transport utive (STIB) can be obtained in the king hall at the Gare du Midi. Information and tickets for SNCV are also able at Rue Ravenstein 60, tel: 26 41, and for STIB on the 6th of the Galeries de la Toison d'Or, 515 20 00, as well as at the Metro ons Porte de Namur, Rogier and . You can also purchase train tickets in any of the larger Metro stations, merous newspaper kiosks and in Town Hall (TIB). Route maps are lable free from the tourist office information kiosks at Porte de ur, Rogier and Midi.

here are several different types of ts, including single-fare or multi-hey tickets, for five or 10 rides, a 24-hour ticket that can be used where within the city centre.

or passengers travelling to any of outlying districts it is necessary to an additional "Z" ticket. There is xtra charge for transferring. Passengers caught riding without a valid et by one of the many roaming pa-s can expect to pay a hefty fine.

he Brussels Passenger Transport cutive offers a variety of interesting irsions under the heading "Rose Vents". Destinations include some e more beautiful areas surround-Brussels and are conducted via ro, bus and tram.

ervices run from 6am until mid-t, with a sporadic night service.

Domestic Flights

possible to fly from Zaventem Air-: in Brussels to different cities in gium. However, as the country is tively small and thus distances veen places fairly short, the best le of transport is by rail. Many el agencies offer day excursions to er cities in the country.

Taxis

ng a taxi in Belgium is not particu-' expensive and can often present ractical alternative to using some of public transport. The most con-ient way to get a taxi is to ask the el reception to order you one. The base rate is 95 Bfr; for each additional kilometre there is a 38 Bfr charge within the city-limits. For journeys extending beyond city perimeters, this rate can be increased to as much as 76 Bfr per kilometre. If you'd like the taxi driver to wait for you, expect to pay around 600 Bfr for each hour. Some taxi companies charge reduced fares for the journey to Zaventem Airport. Ask for details before you set off. Taxis in Brussels can be picked up from taxi stands, notably at Bourse, Brouckère, Grand Sablon, Porte de Namur and at railway stations and hotels.

Taxis can be ordered from the central dispatch service of the following companies:

ATR, tel: 647 22 22.
Autolux, tel: 512 31 23.
Taxis Bleus, tel: 268 10 10.
Taxis Verts, tel: 349 49 49.

Waterways

Many boating companies cruising the waterways of Belgium offer excursions to different places. Tourist information centre agents will be happy to provide you with further information.

Private Transport

The fact that Brussels is situated in the very heart of Belgium definitely influences the country's traffic patterns. A ring-shaped motorway encircles the city, providing both direct access and the opportunity for vehicles in transit to skirt the city entirely.

The following is gives distances between Brussels and other important Belgian cities. Antwerp 48 km (30 miles), Bruges 97 km (61 miles), Charleroi 61 km (38 miles), Ghent 55 km (35 miles), Liège 94 km (59 miles), Mechelen 27 km (17 miles), Mons 67 km (42 miles), Namur 63 km (40 miles), Ostend 114 km (71 miles) and Tournai 86 km (54 miles).

Traffic Regulations: The maximum speed limit in Belgium within populated areas is 50 kph (31 mph); outside these areas it increases to 90 kph (55 mph). On motorways and other major thoroughfares of at least two lanes the speed-limit is 120 kph (75 mph). The general rule of thumb is that those to the right of you have right of way. Wearing seatbelts is mandatory. It is illegal for children under the age of 12 to sit next to the driver if there is adequate space in the back of the vehicle. Motorcyclists and moped riders are required by law to wear helmets; parking on yellow lines is not allowed. Trams always have the right of way. Foreign visitors caught transgressing traffic regulations will be required to pay any fines on the spot.

Car Hire

In Brussels it is possible to reserve a rental car either in the capital itself, or in an entirely different city by calling one of the following agencies between 7am–11pm:

Auto Rent: Sint-Lazarusplaats 5, tel: 2-217 15 50.
AT Rent-a-Car: (Auto Technique Belgique S.A.): Avenue d'Auderghem 33, tel: 2-230 89 89; Boulevard du Midi 41, tel: 2-513 69 69.
Avis: Brussels Airport, Arrival Hall, Zaventem, tel: 2-720 09 44; Brussels Hilton, Boulevard de Waterloo 38, tel: 2-513 10 51, fax: 2-513 72 33.
Budget: Central Reservations Headquarters, tel: 2-376 85 31, fax: 2-378 40 15; Brussels Airport (Arrival Hall), Zaventem, tel: 2-720 80 50, fax: 2-721 19 70; Avenue Louise 93, tel: 2-538 80 75, fax: 2-538 80 71; Rue de Lombard 57, tel: 2-507 28 45, fax: 2-507 28 00.
Europcar: Avenue Louise 235, tel: 2-640 94 00, fax: 2-648 61 63; Brussels Airport, Zaventem, tel: 2-721 11 78; Avenue Louise 235, tel: 2-640 94 16.
Hertz: Brussels Airport, Zaventem, tel: 2-720 60 44; Boulevard Maurice Lemonier 8, tel: 2-513 28 86; Rue Defacqz 131, tel: 2-538 33 21.

AUTOMOBILE ASSOCIATIONS

The following are represented in Belgium:
Royal Automobile Club de Belgique (RACB), Rue d'Arlon 53, 1000 Brussels. Tel: 02-287 09 11.
Touring Club de Belgique (TCB), Rue Joseph II 25, 1000 Brussels. Tel: 02-512 78 90.
Vlaamse Automobilistenbond (VAB), Sint Jacobsmarkt 45, Antwerp. Tel: 03-234 34 34.

BREAKDOWN SERVICES

If you should have car trouble while on the motorway, call the Breakdown Patrol Service from the nearest emergency telephone.

For breakdowns occurring on roads other than motorways, contact the nearest breakdown service (*Touring Secours*) in:

Antwerp, tel: 31 538 888.
Ardennes, tel: 62 212 333.
Bruges, tel: 50 811 717.
Brussels, tel: 2 233 2211.
Charleroi, tel: 71 310 025.
Hainaut, tel: 64 663 301.
Limburg, tel: 11 225 533.
Leuven, tel: 16 466 821.
Liège, tel: 41 325 810.
Namur, tel: 81 433 363.
East Flanders, tel: 91 626 565.
West Flanders, tel: 51 778 140.

Cycling

Cycling in Belgium is one of the best ways of getting around. Distances are short and the country relatively flat. Most roads have bicycle lanes and tourist offices can supply details and maps of local routes. For a charge you can take your bike on the train.
Rent-a-bike: You can rent bicycles from the 60 or so railway stations, open 7am–9pm, and return them to any station of your choice.

Belgium Railways Train & Vélo (Trein & Fiets) leaflet is available from the Belgian Tourist Office in London, tel: 0171-629 0230, fax: 0171-629 0454.

Hitchhiking

The Belgians are generally keen to give lifts to hitchhikers, but remember that hitchhiking on motorways is illegal.

Where To Stay

Hotels

Visitors to Belgium will find a large selection of hotel accommodation in every price range. Many of the larger hotels offer special bargain rates for weekend stays. Every hotel is required to post their room rates at the reception desk and are permitted to charge only these prices on your final bill.

The BTR (Belgian Tourist Reservations) will book a room for you anywhere in Belgium. It is possible to reserve a room through them (free of charge) right up to the last minute. They can be contacted at Boulevard Anspach III, 1000 Brussels, tel: 02-513 74 84, fax: 02-513 92 77. Various tourist associations and local tourist information offices will also make hotel reservations for you free of charge. However, you will be required to pay a deposit which will be deducted from your final hotel bill.

Brussels

In the city's official hotel guide, available at the Reception Service, Rue du Marché aux Herbes (Grasmarkt) 61, and in the Town Hall (TIB), you will find a complete list, including addresses, of the 120 or so hotels in the capital. It is possible to book accommodation at both places.

The Nine Provinces

Hotel rooms can be booked free of charge through the following agencies:
Antwerp: Toeristische Federatie van de Provincie Antwerpen, Residentie Warande, Karel Oomsstraat 11, 2018 Antwerp. Tel: 03-216 28 10.
Brabant: Féd. Touristique de la Province de Brabant/Toeristische Federatie van de Provincie Brabant, Rue du Marché aux Herbes 61, Grasmarkt, 1000 Brussels. Tel: 02-513 07 50.
Hainaut: Féd. Touristique de la Province du Hainaut, Rue des Clercs 31, 7000 Mons. Tel: 065-36 04 64.
Liège: Féd. Touristique de la Province de Liège, Boulevard de la Sauvenière

77, 4000 Liège. Tel: 041-22 42 1
Limburg: Provinciaal Verbond Toerisme in Limburg, Domein Bok 3600 Genk. Tel: 011-22 29 58.
Luxembourg: Féd. Touristique du embourg-Belge, Quai de l'Ourth 6980 La-Roche-en-Ardenne. Tel: 0 41 10 11.
Namur: Féd. Touristique de la Prov de Namur, Rue Notre Dame 3, 5 Namur. Tel: 081-22 29 98.
East Flanders: Federatie Toerisme in Oost-Vlaanderen, Koni Maria-Hendrikaplein 64, 9000 Gh Tel: 091-22 16 37.
West Flanders: Provinciale V vlaamse Vereiniging voor Toeris Kasteel Tillegem, 8200 Bruges 2. 050-38 02 96.

At Border Crossings

Hotel rooms can be booked at the lowing border crossings: on the E (Breda-Antwerp-Brussels); on the (Aachen-Liège-Brussels); on the E (Paris-Valenciennes-Mons-Brusse and at the Zaventem National Air (in the arrival hall).

Hotels in Flanders

Price categories for the cost of a night stay, including breakfast, room: $=£20–£50; $$=£50–£1 $$$=£100–£150; $$$$=over £1

AALTER

Capitole, Stationsstraat 95, 9 Aalter. Tel: 09-374 10 29, fax: 09-77 15. 34 rooms. $

ANTWERP

Alfa de Keyser, De Keyserlei 66 2018 Antwerp. Tel: 03-234 01 35, 03-232 39 70. 115 rooms. $$$$
Holiday Inn Crowne Plaza, G. L rellelaan 10, 2020 Antwerp. Tel: 237 29 00, fax: 03-216 02 96. rooms. $$$$
Switel, Copernicuslaan 2, 2018 werp. Tel: 03-231 67 80, fax: 03-02 90. 301 rooms. $$$
Villa Mozart, Handschoenmark 2000 Antwerp. Tel: 03-231 30 31, 03-231 56 85. 25 rooms. $$$
Alfa Congrès, Plantin en Moretu 136, 2018 Antwerp. Tel: 03-235 00, fax: 03-235 52 31. 66 rooms
Cammerpoorte, Nationalestraat 2000 Antwerp. Tel: 03-231 97 36, 03-226 29 68. 39 rooms. $$
Plaza, Charlottalei 43, 2018 Antw

3-218 92 40, fax: 03-218 88 23.
oms. $$

BLANKENBERGE

t, Molenstraat 51, 8370 Blan–
erge. Tel: 050-41 15 99, fax:
2 91 46. 53 rooms. $$
Zeedijk 244, 8370 Blankenberg.
50-42 86 00, fax: 050-42 97 46.
oms. $$
nn, Kerkstraat 92, 8370 Blanken-
. Tel: 050-41 81 72, fax: 050-42
. 70 rooms. $

BREDENE

of, Zegelaan 18, 8450 Bredene.
59-33 00 34, fax: 059-32 59 59.
oms. $

BRUGES

angerie, Kartuizerinnenstrat 10,
Bruges. Tel: 050-34 16 49, fax:
3 30 16. 18 rooms. $$$
ilerieen, Dijver 7, 8000 Bruges.
50-34 36 91, fax: 050-34 04 00.
oms. $$$–$$$$
Swaene, Steenhouwersdijk 1,
Bruges. Tel: 050-34 27 98, fax:
3 66 74. 20 rooms. $$$
otel, Vrijdagmarkt 5, 8000
s. Tel: 050-33 33 64, fax: 050-
7 63. 86 rooms. $$$
an, Boeveriestraat 2, 8000
s. Tel: 050-34 09 71, fax: 050-
0 53. 155 rooms. $$$
ia, Korte Zilverstraat 3A, 8000
s. Tel: 050-34 44 11, fax: 050-
317. 28 rooms. $$
jer, Bisjkajerplein 4, 8000
s. Tel: 050-34 15 06, fax: 050-
9 11. 17 rooms. $$
astillion, Heilige Geeststraat 1,
Bruges. Tel: 050-34 30 01, fax:
3 94 75. 20 rooms. $$
Hotel, Augustijnenrei 18, 8000
s. Tel: 050-33 79 75, fax: 050-
2 66. 28 rooms. $$
tel Bruges Zuid, Chartreuseweg
200 Bruges. Tel: 050-38 28 51,
50-38 79 03. 101 rooms. $$
s Oud Huis Amsterdam, Spie–
3, 8000 Bruges. Tel: 050-34 18
x: 050-33 88 91. 22 rooms. $$–

hotel, Pandreitje 16, 8000
s. Tel: 050-34 06 66, fax: 050-
5 56. 24 rooms. $$
nari, 'T Zand 15, 8000 Bruges.
50-34 10 34, fax: 050-34 41 80.
s. $$
Duinen, Langerei 52, 8000

Bruges. Tel: 050-33 04 37, fax: 050-
34 42 16. 18 rooms. $$
Jacobs, Baliestraat 1, 8000 Bruges.
Tel: 050-33 98 31, fax: 050-33 56 94.
26 rooms. $

BRUSSELS

The Best Hotels
Amigo, Rue de l'Amigo, 1000 Brus-
sels. Tel: 02-547 47 47, fax: 02-513
52 77. 165 rooms. $$$$
Brussels Hilton, Boulevard de Water-
loo 38, 1000 Brussels. Tel: 02-504 11
11, fax: 02-504 21 11. 416 rooms.
$$$$ Luxury-class hotel with 4 restau-
rants, a bar and conference facilities.
All rooms have a view of the city and a
park.
Sheraton, Place Rogier 3, 1210 Brus-
sels. Tel: 02-224 31 11, fax: 02-224
34 56. 484 rooms. $$$$ Luxury-class
hotel with 2 restaurants, a piano
lounge, swimming pool, sunbathing
terrace and fitness studio. Rooms con-
tain a colour television and telephone;
there is a breakfast buffet each morn-
ing.
Président World Trade Center, Boul-
evard E. Jacqmain 180, 1210 Brus-
sels. Tel: 02-217 20 20, fax: 02-218
84 02. 309 rooms. $$$–$$$$ New
Luxury-class hotel with conference fa-
cilities. All rooms have a mini-bar, col-
our television set, radio, telephone,
sauna and solarium.
Hotel Metropole, Place de Brouckère
31, 1000 Brussels. Tel: 02-217 23
00, fax: 02-218 02 20. 395 rooms.
$$$$ Luxury-class hotel rich in tradi-
tion. It has a restaurant, bar and fit-
ness floor. All rooms have colour TV,
telephone and a mini-bar; a breakfast
buffet is offered each morning.
Pullman Astoria, Rue Royale 103,
1000 Brussels. Tel: 02-217 62 90,
fax: 02-217 11 50. 113 rooms. $$$
Comfortable hotel with its own restau-
rant and piano lounge. Each room has
a colour TV, mini-bar, radio and telephone.

Additional Luxury Class Hotels
Copthorne Stephanie, Avenue Louise
91, 1050 Brussels. Tel: 02-539 02
40, fax: 02-538 03 07. 141 rooms.
$$$$
Jolly Hotel Atlanta, Boulevard Adolphe
Max 7, 1000 Brussels. Tel: 02-217 01
30, fax: 02-217 37 58. 240 rooms.
$$$$
Royal Windsor Hotel, Rue Duquesnoy

5, 1000 Brussels. Tel: 02-511 42 15,
fax: 02-511 60 04. 266 rooms. $$$$
SAS Royal Hotel, Rue du Fossé-aux-
Loups, 1000 Brussels. Tel: 02-219 28
28, fax: 02-219 62 62. 263 rooms.
$$$$
Tagawa, Avenue Louise 321, 1050
Brussels. Tel: 02-640 80 29, fax: 02-
646 12 57. 77 rooms. $$$$

Good Hotels
Albert Première, Place Rogier 20,
1210 Brussels. Tel: 02-217 21 25,
fax: 02-217 93 31. 285 rooms. $$ A
luxurious hotel located not far from the
North Railway Station, with conference
facilities and a tavern. Rooms come
with a mini-bar and colour TV; there is
a breakfast buffet served daily.
Arenberg, Rue d'Assault 15, 1000
Brussels. Tel: 02-511 07 70, fax: 02-
514 19 76. 155 rooms. $$$ Near the
Central Railway Station. Rooms with
bathroom/shower/WC.
Chambord, Rue de Namur 82, 1000
Brussels. Tel: 02-513 41 19, fax: 02-
514 08 47. 69 rooms. $$ Comfort-
able hotel with a piano lounge. All
rooms have a bathroom/WC, tel-
ephone, colour television and mini-bar;
some have a balcony.
Diplomat, Rue Jeans Stas 32, 1060
Brussels. Tel: 02-537 42 50, fax: 02-
539 33 79. 68 rooms. $$$ Modern
hotel located in the midst of the el-
egant shopping area along the Avenue
Louise. Rooms with bathroom/
shower/WC.
Manos, Chaussée de Charlcroi 100-
104, 1060 Brussels. Tel: 02-537 96
82, fax: 02-539 36 55. 38 rooms. $$
Mansion-style hotel near Avenue
Louise.
New Siru, Place Rogier, 1210 Brus-
sels. Tel: 02-217 75 80, fax: 02-218
33 03. 101 rooms. $$ Not far from the
North Railway Station with restaurant
and conference facilities. The rooms
have been furnished and decorated by
different artists and have either a
bathroom/WC, or shower/WC, telephone, radio and colour television.
Queen Anne, Boulevard Emile
Jacqmain, 1000 Brussels. Tel: 02-217
16 00, fax: 02-217 18 38. 60 rooms.
$$ Close to Grand'Place. Rooms each
have a colour television and tel-
ephone; there is a breakfast buffet
offered each morning.

At the Airport
Holiday Inn Brussels Airport, Holi–daystraat 7, 1831 Diegem. Tel: 02-720 58 65, fax: 02-720 41 45. 309 rooms. $$$$
Novotel Brussels Airport, Olmen–straat, 1831 Diegem. Tel: 02-725 30 50, fax: 02-721 39 58.

Reasonably Priced Hotels
Argus, Rue Capitaine Crespel 6, 1050 Brussels. Tel: 02-514 07 70, fax: 02-514 12 22. 41 rooms. $$
Derby, Avenue de Tervuren 24, 1040 Brussels. Tel: 02-733 75 81, fax: 02-733 74 75. 28 rooms. $
Des Esperonnes, Rue des Esperonnes 1, 1000 Brussels. Tel: 02-513 53 66. 16 rooms. $
Du Congrès, Rue de Congrès 42, 1000 Brussels. Tel: 02-217 18 90, fax: 02-217 18 97. 52 rooms. $$
Gascogne, Boulevard Adolphe Max 137, 1000 Brussels. Tel: 02-217 69 62. 15 rooms. $
Grande Cloche, Place Rouppe, 1000 Brussels. Tel: 02-512 61 40, fax: 02-512 65 91. 45 rooms. $$
Van Belle, Chaussée de Bergense Mons 39, 1070 Brussels. Tel: 02-521 35 16, fax: 02-537 00 02. 126 rooms. $$
Vendome, Boulevard Adolphe Max 98, 1000 Brussels. Tel: 02-218 00 70, fax: 02-218 06 83. 118 rooms. $$

DE HAAN

Grand Hotel Belle Vue, Koningsplein 5, 8420 De Haan. Tel: 059-23 34 39, fax: 059-23 75 22. 45 rooms. $$

DE PANNE

Hostellerie Le Fox, Walckierstraat 2, 8660 De Panne. Tel: 058-412 855, fax: 058-415 879. 14 rooms. $

DEURLE

Auberge du Pêcheur, Pontstraat 41, 9831 St-Martens-Latem. Tel: 09-282 3144, fax: 09-282 9058. 13 rooms. $$

GENK

Atlantis, Fletersdel 1, 3600 Genk. Tel: 089-35 65 51, fax: 089-35 35 29. 24 rooms. $$

GHENT

Holiday Inn, Ottergemseesteenweg 600, 9000 Ghent. Tel: 091-22 58 85, fax: 091-20 12 22. 165 rooms. $$$

Arcade Opera, Nederkouter 24, 9000 Ghent. Tel: 091-225 07 07, fax: 091-223 59 07. 134 rooms. $$
Astoria, Achilles Musschestraat 39, 9000 Ghent. Tel: 091-228 413, fax: 091-204 787. 15 rooms. $$
Carlton, Koningin Astridlaan 138, 9000 Ghent. Tel: 091-222 88 36, fax: 091-220 49 92. 22 rooms. $$
Novotel Ghent Centrum, Gouden Leeuwplein 5, 9000 Ghent. Tel: 091-224 22 30, fax: 091-224 32 95. 113 rooms. $$

GERAARDSBERGEN

Geeraard, Lessensestraat 36, 9500 Geraardsbergen. Tel: 054-41 20 73, fax: 054-41 71 99. 9 rooms. $

HALLE-ZOERSEL

St-Martinushoeve, Sniederspad 133, 2980 Halle-Zoersel. Tel: 03-384 02 23, fax: 03-384 02 71. 30 rooms. $$

HAMONT-ACHEL

Koeckhofs, Michielsplein 4, 3930 Hamont-Hachtel. Tel: 011-64 31 81, fax: 011-64 42. 27 rooms. $

HASSELT

Hassotel, St-Jozefstraat 10, 3500 Hasselt. Tel: 011-22 64 92, fax: 011-22 94 77. 30 rooms. $$

IEPER

Regina, Grote Markt 45, 8900 Ieper. Tel: 057-218 888, fax: 057-219 020. 17 rooms. $$

KASTERLEE

Den En Heuvel, Geelsebaan 72, 2460 Kasterlee. Tel: 014-85 04 97, fax: 014-85 04 96. 24 rooms. $

KNOKKE-HEIST

Auberge St-Pol, Bronlaan 23, 8300 Knokke-Heist. Tel: 050-601 521, fax: 050-621 760. 14 rooms. $–$$
Du Soleil, Patriottenstraat 15, 8300 Knokke-Heist. Tel: 050-51 11 37, fax: 050-51 69 14. 27 rooms. $$
Lido, Zwaluwenlaan 18, 8300 Knokke-Heist. Tel: 050-60 19 25, fax: 050-61 04 57. 40 rooms. $
Malibu, Kustlaan 43, 8300 Knokke-Heist. Tel: 050-61 18 03, fax: 050-61 06 78. 25 rooms. $–$$
Square, De Kinkhoorn 21, 8300 Knokke-Heist. Tel: 050-51 12 37, fax: 050-51 73 32. 32 rooms. $

Ter Zaele, Oostkerkestraat 40, Knokke-Heist. Tel: 050-60 12 37 050-61 19 73. 22 rooms. $$

KOKSIJDE

Soll Cress, Koninklijke Baan 8670 Koksijde. Tel: 058-51 27 fax: 058-51 91 32. 23 rooms. $

KORTRIJK

Broel, Broelkaai 8, 8500 Kortrij 056-21 83 51, fax: 056-20 03 0 rooms. $$

LEUVEN

Begijnhof Congreshotel, Tervu vest 70, 3000 Leuven. Tel: 016-2 10, fax: 016-29 10 22. 67 room **Binnenhof**, Maria-Theresiastraa 3000 Leuven. Tel: 016-20 55 92 016-23 69 26. 54 rooms. $$

MECHELEN

Gulden Anker, Ridder Dessainla 2800 Mechelen. Tel: 015-42 31 fax: 015-42 34 99. 28 rooms. $

MOL

Mollenhof, Groeneweg 4, 2400 Tel: 014-31 45 53, fax: 014-31 2 12 rooms. $

NIEUWPOORT-BAD

Cosmopolite, Albert 1, laan 8620 Nieuwpoort-Bad. Tel; 058-2 66, fax: 058-23 81 35. 80 room

OOSTDUINKERKE

Albert I, Astridplein 11, 8670 C duinkerke. Tel: 058-52 08 69 058-52 09 04. 22 rooms. $$

OSTENDE

Bero, Hofstraat 1A, 8400 Ostene 059-70 23 35, fax: 059-70 25 9 rooms. $$
Europe, Kapucijnenstraat 52, Ostend. Tel: 059-70 10 12, fax: 80 99 79. 55 rooms. $
Glenmore, Hofstraat 25, Ostend. Tel: 059-70 20 22, fax: 70 47 08. 40 rooms. $
Lido 2000, L. Spilliaertstraat 1, Ostend. Tel: 059-70 08 06, fax: 80 40 07. 66 rooms. $
Louisa, Louisastraat 8B, Ostend. Tel: 059-50 96 77, fax: 31 77 66. 18 rooms. $
Melinda, Mercatorlaan 21, Ostend. Tel: 059-80 72 72, fax: 80 74 25. 40 rooms. $$

ess, Boekareststraat 7, 8400
nd. Tel: 059-70 68 88. Fax: 059-
5 66. 45 rooms. $

SINT-NIKLAAS

Flandres, Stationsplein 5, 9100
Niklaas. Tel: 03-777 10 02, fax:
7 05 96. 20 rooms. $$

SINT TRUIDEN

dria, Abdijstraat 6, 3800 Sint
en. Tel: 011-68 13 44, fax: 011-
38. 26 rooms. $$

TIENEN

Hotel, Leuvensestraat 95, 3300
n. Tel: 016-82 28 00, fax: 016-
54. 18 rooms. $

VILVOORDE

olleycenter, Beneluxlaan 22,
Vilvoorde. Tel: 02-252 11 50,
2-252 04 58. 19 rooms. $

WESTERLO

ts, Grote Markt 50, 2260
erlo. Tel: 014-54 40 17, fax: 014-
80. 10 rooms. $$

ZEERBRUGGE

ime, Zeedijk 6, 8380 Zeebrugge.
50-54 40 66, fax: 050-54 66 08.
oms. $$
ime Palace, Brusselstraat 5,
Zeebrugge. Tel: 050-54 54 19,
50-54 66 08. 18 rooms. $

Hotels In Wallonia

BEAURAING

Aubépine, Rue des Gendarmes 5,
Beauraing. Tel: 082-71 11 59,
82-71 33 54. 79 rooms. $

BOUILLON

rge d'Alsace, Faubourg de
e, 6830 Bouillon. Tel: 061-46
8, fax: 061-46 83 21. 81
s. $
Ardennes, Rue des Abattis 43,
Bouillon. Tel: 061-46 66 21, fax:
6 77 30. 30 rooms. $$
de la Poste, Place St-Arnould,
Bouillon. Tel: 061-46 65 06, fax:
6 72 02. 80 rooms. $

CHARLEROI

, Place E. Buisset 13, 6000
eroi. Tel: 071-31 98 70, fax: 071-
40. 30 rooms. $$

Socatel, Bd. Tirou 96, 6000 Charleroi.
Tel: 071-31 98 11, fax: 071-31 98 11.
65 rooms. $$

COMBLAIN LA TOUR

Hostellerie Saint-Roch, Rue du Parc 1,
4180 Comblain La Tour. Tel: 041-69
13 33, fax: 041-69 31 31. 11 rooms.
$$

DINANT

Couronne, Rue Sax 1, 5500 Dinant.
Tel: 082-22 24 41, fax: 082-22 70 31.
22 rooms. $–$$
Moulin de Lisogne, Rue de la
Lisonnette, 5500 Dinant. Tel: 082-22
63 80, fax: 082-22 21 47. 9 rooms.
$$

DURBUY

Le Sanglier des Ardennes, Rue Comte
d'Ursel, 6940 Durbuy. Tel: 086-21 32
62, fax: 086-21 24 65. 24 rooms. $$

GEMBLOUX

Les Trois Clés, Chaussée de Namur
17, 5030 Gembloux. Tel: 081-61 16
17, fax: 081-61 41 13. 45 rooms. $

GESVES

Hostellerie La Pichelotte, Rue de la
Pichelotte 5, 5340 Gesves. Tel: 083-
67 78 21, fax: 083-67 70 53. 53
rooms. $$

HERSTAL

Post House, Rue Hurbise, 4040
Herstal. Tel: 041-64 64 00, fax: 041-
48 06 90. 96 rooms. $$–$$$

LA ROCHE

La Claire Fontaine, Rue de Hotton 64,
6980 La Roche. Tel: 084-41 24 70,
fax: 084-41 24 72. 25 rooms. $$

LIBIN

Les Roses, Quartier Latin 2, 6890
Libin. Tel: 061-65 50 03, fax: 061-61
25 00. 13 rooms. $

LIÈGE

Le Cygne d'Argent, Rue Beeckman
49, 4000 Liège. Tel: 041-23 70 01,
fax: 041-22 49 66. 22 rooms. $
Holiday Inn, Esplanade de l'Europe 2,
4020 Liège. Tel: 041-42 60 20, fax:
041-43 48 10. 214 rooms. $$$
Ramada, Bd. de la Sauvenière 100,
4000 Liège. Tel: 041-22 49 10, fax:
041-22 39 83. 105 rooms. $$$

Univers, Rue des Guillemins 116,
4000 Liège. Tel: 041-52 26 50, fax:
041-52 16 53. 49 rooms. $$
Ibis, Pl. de la République Française
41, 4000 Liège. Tel: 041-23 60 85,
fax: 041-23 04 81. 78 rooms. $$

MAISSIN

Hotel Roly du Seigneur, Avenue du
Roly du Seigneur 12, 6852 Maissin.
Tel: 061-65 50 49. 16 rooms. $–$$

MOUSCRON

Elberg, Grand'Place 27, 7700 Mous–
cron. Tel: 056-330 874, fax: 056-341
907. 6 rooms. $

NAMUR

Beauregard, Av. Baron Moreau 1,
5000 Namur. Tel: 081-23 00 28, fax:
081-24 12 09. 51 rooms. $$
Château de Namur, Avenue de
l'Ermitage 1, 5000 Namur. Tel: 081-74
26 30, fax: 081-74 23 92. 29 rooms.
$$
Queen Victoria, Avenue de la Gare 11,
5000 Namur. Tel: 081-22 29 71, fax:
081-24 11 00. 21 rooms. $
Saint-Loup, Rue St-Loup, 5000 Namur.
Tel: 081-23 04 05, fax: 081-23 09 43.
10 rooms. $$

NASSOGNE

Beau Séjour, Rue de Masbourg 30,
6950 Nassogne. Tel: 084-210 696,
fax: 084-214 062. 21 rooms. $

SPA

Cardinal, Place Royale 21-27, 4900
Spa. Tel: 087-77 10 64, fax: 087-77
19 64. 30 rooms. $

TOURNAI

Cathédrale, Place St Pierre 11, 7500
Tournai. Tel: 069-215 077, fax: 069-
21 50 77. 53 rooms. $$

VERVIERS

Amigo, Rue Herla 1, 4800 Verviers.
Tel: 087-22 11 21, fax: 087-23 03 69.
50 rooms. $$

VIEUX VILLE

Le Lido, Rue de Logne 8, 4190 Vieux
Ville. Tel: 086-21 13 67, fax: 086-21
34 22. 13 rooms. $

VRESSE

Hostellerie de la Semois, Rue Raty 63,
5550 Vresse. Tel: 061-50 00 33, fax:
061-50 16 91. 21 rooms. $

Novotel, Chaussée de Dinant 1149, 5100 Wépion. Tel: 081-46 08 11, fax: 081-46 19 90. 110 rooms. $$

Bed & Breakfast

One of the most enjoyable ways of discovering the country and its people is to stay in a family home for one night or even a few days. Bed & breakfast accommodation usually offers comfort and good value for money. Information booklets can be obtained from tourist offices and, in particular, from:

Flanders: Taxistop, Onderbergen 51, B-9000 Ghent. Tel: 09-223 23 10, fax: 09-224 31 44.
Wallonia: Taxistop, Place de l'Université 41, 1348 Louvain-La Neuve. Tel: 10-45 14 14, fax: 10-45 51 20.
Brussels: Promenade de l'Alma 57, 1200 Brussels. Tel: 02-779 08 46, fax: 02-779 08 32; Gites de Wallonie, Rue du Millénaire 53, B-6941 Villers-Sainte-Gertrude. Durbay). Tel: 86-49 95 31, fax: 86-49 94 07.

Self-Catering

It is possible to rent furnished houses and flats in resorts along the Belgium coast and in the Ardennes. There are also many holiday villages with self-catering chalets, sporting and leisure facilities. The following agents in Britain arrange self-catering holidays in Belgium:

AA Motoring Holidays, PO Box 128, Fanum House, Basingstoke, Hants RG21 2EA. Tel: 01256 493878. Self-catering at SunParks Vielsalm in the Ardennes.
Angel Travel, 34 High Street, Borough Green, Kent TN15 8BJ. Tel: 01732-884109. Self-catering holidays in various centres in the Belgian Ardennes in conjunction with Belsud.
Belgian Holidays, 175 Selsdon Park Road, South Croydon, Surrey CR2 8JJ. Tel: 0181-651 5109. Self-catering on the Belgian Coast at Ostend, De Panne, Nieuwpoort, Blankenberg and SunParks De Haan. In Bruges at the Holiday City Centre apartments, and in the Ardennes in all the major holiday villages.
Belgian Travel Service, Bridge House, Ware, Herts SG12 9DG. Tel: 01920-

467345. Self-catering holidays in the Belgian Ardennes in the holiday village of La Bouverie, and at SunParks Vielsalm. On the coast in the SunParks holiday villages of De Hann and Groendyk, in Bruges in City Centre Apartments and at Rauwse Meren SunParks in the Belgian Kempen.
Cresta Holidays, Cresta House, 32 Victoria Street, Altringham, Cheshire WA14 1ET. Tel: 0161 953 2008. Self-catering on the coast at SunParks De Haan and Groendijk.
David Newman Tours, PO Box 733, Upperton Road, Eastbourne, Sussex BN21 4AW. Tel: 01323-410347. Self-catering apartments in Bruges.
Eurosites, Wavell House, Holcombe Road, Helmshore, Rossendale, Lancs BB4 4NB. Tel: 01706 830888. Mobile homes and tents at La Rochette in the Ardennes.
Gîtes de France, 178 Piccadilly, London W1V 9DB. Tel: 0171-493-3480. Centres in the Belgian Ardennes for self-catering Gîtes.
Hoseasons Holidays Abroad, Sunway House, Lowestoft, Suffolk NR32 3LT. Tel: 01502-500555. Self-catering holidays on the coast in the SunParks holiday villages of De Haan and Groendyk, and at the Holiday City Centre apartments in Bruges. In the Ardennes at SunParks Vielsalm, and at Rauwse Meren SunParks in the Kempen.
Interhome, 383 Richmond Road, Twickenham, Middlesex TW1 2EF. Tel: 0181-891 1294. Self-catering apartments and houses in Bredene and Knokke on the Belgian coast, in Bruges, Brussels and Damme, as well as in the Ardennes at Waulsort and St Vith.
Motours, The Coach House, 21 Landsdowne Road, Royal Tunbridge Wells, Kent TN1 2NG. Tel: 01892 518555. Self-catering in Sun-Parks and Park Atlantis on the coast, Molenheide and Sun-Parks Rauwse Meren in the Kempen, Val d'Arimont and L'Hiron–delle Holiday Villages and SunParks Vielsalm in the Ardennes.
Stena Sealink Holidays, Charter House, Park Street, Ashford, Kent TN24 8EX. Tel: 01233-647033. Self-catering in the Ardennes at SunParks Vielsalm and SunParks Rauwse Meren and the Molenheide Holiday Village in the Kempen. Also City Centre apartments in Bruges and the De Haan and Groendijk SunParks on the coast.

Select Site Reservations, ┐
House, Monmouth Road, Abergav
Gwent NP7 5HL. Tel: 01873-859
Camping at the Blaarmeersen sit
outside Ghent, as well as at Pa
Closure near Bure in the Ardenn

House Swapping

An alternative to the more tradit
accommodation options in Belgi
house-swapping. This is a sy
whereby you can spend the holida
the private house of a host family
they are making themselves con
able in your house. Additional info
tion is available from:
Centrum voor Positieve Aanwe
vzw, Onderbergen 51, 9000 Ghe

Camping

There are more than 500 lice
campsites in Belgium. They are c
fied into categories from one to
stars depending upon overall q
and the degree of comfort offered
majority are one-star, but all are g
ally well-equipped. As a rule, yo
check into a campsite any time
2pm; check-out time is no later
noon. A leaflet is available from
Belgium Tourist Office, 29 Pri
Street, London W1R 7RG (Tel: 0
629 0230) listing details of sites
facilities.
Brussels: There are no campsit
the city itself. However, the follo
three sites are located nearby an
within easy reach by public trans
Huizingen, 13 km (8 miles) sou
Brussels, Provinciaal Domein 6
380 14 93.
Neeerijse, 20 km (13 miles) ea
Brussels, Kamstraat 46. Tel: 01
75 13.
Wezembeek-Oppen, 10 km (6 n
east of Brussels, Warandeberg
782 10 09.

Youth Hostels

There are a number of youth host
Belgium. Those in Flanders tend
large and cater for parties, while t
in Wallonia are smaller and more
mal. If you plan to stay in several
hostels it is worth joining the Y
Hostel Association at home befor
depart and obtaining a complete

BRUSSELS

Eating Out

What To Eat

...eople of Belgium have a reputa-
...for possessing especially fine
...buds and this fact is attested to
...e number of excellent restau-
..., particularly in Brussels. The
...rous, relatively inexpensive gas-
...mic specialities of Belgium are
...e only dishes that come highly
...mmended; the plain, home-style
...served throughout the country will
...ably prove to be just as delicious.
...y all restaurants offer daily spe-
...children's portions and complete
...t menus. The big meal of the day
...ually consumed in the evening.

Along the coast the culinary empha-
sis is, as might be expected, on seafood, while the cuisine indigenous to
the city of Brussels tends to be international in flavour. Belgium's capital
city boasts a bewildering number of
fine dining establishments. Among
these, restaurants serving French food
are especially well represented. Brussels is world famous for its fresh mussels, oysters and lobster. Fish dishes,
made form sole, cod and turbot, are
prepared in a variety of tasty ways.
Belgian chicory also enjoys an international reputation, served frequently in
a form of casserole. Two more delicious dishes which can be recommended are red cabbage prepared in
the traditional Flemish style and asparagus from Mechelen. A "Gourmet"
dining guide to eating out in Brussels
is available from the Tourist Information Centre (TIB); this booklet contains
a list of restaurants in the city along
with their addresses, hours, prices
and particular house specialities.

A culinary "must" while visiting
Ghent and Antwerp is *Waterzooi*, small
pieces of chicken in chicken broth,
served with a selection of vegetables
and cream. In the forested regions,
particularly in the Ardennes, adventur-
ous diners will find a wide variety of
game offered in local restaurants during the hunting season. Pheasant prepared in the old Brabant tradition is a
particularly lauded dish. The Ardennes
is also known for its hearty soups,
cured ham and pâté.

Sweet rice cakes take the first prize
among the wide assortment of baked
goods and pastries. Waffles are another typical treat; in Brussels they are
usually served with cream, in Liège
with caramelised sugar.

In the centre of the capital along the
boulevards around the opera house
and stock exchange, as well as around
the Grand Place, there are numerous
places to sit down and enjoy a waffle,
slice of pie or cake, or a cold drink. The
larger hotels also serve various bever-
ages and snacks.

Beer – and there are well over 200
different kinds to choose from! – is the
beverage most typically consumed in
Belgium. However, the wine, primarily
imported from France, is also recommended.

By the way, a "café" is not necessarily the place to find a cup of coffee.

Generally speaking, a café refers to a
pub where you can get a relatively inexpensive bite to eat – for example, a
bowl of soup, a sandwich or a piece of
home-made quiche. Coffee and tea
are served in special tea rooms (Salon
de Thé, Cafetaria).

Belgium is renowned for its chocolate – it is said that each Belgian con-
sumes 12.5 kg (27.5 lbs) of chocolate
annually – and a visit to a chocolatier
is a must. Godiva and Leonidas,
among others, have shops in the main
towns.

Where To Eat

Flanders

ANTWERP

Alfa Congress, Plantin & Moretuslei
136. Tel: 03-235 3000.
Alfa de Keyser, De Keyserlei 66-70.
Tel: 03-234 0135.
Brasseurs, Britselei 53. Tel: 03-237
6901.
De Molen, Jachthavenweg 2. Tel: 03-
219 3208.
Le Coucou, Breidelstraat 33. Tel: 03-
233 9114
Hippodroom, L. de Waelplein 10. Tel:
03-238 8936.
Popof, Oude Koornmarkt 18. Tel: 03-
232 0038.
Reigershof, Reigersbosdreef 2. Tel:
03-568 9691.
Rubenshof, Groenplaats 9. Tel: 03-
231 5952.
Scandic Crown Hotel, Lt. Lippenslaan
66. Tel: 03-235 9191.
Viskeuken, Korte Koepoortstraat 10.
Tel: 03-233 0866.
Waldorf, Belgiëlei 36–38. Tel: 03-230
9950.

Vegetarian
Facade, Hendrik Conscienceplein 18.
Tel: 03-233 5931.

Blakenberge

Aazaert 2 Relax Hotel, Molenstraat
56. Tel: 050-416 857.
Du Commerce, Weststraat 64. Tel:
050-429 535.
Ideal, Zeedijk 244. Tel: 050-429 474.
La Tempête, A. Ruzettelaan 37. Tel:
050-429 428.
Petit Rouge, Zeedijk Bakkerstraat 1.
Tel: 050-411 006.

Bruges

Biskajer, Biskajerplein 4. Tel: 050-341 506.

'T Bouroensche Cruyce, Wollestraat 41. Tel: 050-337 926.

Condor, Jozef Wauterstraat 61. Tel: 050-380 988.

De Castillion, Heilige Geeststraat 1. Tel: 050-343 001.

La Dentellière, Wijngaardstraat. Tel: 050-33 18 98.

'T Huidevettershuis, Huidevettersplein 10–11. Tel: 050-339 506.

De Karmeliet, Jeruzalemstraat 1. Tel: 050-338 259.

Die Swaene, Steenhouwersdijk 1. Tel: 050-342 798.

Du Sablon, Noordzandstraat 21. Tel: 050-333 902.

Maximilaan van Oostenrijk, Wijn–gaardplein 17. Tel: 050-334 723.

Navarra, St-Jacobsstraat 41. Tel: 050-340 561.

Parkhotel, Vrijdagmarkt 5. Tel: 050-333 364.

'T Pandreitje, Pandreitje 6. Tel: 050-331 190.

Pullman, Boeveriestraat 2. Tel: 050-340 971.

Raspoetin, St Amandsstraat 6. Tel: 050-33 30 36.

'Traptje, Woollestraat 39. Tel: 050-33 89 18.

Sint-Joris, Markt 29. Tel: 050-333 062.

Vegetarian

Koffieboontje, Hallestraat 4. Tel: 050-33 80 27.

Zen, Beenhowersstraat 117. Tel: 050-33 67 02.

Brussels

First-Class Restaurants

Bruneau, Avenue Broustin 73, 1080 Brussels. Tel: 427 69 78. Open: noon–1.45pm and 7–9.45pm. Closed: Tuesday evening and Wednesday.

Claude Dupont, Avenue Vital Riethuisen 46, 1080 Brussels. Tel: 426 00 00. Open: noon–2.30pm and 7–9.30pm. Closed: Monday, Tuesday.

Comme Chez Soi, Place Rouppe 23. Tel: 512 29 21. Art Nouveau decor; the speciality here is oysters served with chicory.

La Maison du Cygne, Rue Charles Buls 2 (located at the Grand'Place). Tel: 511 8244. Open: 12.15–2.30pm and 7–10.30pm. Closed: Saturday afternoon and Sunday.

La Truffe Noire, Boulevard de la Cambre, 1050 Brussels. Tel: 640 44 22. Open: noon–2pm and 7pm–midnight.

L'Ecallier du Palais Royal, Rue Bodenbroeck 18–20, 1000 Brussels (at Place du Sablon). Tel: 512 87 51 or 511 99 50. Open: noon–2.30pm and 7–11pm. Closed: Sunday and holidays. Fish and seafood.

Les Quatre Saisons (located in the Royal Windsor Hotel), Rue de l'Homme Chrétien 2, 1000 Brussels. Tel: 511 42 15. Open: noon–2pm and 7pm–12.30am.

Romeyer, Chaussée de Groenendael 109, 1990 Hoeilaart. Tel: 657 05 81. Open: noon–3pm and 7–10pm. Closed: Sunday evening and Monday.

Villa Lorraine, Avenue du Vivier d'Oie 75, 1180 Brussels. Tel: 374 31 63 or 374 25 87. Open: noon–3pm and 6–9.30pm. Closed: Sunday.

Good Restaurants

La Belle Maraîchère, Place Ste-Cathérine. Tel: 512 97 59. Country-style decor; the speciality is seafood.

La Cambodge, Rue Washington 77. Tel: 537 70 98. Light and airy decor with superb Cambodian cuisine.

Chez Léon, Rue des Bouchers. Tel: 513 08 48. The speciality of the house is seafood.

Le Mouton d'Or, Petite Rue des Bouchers 21. Tel: 511 88 39. Country-style decor; the speciality here are salt-water fish dishes.

Mamma Mia, Rue Antoine Dansaert 158. Tel: 512 46 24. Country-style decor, seating for 80; Italian cuisine.

Le Paon, Grand Place 35. Tel: 513 35 82. The building dates back to the 17th-century, seating for 100; the speciality here is rabbit.

Le Paradoxe, Chaussée d'Ixelles 329. Tel: 649 89 81. With a piano lounge, seating for 100; vegetarian dishes are the regular speciality here.

Le Quincaillerie, Rue de Page 45. Tel: 538 25 53. Stylish and high-quality restaurant in a converted hardware store.

La Rose, Rue du Marché aux Herbes 97. Tel: 512 52 66. Country-style decor, seating for 60; the specialities are rabbit and sole.

Scheltema, Rue des Dominicains. Tel: 512 20 84. Traditional Belgian cuisine and seafood specialities.

La Vieux Saint-Martin, Place du G Sablon 38. Tel: 512 64 76. Cou style decor, seating for 75; specia in steak.

Bistros

L'Archiduc, Rue Antoine Dansae Tel: 512 06 52.

La Bécasse, Rue de Tabora 11 511 00 06.

De l'Ogenblik, Galerie des Princ Tel: 511 61 51.

Falstaff, Rue Henri Maus 25. Tel: 97 89.

La Fleur en Papier Doré, Rue Alexiens 53. Tel: 511 16 59.

La Mort Subite, Rue Montagne Herbes Potagères 7. Tel: 513 13

De Ultieme Hallucinatie, Rue R 316, 1210 Brussels. Tel: 217 06

Hotel Restaurants

The following excellent hotel re rants are highly recommended gourmets:

Ambassade Hotel

Arenberg Hotel

Astoria Hotel: the Palais Royal

Bedford Hotel

Hilton Hotel: En Plein Ciel and Café d'Egmont

Metropole Hotel: Z'Alban Chamb

Novotel Hotel: Novotel Grill

Ramada Hotel: Le Bouquet

Royal Windsor Hotel: Les Q Saisons

Sheraton Hotel: Comte de Flan and Le Pavillon.

Genk

Condor, Wiemesmeerstraat. Tel: 355 828.

Europa, Sledderloweg 85. Tel: 354 274.

Steakhouse Rembrandt, Weg a 1. Tel: 011-352 133.

Ghent

Arcade, Nederkouter 24–26. Tel: 250 707.

Condor, Ottegemsesteenweg 703 091-218 041.

Del Hel, Kraanlei 81. Tel: 091-22 40.

Europahotel, Gordunakaai 59. 091-226 071.

Het Volk, Poel 7. Tel: 091-242 0

Salons Carlos Quinto, Kammers 20. Tel: 091-255 929.

St-Jorishof, Botermarkt 2. Tel: 242 424.

ing, Maaltkekouter 3. Tel: 091-141.

Eyck, Lange Kruisstraat 4. Tel: 258 371.

tarian
hasbelly, Hoogpoort. Tel: 091-17 32.

Iepe and Ypres

weerd, Grote Markt 2. Tel: 057-475.

na, Grote Markt 45. Tel: 057-218

oria Palace, St-Jacobsstraat 3. 057-201 747.

Knokke-Heist

ir, Patriottenstraat 24. Tel: 050-300.

soleil, Patriottenstraat 15. Tel: 511 137.

de Bourgogne, Zoutelaan 175. 050-613 624.

stic, Zeedijk 697. Tel: 050-611

ling Palace, Albertplein 23. Tel: 601 164.

lon du Zoute, Bronlaan 4. Tel: 611 061.

re Hoel, De Kinkhoorn 21. Tel: 511 237.

Zaele, Oostkerkestraat 40. Tel: 601 237.

Leuven

allieter, Oude Markt 7. Tel: 016-722.

Mechelen

en Anker, Ridder Dessainlaan 2. 015-422 535.

iera, Veemarkt 20-24. Tel: 015-046.

r den Toren, Onder den Toren 4. 015-202 393.

ns van Dijk, Fr. de Merodestraat el: 015-204 517.

Nieuwpoort

s Portus, Goethealsstraat 2. Tel: 234 153.

monde, Victorlaan 1. Tel: 058-236

Ostend

omeda, Kursaal Westhelling, t I Promenade 5/60. Tel: 059-611.

in, A. Buylstraat 1A. Tel: 059-700

Ensor, Christinastraat 33-35. Tel: 059-504 013.

Glenmore, Hofstraat 25. Tel: 059-702 022.

Imperial, Van Iseghemlaan 76. Tel: 059-806 767.

Princess, Boekareststraat 7. Tel: 059-706 888.

Royal Albert, Zeedijk 167. Tel: 059-704 236.

Thalassa, Henegouwenstraat 1. Tel: 059-506 427.

Wiener Caffee, Christinastraat 20. Tel: 059-809 969.

Zeezicht, Zeedijk 161. Tel: 059-707 671.

Wallonia

BOUILLON

Hôtel de la Semois, Rue du Collège 44. Tel: 061-466 027.

La Vielle Ardenne, Grand' Rue 9. Tel: 061-466 277.

CHARLEROI

Gourmet Gourmand (Hôtel Pim's), Place Buisset 13. Tel: 071-319 870.

Hippopotame, Rue du Comptoir 4-6-8. Tel: 071-321 902.

DINANT

La Licorne, Rue Sax 50. Tel: 082-225 271.

Mont-Fat, Rue en Rhee 15. Tel: 082-222 783.

Villa Mouchenne, Av. des Combattants 30. Tel: 082-226 751.

LIÈGE

Fiacre, Place Saint-Denis 2. Tel: 041-231 545.

Mama Vi Cou, Rue de la Wache 9. Tel: 041-237 181.

Métropole, Rue des Guillemins 143. Tel: 041-524 293.

MONS

No Maison, Grand'Place 21. Tel: 065-347 474.

La Petite Provence, Grand'Place 26. Tel: 065-337 057.

Table Ronde, Place Léopold 5. Tel: 065-353 168.

NAMUR

Beffroi, Rue Jardin d'Harscamp 2. Tel: 081-224 847.

Le Belvédère, Av. Milieu du Monde 1. Tel: 081-223 824.

Côté Jardin, Rue de la Halle 2. Tel: 081-223 177.

L'Espièglerie, Rue des Toimeries 10. Tel: 081-223 024.

SPA

Le Cardinal, Place Royale 25-27. Tel: 087-771 064.

Source de Barisart, Route de Barisart 299. Tel: 087773 298.

TOURNAI

Château de Cartes, Rue St-Bruno 20. Tel: 069-235 605.

Le Richelieu, Pl. St-Pierre. Tel: 069-215 077.

Drinking Notes

Beer

The Belgians' favourite drink is beer. It has been brewed in Belgium since the Middle Ages when a Benedictine monk, St Arnold, discovered that the noblemen had a considerably higher life expectancy than the common people because they were able to quench their thirst with beer rather than the often contaminated water. He exhorted his flock to drink beer and for centuries afterwards the art of brewing remained firmly in the hands of the various religious communities. The craft has now become a major industry. Today there are no fewer than 400 breweries scattered across Belgium, producing 200 kinds of beer. It is usually served in small glasses. Stella Artois from Leuven, Jupiler from Liège and Maes are the most common.

Local draft pilsner is relatively mild in flavour; the speciality beers, usually served by the bottle, tend to be strong. The Rodenbach Brewery in West Flanders brews a beer known as Dobbelen Bruinen which is stored in oak barrels and subsequently filled into champagne bottles.

An unusual beers is Lambic. This also forms the basis for a number of other brews: Gueuze, Faro, Kriek and Framboise. Of the beers produced by Belgium's Trappist monasteries, Chimay, brewed in Hainaut, is the most widely available. Orval, from Luxembourg, is fruitier; Westmalle, from Antwerp is rich and malty.

Wines And Spirits

Wines are widely available and generally imported from France. However, the southern province of Luxembourg produces very drinkable white wines from the banks of the Moselle.

The Belgians' favourite chaser is *jenever* (juniper-flavoured gin). Be warned, *jenever* can cause a thundering hangover when consumed in quantity.

Attractions

Belgium is a country rich in art, architecture and culture. Each of the towns has its own history, traditions and treasures. Antwerp is a lively city of Baroque elegance; the entire centre of medieval Bruges is a living museum; Ghent, with its canals and ancient architecture, has been compared to Venice; Brussels boasts the country's best art collections; Leuven is the seat of the oldest university in Belgium; Mons is surrounded by castles; Namur, gateway to the Ardennes, is dominated by its massive citadel, to name just a few of the places of interest. Museums and art galleries abound and performance art is thriving.

The daily newspapers contain information about events and entertainment. In Brussels, visitors can reserve tickets for the opera, concerts and theatre productions at the Brussels Tourist Information Centre (TIB). There are theatres in the capital which perform dramatic pieces in both the French and Dutch languages. Most of the important concerts take place in the Palais de Beaux Arts. Opera and ballet productions are performed at the Théâtre Royale de la Monnaie (the National Opera House), the most famous stage in Brussels. Puppet shows played out in the Brussels dialect have been performed at the Toone Puppet Theatre since 1830.

Museums and Art Galleries

Please note that most museums are closed on Monday.

ANTWERP

Diamondland, Appelmanstraat 33 A. Tel: 03-234 3612. Centre for diamonds including diamond-cutting demonstrations.

The Royal Museum of Fine Arts, Leopold de Waelplein. Tel: 03-238 7809. Paintings dating from the 14th to 20th century

The Mayer van den Bergh Museum, Lange Gasthuisstraat 19. Tel: 03-232 4237. Reconstructed patrician apartment.

Vleeshuis Museum, Vleeshouwersstraat 38-40. Tel: 03-233 6404. Late Gothic building once serving as butcher's guild, presently housing an archaeological museum. Hours: 10am–5pm, closed: Monday.

The Museum of Contemporary Art (MUKHA), Leuvensestraat 32. Tel: 03-238 5960. Artworks produced by both Belgian and foreign artists, dating for the most part from the 1980s.

The National Shipping Museum "Steen", Steenplein 1. Tel: 03-232 0850. Hours: 10am–5pm.

The Plantin-Moretus Museum, Vrijdag–markt 22. Tel: 03-233 0294. Famous prints by Plantin; printing works, foundry, office and correcting rooms. The museum also contains some very old printing presses and paintings by Rubens. Hours: 10am–5pm.

The Rubens House, Wapper 9–11. Tel: 03-232 4747. Former residence and studio with historical garden; paintings, furniture and artworks dating from the 17th century. Hours: 10am–5pm daily.

BINCHE

International Carnival and Mask Museum, Rue de l'Eglise. The Carnival tradition as it is carried on in Binche and the tradition of masks throughout the entire world. Hours: 1 February–31 March 2–6pm Saturday; on weekdays and for groups by prearranged appointment only. 1 April–15 November 10am–noon and 2–6pm daily, except Friday.

BRUGES

The Groeninge Museum, Dijver 12. Survey of southern Dutch and Belgian painting from the 15th to 20th century. Hours: 1 April–30 September daily 9.30am–6pm; 1 October–31 March 9.30am–noon, 2–5pm daily, clo Tuesday.

The Grunthouse Museum, Dijver Flemish lace, musical instrume 16th and 17th century tapest housed in a 15th-century mans April–September daily 9.30am–5 October–March 9.30am–12.30pm 5pm, closed: Tuesday.

Brangwyn Museum, Dijver 16. Ho the work of the Welsh artist Sir F Brangwyn.

BRUSSELS

The 70 or so museums loc throughout the city of Brussels h a wide variety of art objects da from many different periods. M museums are open every day (ex Monday) 10am–5pm and often discount admission prices for gro children and senior citizens.

The following list includes som the most important museums:

Atomium, Boulevard du Centen Built on the occasion of the 1 World Exhibition it symbolises atomic structure of an iron mole enlarged 165 billion times; the ex tion inside traces the developme nuclear energy. Hours: the exhibiti open daily 9.30am–6pm; the obse tion sphere is open 1 May–31 Au daily 9.30am–10pm.

Autoworld, Parc du Cinquanter (Jubilee Park), Palais Mondial. M ised vehicles dating from 1886 approximately 1960. Hours: 1 No ber–31 March daily 10am–5pm April–31 October 10am–6pm.

The Beer Museum (Musée d Gueuze), Rue Gheude 56. Gu beer is brewed here from a re handed down through the ages. H 15 October–15 May 11am–2pm S day, or by pre-arranged appointm **The Museum of Brewing**, Grand'P 10. A 17th-century brewery; the tory, theory and techniques of production in Belgium are on dis here. Hours: 10am–noon and 2– Monday–Friday; 10am–noon Satu **The Brueghel Museum**, Rue Ha The residence of Pieter Brueghe Elder, complete with paintings, d ments and various memorabilia longing to this painter who die Brussels. Hours: 2–6pm Wednes Saturday.

The Charlier House (Musée Char

...sse, Avenue des Arts 16. Villa of famous art nouveau architect Victorta, complete with silver, furni... etc. In addition to these items, e are also paintings by Ensor and nier, among others. Hours: 1–5pm day–Friday.

Museum of Comics (Centre Belge a Bande Dissinée), Rue des Sa- 20. Wonderfully amusing mu-n in a renovated house designed orta; fun and enjoyment for both oung and young-at-heart. Hours: n–6pm Tuesday–Sunday.

Railway Museum (Musée du nin de Fer Belge), Gare du Nord h Railway Station), Rue du Prog- '6. Exhibition of Belgian railways. s: 9am–4.30pm Monday–Friday.

**Fire Brigade Museum (Musée du , Rue Simons 23. Hours: May– er 10am–4pm every weekend.

Museum of Flemish Folklore ée de la Vie Flamande à elles), Rue des Poissoniers 13. Flemish tradition in Brussels. s: 9am–4.30pm Monday–Friday.

City of Brussels Municipal Mu- (Musée Communal), d'Place. Exhibits trace the histori-nd archaeological development of ity and include collections of por-n and stoneware as well as the eken Pis wardrobe. Hours: n–12.30pm and 1.30–5pm Mon-Friday; the museum closes at 1 October–31 March.

Woluwe-St Lambert Municipal um (Musée Communal de ve-St Lambert), Woluwe-St-Lam-Rue de la Charette 40. Hours: -noon and 2–5pm Monday–Friday.

Horta Museum (Musée Horta), méricaine. Former residence and of Victor Horta; on display are graphs of his best-known build-Hours: 2–5pm Tuesday–Satur-

Museum of Musical Instruments ée Instrumental), Place du Petit n 17. Contains over 6,000 musi-struments from a wide variety of ent countries and epochs. Some are exhibited at any time. Hours: -4.30pm Tuesday–Friday; 10am–weekends and holidays; closed: ay.

International Media Museum, ssée de Louvain 696. Collection er 150,000 newspapers pub-d throughout the entire world and

dating from just about every epoch. Hours: 9am–noon and 2–5pm Monday–Friday; closed: 15–31 July.

The Children's Museum (Musée des Enfants), Ixelles, Rue du Bourgmestre 15. An interesting museum for children. Hours: 2.30–5.30pm Wednesday, Saturday and Sunday.

The Museum of the Cinema (Musée du Cinéma), Hortastraat 9. Display of equipment dating primarily from the period of silent films. Hours: 5.30–10.30pm daily, and by pre-arranged appointment.

The Royal Army and Military History Museum (Musée Royal de l'Armée et d'Histoire Militaire), Parc du Cinquantenaire. Weapons and armour dating from the 7th to 18th century; in the aviation section the history of military aviation and parachuting from 1912 up until the present day. Hours: 9am–noon and 1–4pm Tuesday–Sunday.

The Royal Museum of Fine Arts (Musées Royaux des Beaux-Arts), Rue de la Régence 3 and Place Royale 1. One of the largest museums in the world containing paintings, graphics and sculpture from the 15th, 16th and 17th century. The art treasures of the 20th-century housed in the Musée d'Art Moderne (the entrance is located at Place Royale), are available for public viewing 10am–1pm and 2–5pm Tuesday–Sunday. The other part of the museum (visitors enter from the Rue de la Régence), Musée d'Arts Anciens, is open 1–7.30pm Tuesday–Friday and 10am–5pm Saturday and Sunday.

The Royal Museum of Art and History (Musée Royaux d'Art et D'Histoire), Parc du Cinquantenaire. Works dating back to Roman, Greek and Egyptian antiquity, objects originating during the Roman and Frankish periods in Belgium. Hours: 9.30am–12.30pm and 1.30–4.45pm Tuesday–Friday, 9.30am–3.30pm Saturday and Sunday. Different sections of the museum are open alternately on even or odd days.

The Royal Institute of Natural Science (Institut Royal des Sciences Naturelles de Belgique), Rue Vautier 29. Extraordinary collections of minerals, fossils and skeletons help to outline the prehistorical, mineral and zoological development of the country. Hours: 9.30am–4.45pm daily.

The Royal Museum of Central Africa

(Musée Royal de L'Afrique Centrale), Chaussée de Louvain 13. Portrayal of African culture. Hours: 9am–5.30pm; 16 October–15 March 10am–4.30pm.

The Organ Museum (Musée d'Orgues de Kermesse), ·Schaerbeek, Rue Waelhem 104. Tel: 241 2791. Here visitors can admire lovely and original fairground organs. Hours: by appointment only.

The Postal Museum (Musée des Postes et Télécommunications), Place du Grand Sablon. Stamp collections from Belgium as well as from other countries; in addition to these, the entire development of the postal and telecommunications systems are explained in conjunction with a quite varied selection of telecommunications equipment. Hours: 10am–4pm Tuesday–Saturday and 10am–12.30pm Sunday.

The Brussels Town Hall (Hôtel de Ville), Grand'Place. Visitors can tour the reception rooms and councillors' offices which are decorated with tapestries from the 16th, 17th and 18th century. Hours: 9.30am–5pm Tuesday–Friday and 10am–4pm Sunday. Conducted tours are obligatory.

The Toy Museum (Musée du Jouet), Anspach-Center, Boulevard Anspach 36. Hours: 10am–6pm daily.

The Toone Theatre Museum (Musée du Théâtre Toone VII), Petite Rue des Bouchers. On the second floor of the famous "Toone" puppet theatre visitors will find examples of old puppets, posters and manuscripts relating to the history of the theatre. Hours: during theatre performance interval.

The Wax Museum (Musée de Cire), Place de la Monnaie. Life-sized wax figures from the past 2,000 years of history are on display here. Hours: 10am–6pm daily.

The Resistance Museum (Musée de la Résistance), Anderlecht, Rue Van Lint 14. Belgian resistance against occupying forces during World Wars I and II. Hours: 9am–noon and 1–4pm Tuesday–Thursday.

The Wiertz Museum (Musée Wiertz), Ixelles, Rue Vautier 62. The fascinating studio and paintings of the Romantic artist, Antoine Wiertz. Hours: 10am–6pm Tuesday–Sunday.

CHARLEROI

The Museum of Photography, Avenue Paul Pastur 11. Collection of pictures and equipment which illustrate the general history of photography, housed in a former Carmelite monastery. Hours: 10am–5pm daily, except Mondays and holidays.

The Museum of Industry, Rue de la Providence 134. The museum is housed in an old smithy; a forge in action is on display and their are demonstrations of different tools, motors and printing presses. Hours: 9am–4pm and on Saturday by appointment only.

GHENT

The Museum of Fine Arts, Citadel Park. On view are many old Master paintings and a selection of tapestries made in Brussels. Hours: 9am–12.30pm and 1.30–5.30pm daily, except Monday.

HASSELT

National Jenever Museum, Witte Nonnenstraat 19. From grain to drink, see how jenever is made. Hours: 10am–5pm Tuesday–Friday and 2–6pm Saturday, Sunday and public holidays.

KORTRIJK

The Municipal Museum, Broelkaai 6. The Museum of Fine Arts contains more than 700 works of art and the Museum of Archaeology and Arts and Crafts includes an extensive collection of Kortrijk silver, damask and ceramics. Hours: 10am–noon and 2–6pm daily, except Friday; 10am–1pm and 3–6pm Sunday; from 1 October–31 March. The museum closes at 5pm.

The National Flax Museum, E. Sabbelaan 4. The cultivation, development and processing of flax is illustrated on 26 display boards in a restored farmhouse. Hours: 1 March–30 November 9.30am–12.30pm and 1.30–6pm Monday, Wednesday, Thursday and Friday; 1.30–6pm Tuesday; noon–6pm Saturday and Sunday; closed: holidays.

LIÈGE

The Museum of Fine Arts, Rue de l'Académie. Primarily works from the masters of the 19th and 20th century such as Picasso, Gauguin and Ensor.
The Museum of Walloon Art, Parc de la Boverie. Paintings and sculptures from the southern provinces of Belgium. Hours: 1–6pm Tuesday–Satur-

day; 11am–4.30pm Sunday and holidays.

The Aquarium and Zoological Museum, Quai van Beneden 22. Overview of fauna found throughout the entire world, collection of sponges and corals, as well as the skeleton of a 18.5-metre (approximately 62-ft) long finback whale. Hours: 10.30am–12.30pm and 2–6pm daily.

NAMUR

The Archaeological Museum, Rue du Pont. Prehistorical, Roman and medieval collections. Hours: 10am–noon and 2–5pm daily, except Tuesday; closed during the Christmas holidays.
The Museum of Forestry, Route Merveilleuse. On display are the flora and fauna of the Ardennes, a general survey of the damage done to forests and efforts to fight this damage, and a splendid butterfly collection. Different and rare kinds of trees have been planted around the museum grounds. Hours: 1 April–31 October from 9am–noon and from 2–5pm.
The Félicien Rops Museum, Rue Fumal 12. Tel: 081-220 110. Hours: 10am–5pm, closed: Tuesday.

OELEGEM-RANST

Vrieselhof Textile and Costume Museum, Schildesteenweg 79. Tel: 03-383 46 80. A fine collection of lace, costumes, embroidery and printed fabrics. Hours: 10am–5pm March–November, closed: Monday.

OOSTDUINKERKE

The National Museum of Fishing, Pastoor Schmitzstraat 4. The history of fishermen and fishing is traced using fishing boats dating from the period between AD800 to the present and paintings and sculptures produced by artists who worked in Oostduinkerke around 1900. Hours: 10am–noon and 2–6pm daily.

OSTEND

The Museum of Fine Arts, Wapenplein. International modern art with a special section reserved for James Ensor and for Flemish Expressionism. Hours: 10am–noon and 2–5pm daily, except Tuesday; closed: during the month of October.
The Floating School Mercator, Mercatordock. This sailing ship was built in 1932 and was used by the mer-

chant fleet for many years as the ■ ing vessel for its officers. In 196 was established as a floating seum. Hours: during the Easter days and from June–September c in the remaining months the mus is open from 10am–noon and fro 5pm Saturday and Sunday.

TONGEREN

The Basilica Treasure Cham Kloosterplaats. Collection of ■ ments, reliquaries and religious dating from the Merovingian Perio the present day. Hours: 9am–noor 2–5pm daily.

TOURNAI

The Museum of Fine Arts, Enclo St Martin. A 1928 building desi by Horta displaying works by var Weyden, Brueghel, Rubens, Mo van Gogh and Ensor. Hours: 1 Apri October 10am–noon and 2–5.30p November–31 March 10am–noor 2–6pm Sundays and holidays on■

Libraries

The **Albert I Royal Library**, Mon Arts, is located in Brussels. Div manuscripts, prints and book c provide a good overview of the hi of books from antiquity until present time. Hours 2–5pm Mo Wednesday and Saturday.

Other libraries in Brussels:
Bibliotheca Wittockiana, Rue B 21. Tel: 02-770 53 33.
Bibliothèque Régionale de Wo■ Saint-Lambert, Rue Saint-Henri Tel: 02-735 28 24.
Bibliothèques Publiques Commu■ d'Uccle Centre, Rue de Doyenn■ Tel: 02-345 86 00.
Bibliothèque de l'Université Lib■ Bruxelles, Avenue F. Roosevelt Tel: 02-642 23 84.
Bibliothèque du Parlament, Pala la Nation, Place de la Nation. Te 519 81 81.

Theatres, Music and Ball

ANTWERP

The Royal Flemish Opera, Frank 3. A well-known theatre for opera operetta performances.
The Royal Young People's The Komedieplaats 19. Has special a for youth.

tres

sschouwburg, Rue Auguste Orts.
513 82 90.

munauté Française, Passage 44.
218 27 35.

es de Schaerbeek, Rue Royale
Tel: 218 00 31.

e Théâtre de l'ULB, Av. Paul Héger
el: 650 38 24.

nklijke Vlaamse Schouburg, Rue
aeken 146. Tel: 217 69 37.

on de Spectacle de la Bellone,
de Flandre 146. Tel: 513 33 33.

eau Théâtre I, Rue de Viaduc
Tel: 640 84 37.

eau Théâtre II, Place des Martyrs
el: 217 99 54.

tre de la Balsamine, Avenue F.
hall 1. Tel: 733 23 02.

tre Molière, Galerie du Roi. Tel:
58 00.

tre National, Centre Rogier. Tel:
03 03.

tre Poème, Rue d'Ecosse 30. Tel:
63 57.

tre Royal des Galeries, Galerie du
el: 513 39 60.

tre Royal du Parc, Rue de la Loi
: 511 41 49.

tre Toone VII, Petite Rue des
hers 21. Tel: 511 71 37.

tre Varis, Rue de Sceptre 78. Tel:
32 58.

c & Ballet

tre Royal de la Monnaie, Place
Monnaie. Tel: 218 12 11.

e Royal, Rue de l'Enseignement
el: 218 20 15.

nne Belgique, Boulevard
ach 114. Tel: 512 59 86.

t National, Avenue de Globe 36.
47 02 30.

GHENT

Royal Dutch Schouwburg, St
plein 7. Theatre performances.

oyal Opera, Schouwburgstraat 3.
and operetta performances.

eke van de Folklore, Kraanlei 63.
t theatre.

LIÈGE

ervatoire Royal de Musique, Rue
e-Ysaye; the concert hall was
ructed in the style of Louis XIV
an accommodate 1,700 people.
tage itself has room enough for
erformers.

NAMUR

The Culture House, Avenue Golen–vaux; concerts, conventions and exhibits all take place in this culture centre.

Cinemas

Many films shown in Belgium are not dubbed. Generally speaking, French movies do not have subtitles, while English films always do.

In Brussels, the greatest concentration of cinemas is in two different area: in the Lower City, between the Place Rogier and the Place de la Bourse, and in the Upper City near the Porte de Namur and in the Avenue de la Toison d'Or. In addition there is the Kinepolis complex at Bruparck, with 24 screens, including an IMAX wrap-around theatre.

Foreign films are often shown at the Actor's Studio, Petit Rue des Bouchers 16, and at the Arenberg/Galeries, Galerie de la Reine 26. The Musée du Cinema, rue Baron Horta 9, shows a selection of old silent films.

On Monday nights entrance to some cinemas is half-price. For an up-to-date list of what's on consult *Le Soir*, *De Standard* and the weekly English language *The Bulletin*.

Cinemas

Eldorado. Newly rebuilt 8-screen complex. 38 Place de Broukère. Tel: 218 04 34.

Kinepolis. The biggest cinema complex in the world with 24 screens. Bruparck Centre, Boulevard du Centenaire. Tel: 478 04 50 and 478 15 00.

Acropole. An 11-screen complex in the Upper Town. 17 Avenue de la Toison d'Or. Tel: 511 43 28.

EU Buildings

European Union buildings are located in Brussels at the Robert-Schumann-Platz. The EU Council of Ministers maintains offices at Rue de la Loi 100, tel: 234 61 11. The Commission also has its headquarters in Rue de la Loi 200, tel: 235 11 11. Call these numbers if you would like to sign up for a tour or call for information.

Breweries

Please contact the breweries direct for opening times and tours.

Oud Beersel, Laarheidestraat 230,

1650 Beersel. Tel: 2-380 33 96.

Straffe Hendrik Brewery, Walplein 26, 8000 Brugge. Tel: 50-33 26 97.

De Dolle Brouwers Brewery, Roese–larestraat 12b, 8600 Esen. Tel: 51-50 27 81.

Brasserie d'Achouffe, Rue W. Achouffe 32, 6660 Houffalize. Tel: 61-28 81 47 and 61-28 94 55.

Interbrew Brewery (Stella Artois), Vaarstraat 94-96, 3000 Leuven. Tel: 16-24 74 61.

Liefmans Brewery, Aalststraat 200, 9700 Oudenaarde. Tel: 55-31 13 91.

Belle-Vue Brewery, Henegouwenkaai 43, 1080 Sint-Jans-Molenbeek. Tel; 2-410 19 35.

De Gouden Boom Brewery, Lange–straat 45, 8000 Brugge. Tel: 50-33 06 99.

Cantillon Brewery and Museum, Gheudestraat 56, 1070 Brussels. Tel: 2-521 49 28.

Floreffe Abbey (Mill Brewery), Rue de Seminaire 7, 5750 Floreffe. Tel: 81-44 53 03.

Domestic Brewery Domus, Tiense–straat 8, 3000 Leuven. Tel: 16-29 14 49.

Gouden Carolus Brewery, Guido Gezellelaan 49, Krankenstraat 2, 2800 Mechelen. Tel: 15-20 38 80.

Du Bocq Brewery, Rue de la Purnode 49, 5530 Purnode. Tel: 82-61 37 37, fax: 82-61 17 80.

Brasserie Fantome, Rue Preal 17, 6977 Soy. Tel: 86-47 75 86, fax: 86-47 70 32.

Musée de la Cervoise du Gruyt et des Bières Medievales, Avouerie d'An-thisnes, Avenue de l'Abbaye 19, 4160 Anthisnes.

Brewery and Malthouse Museum, Verbrand Nieuwland 10, 8000 Brugge. Tel: 50-33 06 99.

Bier-o-Rama, Domein Kelchterhoef, Kelchterhoefstraat 9, 3550 Hout-halen.

Museum of Belgian Beers, Rue de la Gare 19, 5170 Lustin. Tel: 81-41 11 02.

Beer Museum, Rodt-Thommberg, 4780 Sankt-Vith. Tel: 80-22 63 01.

Brewery Museum, Dorpsstraat 53, 3950 Bocholt. Tel: 89-47 29 80.

Beer and Regional Museum 't Nieuwhuys, c/o Gemmentelijke Dienst voor Toerisme, Gemmenteplein 1, 3320 Hoegaarden. Tel: 16-76 61 11.

City Brewery Museum, Naamsestraat 3, 3000 Leuven. Tel: 16-22 69 06.

National Hop Museum, De Stads-waag, Gasthuisstraat 71, 8970 Poperinge. Tel: 57-33 40 81.

Nature Reserves

Botrange Nature Park, situated in the province of Luxembourg at the highest point in Belgium, organises walking and bicycle tours on request and offers mountain bikes, skis and boots for hire. Exhibitions, nature films and a multivision slide show can be viewed in the Park Centre where there is a "Green Shop" and cafeteria. Picnicking facilities. Botrange Nature Park, B-4950 Robertville. Tel: 080-44 57 81. Open: daily 10am–6pm, closed: late November–early December.

Het Zwin Nature Reserve in West Flanders is the largest salt marsh in Belgium. Several thousands of birds breed in the sanctuary. B-8300 Knokke-Heist, Het Zwin, Ooievaarslaan 8. Tel: 050-60 70 86. Open: Easter–September 9am–7pm; October–Easter 9am–5pm, closed: Wednesday, November–March.

Westhoek Nature Reserve southwest from De Panne in West Flanders is an unspoilt stretch of coastline and sand dunes with marked footpaths for walking and enjoying the local flora and fauna. Maps available from the tourist office in De Panne.

L'Eau d'Heure lakes at Boussu-lez-Walcourt in Hainaut is a popular centre for watersports (windsurfing, sailing, fishing, waterskiing, speedboat racing, jet-ski, diving, go-karting) and walking. Other attractions include guided visits to the dam of Plate Taille and a film of the history of the site, aquariums and boat trips. The recreation centre offers train rides, canoes, pedalos, mini-golf, BMX track, tennis, sandy beaches and a cafeteria. Centre d'accueil de la plate Taille, B-6440 Boussu-lez-Walcourt. Tel: 071-63 35 34.

The Virelles Lakes in Hainaut is a 250-acre nature reserve offering guided tours on foot, observation posts, restaurants, barbecue area, children's games, pedalos and boats. B-6200 Bouffioulx, rue E. Hermant 20. Tel: 060-21 13 63. Open: May–September daily 10am–6pm; October–April Sunday only.

Beguine Convents

In the 13th-century single women were given the opportunity to live together, well looked after, in secular convents. These "worldly nuns" could choose to leave the Beguine Convent any time they pleased. Most of these convents remain well-preserved and are well worth visiting. You'll find them located in the following cities: Aarschot, Antwerp, Bruges, Brussels, Diest, Diksmuide, Ghent, Kortrijk, Lier, Leuven.

Military Cemeteries

There are many war cemeteries in Belgium, most centred on the World War I battlefields around Ieper (Ypres), and others dating back to the World War II in the Ardennes. For information pertaining to war graves contact:

War Graves Commission, 2 Marlow Road, Maidenhead, Berkshire, UK. Tel: 0628-34221.
Volksbund deutscher Kriegsgräber–fürsorge, Werner-Hilpert-Strasse 2, 3500 Kassel, Germany. Tel: 0561-79 41.

Tours

AROUND BRUSSELS

Tervuren is located only 13 km (8 miles) from Brussels. Tervuren Park is well worth visiting, as is St Hubert's Chapel (built in the 17th-century) and the Museum of Central Africa (Musée Royal de l'Afrique Centrale) with its impressive collection of items dating back to the period when Belgium was a colonial power.

The university city of Leuven (Louvain) is also not far from Brussels. While strolling through the main market, be sure to take a look at the town hall (Hôtel de Ville), and St Peter's church. The university itself was founded in the year 1425.

Children will have fun visiting the town of Wavre (located 25 km/15 miles) from Brussels. Young and old alike are sure to enjoy a day spent at "Walibi", Belgium's largest amusement park.

The country's most frequently visited tourist attraction, the battlefield at Waterloo, is located in the province of Brabant.

Nivelles is situated 35 km (22 miles) away from Brussels; it's worth your while to make an excu to the St Gertrude Abbey, found the 7th-century. And those who get enough of the Manneken P Brussels should make it a po track down the "Jean de Ni Tower" in Nivelles, where the fa copper figure emerges to strike hour.

The ruins of the Cistercian abb **Villers-la-Ville**, located east Nivelles, is also sure to make f interesting excursion. The abbey established in the 12th-century.

There are many artistic treas on view in the pilgrimage city of I 15 km from Brussels, at the chu Our Lady.

The extensive park ground **Huizingen** positively invite the vis take time out for a relaxing stro medieval **Beersel Castle** (a mo castle) is located close by **Anderlecht** tourists can admire S ter's church, built in the 15th-ce and the House of Erasmus (M d'Erasmus).

The city of **Mechelen** lies t north of Brussels and is home t almost 100-metre (333-ft) Rombout church tower with its site carillon. Additional tourist a tions in Mechelen include the tow (Hôtel de Ville) on the Grand'Place Palace of Justice and the church John.

Thanks to two of its citizens, th of **Lier/Lierre** also enjoys a ce claim to fame: Felix Timmermans both a writer and painter and Zimmer invented the astrono clock. The Timmermans-Ops House and the Zimmer Tower, the hall (Hôtel de Ville), church Gummarus and the Wuyts Campen-Caroly Museum are all visiting. In Lier you'll find the bes served Beguine convent in all o gium.

IN FLANDERS

Flandria Boat Tours. Excursion fered include a "Scheldt Tour", a tended Scheldt Tour" and a "Ha Tour". Toeristisch Gebouw. Steen 2000 Antwerp. Tel: 03-233 74 2 **Boat Cruises Along Antwerp' nals**. Departures from Rozenhoe Dijver and Mariaburg. **Boat Tours "De Lamme Goed**

rsions from Bruges to Damme vice versa, from April until September. Dienst voor Toerisme Damme, huis Markt 1, 8340 Damme. Tel: 35 33 19.

t by Boat. Korenlei, 9000 Ghent. 091-23 88 53.

rsions on the Meuse around ec. Maasdijk, 3640 Konrooi. Tel: 56 75 03.

Tours and Sea Fishing. Fishing er Vieren, Albert I-Laan 90, 8620 wpoort. Tel: 058-23 47 30.

Park. An amusement park for the e family. De Pannelaan 68, 8660 kerke-de Panne. Tel: 058-42 02

dewijn Park. A family park containa dolphin aquarium and reptile se. A. De Baeckestraat 12, 8200 es. Tel: 050-38 38 38.

etum. Famous collection of more 6,000 trees, shrubs and plants. vel 2, 2920 Kalmthont. Tel: 03-67 41.

Park. An adventure park with imsive suspended bridges, climbing mids, trampolines, huge slides more. Moorsledestraat 6, 8890 zele. Tel: 065-50 05 05.

waerde Amusement Park. Safari s, lions, tigers, crocodiles and r animals, a cowboy village, white-r slide and playground. Meen–g 497, 8902 Zillebeke-Ieper. Tel: 46 86 86.

ora. Plants, birds, fish, monkeys – opportunities for both the young young at heart. Bruggestraat 218, Ingelmunster. Tel: 051-30 15

ejaanland Amusement Park. Fun he family with over 40 different ctions. Olensesteenweg 45, 2460 aart. Tel: 014-55 78 11.

n Biesen Bilzen. Commandery of Teutonic Order from 1317 in the e-Meuse region. Kasteelstraat 6, Bilzen (Rijkhoven). Tel: 011-41 4.

onk Castle. Flemish-Spanish aissance castle dating from the -century. 9800 Deinze. Tel: 091-1 23.

sbeek Castle. Construction comced back in the 13th-century. The e houses a unique collection of reasures, antique furniture, stone-e and porcelain, wood carvings, ur, brass, silver, glassware and stries. Groenstraat, 1750

Gaasbeek. Tel: 02-53 243 72.

Sint-Truiden Bicycle Tour. The Trudo cycle route takes you via historic fortresses and country houses. Stadhuis, Grote Markt, 3800 Sint-Truiden. Tel: 011-68 62 55.

Gravensteen Castle. One of the best-preserved castles in Belgium. Sint-Veerleplein 11, 9000 Ghent. Tel: 091-23 99 82.

Loppem Palace. Jean Béthune designed the building itself, the furniture and decorations contained in this palace dating from the year 1859. There is a unique labyrinth located in the palace grounds. Steenbrugsesraat 26, 8210 Zedelgem-Loppem. Tel: 050-82 22 45.

Horst Castle. One of Belgium's most beautiful medieval castles. A castle festival takes place every year on the first Saturday and Sunday following the 15 August. Horststraat 28, 3320 St-Pieters-Rode. Tel: 016-635 911.

Laarne Castle. A 13th-century castle containing 16th-century furniture and tapestries and a collection of silver-ware. 9270 Laarne. Tel: 09-230 91 55.

Wijnendale Castle Museum. A moated castle with a guard-room and kitchen dating back to the 17th-century, a Burgundian hall, torture chamber, attic and cheese museum. Oostendestraat 390, 8820 Torhout. Tel: 050-212 377.

Het Zwin National Park, Ooievaar–slaam 8, 8300 Knokke-Heist. Tel: 050-60 70 86.

Butterfly Garden, Bronlaan 14, 8300 Knokke-Heist. Tel: 050-610 472.

IN WALLONIA

Ecaussinnes-Lalaing Castle. This castle dates from between the 11th and 15th century and houses a wide variety of paintings, sculpture, porcelain, ceramics and glass. 7191 Ecaus–sinnes-Lalaing. Tel: 067-44 24 90.

The Slope of Ronquières, Rue des Clercs 31, 7000 Mons. Tel: 065-360 464.

L'Orient Recreational Centre. Water sports, playground and barbecue facilities. Chemin de Mons 8, 7500 Tournai. Tel: 069-22 26 35.

Parc Paradisio. A bird sanctuary set in beautiful parkland among the ruins of a 13th-century Cistercian abbey. Domaine de Cambron, 7940 Cambron Casteau. Tel: 68-45 46 53 and 45 57 87.

Belœil Castle. Precious collections from the 15th and 19th century, a library with 25,000 volumes, French-style park and the "Minibel Kingdom", Belgium's tourist attractions presented on a scale of 1:25. Rue du Chateau 11, 7970 Belœil. Tel: 069-68 94 26.

Horse-drawn Boat Rides. A century-old barge is towed along by a horse. Departure: "Cantine des Italiens", Rue Tout-y-Faut, 7070 Houdeng Goegnies-La Louvière.

Naval Yard in La Louvière. History of the hydraulic ship canal lift. Rue Tout-y-Faut, 7070 Houdeng Goegnies-La Louvière. Reservations: tel: 064-66 25 61.

Marcinelle Recreational Park. Swimming-pool, various water sports, tennis and opportunities for hiking. Avenue des Mugets 16, 6001 Marcinelle. Tel: 071-36 22 89.

The Virelles Lakes. Nature reserve, playgrounds, peddle boats, tours on foot or by jeep. Rue E. Hermant 20, 6260 Bouffioulx. Tel: 060-21 13 63.

The Permanent Nature Centre's Observatory. Telescope, planetarium, medicinal herbs and a weather station. Route de Mons 52, 6574 Sivry. Tel: 060-45 51 28.

The L'Eau D'Heure Lakes. A variety of watersports, fishing, parachuting, and a place to rent bicycles. Plate Taille Reception Centre, 6440 Boussu-lez-Walcourt. Tel: 071-63 35 34.

Du Pont D'Arcole Grottoes, Rue d'Inzemont 2, 5540 Hastière. Tel: 082-64 44 01.

Fagnolles Castle. Castle dating from the 13th-century. 6372 Fagnolles. Tel: 060-311 304.

Abime Caves, Rue de la Falaise, 6400 Couvin. Tel: 060-31 19 54.

Neptune Grottoes, Route de L'Adugeoir, 6401 Petigny. Tel: 060-31 19 54.

Rochefort Grotto, Drève de Lorette, 5430 Rochefort. Tel: 084-21 20 80.

Kayak Trips along the Leie (Lesse), Place de L'Eglise 2, 5500 Anseremme-Dinant. Tel: 082-22 43 97.

Game Park. Safari by car through the park. Rue J. Lamotte 2, 5432 Han-sur-Lesse. Tel: 084-37 72 12.

Han-sur-Lesse Grottoes. A train transports visitors through the world-famous grottoes. Rue J. Lamotte 2, 5432 Han-sur-Lesse. Tel: 084-37 72 12.

Kayak Trips. Guided trips followed by a barbecue. Rue du Vélodrome 15, 5500 Anseremme-Dinant. Tel: 082-22 33 44.

Mont-Fat. An amusement park with historical buildings and modern attractions. Rue en Rhée 15, 5500 Dinant. Tel: 082-22 27 83.

Motorcycle Tourism. Motorcycle, scooter and mountain-bike rentals. Rue Defoin 195, 5500 Dinant. Tel: 082-22 57 88.

Vêves Castle. A medieval castle. 5561 Celles-Houyet. Tel: 082-66 63 93.

Spontin Castle. The oldest feudal castle in Belgium. 5190 Spontin. Tel: 083-69 90 55.

Annevoie Gardens. Some of the loveliest gardens in all of Europe. Route des Jardins, 5181 Annevoie. Tel: 082-16 15 55.

Queen Fabiola Attraction Centre. A large playground for children, tourist train, mini-golf, etc. Rond Point Thonar, 5000 Namur. Tel: 081-37 84 13.

Steamship Cruises on the Maas River, Rue Daoust 64, 5500 Dinant. Tel: 082-22 23 15.

Goyet Grottoes. Prehistoric grottoes and caves. 5320 Mozet-Gesves. Tel: 081-58 85 45.

Kayak Trips along the Semois River, Rue Léon Henrard, 6848 Alle-sur-Semois. Tel: 061-50 03 81.

Les Près De Tilff Tourist Centre. Swimming-pool, slide, playground for children, roller-skating rink and mini-golf. Chemin de Halage, 4040 Tilff. Tel: 041-88 12 13.

Mont Mosan. Sea-lion show, Magic Land and a beaver pond. Plaine de la Sarte 18, 5200 Huy. Tel: 085-23 29 96.

Le Trimbleu Recreational Mine, 4570 Blégny. Tel: 041-87 43 32.

Pierre-le-Grand Spring. The famous spring of Spa. Place Royale 41, 4880 Spa.

Hohe Venn-Eifel National Park, 4898 Robertville, Naturparkzentrum Botrange. Tel: 080-44 57 81.

Telecoo Amusement Park. Bob-sleigh run, cable railway, go-carts, bumper boats, old-timers and an Astro-Liner. 4970 Coo-Stavelot. Tel: 080-68 42 65.

Safari and Recreational Park. Rhinoceroses, elephants, hippopotami, lions, tigers, chimpanzees, etc. Fange de Deigné 3, 4960 Deigné-Aywaille. Tel: 041-60 90 70.

Logne Castle. Famous castle in the Ourthe Valley. Route de Logne, 4084 Vieuxville. Tel: 041-84 41 25.

Hotton Grottoes. Some of the most beautiful grottoes to be found anywhere in Europe. 5450 Hotton. Tel: 084-46 60 46.

La Tourelle Lace Centre, Rue des Brasseurs 7, 5400 Marche-en-Famenne. Tel: 084-31 21 35.

Fourneau Saint-Michel Museum. Iron museum, blast furnace from 1771, old tools, arts and crafts. Fourneau Saint-Michel, 6900 Saint-Hubert. Tel: 084-21 08 90.

"Les Grès de La Roche". Arts and crafts centre. Rue Rompré 28, 6980 La Roche. Tel: 084-41 18 78.

Game Park. Wild animals found in the Ardennes. Rue Saint-Michel, 6900 Saint-Hubert. Tel: 061-61 17 15.

Bouillon Castle, 6830 Bouillon. Tel: 061-46 62 57.

Kayak Trips. Day trips and longer excursions on the Semois River. Quai des Sauls 2, 6830 Bouillon. Tel: 061-46 63 91.

Go-carting. Over 400 metres (approximately 1,300 ft) of asphalt runs for go-cart fans. Voie Jocquée 115, 6830 Bouillon. Tel: 061-46 78 07.

Victory Memorial Museum, Aire de la Victoire, Autobahn E 411/E 25, Hondelange-Arlon. Tel: 063-21 99 88.

Historical Centre. The Battle of Bastogne. Colline du Mardasson, 6650 Bastogne. Tel: 062-21 14 13.

Walibi and Aualibi. Belgium's largest amusement park. Walibi, 1300 Wavre. Tel: 10-41 44 66.

Bupark. Leisure parks within a park. Mini-Europe: Model of European landmarks and buildings in miniature; Oceade: Swirl pool, wave pool, waterslides on a tropical theme. Kinepolis: 24 cinemas on one site. Boulevard du Centenaire, 1020 Brussels. Tel: 2-477 03 77.

Those who start their evening pub tour too early may well find themselves facing locked doors. As in most major cities in Europe, the majority of Belgium's clubs and discothèques do not open until 10pm.

In Brussels, a stroll to the Place Brouckère will help to pass the time. The square is one of the centres of the city's nightlife and a good place to

meet up with friends and enjoy a [...] The bars and discos located in [...] Lower City are on the whole mo[...] laxed and enjoyable than those in [...] Upper City. Prices at places in the [...] ter are generally more expensive, [...] the clientele pays more attentio[...] dressing stylishly. Many of the c[...] are private, but it is possible in s[...] to obtain membership for one eve[...] Night spots in Brussels change h[...] frequently and are often in existe[...] for a short time. It is wise to p[...] before you set your heart on a ce[...] place.

Pubs And Bars

Canne à Sucre, Rue des Pigeons [...]
Cap de Nuit, Place de la Vieille [...] aux Blés 28.
Président Club, WTC, Boulevar[...] Jacqmain 180.
Vol de Nuit, Rue du Magistrat 33[...]
Wine Bar, Rue des Pigeons 9.

Nightclubs

Mirano Continental, 38 Chaussé[...] Louvain. Tel: 218 57 72. The sma[...] dance venue in town.
Cartegena, 70 Rue Marché [...] Charbon. Only hot-blooded Latin t[...] need apply – along with those [...] northerners whose blood could u[...] little heat.
Le Garage, 16 Rue Dusquenoy. [...] 512 66 22. Popular disco with [...] ists.
Happy Few, Avenue Louise 19. [...] swim under the transparent da[...] floor.
L'Ecumes des Nuits, 122a Ga[...] Louise. Tel: 513 53 21. Ambianc[...] funky African and Caribbean.
New Portland, 6 Place de la Chap[...] A nicely-dressed place.
Alexandre, 33 Place du Châtelain. [...] 537 30 92. A touch of nostalgia fo[...] 1960s and 1970s.

Cabarets

Black Bottom, 1 Rue du Lombard. [...] 511 06 08. Small, raffish Parisie[...] style piano cabaret.
Le Show Point, 14 Place Stépha[...] Tel: 511 53 64. A glitzy, platinum-[...] venue, with lots of heavily mad[...] girls go-go dancing.

Casinos

Gambling casinos are a special at[...] tion of Belgian nightlife. You'll

in Blankenberge, Chaudfontaine,
nt, Knokke-Heist, Middlekerke,
ur, Ostend and Spa.

Late-Night Restaurants

rande Porte, Rue Notre-Seigneur
pen: until 2am during the week
until 4am on the weekend.
 Ma Zwet, Rue des Carmélites.
n: until 2am during the week and
 3am Friday and Saturday.
Mozart, Chaussée d'Alsemberg.
n: until 5am during the week and
 6am at weekends.

Jazz

ervation Hall, 3 Rue de Londres.
511 03 04. Programme changes
uently, but the quality remains
 Occasionally features musicians
 its namesake in New Orleans.
taminet du Kelderke, 14
d'Place. Tel: 512 36 94. In a low-
nged, sawdust-floored cellar below
Grand'Place, the Estaminet hops
ome good sounds every evening
 10pm.
drome. 21 Place Fernand Cocq.
512 04 56. Weekend jazz bar.

Blues

s Corner, 12 Rue des Chapeliers.
511 97 94. Dark, dingy, smoky,
, crowded and just about perfect
ome fine blues licks.

Festivals

t of Liberation and Festival of the
s, early September.

Ath

Parade of Giants, the fourth Sun-
n August.

Binche

The Binche Carnival, Sunday–Tuesday
preceding Ash Wednesday.

Blankenberge

Flower Procession, August.

Bruges

Canal Festival, triennial (1995, 1998).
The Sacred Blood Procession, Ascension Day.
Golden Tree Parade, every five years
(1995, 2000).

Brussels

January
Auto-Salon, every two years
Film Festival (Congress Palace)

February
Carnival (in the city centre)
The Antique Fair (Palace of Fine Arts)

March
Belgian Indoor-Tennis Championships
(Exhibition Park)
The Holiday, Tourist and Recreation
Fair
The International Book Fair (Interna-
tional Centre Rogier)

April
Son et Lumière at the Grand'Place

May
Open door at the Royal Greenhouses
open to the public (Laeken)
Queen Elisabeth International Music
Competition (Palace of Fine Arts)
Foire Commerciale (Trade Fair)
Petro-Mobile-Oldtimer-Rallye
International Comic Festival

June
The 20-km Brussels Run (Jubilee Park)
Re-enactment of the Battle at Water-
loo (Waterloo)
Europe Festival

July
Ommegang (Grand'Place). Originally a
religious procession in the 14th-cen-
tury, Ommegang today is like a Carnival procession.
National Holiday (21 July, celebrations
in city parks) and the Brussels Fair
(Midi Quarter)

Foire du Midi, big annual market held
at the Gare du Midi.

August
Raising the Meiboom (Grand'Place)
Brosella Folk & Jazz (Théâtre de Ver-
dure)
Carpet of Flowers (Grand'Place), held
every two years
International Carillon Competition in
Mechelen

September
The Eddy Merckx Grand Prix (Wald La
Cambre)
The Brussels Marathon
Brueghel Festival
Dressage and Team Competition
(Wald La Cambre)
Food Fair, Eureka Hobby Fair (Exhibi-
tion Park)
Ommegang (Grand'Place)

November
International Show Jumping Tourna-
ment (Exhibition Park)

December
Christmas Market (Zavel)
Manger and Christmas Tree
(Grand'Place)
Arrival of St Nicholas, processions
and the giving of sweets to children,
December 6.

Diksmuide

Beer Festival, September.

Genk

Grand Procession, May.

Ghent

Flanders Festival, from the mid-August
to mid-September.
Floralies of Ghent, International flower
show in April.

Knokke-Heist

International Cartoon Festival, June–
September.

Lembeke

Windmill Festival, May.

Leuven

International Folklore Festival, Easter weekend.
Marktrock Rock Festival, August.

Liège

Outremeuse Folklore Festival (in the Outremeuse district), 15 August.
Walloon Festival, the fourth Sunday in September.

Mechelen

Handswijk Procession, May.

Mons

The Parade of the Golden Wagon and the "**Battle Against the Dragon Lumecon**", Trinity Sunday.

Moselle Valley

Wine Festivals, August–October.

Oostduinkerke

Shrimp Festival, the second-to-last weekend in June.

Ou De Naarde

Adriaen-Brouwer Feest, beer festival end of June.

Ostend

The Dead Rat Ball, Carnival on the first Sunday in March.

Poperinge

Hops Festival, first Sunday in September.

Theux

Medieval Fair at Franchimont Castle, August.

Tournai

The "Four Parades", the second Sunday in June.
Procession of the Plague, the second Sunday in September.

Turnhout

The Peasants' Festival, the second weekend in June.

Verviers

International Costumed Parade, third Sunday in July.

Ypres

Cat Festival, the second Sunday in May.
The Procession of the Holy Cross and Our Lady of Succour, the Sunday following 8 September.

Shopping

Belgium enjoys an international reputation for its fine dipped chocolates and chocolate in general, crystalware, firearms, diamonds and, of course, the world-famous lace made in both Brussels and Bruges. Most shops are open 9am–6pm, some close for a lunch break between noon and 2pm, and others remain open late.

You will find a variety of markets which take place on certain days in every city. A visit to any one of these nearly always proves to be well worth the effort.

Shopping Areas

Antwerp

The Bird Market: Sunday.

Brussels

The main shopping districts detailed below sell speciality Belgian products, including lace, crystal, diamonds, chocolates, beers and foodstuffs such as cheeses, Ardennes hams and pâté.

Non-EU residents may be ab[…] claim back some of the tax they pa[…] purchases. It is worth asking a[…] this in the main shopping areas, e[…] cially if you are spending a l[…] money.

If you are looking for a bargain[…] magic words to look out for are *so[…]* and *solden*. Even better, though r[…] are *liquidation totale* and *t[…] uitverkoop*, announcing that "e[…] thing must go".

RUE NEUVE

What this area lacks in cool sophis[…] tion, it makes up for in popular pr[…] Beginning at Place Rogier, City 2[…] shopping mall on three floors off[…] everything under one roof with p[…] rias, hot-dog stalls, ice-cream parl[…] coffee stands and bar terraces. E[…] cially notable are FNAC, Belgi[…] good-value books-magazines-CDs-[…] puter-video-photo shop (where you[…] also buy concert tickets); We[…] honey shop; Le Jardin d'Apollon, w[…] specialises in bonsai trees; and I[…] Belgium's department store.

At the far end of Rue Neuve, […] another entrance to Inno, are r[…] department stores, C&A, Marks[…] Spencer, Peek & Cloppenburg (P[…] Sarmalux and Maison d'Oreé, foll[…] by two more malls, the Ce[…] Monnaie and the Anspach Centre[…]

IN THE CENTRE

Here the pace slows down a little[…] Rue des Fripiers are some s[…] clothes boutiques and a charming[…] shop, In Den Olifant. Samoka […] place to rest over a cup of fre[…] milled coffee or linden tea.

The Galerie du Centre attrac[…] regular clientele thanks in pa[…] Leonidas pralines shop, serving s[…] of the best of Belgium's wond[…] chocolates. One exit from the Ga[…] leads straight into Au Bon V[…] Temps, a typical Brussels bar.

Rue de Tabora sports the Nic[…] wine shop and Le P'tit Norn[…] cheeses. On Rue du Marché […] Herbes there is Michelangeli for […] fumery and handbags; Dandoy for[…] ciality biscuits; and Eurolines, for[…] rything you ever wanted.

Rue du Midi is home to stamp[…] coin dealers.

...e's first shopping mall, built be-
...n 1846 and 1847 in Italian neo-
...issance style, the Galeries offer
...y shopping, at a price. Here are
...en-Dazs for ice-cream; Libraire
...Galeries for art books; Tropismes
...aperbacks; Ganterie Italienne for
...s; Oriande for crystal and jewel-
...Delvaux for handbags and
...aus for chocolates.

RUE ANTOINE DANSAERT

...is where some of the well-known
...ners have their boutiques – Della
..., Knokke, Stijl and Romeo Gigli to
...e a few.

PORTE DE NAMUR

...upmarket shopping district in-
...s the nearby Avenue de la Toison
...the Boulevard de Waterloo, Av-
...Louise and Place Stéphanie.
...known designers, including Gucci,
...ni Versace and Nina Ricci are lo-
...d on Boulevard de Waterloo. Oppo-
...hem gallery entrances lead to a
...ring maze of shops. From Place
...hanie there is Galerie Louise,
...ce Louise, Galerie de la Toison
...(Gallery of the Golden Fleece) and
...rie Porte de Namur.

MARKETS

...ic market: Sunday morning, Gare
...idi. Daily, except Monday.
...er market: Sunday mornings,
...d'Place.
... market: daily, Place du Jeu de
....
...que market: weekends, Place du
...on.
... markets: first Sunday in the
...th, Place St Lambert; Tuesday
...ing, Place Dailly, Schaarbeek.
... market: Sunday morning,
...d'Place.

Leuven

...ket day: Friday, Oude Markt.

Liège

...market "La Batte": Sunday morn-

Nieuwpoort

...market: early every morning.

Tongeren

...ea market and junk market: Sun-
...morning.

Sports & Leisure

Belgium's favourite sport is bicycle racing. This being the case, you can rent a bicycle anywhere in the country, even at railway stations. Most regions have marked cycle routes and maps are available from tourist offices.

Facilities for different athletic activities such as bowling, ice-skating, soccer, golf, mini-golf, roller-skating, tennis, swimming and squash can be found in every city and in many villages.

The Belgian coastline provides excellent opportunities for sailing, surfing and fishing. A variety of boating companies offer excursions to other cities via the country's numerous waterways. Along the coastline sea tours are also available.

Skiing

You can obtain a copy of the map "Ski Ardennes" from the Office de Promotion du Tourisme, Rue du Marché aux Herbes 61, 1000 Brussels.

Ski Areas
Spa–Francochamps–Trois-Ponts
Vielsalm
Baraque de Fraiture–Plateau des Tailles
Plateau de Bastogne
Anlier–Martelange
Libramont–Champlon–Saint-Hubert
Croix-Scaille
Haute Fagnes–Cantons de L'Est

Ice-Skating Rinks

Poisedon, Dapperenlaan 4, Brussels. Tel: 02-762 16 33.
Vorst Nationaal, Globelaan 36, Brussels. Tel: 02-346 16 11.

Golf

Brussels Golf School and Training Center, Ter Hulpsesteenweg 53A, 1170 Brussels.

Royal Golf Club of Belgium, Route de la Marache 19, 1328 Ohain.

Spectator Sports

Information about local sporting events is available at tourist information agencies.

The most popular spectator sports in Belgium include bicycle racing, soccer and horse events, especially galloping and trotting races.

Soccer

Heizel Stadium, Marathonlaan 135, 1020 Brussels.
Royal Belgian Football Association, Wetstraat 43, 1040 Brussels.
Racing White Daring de Molenbeek, Charles Malisstraat 61, 1080 Brussels.
Royal Union Saint-Gilloise, Brussels–esteenweg 223, 1190 Brussels.
Sporting Club Anderlechtois, Thé Verbeecklaan 2 (Park Astrid), 1070 Brussels.

Horse Racing

Boitsfort, Terhulpsesteenweg 51, 1170 Brussels.
Groenendael, Sint-jansberglaan 4, Hoeilaart.
Sterrebeek, Avenue du Roy de Blicquylaan 43, Brussels.

Health Spas

There are three health spas in Belgium:
Chaudfontaine: Thermal spring, 36.6°C, recommended for cases of rheumatism and gout.
Ostend: Especially good for those suffering from rheumatism, asthma, neuralgia and hay fever.
Spa: Recommended for people with rheumatism, heart and circulatory troubles and metabolic disorders.

Language

French

Good day/*Bonjour*
Good evening/*Bonsoir*
Good-bye/*Au revoir*
I/*je*
me/*moi*
we/*nous*
yes/*oui*
no/*non*
please/*s'il vous plaît*
thank you/*merci*
excuse me/*pardon*
where/*où*
when/*quand*
how long?/*combien de temps?*

Time

today/*aujourd'hui*
yesterday/*hier*
tomorrow/*demain*
day/*jour*
week/*semaine*
month/*mois*
year/*année*
Monday/*lundi*
Tuesday/*mardi*
Wednesday/*mercredi*
Thursday/*jeudi*
Friday/*vendredi*
Saturday/*samedi*
Sunday/*dimanche*

Opposites

left/right/*à gauche/à droite*
open/close/*ouvert/fermé*
big/little/*grand/petit*
cheap/expensive/*bon marché/cher*
early/late/*de bonne heure/tard*
old/new/*vieux/nouveau*
cold/hot/*froid/chaud*

Numbers

0/*zéro*
1/*un/une*
2/*deux*
3/*trois*
4/*quatre*
5/*cinq*
6/*six*
7/*sept*
8/*huit*
9/*neuf*
10/*dix*
11/*onze*
12/*douze*
13/*treize*
14/*quatorze*
15/*quinze*
16/*seize*
17/*dix-sept*
18/*dix-huit*
19/*dix-neuf*
20/*vingt*
30/*trente*
40/*quarante*
50/*cinquante*
60/*soixante*
70/*soixante-dix (belg. septant)*
80/*quatre-vingt (belg. huitant)*
90/*quatre-vingt-dix (belg. nonant)*
100/*cent*
200/*deux cents*
500/*cinq cents*
1000/*mille*

Nouns

railway/*gare*
airport/*aéroport*
mail office/*poste*
mailbox/*boîte aux lettres*
stamps/*timbre-poste*
police/*police*
bank/*banque*
chemist's/*pharmacie*
petrol station/*station-service*
supermarket/*supermarché*
hairdresser's/*coiffeur*
hospital/*hôpital*
doctor/*médecin*

Short Sentences

What's your name?
Comment appelez-vous?
I don't understand
Je ne comprends pas
Do you speak English?
Parlez-vous anglais?
How much does that cost?
Combien ça coute?

Dutch

General Terms

Good morning/*Goedemorgen*
Good day/*Goedendag*
Good evening/*Goedenavond*
Good-bye/*Tot ziens*
I/*ik*
we/*wij*
yes/*ja*
no/*nee*
please/*alstublieft*
thank you/*dank u wel*
excuse me/*pardon*
where/*waar*
when/*wanneer*
how/*hoe*
how long?/*hoelang?*
how much?/*hoeveel?*

Time

today/*vandaag*
yesterday/*gisteren*
tomorrow/*morgen*
week/*week*
month/*maand*
year/*jaar*
Monday/*maandag*
Tuesday/*dinsdag*
Wednesday/*woensdag*
Thursday/*donderdag*
Friday/*vrijdag*
Saturday/*zaterdag*
Sunday/*zondag*

Opposites

left/right/*links/rechts*
open/closed/*open/gesloten*
big/little/*groot/klein*
cheap/expensive/*goedkoop/duu*
early/late/*vroeg/laat*
old/new/*oud/nieuw*
cold/hot/*koud/heet*

Numbers

0/*nul*
1/*één*
2/*twee*
3/*drie*
4/*vier*
5/*vijf*
6/*zes*
7/*zeven*
8/*acht*
9/*negen*
10/*tien*
11/*elf*
12/*twaalf*
13/*dertien*
14/*veertien*
15/*vijfteen*
16/*zestien*
17/*zeventien*
18/*achttien*
19/*negentien*
20/*twintig*
30/*dertig*
40/*veertig*
50/*vijftig*
60/*zestig*

0/zeventig
0/tachtig
0/negentig
00/honderd
00/tweehonderd
00/vijfhonderd
000/duizend

Nouns

ay station/station
rt/vliegveld
office/postkantoor
box/brievenbus
ps/postzegel
e/politie
/bank
nist's/apotheek
l station/tank station
rmarket/supermarkt
resser's/kappa
ital/ziekenhuis
or/arts

Short Sentences

's your name?/Hoe heet u?
't understand/Ik versta u nit
ou speak English?
ekt u Engels?
much does that cost?
kost dat?

urther Reading

General

sation by Kenneth Clark, Penguin.
ntful commentaries on the major
s of the Flemish Masters.
Sorrow of Belgium by Hugo Claus,
g. A novel charting the effects of
Nazi occupation of Flanders
gh the eyes of a young boy.
Van Eyck to Bruegel by Max J.
ander, Phaidon. Definitive ac-

count of the Flemish Masters.
A New Guide to the Battlefields of Northern France and the Low Country by Michael Glover, Michael Joseph.
Battlefields of the First World War by T.&V. Holt, Pavilion.
History of the Belgians by A. de Meeiis. A colourful and wide-ranging history of the Belgians.
Bruegel by Gregory Martin. An introduction to the works of Pieter Bruegel.
The Renaissance and Mannerism Outside Italy by Alastair Smart.
Defiant Dynasty: The Coburgs of Belgium by Theo Aronson. A gossipy history of the kings of the House of Saxe-Coburg-Gotha from 1831 to 1950.
Twelve Cities by John Gunter. Includes a lively if dated essay on the temperament of Brussels and its citizens.
The Low Countries: 1780–1940 by E.H. Kossman. A thorough history.

Other Insight Guides

Nearly 200 Insight Guides cover the world, complemented by more than 100 Insight Pocket Guides and a new series of Insight Compact Guides.

In more than 200 pages, *Insight Guide: Brussels* covers in comprehensive detail every aspect of the city: history, culture, people and places. It's the ideal companion.

For those on a tight schedule, *Insight Pocket Guide: Brussels* sets out carefully crafted itineraries designed to make the most of your visit. It contains recommendations from a local expert and comes with a full-size fold-out map showing the itineraries.

Insight Compact Guides to *Belgium* and *Brussels* are ideal on-the-spot reference guides – in essence, mini-encyclopedias. Highly portable, each is packed with detailed text, photography and maps, all meticulously cross-referenced for ease of use.

Art/Photo Credits

Photography by

Ingeborg Knigge *3*, 16/17, 55, 56, 57, 58, 62, 64, 65, 69, 71, 78, 95, 96, 99, 100, 101, 107, 108, 112/113, 128, 131, 133, 136, 137, 139, 141, 143, 144, 145, 150, 153, 154, 155, 156, 160, 167, 171, 198, 199, 200, 201, 203, 204, 205, 206, 207, 209, 211, 213, 222/223, 225, 228, 229, 230, 231, 233, 235, 237, 263R, 282, 283, 286, 287, 298, 299R, 299L

Wolfgang Frtiz 9, 14/15, 20/21, 22, 27, 38, 39, 41, 54, 66, 68, 70, 72, 73, 74, 76, 79, 116/117, 118/119, 126, 132, 134, 135, 148, 149, 151, 157, 158, 159, 161, 174, 176, 177, 178, 179, 188, 191, 193, 202, 210, 214, 216, 218, 219, 220, 252, 255, 268, 271, 280, 281L, 297R, 304

Wieland Giebel 18/19, 242/243, 245, 246R, 247R, 247L, 248, 249, 250, 254, 266, 267, 270, 272, 273, 274, 275, 277, 278R, 278L, 279, 284/285, 288, 289R, 289L, 290, 291, 292, 293, 294, 295, 296, 300, 301

Bodo Bondzio 1, 29, 36, 60/61, 63, 75, 85, 92, 93, 111, 138, 140, 180/181, 189, 221, 224, 227, 234, 236R, 236L, 238, 239, 241, 246L, 251, 263L

Hans Höfer 28, 114/115, 184

Archiv für Kunst und Geschichte 45, 88/89

Institut Belge d'Information et de Documentation 49, 51, 165, 166

Christoph Henning 59, 80, 81, 82, 84, 86, 87, 98, 120, 186, 187, 212, 217

Thomas Mayer 91, 94, 105, 106, 147, 163, 170, 173

Jochen Kente 127, 129, 130, 146

Wiener 142, 181R, 190, 192

dpa 164

Michael Bengel 194, 197, 208

Wiener 232

Zdenka Bondzio 240

Jörn Sackermann 256/257, 265

Johannes Weber 260

Peter Brückmann (Sven Simon/ Diogenes) 264

Auschwitz Stiftg., Antwerp 47, 48

Maps Berndtson & Berndtson

Visual Consultant V. Barl

334

Index